Trump and Iran

Trump and Iran

From Containment to Confrontation

Nader Entessar and Kaveh L. Afrasiabi

LEXINGTON BOOKS
Lanham • Boulder • New York • London

Published by Lexington Books
An imprint of The Rowman & Littlefield Publishing Group, Inc.
4501 Forbes Boulevard, Suite 200, Lanham, Maryland 20706
www.rowman.com

6 Tinworth Street, London SE11 5AL, United Kingdom

British Library Cataloguing in Publication Information Available

Library of Congress Cataloging-in-Publication Data Available

ISBN: 978-1-4985-8886-7 (cloth)
ISBN: 978-1-4985-8887-4 (electronic)

Contents

List of Figure and Table

FIGURE

TABLE

Abbreviations

HEU	Highly Enriched Uranium
IMF	International Monetary Fund
INSTEX	Instrument in Support of Trade Exchanges
GCC	Gulf Cooperation Council
IAEA	International Atomic Energy Agency
JCPOA	Joint Comprehensive Plan of Action
LEU	Low-Enriched Uranium
NATO	North Atlantic Treaty Organization
NPT	Treaty on the Non-Proliferation of Nuclear Weapons
NWFZ	Nuclear-Weapons-Free-Zone
SCO	Shanghai Cooperation Organization
SPV	Special Purpose Vehicle
UN	United Nations
UNSC	United Nations Security Council
WMD	Weapons of Mass Destruction
WTO	World Trade Organization

Introduction

This is our third collaborative work and is conceived as a timely complement to our previous books. In *Iran Nuclear Negotiations: Accord and Detente Since the Geneva Agreement of 2013*, we provided a detailed examination of the decade-long and arduous multilateral negotiation process between Iran and the world powers, which culminated in an interim nuclear agreement in 2013—that laid the groundwork for the final agreement of two years later, known as the Joint Comprehensive Plan of Action (JCPOA). We also discussed the evolution of the relationship between the United States and Iran, that is, a new thaw, as a result of the nuclear breakthrough, as well as the nature of connections between the Iranian nuclear crisis and the country's national security. The JCPOA merited the widespread praise it received in the international community because it averted war, to paraphrase US Secretary of State John Kerry, one of the main architects of the multilateral agreement, who devoted considerable personal focus and energy to end the vexing Iran nuclear crisis in a manner satisfactory to both sides, that is, a "win-win." The agreement obliged Iran to limit its nuclear program in exchange for the suspension of economic sanctions. It also required from the United States and other parties not to inhibit Iran's reintegration into the global economy. In a certain sense, the JCPOA had the attributes of a multilateral trade agreement. It committed the parties "to prevent interference with the realization of the full benefit by Iran of the sanctions lifting specified" in the deal. Also, it committed the United States and Europe to "refrain from any policy specifically intended to directly and adversely affect the normalization of trade and economic relations with Iran." The agreement committed them to "agree on steps to ensure Iran's access in areas of trade, technology, finance, and energy." In our next book, *Iran Nuclear Accord and the Remaking of the Middle East*, we contextualized the JCPOA and focused on the short- and

1

long-term implications of the Iran nuclear agreement for the broader region in the Persian Gulf and the Middle East. The JCPOA was reached at a crucial historical juncture in Middle East politics, rife with unresolved tensions and conflicts, and was considered a milestone in conflict-management. Today, in the middle of the Trump "era," it is impossible to recapture the exhilarating international atmosphere of the 2015–2016 when the euphoria over the Iran nuclear breakthrough was at its highest. The switch from optimism to cynicism and a related sense of despair about the deteriorating relations between the United States and Iran has been rapid and ruthless. In a word, the Trump "phenomenon" has radically changed the international landscape, its JCPOA "exit wounds" have traumatized not only Iran but also the other signatories, forcing them to act as emergency doctors who must act quickly to regenerate the patient, in this case the "vanishing" agreement, despite the severe injury, to saw back the edges and thus (hoping) to salvage it from the history's butcher's knife.[1]

As is well known, the JCPOA was deliberately limited to the nuclear issue, and other "non-nuclear" issues such as regional issues were not addressed in the agreement. Theoretically speaking, it fits the description of "conditional engagement," that is, is the type of inter-governmental relations where the target state is offered incentives in exchange for specific changes in its (domestic and foreign) behavior.[2] Nonetheless, there was a reasonable expectation that the JCPOA would eventually contribute to regional stability and tranquility and carried the potential to set into motion similar agreements in the future, often referred to as "JCPOA II," thus building on the momentum for peace generated by the landmark nuclear agreement—widely praised as a singular achievement of multilateral diplomacy. While convinced of the basic soundness of this positive reception, our narrative delved into the conflict-management process particularly in Syria, highlighting the need for sustained peace diplomacy in a fractious region where inter-state relations had been strained by perforated sovereignties, uneven development, terrorism upsurge, and a new and unprecedented level of religio-ideological sectarianism permeating traditional power rivalries. With the help of insights from various schools of thought and paradigms in international relations, including critical theory and constructivism, our analysis focused on the balance of forces of disintegration and discord on the one hand and, on the other, the forces of integration and cooperation, opting for a rather optimistic interpretation of the (modernist) impact of the nuclear agreement for a future-oriented *remaking* of the fractious Middle East more in tune with international norms and principles. However, this optimism was tempered by the recognition of the diverse, and contradictory, receptions of the JCPOA throughout the Middle East, above all in Persian Gulf region, due to the on-going rivalries between and among the various contenders for regional dominance. With the JCPOA turning into a site of contending interpretations, by the time of its implementation in early 2016, it became increasingly clear that there would be no simple "success story" of a peaceful resolution of a vexing nuclear crisis, but rather a paradoxical one, indicating the adverse consequences of the JCPOA for regional balancing, stemming from a widespread perception on the part of Iran's regional rivals that the agreement was a win-lose for them by virtue of strengthening Iran's hands at a time of great uncertainty in Middle Eastern affairs. While cognizant of the contradictory receptions of JCPOA in the region and beyond, our narrative in both those books hammered the historical importance of the pacific settlement of conflicts, aptly demonstrated by JCPOA's achievement, for a region rich in resources and yet rather poor in successful conflict-prevention. Contextualizing the nuclear breakthrough was, and continues to be, highly important for an apt understanding of the "next stage" in the region's inter-state patterns of interaction, in the direction of a modernist state system based on national sovereignty, instead of melting in the quagmire of transboundary sectarianisms, failed states, and failed or failing peace processes. We hasten to add, however, that in both of our aforementioned books, we were primarily concerned with the social scientific study of what "is" rather than what "ought to be." Taking stock of the past and present history and using appropriate theoretical and methodological tools of analysis has been our priority, in order to shed light on an important aspect of today's international affairs. The latter point brings us to the subject of the present book, which we have written to cover the first two years or so of the Trump administration and its drastic re-working and re-scripting the relationship between the United States and the Islamic Republic of Iran. To what extent was this attributable to the uncertainties and anxieties of a "superpower in decline" and the perceived need to reassert the American power, and leadership, in a Middle East that had experienced the dramatic post-9/11 infusions of American power followed by a period of self-extrication, restraint, and cautious diplomacy?

Our present narrative has been undertaken with a conscious effort to illuminate an unfolding process dealing with a highly fluid situation pertaining to a "mercurial" US president who has been highly controversial, unpredictable, and prone to policy reversals and even "flip-flops." Adopting a process-oriented approach, we have sought to take contingency as a primary parameter that guards against certain conclusions that may be premature and unsubstantiated by either the regional dynamic or the fluidity of foreign policy decisions in Trump's era. One of the drawbacks of writing about a present (and tumultuous) reality is that historical proximity has a tendency to occlude a deeper understanding and detection of ebbs and flows of policy that require the sufficient passage of time for an apt analysis. Although we can state with a degree of certainty that since Trump's presidency, US-Iran relations have substantially deteriorated and may soon spiral toward a full-blown crisis, on the other hand, it is far from certain that a US-Iran war is imminent. Having examined in-depth the various war scenarios, we admit we were initially skeptical about the possibility of a war between the United States and Iran during Trump's presidency and, yet, the subsequent developments—such as the designation by the United States of Iran's revolutionary guards as terrorist followed by a greater infusion of US military forces in the region in direct response to the perceived Iran threat—have steered us toward the opposite conclusion that a US-Iran war was a distinct possibility and the two countries were edging closer to the precipice of the boiling cauldron of Middle East war, unless of course, both sides took the necessary adjustments needed to de-escalate tensions between them. Given the asymmetry of both economic and military power between the Western superpower and the "regional pivot" Iran, Iran's leaders were confronted with a dire situation not unlike the Melians in the *Peloponnesian War*, recalling Thucydides's famous "The strong do what they can, and the weak endure what they must."[3] Still, Iran's "Melian dilemma" has special characteristics in the broader canvas of Middle East politics (where Iran has considerable influence beyond its borders) that, as a result, sets it apart from the ancient tragedy, in which an aggressive imperial power ruthlessly crushed a smaller state into oblivion. By all account, Iran was not a trivial and or failed state and, militarily speaking, posed a formidable challenge to its adversaries.

Indeed, our examination of the various (internal and external) variables or factors that hamper the war scenarios has led us to question the facility with which some experts, especially in the United States, have predicted the outbreak of war between United States and Iran in the proximate future. A synthetic analysis that is not reductionist and does not infer the probability of a US-Iran war from each side's incendiary rhetoric and public postures is attempted here, with due attention to alternative scenarios, including re-engagement and the dawn of a new phase in US-Iran diplomacy. Sifting through the complex, and at times convoluted, history of US-Iran relations, our observation has detected a systemic source for the sustained rivalry between the two countries that has reached a new apex under the Trump administration. Above and beyond the role of specific presidents and leaders and their policies on both sides, the structure of conflict between the United States and Iran requires close examination. Once this systemic or structural source, pertaining to post-revolutionary Iran's revisionist ethos, and the regional sub-system's post-Cold War changes toward multipolarity, is properly examined, then it is possible to gain better, and certainly deeper, insights about the extent of probability of war and other contrasting scenarios. The overarching theme of this book is that the Trump administration has introduced a shift of emphasis in the relations of the United States with Iran, which can be summed up as a turn from containment to compellence. Following Thomas Schelling and others, we define "compellence" as a method to force an opponent into doing something against its will under the duress of threat or coercion.[4] Closely identified with "coercive diplomacy," compellence as a strategy aims to get an adversary to do or cease doing something, which it normally considers inexpedient. This contrasts with the aim of containment, which is to prevent an adversary from expanding its power and influence. Extended compellence, on the other hand, refers to secondary coercion or "indirect coercion" directed at third parties in order to garner their cooperation with the coercive strategy against the primary target. In this context, this term applies to the arm-twisting and "bullying" tactics of the United States with respect to other nations that preferred to maintain normal relations with Iran, compelling them to bend in the direction of the United States through a combination of soft and hard power tactics. The Trump administration has unleashed the "fire and fury" of a rollback strategy against Iran, rolling back not only the nuclear agreement, but also the very foundation of previous "containment strategy" that had informed Washington's approach toward Tehran for the past decades, stretching (with remarkable consistency) from the presidency of Jimmy Carter through Barack Obama. Thus, conceptually speaking, the Trump administration has introduced an unprecedented policy discontinuity with the past, in a word, by transgressing the boundaries and limits of containment in favor of a confrontational rollback strategy, defined here in terms of full-fledged compellence, in contrast to the partial, nuclear-focused compellence strategy of the Obama administration. Examining the nature and scope of this discontinuity, this book sheds light on the perennial question of "incremental change or re-orientation" in the remaking of the policy of the United States for Iran under the Trump administration, which has been turned relatively opaque by virtue of the volcanic eruption of hateful, incendiary rhetoric by both sides.

This policy shift has resulted in the withdrawal of the United States from the JCPOA, re-imposition of nuclear sanctions, US attempts to isolate Iran in the international community, and to apply "maximum pressure" aiming to bring about fundamental changes in the foreign behavior of Islamic Republic, accused of fomenting regional stability, sectarianism, and human rights abuse at home. But, while the main contours of Trump administration's hostile policies against the Iranian government are relatively well-known and transparent to the public, what is less known and subject to critical scrutiny is both the nuanced nature of these policies and, moreover, the net results of these policies, that is, whether or not they will ultimately yield the intended results? Will these Trumpian policies aggravate the situation by undermining Iran's political moderates, emboldening the hard-liners, and instigating further Iranian mischief in retaliation against American pressures? In other words, could the Trumpian strategy of compellence end up provoking the kind of Iranian behavior it was intended to prevent, that is, a case of "self-fulfilling prophecy"?

In order to do justice to these key questions, it is important to have an adequate understanding of the Trump "phenomenon," which is why in chapter 1, we have probed the growing literature on Trump's "worldview" and foreign policy priorities, focusing on Trump's contradictory foreign impulses. One of the main points of contention in the emerging body of work on Trump's foreign policy is about the latter's connection with its predecessor, that is, Obama's foreign policy, which counted on the Iran nuclear deal as one of its crowning achievements. Intent on reversing Obama's legacies, Trump has been widely regarded as Obama's antithesis, yet our analysis shows this to be an exaggeration, particularly as it pertains to Iran. Compared to some other authors, our narrative is critical of the Obama administration for losing the Iran focus after reaching the Iran deal and for failing to make use of a historic opportunity to telescope the agreement to a diplomatic rapprochement with Iran, instead of a "half-pivot." Iran is also fully responsible for playing its share of responsibility for this missed opportunity, which, in turn, raises the issue of domestic sources of foreign policy decisions. Trump's reaction against Obama's Iran legacy must be viewed in connection not only with Trump's anti-Islamic Republic agenda but also with the basic shortcomings and lacunae of Obama's Iran engagement approach. Above and beyond their differences, however, Trump and Obama shared a good deal in common, resulting in Trump's cautious Middle East decisions, such as the decision to refrain from getting deeply involved in the Syrian theater of conflict. But, of course, we need an overall understanding of the tumultuous US-Iran relations during the past several decades since the Islamic Revolution of 1979, which is why we have provided an overview of the changing Washington approach toward Iran under different administrations prior to Trump. The overarching theme of "Iran containment" during the pre-Trump presidencies stretching back to Carter (and the Carter Doctrine) has now become a candidate for reconsideration by a (post-containment) confrontational approach by Trump administration. This approach, which we have identified as a "rollback" strategy giving the impression of a "grand strategy," has faced numerous challenges, ironically some of them by Trump himself, as a result of which the overall Iran strategy has been oscillating between the two poles of containment and (rollback) confrontation (chapter 2). This oscillation has culminated in certain ambiguities and incoherence, particularly with respect to the possibility of a new dialogue between Tehran and Washington. In order to grasp these ambiguities, our narrative ventures in the dimension of political economy to get an overall sense of economic warfare currently waged relentlessly against Iran by the US government. Chapter 3 has been devoted to this subject, equipping the readers with a full knowledge of the devastating impact of unilateral US sanctions on the Iranian economy, which nonetheless have fallen short of completely busting up the Iranian economy, partly as a result of (crucial oil and non-oil) waivers granted to a number of other nations, including some of Iran's neighbors and "near neighbors" such as Iraq and India. In this chapter, we argue that these waivers are relatable to the uneasy intersection of the policy of the United States for Iran with other ramparts of US foreign policy, including the policies of the United States for South Asia and Iraq. The resulting chasm between rhetoric and actual policy has been counterproductive for US foreign policy, raising the risk of impulsive decisions that could aggravate the climate of hostility between the two nations. Following a well-established international relations perspective on the role of "misperceptions," we have sought to "deconstruct" the Trumpian discourse on Iran's nuclear program, distinguishing between facts and misinformation and subjecting Trump's stated positions on the JCPOA to a rigorous critical analysis. The evolution of these positions from Trump's presidential candidacy, through the tenure of Iran policy "doves" uprooted by the upsurge of Iran "hawks," has been studied, as well as Iran's counter-measures and the possibilities for a new nuclear negotiation between the two powers. In chapter 4, we turn to an examination of the emerging transatlantic rift between the United States and Europe over Iran, looking in particular at European diplomacy and the possibilities for a "JCPOA minus United States." This is followed in chapter 5 by a treatment of the "regional dimension" in the current US-Iran hostilities, which have been presented by some politicians, experts, and pundits on both sides as a pure, that is, zero-sum, hostility. A new, post-JCPOA sharpening and polarization of political loyalties can be discerned, reflecting to some extent the continued infections of Middle East politics by "big powers" politics. This polarization is inherently dangerous and has pitted the region's nations against each other in what is nowadays commonly referred to as "proxy wars." At the same time, it is a mistake to maintain that the volatile Middle East is helplessly caught by the fissures of this new polarization traversing religious fault lines. There are also important counter-trends that operate against this polarization and, in fact, give rise to a guarded optimism that the future of the region is not necessarily bleak and the potential for greater conflict-management actually exists. Looking in particular at Iran-Saudi Arabia relations, this chapter identifies the various variables conducive to both sustained rivalry as well as a new thaw, which could emerge, ironically, as a result of the fractious Persian Gulf, where the US government has pursued its anti-Iran objectives by seeking to establish an "Arab NATO." In our estimation, the prerequisite unity for this objective has been absent and, therefore, it is unlikely that it can materialize in the manner foreseen by the United States. We conclude the book with a set of recommendations in chapters 6 and 7 that basically advise on how to retrieve the US-Iran dialogue and neutralize the present crisis in their inter-state relations, essentially by returning to the status quo ante of mutual containment and dispensing with the dangerous parameters of (extended) compellence strategy, wedded to the "grand illusion" of regime change in Iran, which has a decent probability of culminating in egregious foreign policy errors, above all another "war of choice," not necessity.

NOTES

1. We draw attention to Hirschman, who in his classical theoretical text on "exit" claims that the "agony" or "ideology of exit" has been a dominant and powerful narrative in the United States. See Albert O. Hirschman, *Exit, Voice, and Loyalty: Responses to Decline in Firms, Organizations, and States* (Cambridge, MA: Harvard University Press, 1970).

2. John Lewis Gaddis, *Strategies of Containment: A Critical Appraisal of American National Security Policy during the Cold War*, revised edition (New York: Oxford University Press, 2005).

3. Thucydides, *History of the Peloponnesian War* (New York: Penguin Books, 1972).

4. Thomas C. Schelling, *Arms and Influence* (New Haven, CT: Yale University Press, 1966); Richard Ned Lebow and Janice Gross Stein, "Deterrence: The Elusive Variable," *World Politics* 42, no. 3 (April 1990), 336–369; Alexander L. George and William E. Simon, *The Limits of Coercive Diplomacy* (Boulder, CO: Westview Press, 1994).

Chapter 1

Trump and Obama's Mixed Iran Legacy

At first glance, it is relatively easy to sum up the nature of dramatic changes in the attitude of the United States toward Iran under the Trump administration. The paradigm of "engagement" spearheaded by President Barack Obama had experienced a devastating blow, replaced with the paradigm of confrontation.[1] The United States was no longer seeking even partial engagement with the Islamic Republic, or merely the containment of the old adversary. Confrontation and economic strangulation of Iran were the order of the day. This had all the features of an emerging grand strategy,[2] in sharp contrast to the half-measures of the Obama administration—that essentially left a bulk of US problems with Iran unresolved, despite the outward appearance of being "committed to diplomacy that addresses the full range of issues before us," to paraphrase Obama's 2009 new year message to Iran.[3] But, once the nuclear agreement was reached, little of that purported commitment showed its feather, reflecting an administration that was content to pitch its short lance on the nuclear standoff, instead of using it as a spigot for the frozen pipeline of rapprochement. "The JCPOA was never intended to solve all of our problems with Iran," Obama said in the aftermath of withdrawal of the United States from the deal, thus confirming the incremental nature of his Iran policy.[4] Accordingly, the JCPOA was conceived as a crucial step forward in de-escalation of tensions with Iran, by essentially putting the genie of Iran's nuclear weapon back in the bottle and thus removing, at least for a decade, what was perceived as a clear and present danger to the national security of the United States. In a certain sense, Obama's approach resembled the limited engagement policy of the Clinton administration toward North Korea that had focused first and foremost on de-nuclearization, albeit under the guise of a "grand security strategy."[5] Initially, particularly as the marathon negotiations for the JCPOA were proceeding, there was a reasonable expectation that a final deal would carry dividends for a whole host of other issues, including the conflict in Syria, counter-terrorism, broader disarmament in the Middle East, the future relations of Iran with the West, as well as Iran's relations with its Arab neighbors in the Persian Gulf. A clue to these was given by Iran's President Hassan Rouhani at the UN's General Assembly in September 2104, promising cooperation with the United States against terrorism "only after nuclear crisis is resolved."[6] Iran's supreme leader, Ayatollah Seyed Ali Khamenei, echoed this sentiment in April 2015, by stating that if the United States "stops its usual obstinacy, this [deal] will be an experience [for Iran], and we will find out that we can negotiate with it over other matters as well."[7] In the preface to the JCPOA, the signatories had anticipated that "full implementation" of the JCPOA would "positively contribute to regional and international peace and security." Subsequently, Iran's lead negotiator, foreign minister Mohammad Javad Zarif, drew attentions to the threats posed by terrorism and called on the Western governments to "open new horizons to address important, common challenges" after having resolved the nuclear dispute with Iran.[8] But, as time passed, the initial enthusiasm for the JCPOA and its future potential was gradually replaced with a more restrictive American interpretation that can be best described as minimalist in nature. This was reflected in the assessment of Obama's national security adviser, Susan Rice: "The Iran deal was never primarily about trying to open a new era of relationship between the United States and Iran. It was far more pragmatic and minimalist."[9] Another official of the Obama administration, Deputy Secretary of State Anthony Blinken, emphatically hammered the same point in a lecture at the Council on Foreign Relations by stating categorically that the purpose of nuclear negotiations of the United States was not "about trying to forge a broader and deeper relationship with Iran."[10]

In contrast, the Trump administration, keen on correcting the perceived "strategic atrophy" of its predecessor,[11] was not content with any piecemeal approach. The new administration had retooled its strategic assumptions to confront the threat of a "resurgent" Iranian power, conceived essentially as a strategic threat. This stemmed from the understanding that in the JCPOA was a "fantastic" deal for Iran that had "emboldened" its foreign policy by relaxing the constraints on Iranian power and thus enabled it to expand its strategic alliance, with both state and non-state actors, across the region at the expense of Western powers and their regional allies, thus warranting a new approach—that fit the description of a grand plan or "grand strategy," one that almost inevitably increased the risk of an open confrontation with Iran. And yet, this was in a jarring contrast with Trump's own oft-stated war-weariness, which he inherited from Obama, and was a bedrock of his "America First" ethos.[12]

To elaborate, Trump had campaigned as a "populist outsider,"[13] promising to "upend the international order," to paraphrase a *New York Times* editorial after his victory,[14] while criticizing the involvement of the United States in the Iraq war and lamenting "we've made the Middle East more unstable and chaotic than ever before."[15] He repeatedly promised to avoid getting involved in foreign wars and in one of his first post-election "thank you" tours around the nation laid out a US military policy that would "stop racing to topple foreign regimes we know nothing about, that we shouldn't be involved with."[16] The real estate tycoon and reality TV star-turned-president had no prior background in diplomacy and displayed contradictory foreign policy impulses, reflecting a bifurcated pattern. Thus, for example, Trump launched missile strikes against the Bashar al-Assad regime in Syria before announcing he was withdrawing US troops from the region and then, subsequently, amending himself. He threatened apocalyptic war with North Korea—telling its leader Kim Jong-un that there would be "fire and fury" if he kept threatening America—and yet at other times flirted with withdrawing all US troops from the Korean Peninsula. He leveled similar threats against Iran and demonized its leaders in the strongest language and then offered to hold talks with them without any preconditions. Aside from his heavy focus on correcting the trade imbalances, building a wall at the US-Mexico border, rebuilding the "depleted" US military, and defeating the terrorist Islamic State (ISIS),[17] Trump had no clear foreign policy road map. He brought with him an odd mixture of dogmatic Islamophobia[18] and "new transactional openness,"[19] paving the way to a "new combination of globalism and nationalism"[20] while at the same time downplaying expectations by stating: "We cannot purge the world of evil or act everywhere there is tyranny . . . . No amount of American blood or treasure can produce lasting peace and security in the Middle East. It's a troubled place."[21] Yet, according to a White House insider, "If Trump had one fixed point of reference in the Middle East, it was . . . that Iran was the bad guy."[22] In line with the Iran-centric strategic outlook of Israeli and Saudi leaders, Trump believed that Iran was the principal enemy in the Middle East and that the nuclear deal was deeply flawed because it fueled Iranian expansionism. Inevitably, this would put Trump (unilaterally) against the multilateral agreement, widely viewed as one of the biggest foreign policy achievements of Obama's presidency. Not only that, in a matter of months in the office, Trump had reversed Obama's strategy of encouraging a regional equilibrium of power between Sunni Saudi Arabia and Shiite Iran, siding unequivocally with the Saudis, who harbored their own hegemonic ambitions in the region, that is, a *Pax Saudica*. He had also abandoned decades of US attempts to balance Israeli interests with those of the Palestinians, by moving the US embassy in Israel to Jerusalem, cutting off aid for Palestinian refugees, and closing the Palestinian diplomatic mission in Washington. He had put his inexperienced son-in-law, Jarred Kushner, in charge of the Middle East policy, promising a new Middle East peace plan, while taking partisan steps that catered to the Israeli far-right on the one hand, and a young but recklessly aggressive Saudi crown prince on the other hand—with predictable sub-optimal results.[23] Still, as stated earlier, there was one aspect of his predecessor's Middle East legacy that appeared to endure Trump's era, that is, Obama's war-weariness, which was connected to Trump's stated determination to "shake the rust off of America's foreign policy."[24]

IRAN AND THE "TRUMP DOCTRINE"

Trump's secretary of state, Mike Pompeo, has invoked the term "Trump doctrine," describing it as a timely corrective to Obama's "accommodationist" strategy that incorrectly signaled "diminished American power and influence."[25] But, a number of other authors have questioned the existence of any (coherent) doctrine on Trump's part, citing the chaotic and messiness of Trump's foreign and domestic politics. Case in point, Randal Schweller has stated: "There is no Trump doctrine. Prudence is the Trump buzzword for foreign policy."[26] There is, of course, no consensus on interpreting Trump and in the growing literature on Trump's presidency divergent images of Trump as "realist" or "closet realist" or "deconstructionist" (of the world order), and so on, can already be found aplenty.[27] Scholars of international institutions, for instance, view Trump's presidency as a test of the theory that institutions and long-standing strategic bargains will prove resilient. Trump has been accused of harboring "Nazi dispositions" by Iran's president. The outside fear about Trump's rupture to the post-Cold War new international order has been articulated by even some of America's Western allies, epitomized by the *Economist*'s depiction of "Trump's wrecking ball theory of foreign policy."[28] After all, in addition to the Iran nuclear deal, Trump had also managed to withdraw the United States from a number of other international agreements, including the Paris Climate Accord, the Trans-Pacific Partnership (TPP), the Intermediate-Range Nuclear Forces Treaty (INF), the Geneva-based U.N. Human Rights Council, and the UN Educational, Scientific and Cultural Organization (UNESCO). Also, the United States had refused to sign the Global Compact on Migration. The Trump administration had made cutbacks in voluntary funding for the UN Population Fund (UNFPA), the UN Relief and Works Agency (UNRWA) and limited some UN peacekeeping funds. Notwithstanding these actions and Trump's strong criticisms of global institutions, the negative appraisals of Trump's presidency, especially in the realm of foreign affairs, often assumed the predominance of policy discontinuity rather than continuity by his administration, relative to his predecessor(s), but our contention is that this too is a contested question and requires the sufficient passage of time for a final verdict. This is so because on many foreign policy issues, such as the viability of NATO and America's Cold-War related strategic commitments, Trump had eschewed his campaign rhetoric and opted for policy continuity, albeit with incremental adjustments, for example, pushing more vigorously for allied "burden-sharing" instead of abandoning NATO altogether. This was even discernible with respect to, among other issues, the North American Free Trade Agreement (NAFTA), that Trump successfully renegotiated with Canada and Mexico in the Summer of 2018 after months of denouncing it as "one of the worst deals" ever negotiated by the United States. The "new" NAFTA has turned out to be a modified version of the old NAFTA, reflecting Trump's actual commitment to the preservation of the status quo despite the substantial jolts of his rhetoric to the contrary.[29] In other words, there was a chasm between Trump's political rhetoric and discourse on the one hand and, on the other, the actual policy decisions and output by Trump's White House—that showed signs of willingness to retreat from some of Trump's early decisions, such as on the Paris Climate Agreement and the TPP, increasingly less prone to "rocking the boat" let alone "sinking it," to speak metaphorically. A big question was, of course, if during the remainder of his presidency, Trump would similarly entertain a U-turn on his other foreign policy priorities, such as with respect to China and Iran?

On both these issues, Trump had fulfilled his campaign pledges, by triggering a full-scale trade war with China, which retaliated in kind by imposing reciprocal tariff on American goods, and by unleashing the fury of a comprehensive economic warfare against Iran following the decision to quit the JCPOA. Given China's status as Iran's number one energy partner, Beijing's on-going dispute with the United States in the Pacific Ocean and South China Sea, and Washington's misgivings about "rising China"—that vigorously pushed forward its ambitious One Belt, One Road trans-regional policy encompassing Iran—there was an interconnection between China and Iran policies of United States. These policies would need to be contextualized in terms of the relative decline of US power, emerging global power blocs, and regional re-balancing particularly in the Middle East and, more specifically, the Persian Gulf region. Indeed, the new American pressures simultaneously applied on China and Iran needed to be correctly analyzed with the help of appropriate theoretical tools from the field of foreign policy analysis, for example, system level analysis, hegemonic stability theory, complex interdependence, balance of power, and the like. Thus, instead of an actor-centered analysis that extrapolates the main contours of Trump's foreign policy from his personal traits or "world-view," we opt in this book in favor of a more complex analysis that contextualizes the administration's policies and behavior by focusing on the shifting winds of changing balance of power connected to an emerging multi-polar world, raising new challenges for American foreign policy.

In their insightful book, *Donald Trump: The Making of a World View*, Charlie Laderman and Brendan Simms have traced Trump's strong cognitive antipathy toward Iran to "the trauma of the hostage crisis and the sense of US decline in the late 1970s and 1980s."[30] As the economic historian Daniel Yergin has put it, during those decades, many Americans "feared that the end of an era was at hand," as the world's "foremost superpower" had been "thrown on the defensive, humiliated, by a handful of nations."[31] Ironically, all this had happened precisely at a time when the Persian Gulf region had been elevated in the American national security discourse to the level of "the third strategic zone after Europe and East Asia for US strategy."[32] With the collapse of the Bretton Woods international monetary system in 1971, the traumatic effects of the OPEC oil shock of 1973, followed a few years later by the seismic shocks of the Islamic revolution in Iran dislodging a reliable US ally,[33] the conventional wisdom at the time was that America had passed its apex of global power, experiencing a downward trend. However, here, one is tempted to challenge that wisdom for operating with assumptions far too narrow. For one thing, this ignores that the collapse of the Soviet Union in 1991 coupled with US victory in the first Iraq war (1991) "suggested a brighter future for the American empire, especially as Iran was being seriously weakened by US sanctions."[34] Hal Brands has convincingly argued that the 1970s "were the prologue to America's post-Cold War unipolar moment."[35] Arguably, the latter found its expression in the second Iraq war (2003) and the "Bush doctrine" that was centered on the use of unilateral preemptive strike as a defense strategy against a perceived immediate threat to the security of the United States. It has become a commonplace in the United States that one of the main outcomes of the "Bush Doctrine" (that led to the post-9/11 invasions of Afghanistan and Iraq) was the strengthening of Iran, since its most deadly regional competitors were removed. There is no evidence that Trump deviated from this assessment, adopted as an article of faith in United States, which is incidentally almost never gleaned from Iran's national security lens; the latter leads to a greater appreciation of Iran's national insecurities on a long-term basis caused by the invasions of this superpower (United States) of its neighbors, which stood in sharp contrast to any short-term gains. This aside for the moment, the argument that Trump's aggressive Iran policy had been shaped by the generational impact of the hostage crisis on Trump's political identity smacks of methodological individualism. A critique of this line of reasoning can be found in the works of Max Weber, whose theory of "social action" leads us to decipher a political decision by taking into consideration "the expectation of others."[36] This is an important factor dealing with the interplay of individual and extra-individual, for example, institutional, motivations behind a policy decision, and compelling a decision-maker, in this case President Trump, to behave in a certain way.[37] The significance attributed to Trump's subjective molding by the decades-old hostage crisis appears to be exaggerated and does not adequately take into account the interconnection of multiple causation, that is, how Trump's anti-JCPOA was obtained as a result of the confluence of a variety of personal, interpersonal,[38] political, institutional, and external power variables, such as a desire to recuperate America's "primacy" in the Middle East, each acting as equivalent to a policy "input," irreducible from one another.[39]

THE ADMINISTRATION'S IRAN HAWKS

From the outset, Trump's foreign policy circle had been populated by ardently anti-Iran and anti-Muslim voices, including his campaign manager-turned policy adviser, Steve Bannon, who called for "a global war against Islamic fascism"[40] citing Iran as one of its manifestations. Another administration hawk was the vice-president Mike Pence, who had previously served on the Subcommittee on Middle East and Central Asia of the House Foreign Affairs Committee while in Congress and was a strong supporter of the US invasion of Iraq as well as an outspoken opponent of the nuclear deal with Iran. The initial national security adviser, Michael Flynn, was equally hostile and depicted Islam as a "vicious cancer inside the body of 1.7 billion people." Flynn even expounded support for forcing American Muslims to register with the government.[41] Both Bannon and Flynn compared America's struggle against "radical Islam" to Ronald Reagan's struggle against communism, with Flynn depicting Iran as the "centerpiece" of a global "Enemy Alliance" against the United States, warranting a full-fledged campaign to bring about its demise. Flynn's tenure was short-lived, and he was one of the early targets of the on-going Russia investigation that bedeviled the Trump administration during the first two years of his presidency. Reshuffling his foreign policy team, Trump subsequently replaced his second national security adviser, H. R. McMaster, and the secretary of state, Rex Tillerson, both of them supporters of the nuclear deal, with the more hawkish voices, namely, John Bolton and Michael Pompeo, respectively. Both Bolton and Pompeo were on record opposing the Iran nuclear deal and had shared Trump's criticism of the Obama administration for "appeasing" Iran's rulers. As it turned out, the Bolton-Pompeo duet would play a key role in shaping the new Iran policy from a White House platform, which uniformly pushed back against Iran's "rogue behavior."[42] The Trump administration's strategy, Pompeo stated on more than one occasion, was to "fundamentally alter the behavior of the Islamic Republic of Iran's leadership," and to "convince

the regime to abandon its current revolutionary course."[43] *Aggressive* sanctions were just one of the tools the United States was deploying to pressure
Iran. In August 2018, the US State Department announced the creation of
the Iran Action Group (IAG), which openly supported opposition forces
within Iran,[44] and Bolton promised that the United States would do "other
things" to force a "massive change in the regime's behavior."[45] Increasing
support for Iranian dissident groups seeking regime change in Iran was on
the administration's agenda as well, notwithstanding the explicit support of
the dissident group known as MEK (*Mojahedin-e Khalgh Organization)* by
Bolton, Pompeo, and Trump's legal counselor Rudy Giuliani.[46] Iran, on the
other hand, asserted that the United States was making instrumental use of
the "human rights card" as a hegemonic soft power and that Washington's
democracy promotion represented a violation of the 1981 Algiers Accord that
settled the hostage crisis and committed the United States to noninterference
in Iran's internal affairs. Accusing Washington of "abusing the human rights
of all Iranians" by waging "economic terrorism" that "targeted innocent Iranians," Iranian officials tried to turn the human rights issue in their favor by
emphasizing the economic an humanitarian consequences of US sanctions.[47]
Given the fact that the United States did not apply the democracy and human
rights standards toward some of Iran's neighbors allied to the United States,
such as Saudi Arabia and Bahrain, lend itself to charges of hypocrisy and
double standards and also raised the question of the place (and importance)
of human rights in the conduct of the policies of the United States for Iran
and Middle East, which prioritized non-proliferation, counter-terrorism, and
regional stability.[48]

An extended treatment of this subject requires, of course, making recourse
to the voluminous literature in political science devoted to the study of foreign policy decision-making process, reflecting divergent interpretations and
methodological tools for research.[49] Thus, to illustrate the matter, the White
House statement on the JCPOA withdrawal accused Tehran of being "in
pursuit of the most dangerous task—acquisition of nuclear weapon and the
means of delivering them."[50] This followed an Israeli disclosure of purported
evidence stolen from an Iran nuclear warehouse, which the Prime Minister
Benjamin Netanyahu claimed to represent a major intelligence coup shown
to the US government beforehand to "vouch for its authenticity."[51] While
there is no direct evidence that this revelation influenced Trump's decision
on Iran, the mere fact that Trump cited it in his speech on JCPOA withdrawal
shows its relevance—at a minimum as a supporting rationalization.[52] Another
important variable is the exigencies of presidential elections. Suffice to say
that Trump in his presidential campaign successfully turned the Iran nuclear
deal into a domestic political issue against his Democratic opponent Hillary

Clinton, who backed the deal.[53] During the primaries, Trump and another republican contender, Ted Cruz, rallied against the Iran nuclear deal and vied with each other for crucial evangelical and Jewish votes.[54] It has been noted that some of Trump's biggest campaign donors were powerful Jewish lobbyists known for their pro-Israel and anti-Iran advocacy.[55] This anti-Iran front viewed the collapse of the JCPOA as the trigger for a wider policy aimed at confronting Iran. According to Adam Entous, Trump had essentially adopted the Israeli "grand Middle East strategy" of sidelining the Palestinian issue, rejecting Obama's nuclear deal with Iran, and forging a strategic alliance against Iran that included a Saudi-Israeli cooperation against the common enemy.[56] The problem with this interpretation is that it places the emphasis almost entirely on the external variables, thus ignoring that irrespective of the latter, Trump may well have moved against the nuclear deal, notwithstanding how Trump's *Weltanschauung* received its political socialization on Iran in an "agonistic deliberative democracy" that had agonized for more than three decades over the "Iran question," what author Donette Murray aptly refers to as the "Iran Syndrome" built largely on the "carcass of dead policies."

In the book, *US Foreign Policy and Iran: American-Iranian Relations Since the Islamic Revolution,*[57] Murray has provided a sober assessment of the policy of the United States for Iran through the presidency of Jimmy Carter, Ronald Reagan, George H. Bush, Bill Clinton, and George W. Bush, all of whom prioritized "Iran containment" albeit with different nuances and degrees of attention and intensity. Case in point, ample evidence suggests that the Reagan administration initially favored a deadly stalemate in the bloody Iran-Iraq conflict (1980–1988) and thus deliberately stonewalled the efforts at the United Nations to bring about a speedy cease-fire. Even after Saddam Hussein used chemical weapons "on a scale not seen since World War I," the United States continued to support him, by shielding him from a UN investigation and, more importantly, by providing Baghdad with economic aid and crucial intelligence on Iran's battle plans.[58] Like Walt and Mearsheimer in their book, *The Jewish Lobby,*[59] Donette delves into the role of Israel and pro-Israel interests in shaping the US government's Iran policy, aptly concluding that these "limited what the US could do unilaterally with regard to Iran."[60] Walt and Mearsheimer have credited the Israeli lobby for articulating the "dual containment" approach for US policy consumption, a policy that was designed to do more than just contain Iran, "it also aimed to cause "dramatic changes in Iran's behavior."[61] Political scientist Stephen Zunes, on the other hand, has aptly turned our attention to the role of "other special interests" such as the oil companies, the arms industry, and the Gulf Arab monarchies led by Saudi Arabia, that influence the policy of the United States in Persian Gulf region.[62]

US-IRAN DIPLOMACY AT A GLANCE

Briefly, the nature and dynamic of US-Iran relationship in modern history has been shaped by the region's changing realities. Here, we must distinguish between the Cold War and post-Cold War eras, the two nearly corresponding with another important periodization, that is, the pre and post-revolution chapters in the (tortured) relationship between the United States and Iran. Although the Islamic Revolution preceded the collapse of the Berlin Wall by more than a decade,[63] nonetheless it is possible, conceptually speaking, to regard it as a "post-Cold War" phenomenon, insofar as the revolution was unhinged from the Cold War parameters as its "neither West, Nor East" defining ethos posited the country's break from post–World War II Middle East "subordinate system." Concerning the latter, it is worth recalling that one of the early Cold War crises transpired in Iran, beginning with the 1946 crisis, when the Iranian government refused to grant Russia an oil concession equal to that given to Britain, the Soviets then refused to withdraw their troops from northern Iran—the allied forces had jointly occupied Iran during World War II in order to deprive Germany of access to Iranian oil. After the Soviets withdrew under American pressure, Iran with US backing reneged on the oil agreement with Moscow and settled back into the western sphere of influence.[64] Then came the Anglo-American engineered coup against the democratically elected premier Mohammad Mossadegh following the latter's nationalization of Iran's oil industry, resulting in a quarter of century of the US-backed monarchical dictatorship, which played a subordinate role in the Cold War containment strategy vis-à-vis Soviet expansionism.[65] In *All the Shah's Men*, Stephen Kinzer cogently argues that Iran's current rulers have taken up Mossadegh's emphasis on national sovereignty, in the form of anti-Americanism, while rejecting his beliefs in secularism and Western-style pluralism.[66] The Pahlavi dynastic rule's downfall in 1979 and its replacement by an anti-western Islamist order sounded the death knell for US policy of "twin pillar" stability, that relied on Iran and Saudi Arabia for regional stability (attributed to the Nixon administration), toward the more interventionist "Carter Doctrine;" the latter's aim was for the United States to directly fill the vacuum of Iranian power and simultaneously build up the US forces in the region to forestall conscious attempts by Iranians to "export" their "identity" revolution beyond their borders.[67] The subsequent "Reagan doctrine" and the (more unilateralist) "Bush doctrine" can and should be interpreted as consistent follow-ups to the Carter doctrine, all stemming from the perception of a new post-Cold War geostrategic vulnerability that put a high premium on deterring Iran and limiting its regional influence.[68] Dilip Hiro, Gregory Gause, and a number of other authors have provided detailed accounts of the increasing pro-Iraq tilt of the Reagan administration that viewed the Baathist regime in Baghdad as a counterweight to revolutionary Iran, thus assigning to it a functional role as a "containment" actor.[69] A minor, and passing, self-reversal under Israeli pressure, stemming from the latter's concerns over an Iraqi victory, was the Reagan administration's consent to secret arms shipment to Iran in mid-1980s, in the so-called Iran-Contra affair—that, in turn, drew a very thin line between cross-cutting allegiances, if not alliances.[70] But, with the eight-year war ending in terms largely favorable to Iraq, which was nonetheless economically impoverished and thus turned predatory against its conservative Arab neighbors who had bankrolled it, the US policy transitioned toward a more differentiated "dual containment" approach, geared to checking both regional "hegemons." But, this met with only partial success, in light of Iraq's invasion of Kuwait in 1990 and Iran's ability to make significant inroads in Lebanon through its Shiite protégé force, the Hizbollah, which was accused of a role in the attack at the US military compound in Khobar, Saudi Arabia, in 1996.[71] In the aftermath of events of September 11, 2001, the US basically dropped "dual containment" following the neo-conservative argument that regime change in Iraq was essential in order to trigger a far-reaching process of change throughout the Middle East.[72] As with the Soviet containment strategy, this showed that there was a rather precious thin line separating containment (prescribing deterrence) from outright rollback vis-à-vis the so-called backlash states.[73] As is well-known, in Iraq, this policy was tantamount to opening a dangerous Pandora's Box, instigating a ruinous "war of choice" and, with it, an endemic, long-term instability that continues to exact a heavy toll on the region till this day.[74] In her book, *Bitter Friends, Bosom Enemies: Iran, the US, and the Twisted Path to Confrontation*, Barbara Slavin has provided a detailed account of thwarted efforts at reconciliation by both the Clinton and Bush presidencies and opportunities for a "grand bargain"[75] rebuffed by the Bush administration in its belief that the "axis of evil" Iran would be weakened by the invasion of Iraq—a dubious assumption debunked by the subsequent history.[76] A more recent book by Mehran Kamrava on the sources of the Persian Gulf insecurity, probes the structural dimensions of the US-Iran conflict, its emphasis being on shared/clashing interests and competing narratives on regional security.[77]

The foregoing discussion is not meant as a substitute for a thorough analysis of the complex, convoluted, and often dramatic developments between the United States and Iran, nations that have lacked diplomatic ties since the whirlwind Islamic Revolution of 1979. Rather the aim is to simply highlight the main outline of a "reciprocal containment" strategy by both Washington and Iran, mirror-imaging each other.[78] Emerging as a historic challenge to US regional interests and objectives, the Islamic Republic of Iran has throughout its history been guided by the principle of deterrence vis-à-vis American power, increasingly in tandem with Russia and other powers. The latter was reflected in the statement of Supreme leader in September 2018 at a meeting with Russia's president, Vladimir Putin: "One of the cases that the two sides can cooperate with each other is to contain the United States, because it is a danger to humanity and it is possible to contain it."[79] Still, despite the durability of reciprocal containment as the principal feature of US-Iran relations since 1979, there have been some "missed opportunities" for a détente, such as when the White House under both the second Bush administration and the Obama administration turned its backs on decent chances to explore the possibility of improving relations with Iran, which would have affected the strategic force posture of the United States in the Persian Gulf.[80] This has been attributed to, among other things, a "constructive ambiguity" in the attitude of the United States toward Iran, reflecting a built-in ambivalence on the part of various administrations including the Obama administration, with respect to the long-standing "Iran question." This ambivalence is rooted in the dialectical complexities of an evolving Middle East that over time has sustained the animosity between an intrusive Western superpower and an assertive regional power and, ironically, occasionally has made the two nations into strange bedfellows,[81] as they cooperated with each other during the Kuwait crisis, in order to restore Kuwait's sovereignty, and also in Afghanistan after the events of September 11, resulting in a peaceful takeover of Kabul by anti-Taliban forces.[82] James Dobbins, US special envoy to Afghanistan at that time, has praised the role of Iranian diplomats, stating that "none was more helpful than the Iranians," referring to their input over the new post-Taliban political order in Afghanistan.[83] Even in post-invasion Iraq, where the US-led coalition forces often clashed with the pro-Iran militias, there was sufficient ground for a security dialogue between Tehran and Washington, both supporting the new Iraqi political order. In point of fact, the problems of transition to a pluralistic Iraq might not have been overcome in the absence of a *modus vivendi* between American and Iranian-backed forces, which became increasingly manifest after the emergence of Islamic State (ISIS) in 2014; this was highlighted in March, 2015 in a *New York Times* report under the heading "U.S. Strategy in Iraq Increasingly Relies on Iran."[84] Even candidate Trump, in his third televised presidential debate with Hillary Clinton, readily admitted that Iran was "fighting ISIS," that is, a rare admission of Iran's contribution to counter-terrorism.[85]

Yet, as it turned out, Trump's aforementioned insight on Iran lacked a firm footing and was soon eclipsed by the more pronounced enemy image of Iran that defined his presidency, attributable in part to the half-steps, or put in other word "half-pivots," of his predecessor—reflected in the words of Obama's secretary of state Hillary Clinton that Obama's "priority was to extend our military partnership in the Gulf and deploy new military resources across the region to reassure our partners and deter Iranian aggression."[86]

In her book, *Hard Choice*, focusing on her foreign policy role from 2009 through 2013, Clinton has credited Obama's "dual-track strategy of engagement and pressure"[87] for bringing Iran to the table, a strategy that presented Iran with the prospect of "improved relations" with the United States if Tehran reached for a major compromise in the nuclear standoff.[88] Yet, despite the nuclear breakthrough, there would be no parallel diplomatic improvement, the so-called primary sanctions on Iran over its "rogue behavior" and human rights issues remained in place,[89] and there was an attrition of focus on Iran as Obama spent the last year of his presidency to create another important legacy, namely, normalization with Cuba.

For sure, this does not tell the entire story and equal attention must be paid to the developments inside Iran, where the faction-ridden Iranian politics dominated by the hard-liners around the Supreme Leader played its own fair share in perpetuating the post-JCPOA diplomatic quagmire with the United States. A new opening to the West afforded by the nuclear deal carried an ideological side-effect, by perpetuating the impression that it "was allowing the Revolution to drift from its moorings back into a relationship with the Great Satan," to paraphrase a former American diplomat held hostage in Iran.[90] Also, the JCPOA carried "the potential to energize the struggle for democracy in Iran," to paraphrase a prominent Iranian dissident Akbar Ganji, and was widely regarded as a catalyst for improvement in the rather abysmal record of the Islamic Republic on human rights, the argument being that in the post-JCPOA era of new trade opening, the outside world would be better able to influence the Iranian government on rights issues.[91] From the vantage of Iran's hard-liners however, the JCPOA was both a blessing and a curse, entailed major concessions on Iran's part for the sake of survival in the sanctions-ridden environment, and could spell even further "normative" compromises as Iran began to reintegrate in the international community in the post-JCPOA milieu; the latter imperiled a new Western "cultural invasion" accompanying new foreign investments and import-led market liberalizations spearheaded by the Rouhani administration.[92] Besides, the United States was aligned with Iran's rivals in the region infested with Sunni terrorism, which was suspected of receiving aid from the United States and Saudi Arabia in places such as Syria in order to weaken the Iran-led "axis of resistance." As a result of this Iranian threat assessment, drawn from the fluid and confusing crises in Iran's vicinity, the United States remained in Iranian cognitive radar as an enemy state requiring distance and deterrence. In the United States, on the other hand, a main concern was how the JCPOA affected the geopolitical and geostrategic calculus of the United States? A JCPOA-induced conundrum, it was reflected in the official concerns that Iran was directing some of the frozen assets released to it under the JCPOA for financing its proxies throughout the Middle East—one of the principal reasons why the Obama administration showed a deliberate procrastination in issuing licenses for trade with Iran, dragging its feet in some instances, and imposing new sanctions over Iran's ballistic missile tests, decried by Iran. US officials, on the other hand, complained that Iran's rogue behavior in the region had continued unabated since the JCPOA, that Tehran's rulers had failed to recalibrate their "offensive foreign policy" that showed nothing but disdain toward American presence in the area. As a result, suspicion and hostility continued to permeate the post-JCPOA US-Iran relations, and there was little attempt by the Obama administration to upgrade its minimalist approach toward anything signifying a departure from the previous containment strategy.

At this juncture, a dose of history regarding the Iran containment strategy of the United States may be helpful. There were occasional flirtation with Iran engagement prior to Obama, ranging from a meeting of Carter's National Security Adviser, Zbigniew Brzezinski and Iran's post-revolutionary prime minister, Mehdi Bazargan, in Algiers in 1979, to the "Iran-Contra" arms sales to Iran in mid-1980s, to a very noticeable overture by the Clinton administration with Iran, reflected in Secretary of State Madeleine Albright's apology for the American role in the 1953 coup in Iran, admitting "it is easy to see now why many Iranians continue to resent this intervention by America in their internal affairs."[93] Still, despite such conciliatory gestures, it was during the Clinton administration that tough new Iran sanctions laws were passed, such as the 1996 enactment of the first oil sanctions on Iran, which was levied precisely at a time when Iran's then president, Hashemi Rafsanjani, was actively seeking investment by American oil companies, notably Conoco.[94] In effect, this meant institutionalizing the US-Iran dispute at a more entrenched level—that persisted throughout the two-term presidency of George W. Bush, and then became a candidate for (a partial or minimalist) reconsideration by Obama.

OBAMA'S MIDDLE EAST LEGACY REVISITED

Already much has been written about Obama's foreign policy including by those who worked in his administration as well as by academics and policy experts. According to Mearsheimer, "Except for the Iran nuclear deal, under President Obama we have helped create a zone of disaster" in the Middle East.[95] A pragmatic realist, Obama's foreign policy was guided by what the commentator Fareed Zakaria has characterized as "strategic restraint" and war-avoidance. A *Washington Post* editorial characterized the "Obama doctrine" as one that "relies on the U.S. deploying every possible economic and institutional lever before resorting to armed force."[96] Walt on the other hand has praised Obama for refraining from "naive realism" and also from "threat-mongering and the misguided military engagements that flow from both tendencies."[97] Examples of Obama's "botched" Middle East policies included Libya, where his administration and NATO allies bore responsibility for a post-Kaddafi mess as they swiftly exited after helping the rebels overthrow the entrenched Libyan dictator "without making a serious effort to help Libyans establish security and build a new political order." Obama himself has called the failure to plan for a post-Kaddafi Libyan government the biggest mistake of his presidency.[98] By all indications, this was a foreign policy mistake that was replicated in other instances of Obama's Middle East policy, by virtue of abstaining from feasible alternatives that somehow were not followed as a rational course of action, guaranteeing a blowback.[99] Obama had promised "change you can believe in," and yet, was unable to deliver on so many fronts, some of it due to the external challenges he faced, and some due to the fact that often for him foreign policy "was an afterthought."[100] Thus, Obama's "reset" with Russia leaped backward into the cold war past after Russia's annexation of Crimea in 2014, the Middle East peace process remained deadlocked, the bloody war in Syria flummoxed, the Arab Spring in Egypt culminated in a military dictatorship, a Saudi-led war on Yemen went on uninterrupted, and North Korea's steady nuclearization resisted any solution. Furthermore, prioritizing traditional US alliances in the Middle East over worries for democracy and or human rights, the US government under Obama turned a blind eye to the Saudi military intervention in Bahrain in 2011 and the Bahraini government's brutal suppression of the Shiite uprising within days of visit by Obama's defense secretary, Robert Gates. The West's silence on Bahrain smacked of a double standard, underscoring the aversion of the United States toward the democratization of the Gulf's oil monarchies.[101]

The so-called drone president was, however, locked in a serious of "shadow wars"—undeclared conflicts against non-state actors fought by covert means, proxy armies, special forces, drones and other means—that in the end proved more successful in some theaters, such as Iraq, than others, such as Afghanistan.[102] His planned troop withdrawal from both Iraq and Afghanistan in 2011 and 2014, respectively, did not materialize and in both cases he found himself backing the same political horses in Baghdad and Kabul as the Iranians.[103] Strange bedfellows, United States and Iran tacitly cooperated with each other in backing the Shiite-led political order in Iraq against the (Saudi-backed) Sunni forces, while at the same time competing against each other in other theaters of conflict in the region including in Syria and Yemen. Under the veneer of its self-imposed definition of legal authority, the Obama administration engaged in untold number of drone strikes—in Afghanistan, Syria, Iraq, Pakistan, Yemen, Libya, and Somalia—targeting al-Qaeda and ISIS terrorists and in the process killing a number of civilians, deemed as "collateral damage." This lowered the threshold for military intervention abroad and

undermined the sovereign right of noninterference that the Obama administration much like its predecessors nominally professed to respect.

In fact, a fundamental problem with Obama's Middle East policy was the
wide gap between its rhetoric and actual policies, undermining the influence
of the United States in the region.[104] Thus, although the Obama administration routinely signaled its intention to remain engaged in the region by maintaining its military bases and keeping the traditional alliances intact, it also
opened a space for doubt and questions about the commitment and sustained
presence of the United States due to the administration's war-weary talk of
withdrawal and disengagement that, in turn, fueled the sectarian competition
for regional dominance (between Iran and Saudi Arabia) as well as Russia's
determination to insert itself in the regional balance and thus introduce new
constrains on US Middle East policy choices. Coinciding with Obama's
self-restraint in Syria, stemming from the fear of getting dragged in another
Middle East quagmire, was Russia's new Middle East policy, featuring a
realignment of forces that increasingly put the NATO ally Turkey in the
same equation as with Russia and Iran, in turn, raising new questions about
the "Russia containment" policy of the United States that had been in place
since the end of World War II. To reiterate, the containment policy of the
United States for Soviet showed its teeth first in Iran, when the Soviet forces'
refusal to vacate post-war Iran reportedly met the first American exercise of
power that successfully forced the Soviet withdrawal from Iran and the restoration of Iran's territorial sovereignty, followed by more than thirty years
of consistent US policy of shielding Iran under the umbrella of containment.
A historical departure, Iranian revolution of 1979, heralding the rise of an
assertive Islamic state, spelled the end of the country's subordinate role in
the cold war architecture and the concomitant rise of a new US policy of
containment vis-à-vis revolutionary Iran—that has remained basically intact
until now despite its ebbs and flows through six US presidents before Trump.
In a nutshell, this policy stemmed from a novel threat perception, reflected
in Brzezinski's statement: "The Iranian crisis has led to the collapse of the
balance of power in Southwest Asia, and it could produce Soviet presence
right down to the edge of the Arabian and Oman Gulfs."[105] Accordingly, the
United States revised its military strategy in the region by the creation of a
"rapid deployment force", which would in the early 1980s evolve into the
Central Command, better known as CENTCOM in its military jargon, as
well as base-building in the area and contingency plans for a "two-pronged"
attack on Iran by US and Arab forces. Iran Containment and military options
on Iran have been constant staples in the policy of the United States for
Middle East since the late 1970s, resulting in military clashes in the Persian
Gulf during the final stages of Iran-Iraq war. The Iran containment policy has
since then been articulated by a fairly large number of US officials, such as

then-Secretary of State James Baker during his trip to Central Asia in 1992, declaring that containing Iran's influence in the region constituted a major objective of US foreign policy.[106]

Dispensing with a long historical detour already well-covered in the literature on US-Iran relations, suffice to say here that Obama's Middle East and Iran policies were not distinguished by any wholesale change and or any remarkable creativity in terms of redesigning US policy in the region, but rather by wholly incremental changes that were for the most part tactical and or reactive rather than strategic. Obama continued, albeit in a modified form, his predecessor's plan to deploy anti-ballistic missiles and radars on European soil, ostensibly to deter Iran's ballistic missile threat, although this was regarded as a security threat by Russia. As he explained in 2009, the European missile defense was necessary to protect "the United States and Europe from an Iranian ballistic missile armed with a nuclear warhead."[107] The association between Iran and missile defense dated back to the US withdrawal from the Anti-Ballistic Missile Treaty (ABM) in 2002. The 1972 treaty embodied a shared understanding between the United States and the Soviet Union that strategic balance required some restrictions on the development of missile defenses, and was subsequently shelved by the United States following the justification that it and its allies needed protection against "future terrorist or rogue-state missile attacks."[108] Thus, while the United States under Obama tapped into the "Iran threat" for its Russia containment strategy, at the same time it took advantage of the (Sunni versus Shiite) sectarian conflict in the Middle East to contain Iran's influence, notably by nodding to a de facto partnership between Israel and the conservative Sunni states of the Persian Gulf against what Jordan's King Abdullah ominously referred to as the "Shia Crescent."[109] It is noteworthy that the majority of Muslims in the Middle East are Sunnis, constituting around 90% of the population in countries such as Egypt, Jordan, and Saudi Arabia, while Shiites form the majority population in Iran, Iraq, and Bahrain. There are also sizable Shiite communities in Kuwait, Yemen, Lebanon, Qatar, Syria, Saudi Arabia, and the UAE.[110]

However, the outbreak of the "Arab Spring" in 2010–2011 caught the Obama administration by surprise and was initially embraced by Obama, who vowed to "use all our influence to encourage reform in the region" and, yet subsequently, nuanced himself and partially stepped back as a result of "discouraging developments" such as the electoral victory of the Muslim Brotherhood in Egypt and post-Kaddafi warlordism and havoc in Libya, exacting the lives of an American diplomat. Critics of the Obama administration such as Fawaz Gerges have pinpointed instances of "policy blunders" and policy selectiveness in championing reform in the Arab world, for example, by failing to include the oil sheikhdoms of the Persian Gulf, which was attributable to Washington's priority of geopolitical and economic interests overshadowing the concerns for democracy and human rights.[111] In 2009, in the aftermath of controversial presidential elections in Iran igniting mass protests, the Obama administration extended little more than moral support, focusing instead on nuclear negotiations with Tehran's rulers, using the sticks of sanctions, military threat, cyberwarfare, and diplomatic isolation, as well as the carrots of economic relief and "constructive dialogue" centered on how (to paraphrase Obama) the Iranians "can align themselves with international norms and rules and re-enter as full members of the international community."[112] Over time, this hybrid approach that used America's both soft and hard powers would yield results, initially in the form of an interim agreement in Geneva in 2013, which acted as the springboard for the final agreement, the JCPOA, in July, 2015. Obama praised the results by stating: "For the first time in nearly a decade, we have halted progress of the Iran nuclear program, and key parts of the program will be rolled back." Obama had earlier insisted, "We do not have a policy of containment when it comes to a nuclear Iran."[113] Essentially, this meant a bifurcated approach, one in which a nuclear rollback strategy was actively pursued in tandem with a broader and yet less clearly defined containment strategy that assured Tehran that Obama's intention was not to superimpose a regime-change; Obama and his officials had disavowed any intent to impose "freedom" on Iran, in sharp contrast to the subsequent declaration by the Trump administration officials that their intention was to "restore democracy" to Iran.[114] To reiterate, above and beyond his disarmament agenda with Iran Obama did not have a plan of action for a post-JCPOA normalization of relations with Iran. The nuclear issue was just a part of a multi-pronged Iran's containment strategy that required a flexible response on the question of prioritization and how to adjust and re-adjust the pieces of policy and, in a word, sequencing them. With the priority given to the disarmament issue, the Obama administration was forced to step back from détente with Iran even if that was the desired end-game of the president. This was highlighted at a Camp David summit with the heads of the GCC states prior to the final nuclear agreement, where Obama assured his guests that the nuclear deal did not mean a normalization of relations between Tehran and Washington or any diminishing importance of commitment of the United States to contain the Iran threat. This was reflected in the summit's joint communique that stressed the US-GCC strategic partnership and declared that "the United States and GCC states oppose and work together to counter Iran's destabilizing activities in the region."[115] Still, this did not assuage the growing concerns of the GCC states that a post-deal Iran would enable it to gain leverage vis-à-vis its regional rivals by the infusion of Iran's frozen assets and the related ability to build Iran's conventional capability. The glaring absence of several heads of the GCC states at the Camp David summit reflected the Arab misgivings about a "Faustian bargain" on Iran by the Obama administration, shared by the Israeli government and some members of US Congress.[116] Pointing to such negative "trade-offs," some critics of the Obama administration argued that Obama's Iran policy actually exacerbated inter-state conflicts along the Sunni-Shiite divide by "appeasing" Iran on regional issues such as the civil war in Syria for the sake of the nuclear deal.[117] But, this overlooks that the fact that the Obama administration ended up placating the Saudis by granting more arms sales to them and also by tacitly consenting to the Saudi-led war on Yemen, partly as a result of fear that "a major fissure between the United Sates and Saudi Arabia could weaken the Iran deal."[118] Also disconcerting to the Saudis was when in 2016 Obama accused them of being security "free riders," called for a "cold peace" between Tehran and Riyadh, and also urged the latter to "share the neighborhood" with Iran.[119] Still, despite such rhetoric, the United States under Obama never scrapped the American military footprint in the Persian Gulf region—the Saudi-led GCC bloc is a source of gigantic profit for the US military-industrial complex—and thus never wavered from its commitment to stop what it repeatedly characterized as Iran's "imperial ambitions." Keen on maintaining the status quo, whereby the GCC states' necessity for American protectorate power stemmed from the durability of perceived "Iran threat," the United States was at best interested in a "cold peace" between Tehran and Riyadh and not necessarily a warm and cooperative relationship between them. After all, the United States had its own geostrategic calculations vis-à-vis post-revolutionary Iran that openly yearned for the expulsion of US forces from the region, that is, a hostile posture that did not undergo any noticeable transformation even after the nuclear deal, thus guaranteeing the stalemate in overall US-Iran relations irrespective of progress on the nuclear front. This stalemate was tantamount to the perpetuity of "primary sanctions" on Iran, which were in fact augmented during the nuclear negotiations, as, for instance, immediately after reaching the interim nuclear agreement, the administration renewed the oil and banking sanctions on Iran and also decided to sequester 20 airplanes sold to Iran's Mahan Airline and to sanction companies that were behind the deal, arguing that such measures were imposed on Iran because of its rogue behavior, a policy that it continued even after the final deal was reached in 2015. A complicating factor, the two types of "primary" and "secondary" sanctions were interconnected and it was not always easy to distinguish between the nets cast by them, overlapping in some instances, which then became an excuse for procrastination and "foot dragging" by the US Treasury responsible for issuing guidelines on removing the latter category, eliciting complaints from Iran's head of Central Bank, who visited the United States in April 2016, three months after the implementation phase of the JCPOA began.[120] Still, despite such complaints, the JCPOA was in "moderately healthy" state during the final stages of Obama administration, which devoted attention to creating another last-minute legacy, by normalizing diplomatic relations with another "rogue regime," namely, Cuba. Thus, the previous, pre-JCPOA focus, which was taxing on the US diplomats who shouldered the negotiation chores, experienced a certain attrition, which was at any rate required in order to take it to the next level of rapprochement. With both initiatives toward Iran and Cuba heavily criticized in a Republican-dominated Congress, one may argue (with a degree of hesitation) that the rapid advances in the Cuba story were impediments to a similar diplomatic breakthrough in the relations of the United States with Iran on the part of an outgoing president, who was accused of ignoring his own "red lines" on Syria. Arguably, the JCPOA arrived too late in Obama's presidency, and had it been achieved one or two years earlier, it is conceivable that it could pave the way to a diplomatic normalization of relations. This is, of course, a matter of pure speculation about a "potential past" that we dwell on in passing for future rumination.

A former Obama administration official, Ben Rhodes, has suggested that behind Obama's "hands-off" approach toward Syria was the concern that a more interventionist US policy would risk the Iran nuclear deal, which formed Obama's top priority under a firm conviction that the absence of such a deal would have further destabilized the Middle East.[121] A more cynical take on this view, on the other hand, assumes that Obama deliberately soft pedaled on "hard containment" in order to gain the trust of Iran's leaders and thus garner the nuclear concessions from them, reflected in the JCPOA, in the process allowing a twilight of American power in the Middle East made possible by a Russia-Iran concert in the Syrian theater. The problem with this interpretation is that it overlooks that behind the limited intervention of the United States in Syria, which has continued under the Trump administration, was the underlying fact that the United States had no core national interests at stake in Syria that would in turn warrant a major intervention—as can be inferred from a recent Pentagon's admission that that countering Iran in Syria was not a direct objective of the American-led coalition in the region.[122] Moreover, the alternative option (e.g., massive bombing of Syria and troop deployment) left open the question of "the day after," which according to Rhodes himself Obama posed to his advisers by asking what happens after the US bombs the runaways and Russia, Iran, and Assad rebuild them? Also, the nuclear negotiations in fact proved to be a catalyst for greater Iran-US communication on Syria, yielding some positive results, as, for instance, Iran supported the US-Russia initiative to disarm Damascus of its huge chemical weapons stockpile.[123] Besides, Iran's involvement in Syrian conflict was mostly defensive, following the objective of helping a traditional regional ally against foreign-backed terrorism. Therefore, the assumption of a zero-sum relationship between the United States and Iran in situations such as Syria and Iraq, conveying purely opposite sets of interests, is problematic, particularly since the final chapter on the Syrian conflict has yet to be written, in light of the on-going UN-backed efforts to establish a new constitution and free elections in that war ravaged country—that may have posed a much greater security threat to Western interests had it fallen to ISIS and other jihadist terrorist groups.

Obama was by all indications a political realist who was keenly aware of the limits of American power, prompting him to settle for a nuclear deal with Iran that, by his own admission, did not give the United States all it wanted from the negotiations, such as a complete shutdown of Iran's nuclear fuel cycle, yet was deemed satisfactory by virtue of closing all the pathways to an Iranian bomb and thus averting war. This conclusion subsequently turned Obama into a fierce critic of Trump's Iran policy, criticizing Trump's decision to exit the nuclear deal as a deeply "misguided" decision that ran contrary to American national interests. Yet, the relative facility with which Trump managed to unilaterally walk out of the Iran deal was directly related to Obama's political and legislative maneuvers to save the JCPOA, which was nearly derailed by a hostile Congress that had adopted the Iran Nuclear Agreement Review Act in 2015; this act gave Congress sixty days to review any deal achieved with Iran. The House of Representatives did not approve the agreement and it survived through the Senate only as a result of a successful Democratic filibuster. In the end, not one single Republican senator backed the agreement, all of them applauding the Israeli prime minister, who was invited to Congress without the White House's approval and who urged his audience to stand against the deal. Emerging as an "executive agreement" rather than a treaty, requiring Senate's consent, the JCPOA was on shaky political ground from the outset, as vividly pre-warned in a Senate letter to Iran during the final stages of the negotiations. As aptly predicted in that letter, the next administration proved that it "could revoke such an executive agreement with the stroke of a pen."[124] The only problem was that the legislative authors of that letter to Iran failed to foresee the embeddedness of the Iran agreement in international law, as a result of its open embrace by the UN Security Council, in the form of a unanimously-adopted Resolution 2231, which was adopted with the express purpose of turning it into a more robust agreement than a mere political document, that is, as a legally binding international agreement.

THE JCPOA AS AN INTERNATIONAL AGREEMENT

In fact, the JCPOA fits the description of an "international agreement" by the standards of the United States irrespective of the opposite view presented by its own negotiators—as a mere "political agreement." The accord meets the criteria set by the US Department of State's Directive on International Agreements. The US Directive admits that "forms as such are not normally an important factor." It states: "International agreements require precision and specificity in the language setting forth the undertaking of the parties."[125] Undoubtedly, the JCPOA meets this standard in light of its comprehensive details about the obligations of both sides fully discussed in the previous chapter. Also, the US Directive's emphasis on the "identity" of the parties, that is, "state parties," is met by the JCPOA as the byproduct of diplomatic agreement among seven states, which was then turned international through its adoption by the UN. Another important criterion is the "absence of any provision in the arrangement with respect to governing law," in which case "it will be presumed that it is governed by international law." Similarly, there is no explicit discussion in the JCPOA with respect to "governing law," save references to the UN and the NPT, as a result of which the presumption that the accord is governed by international law applies.

A common misconception regarding the JCPOA is that it is not legally binding because it is not signed by either Iran or the other parties known as the "5 +1," that is, the United States, China, Russia, France, England, and Germany. But this overlooks that signatures on international agreements is not a prerequisite and such an agreement does not have to be signed. The important criterion in this respect is the formal commitment to an agreement by the appropriate officials of a state. It can be safely then stated that Iran and the "5 +1" nations conducted negotiations and have "signed onto" the agreement by reaching it. Also, the negotiators agreed to give the JCPOA the blessing of the UN Security Council, a move which saddled the nuclear deal with much greater signification. We now focus on the legal ramifications of the JCPOA's adoption by the UNSC Resolution 2231, which calls upon all the member states to faithfully implement the JCPOA. To elaborate, prefigured in the JCPOA, Resolution 2231 was adopted exactly one week after the JCPOA was finalized as a result of the intense negotiations in Vienna. The resolution provides for the termination of the provisions of previous (seven) Security Council resolutions on the Iranian nuclear issue, retains a temporary arms embargo and ballistic missile technology ban, codifies the sanctions "snapback" mechanism, under which all Security Council sanctions will be automatically reimposed if Iran breaches the deal, and assigns to the IAEA the necessary verification and monitoring of Iran's nuclear-related commitments under the JCPOA for their full duration. Also, the resolution calls on the UN Secretary General to provide a bi-annual report to the Security Council on the JCPOA's implementation and also sets up a Security Council Facilitator to provide a brief on the JCPOA's implementation parallel to the efforts of the Secretary General.[126] It is noteworthy that this resolution is invoked under Article 41 of Chapter VII of the UN Charter, which authorizes it to adopt measures necessary to maintain international peace and security; all the other previous Iran resolutions, that is, Resolutions 1737, 1747, 1803, and 1929, which imposed sanctions on Iran, invoked Article 41 of Chapter VII as well. Article 41 states:

> The Security Council may decide what measures not involving the use of armed force are to be employed to give effect to its decisions, and it may call upon the Members of the United Nations to apply such measures. These may include complete or partial interruption of economic relations and of rail, sea, air, postal, telegraphic, radio, and other means of communication, and the severance of diplomatic relations.

According to Oscar Schachter and other international law experts, the language in Article 41 is broad enough to cover any type of action not involving the use of force, which is addressed in Article 42.[127] A Security Council resolution is "binding" when it is capable of creating obligations on its addressees. The starting point in interpreting a resolution should be the natural and ordinary meaning of the terms used by the Security Council and the weight and importance attached to its "demands" and or "requests" by the Council. Resolution 2231 "affirms" that the JCPOA's adoption "marks a fundamental shift in its consideration of the issue," urges all member-states to fully comply with the terms of the JCPOA, and "decides under Article 41" that "states shall comply" with the various provisions of the resolution. It "underscores" that "that Member States are obligated under Article 25 of the Charter of the United Nations to accept and carry out the Security Council's decisions" and then goes on to call for the agreement's adoption by the Member-States. Indeed, the "binding" nature of the resolution can be confirmed by the resolution's own explicit reliance on Article 25. Article 25 states: "The Members of the United Nations agree to accept and carry out the decisions of the Security Council." This is a legal obligation, enforceable under international law, which has a broad and evolving scope encompassing the decisions of Security Council increasingly acting as a fount of international law.[128] Given that Article 25 is placed in the Charter's sections dealing with the general powers and functions of the Security Council, it clearly indicates the applicability of Article 25 for any of the Security Council's actions, and not just those taken pursuant to other articles, for example, Articles 39, 41, and 42. Resolution 2231, with its detailed innovation of new tasks for the UN Secretary General and the IAEA Director General, "snapback" mechanism, timetable for arms embargo removal, "Termination Day" and, above all, its call on member-states to adopt and implement the provisions of the JCPOA, clearly meets the standards of a "substantive" rather than merely "hortatory" decision; substantive decisions within the meaning of Article 25 of the Charter are typically referenced to as "legally binding decisions."[129] To elaborate, historically speaking the Security Council has adopted two "types" of resolutions: recommendations of a hortatory nature, and decisions of a mandatory nature. The scope of Council's decisions and their legal nature or effects has been a subject of scholarly debate for years. With respect to Resolution 2231, the implications of this debate are not merely scholastic, but affect the extent to which the JCPOA was legally protected and became *Ergo Omnes*, that is, valid for the world, rather than an ordinary *traité contrat*.

Another misconception regarding the JCPOA is that the UN Resolution 2231 is not binding because it uses the terms "decides" or "calls upon" instead of stronger words such as "mandate." According to Jon Bellinger, "the UNSC "calls on" all UN member states to support implementation of the JCPOA, but it does not obligate the United States to do so as a matter of international law."[130] This is patently incorrect. First, every UN Security Council (adopted) resolution that contains a request is, indeed, binding. Second, as stated earlier, the Resolution 2231 deliberately invokes Article 25, which, in turn, makes it mandatory for the United States and other UN member-states to carry out its decisions with respect to the JCPOA. This Resolution's choice of words is, on the other hand, a rather weak barometer to gauge its significance. Although different tones must be recognized among these terms, it is not always easy to ascertain the legal force of a resolution from the choice of wording in its formulation. Words "may not be associated with probable legal effects."[131] Heinze and Fitzmaurice have rightly stated: "Words such as 'urges' or 'calls upon' are not necessarily of a purely hortatory nature. As will all documents that come under legal analysis, the totality of the document, rather than any particular words, must be given its overall import."[132] Taking the totality of the Security Council Resolution 2231 into consideration means, first of all, it not only endorses the JCPOA but also supplements it through important new provisions that are not in the JCPOA, such as the "snapback" mechanism and arms and missile-technology embargoes, that is, well beyond a mere hortatory modality simply urging or encouraging compliance with the commitments and obligations listed in the agreement. At this point, a detailed examination of the JCPOA is in order.

THE IRAN NUCLEAR AGREEMENT REVISITED

In retrospect, having witnessed Trump's backlash against the JCPOA, it is worthwhile to remember the world-wide euphoria erupting after the agreement was reached following a grueling multilateral negotiation process—that stretched over a decade and had proceeded along a "dual track" western approach, combining the stick of sanctions and military threats and the carrots of sanctions' relief and Iran's economic re-integration in the international community. In Iran, in particular, the spontaneous popular celebrations in the streets of Tehran and other cities throughout the country was in tune with the government's upbeat assessment about the dawn of a new "post-sanctions" era due to Iran's "heroic" diplomacy yielding a "decisive victory." The few Iranians who dared to criticize the JCPOA, including some members of the previous negotiation team or some conservative members of the parliament, were overshadowed by the tidal wave of optimism about the country's future generated by the nuclear breakthrough. Even the country's Supreme Leader offered his blessing for the historic deal, portrayed by the Rouhani government as a "win-win" for both sides, while admitting that Iran had "paid a heavy price" in the nuclear bargain. After a hotly debated delay, the Iranian parliament finally approved the JCPOA, despite powerful concerns on the part of some lawmakers that the agreement had crossed Iran's declared "red lines" by conceding too many concessions, thus mirror-imaging the American critics of the JCPOA, including Trump, who criticized it as being totally lop-sided in favor of Iran. Compared to such negative assessments of the JCPOA, the nuclear expert community in the United States and Europe was largely united in praising the agreement as a "net non-proliferation plus," in light of the ICPOA's strong nuclear safeguards and Iran's pledge in the agreement that it "will not engage in activities that could contribute to the development of a nuclear device"[133]—in conformity with Iran's obligations under Article III of the Non-Proliferation Treaty (NPT). Many nuclear experts have written about the JCPOA as a landmark agreement with the potential for broader implications for the future of NPT and the resolution of other similar nuclear crises in the future.[134]

We must, however, be on guard against reducing the Iran "nuclear deal" to the JCPOA, which was a common error on the part of president Trump, who never bothered to reflect on a second agreement that was closely intertwined with the JCAPOA, namely, the Iran-IAEA agreement(s), which led to the resolution of the contentious issue of so-called possible military dimensions to Iran's civilian nuclear program, as well as to the creation of one of the most robust inspection system in IAEA's history. On the whole, the Iran nuclear deal was broader than the JCPOA, a byproduct of two parallel negotiations, between Iran and the world powers on the one hand and, on the other, Iran and the UN's atomic agency, reinforcing each other, even though the IAEA was not a party to the JCPOA negotiations.[135] In fact, the latter had preceded the Obama administration and stretched back to 2007 Iran-IAEA "work plan" that led to "substantial progress" in tackling the Iran nuclear crisis by virtue of resolving the so-called outstanding issues regarding Iran's nuclear program. Those "outstanding issues" were related to such issues as activities at a uranium mine, sources of contamination of equipment , Iran's centrifuges procurement and work on advanced centrifuges, and a document pertaining to uranium metal, all of which were announced to be "no longer outstanding" per a February 2008 IAEA report. Another issue pertaining to "alleged weaponization studies", which was connected to the "possible military dimension" (PMD) of Iran's civilian nuclear program remained outstanding until December 2015, when the IAEA essentially closed the book on the PMD in its final report. According to that report, Iran had pursued a nuclear weapons program prior to 2003, but did not divert nuclear material from its civilian program as part of any weaponization efforts. The report also stated that some weaponization activities continued through 2009, but these activities "did not advance beyond feasibility and scientific studies, and the acquisition of certain relevant technical competences and capabilities." The report concluded by stating that there were "no credible indications" that any undeclared activities had taken place since 2009. In response to the report, in December 2015, the IAEA Board of Governors voted unanimously to close the investigation into Iran's past activities while continuing to report on Iran's implementation of its obligations under the JCPOA. Here, we use the version of JCPOA, which has been adopted by the European Union.[136] The JCPOA in its Preamble envisions a "step by step" process for the implementation of the agreement, reflecting a pattern of "reciprocal commitments." In a nutshell, it promises that the agreement "will produce the comprehensive lifting of all UN Security Council sanctions as well as the multilateral and national sanctions related to Iran's nuclear program, including steps on access in areas of trade, technology, finance, and energy" in exchange for Iran's fulfillment of its obligations, which are fairly extensive.

REVIEW OF IRAN'S EXTENSIVE OBLIGATIONS UNDER THE JCPOA

The JCPOA calls for a significant reduction in the number and types of Iranian centrifuges for a fifteen-year period. At the time of the interim agreement in November 2013, Iran had installed a total of 19,480 centrifuges at its two enrichment facilities in Natanz and Fordow. Most of these were first generation IR-1 centrifuges and only 1,008 were of the second-generation IR-2. Under the JCPOA, Iran agreed to limit all enrichment-related activities at the Natanz fuel enrichment plant, capped at a maximum of 5,060 IR-1 centrifuges, and to end its current fuel enrichment activities at Fordow. A maximum of 1,044 centrifuges at Fordow for the specific purpose of isotopes' production was allowed. On the whole, under the deal, Iran agreed to dismantle roughly two-thirds of its installed centrifuges and one-third of its operating centrifuges. Under the agreement, Iran was also obligated to get rid of its stockpile of 20 percent enriched uranium, estimated at around 196 kilograms at the time, by converting it into fuel for the Tehran research reactor. The ceiling for the maximum level of enrichment was put at 3.67 percent for a period of 15 years. Also, Iran agreed to limit its stockpile of 5 percent enriched uranium to 300 kilograms, from a stockpile of 10,000 kilograms, that is, a 98 percent reduction.

With respect to centrifuge R & D, Iran agreed that for a period of fifteen years, the only uranium testing would take place at the Natanz Pilot Fuel Enrichment Plant and mechanical testing at the Tehran Research Reactor. There would be no centrifuge R & D at the Fordow facility for a period of fifteen years. During this time period, Iran's uranium testing was limited to IR-4, IR-5, IR-6, and IR-8 centrifuges and Iran would need to seek approval for conducting mechanical tests on new models. Iran was barred from any R & D on alternative forms of uranium separation, such as laser or gaseous diffusion, for a period of 10 years. The JCPOA further stipulates (Annex 1, Para 16) that Iran commits to "not to engage in activities, including at the R &D level which could contribute to the development of a nuclear explosive device, including uranium or plutonium metallurgy activities."

Furthermore, the JCPOA aims to block a "plutonium path" to an Iranian nuclear bomb by imposing significant changes that would "redesign" the heavy-water reactor in Arak. Iran agreed to not undertake the manufacturing of any plutonium separation plant, which is an important prerequisite for a plutonium-based bomb. Also, Iran agreed to reduce the reactor's capacity from 40 MW to 20 MW and to redesign it such that instead of natural uranium it will operate on low-enriched uranium. Iran agreed to ship out of the country all the spent fuel from the reactor during its entire operation. In addition, Iran agreed to submit for approval the design of a new reactor core and to refrain from accumulating heavy water for fifteen years and to export all excess heavy water to the international market.[137]

THE JCPOA'S ROBUST INSPECTION REGIME

The JCPOA is notable for its imposition of a thorough inspection regime on Iran's nuclear program above and beyond the country's safeguards agreement with the IAEA, for example, by extending inspections and verifications to several activities, which do not involve nuclear material. Iran agreed to begin the implementation of the IAEA's intrusive Additional Protocol from the "Adoption Day" and to seek the Protocol's ratification eight years later, on the "Transition Day," which would fall in October, 2023.[138] There is no time limit for Iran's obligations under the safeguards agreement with the IAEA, which will continue after the JCPOA time frame has been reached. Under the

JCPOA, however, the IAEA is equipped with further tools to monitor Iran's nuclear program. The agency is granted the right to raise concerns about undeclared nuclear activities or facilities under the terms of either the comprehensive safeguard agreement or the Additional Protocol. Per the JCPOA, Annex 1, Section 74, the IAEA requests for access cannot be made in "bad faith." This section is worth quoting: "Requests for access pursuant to provisions of this JCPOA will be made in good faith, with due observance of the sovereign rights of Iran, and kept to the minimum necessary to effectively implement the verification responsibilities under this JCPOA. In line with normal international safeguards practice, such requests will not be aimed at interfering with Iranian military or other national security activities but will be exclusively for resolving concerns regarding fulfillment of the JCPOA commitments and Iran's other non-proliferation and safeguards obligations."

In case of a dispute between Iran and the IAEA on the latter's inspection requests, the Joint commission would intervene by consensus or a majority vote of 5 to 4 pursuant to a time-bound mechanism (of twenty-four days) for an Iranian response to a "challenged" request (Annex, para 14); in case Iran refuses to comply with the decision, this would trigger the "snapback" provision (discussed below) on Iran sanctions within three days. In addition, the IAEA will monitor the mining and milling activities in Iran for a period of twenty-five years.[139]

As part of its new transparency commitments, reflected in an Iran-IAEA "roadmap Agreement" signed on the day the JCPOA was reached in July 2015, Iran has also agreed to fully implement the modified Code 3.1 of the Subsidiary Arrangements to its safeguards agreement with the IAEA, according to which Iran would have to inform the atomic agency of any new nuclear facility as soon as the decision to build it is taken, rather than six months prior to the introduction of nuclear material into the facility (as called for by the safeguards agreement). Iran's obligations under Code 3.1 were not time-bound and would be in place as long as Iran was a member-state of the IAEA. Also, Iran's nuclear procurement would be closely monitored as the agreement calls for the UN Security Council's approval for the sale of "all items, materials, equipment, goods, and technology" referenced in the Nuclear Suppliers Group's list of "dual use items."

Finally, in addition to agreeing to not undertake any activities that would contribute to the development of a nuclear explosive device, under the JCPOA Iran agrees (Annex 1, Para 82) to stay clear of a range of other prohibited activities, which are as follows: designing or acquiring using (i) computer models to simulate nuclear explosive devices, (ii) multi-point explosive trigger systems, (iii) explosive diagnostic systems, (iv) explosively driven neutron sources. Also, under the terms of the UN Security Council Resolution

2231 (July 2015), which endorsed the JCPOA and thus put a seal of international acceptability on it, an eight-year restriction on Iran's (nuclear-capable) ballistic missile activities as well as a five-year ban on conventional arms transfers to Iran were imposed. Specifically, Annex B of Resolution 2231 calls upon Iran "not to undertake any activity related to ballistic missiles designed to be capable of delivering nuclear weapons, including launches using ballistic missile technology."

THE JCPOA OBLIGATIONS AND
COMMITMENTS OF THE OTHER PARTIES

Section 4 of JCPOA's Annex II spells out the details of various sanctions on Iran, which were to be removed, that is, lifted, under the agreement. For the Europeans, whose sanctions were directly pegged to the UN Security Council's sanctions, the latter's removal meant that they would nearly dismantle their sanctions regime on Iran, thus allowing the normalization of commercial relations with Iran, save the embargo on sales to Iran of arms, missile technology, and other proliferation-sensitive items. In comparison, as is well known, the United States opted for a more limited approach to sanctions removal by, first and foremost, making the distinction between nuclear-related and nuclear-unrelated sanctions and, second, by agreeing to lift only the "secondary" sanctions—that had been imposed to discourage "non-US" entities from doing business with Iran under the threat of facing punitive measures and being denied access to the US market—as opposed to primary sanctions prohibiting US companies or persons from doing business with Iran.[140] As a result, the structure of US sanctions on Iran remained essentially intact, in sharp contrast to China and Russia, who completely removed all their (nuclear-based) sanctions on Iran.[141]

Per the terms of the JCPOA, the EU committed to terminate, as of the "Implementation Day," a whole array of commercial and financial restrictions that had been enacted into law in the course of the Iran nuclear crisis. Briefly, the following sanctions were designated by the JCPOA to be lifted:

- sanctions on the import of oil, gas, and petrochemical products from Iran;
- sanctions on banking activities with Iran;
- sanctions on investment in the Iranian energy and petrochemical sectors;
- sanctions on insurance activities with Iran;
- sanctions on shipping and shipbuilding;
- sanctions on gold, diamonds, and other precious metals;
- sanctions related to the transpiration sector.

The aforementioned sanctions reliefs did not consume the entire gamut of EU sanctions on Iran, which included human rights-related sanctions, which remained unaffected by the JCPOA. Under the latter's terms, the formal termination of all nuclear-related EU sanctions on Iran would occur on the "Transition Day," which is October 18, 2023. Until then, the EU's arms embargo and restrictions on the transfer of missile technology to Iran also remained in place. With respect to the United States, on the other hand, the JCPOA's Annex II and V spell out the commitments and obligation of the United States.

COMMITMENTS AND OBLIGATIONS OF THE UNITED STATES UNDER THE JCPOA

The United States has made the following commitments under the terms of the JCPOA:

- to suspend its efforts to curb Iran's crude oil sales;
- to lift sanctions with respect to financial transactions between non-US persons or entities and Iranian entities, including the Iranian Central Bank, the National Iranian Oil company, National Iranian Tanker Company, and Naftiran Intertrade Company;
- to lift sanctions on the sale, supply, or transfer of goods and services used in connection with Iran's automotive sector;
- to stop sanctions on non-US persons or entities for engaging in activities in the energy and petrochemical sectors of Iran;
- to lift sanctions on trade with Iran in graphite, raw or semi-finished metals such as aluminum and steel, coal, and software for integrating industrial processes, in connection with activities that are consistent with the JCPOA;
- to stop sanctions on non-US persons or entities engaging in transactions related to the purchase or sale of Iranian currency, rial, or providing of financial services to the Central Bank of Iran and other designated Iranian financial institutions;
- to stop sanctions on non-US persons or entities involved with Iran's shipping and shipbuilding sectors and port operators. This does not apply to persons who knowingly provide support for the transportation of proliferation-sensitive material or terrorism-related activities;
- to lift sanctions on the provision of underwriting services, insurance, or reinsurance in connection with activities that are consistent with the JCPOA;
- The United States agreed to remove certain individuals from the US sanctions lists;

- The United States agreed to allow US and non-US persons and entities to enter into commercial relations with Iran for the sale of commercial passenger aircraft and related parts for exclusively civilian purposes;
- the United States agreed to issue licenses for the import of Iranian carpets and foodstuffs into the United States; also, the United States agreed to begin issuing licenses for foreign subsidiaries of US companies to engage in activities with Iran that are permitted under the JCPOA;
- the United States agreed to seek legislative action with respect to the termination of sanctions under the JCPOA;
- the United States agreed to remove additional groups of persons and entities from its sanctions list on the Transition Day, consistent with normal US interactions with other non-nuclear member-states who are parties to the NPT; also on Transition Day, the United States was obligated to remove sanctions on joint ventures related to mining, production, and transportation of uranium in Iran.
- the United States agreed to refrain from imposing any new nuclear-related sanctions on Iran, or re-imposing the sanctions lifted pursuant to the JCPOA.

In addition to the aforementioned, United States also emerged as a potential nuclear partner with Iran, in light of the JCPOA's Annex III, titled "Civil Nuclear Cooperation," which provides a long list of areas, ranging from nuclear fuel to nuclear waste, to plant modernization, to medical nuclear research, and so on, where the "5 +1" nations have pledged to cooperate with Iran, both bilaterally and multilaterally and mainly, though by no means exclusively, through the IAEA.[142] Accordingly, "The civil nuclear and the scientific cooperation projects envisioned between Iran and the E3/EU+3 as part of this JCPOA may be undertaken in a variety of formats." As a result, United States was initially supposed to partake in the design of a new core for the reactor in Arank, and in 2016 purchased 32 metric tons of heavy water from Iran, since reducing Iran's stockpile of both enriched uranium and heavy water were key components of the JCPOA.[143]

The JCPOA has set up a Dispute Resolution Mechanism to deal with the potential disputes that may arise during the implementation phase of the agreement. In case a party complains that another party is not fulfilling its JCPOA obligations, then the matter can be discussed by the Joint Commission for a period of fifteen days and, in case there is still no resolution, then the matter will be referred to a three-member Advisory Board, comprised one member from each side of the dispute and one independent adviser. The opinion of the advisory board is considered by the Joint Commission for up to five days and then, if after thirty days, the issue is still unresolved to the satisfaction of the complaining party, it can then be referred to the UN Security Council by the Commission as grounds that "it believes the issue constitutes significant non-performance" (JCPOA, Para 36 and 37).

For its part, the UN Security Council has carved out a unique role for itself under the terms of the Resolution 2231, which states that any party can bring a complaint of "significant non-compliance" directly to the Council, which can trigger a new resolution to continue the Iran sanctions relief within 30 days and in case at the end of 30 days no such resolution is adopted, then all the previous UN sanctions resolutions on Iran will be re-instituted. This unique procedure for the so-called "sanctions' snapback" has been innovated to bypass the veto power of the permanent members, which could block such a resolution, and thus facilitate the reapplication of lifted sanctions in the event of a credible complaint of "non-compliance" on Iran's part.[144] However, comparatively little is said about "non-compliance" by other parties, a major lacunae that came to light when the United States, one of the principal architects of the JCPOA, decided to unilaterally exit the agreement.

CONTROVERSY OVER THE JCPOA'S "SUNSET CLAUSE"

The JCPOA's main text provides for the removal of all existing restrictions on Iran's civilian nuclear program after a fifteen-year period. It states: "Successful implementation of this JCPOA will enable Iran to fully enjoy its right to nuclear energy for peaceful purposes under the relevant articles of the Nuclear Non-Proliferation Treaty (NPT) in line with its obligations therein, and the Iranian nuclear program will be treated in the same manner as that of any other non-nuclear-weapon state party to the NPT. This aspect of the JCPOA has been vehemently criticized by the US and Israeli opponents of the agreement, including president Trump, alleging that with the end of JCPOA restrictions, Iran's path to nuclear weapons will be cleared. This criticism has been dismissed by the Obama administration officials as "invalid," "misleading" and "bogus," following the argument that the "Sun never sets on Iran's program," to paraphrase John Kerry, who has pointed out that there is no timeline for some of Iran's obligations, that even after some of the JCPOA restrictions expire, Iran will still be subjected to rigorous IAEA inspections under the Additional Protocol, and that Iran's NPT commitments reiterated in the JCPOA will continue to be binding on the country. Swayed by the opposite argument, the Trump administration rejected such defenses of the JCPOA and decided to terminate the cooperation of the United States with the agreement in August 2018. In the next chapter, we provide a close, and critical, scrutiny of this fateful decision that, in fact, constitutes one of the most controversial decisions of the Trump presidency.

NOTES

1. In the studies of international relations, containment and engagement are often understood as strategies of foreign policy aimed to balance the power of potential adversaries. Containment strategy seeks to limit the power of adversaries by all means. Engagement is defined as "strategic interaction process to encourage an adversary to co-operate" often by offering incentives in order to procure the desired outcome. For more on this see, Richard N. Haass and Meghan L. O'Sullivan, *Honey and Vinegar: Incentives, Sanctions, and Foreign Policy* (Washington, DC: Brookings Institutions, 2000). Also, John L. Gaddis, *Strategies of Containment* (Oxford: Oxford University Press, 1982).

2. For a relevant work on "grand strategy" in American foreign policy thinking, see William C. Martel, *Grand Strategy in Theory and Practice: The Need for an Effective Alternative American Foreign Policy* (Cambridge: Cambridge University Press, 2015). According to Martel, grand strategy "describes how the nation sees its role in the world and the broad objectives that govern its actions." We leave open here the question of whether Trump's Iran approach was actually less than a grand strategy and also whether it contained the coherent "bridging" elements that weaved together a consistent long-term grand strategy. The self-image of this approach as a grand strategy should not be confused with its actuality, however. For a commentary that criticized Trump's Iran policy for lacking in terms of short-term strategy, see Robin Wright, "Trump's New, Confrontational Foreign Policy, and the End of the Iran Deal," *New Yorker*, May 21, 2018, https://www.newyorker.com/magazine/2018/05/21.

3. Thomas Erdbrink and Glenn Kessler, "Obama Message to Iran," *Washington Post*, March 21, 2009, http://www.washingtonpost.com/wp-dyn/content/article/2009/03/20/AR2009032000398.html. Our analysis in this book stands in sharp contrast to Trita Parsi, who has argued that Obama's nuclear diplomacy with Iran aimed to "lose an enemy." This is a naive interpretation and misconstrues the purpose of these negotiations to contain the Iran threat. See Trita Parsi, *Losing an Enemy: Obama, Iran, and the Triumph of Diplomacy* (New Haven, CT: Yale University Press, 2017).

4. Stephanie Liebergen, "Obama Calls Trump's Iran Deal Decision 'Misguided'," *Newsy.com*, August 8, 2018.

5. For more on Clinton's North Korea policy, see C. S. Eliot Kang, "North Korea and the US Grand Security Strategy," *Comparative Strategy* 20, no. 1 (2001), 25–43.

6. "Iran Will Work with US against ISIS Only after Nuclear Crisis Resolved," *Russia Today*, September 26, 2014.

7. "Today, the only matter for negotiation is the nuclear matter. This will become an experience for us. If the other side stops its usual obstinacy, this will be an experience for us and we will find out that we can negotiate with it over other matters as well. But if we see that they continue to behave in the same obstinate and deviant way, well, our previous experience will naturally be strengthened." In "Leader's Speech in Meeting with Panegyrists," *Khamenei.ir*, April 9, 2015, http://english.khamenei.ir/news/2045/Leader-s-Speech-in-Meeting-with-Panegyrists; https://www.newsy.com/stories/obama-criticizes-trump-s-decision-to-leave-the-iran-deal/.

8. George Jahn and Matthew Lee, "Iran to US: Nuke Deal Could Result in Joint Cooperation," *Associated Press*, July 3, 2015, http://bigstory.ap.org/article/0673 b5cdf3a942908ac7c1ec0c9c6197/un-nuke-agency-chief-says-more-work-needed-iran-probe.

9. Quoted in Jeffrey Goldberg, "The Obama Doctrine, R.I.P.," *The Atlantic*, April 7, 2017, https://www.theatlantic.com/international/archive/2017/04/the-obama-doctrine-rip/522276/.

10. Quoted in Teresa Welsh, "Does Nuclear Deal Hold Hope for Future U.S.-Iran Relations?" *US News & World Report*, May 15, 2015, https://www.usnews.com/news/articles/2015/05/15/does-nuclear-deal-hold-hope-for-future-us-iran-relations.

11. John Grady, "Mattis: U.S. Suffering Strategic Atrophy," *USNI.Org*, March 14, 2015, https://news.usni.org/2015/05/14/mattis-u-s-suffering-strategic-atrophy. This view was articulated by a number of Republican politicians, including Dick Cheney and Liz Cheney in their book, *Exceptionalism: Why the World Needs a Powerful America* (New York: Simon and Schuster, 2015). The authors vehemently accuse the Obama administration of abdicating the containment strategy of the United States for Iran in favor of appeasement.

12. For a view that emphasizes continuity between Trump and Obama, see Edward Hunt, "Obama, Trump, and the Future of U.S. Foreign Policy," *Foreign Policy in Focus*, November 23, 2016, https://fpif.org/obama-trump-future-u-s-foreign-policy/.

13. For more on Trump's "populism" and its nuances, paradoxes, and contradictions, see "Trump's Populism: What Business Leaders Need to Understand," *Harvard Business School*, March 22, 2018, https://hbswk.hbs.edu/item/trump-s-populism-what-business-leaders-need-to-understand?cid=wk-rss. Also, Geoffrey Kabaservice, "Wild Populism Has a Long History in US History, But Trump Is Surely Unique," *The Guardian*, January 14, 2017, https://www.theguardian.com/commentisfree/2017/jan/15/wild-populism-long-history-us-politics-trump-surely-unique. Trump's rise is often associated with the anti-tax, anti-Obama Tea Party. See, Vanessa Williamson, "What the Tea Party Tells US about the Trump Presidency," Brookings Institution, November, 2016, https://www.brookings.edu/blog/fixgov/2016/11/09/tea-party-and-trump-presidency/. In our view, the association of Trump with populism is to a large extent questionable, simply because Trump may have been championing the have-nots, but in reality this was a form of cynical exploitation, by an unscrupulous politician, who was surrounded from birth with wealth, his tastes ran to extravagant luxury, and whose economic policies counted the wealthy Americans as the main beneficiaries. It is therefore more apt to speak of Trump's "pseudo-populism."

14. The *New York Times* editorial stated: "For the first time since before WWII, America chose a president who promised to reverse the internationalism practiced by predecessors of both parties and to build walls both physical and metaphorical. Mr. Trump's win foreshadowed an America more focused on its own affairs while leaving the world to take care of itself." See, "Donald Trump's Victory Promises to Upend the International Order," *New York Times*, November 9, 2016, https://www.nytimes.com/2016/11/09/world/donald-trumps-victory-promises-to-upend-the-international-order.html.

15. "Trump: We Spent $6 Trillion in Middle East and We Are Less than Nowhere; Far Worse than 16 years Ago," *Real Clear Politics*, February 27, 2017, https://www.realclearpolitics.com/video/2017/02/27/trump_we_spent_6_trillion_in_middle_east_and_we_are_less_than_nowhere_far_worse_than_16_years_ago.html.

16. Donald Trump, "We Will Stop Racing to Topple Foreign Regimes," *The Guardian*, December 7, 2016, https://www.theguardian.com/us-news/2016/dec/07/donald-trump-we-will-stop-racing-to-topple-foreign-regimes.

17. As a candidate, Trump stated that he wouldn't rule out the use of tactical nuclear weapons against ISIS terrorists. See, "Unpredictability on Nukes among Trump's Keys to Muslim Respect," *Bloomberg*, March 23, 2016, https://www.bloomberg.com/news/articles/2016-03-23/trump-lays-out-vision-for-gaining-respect-from-muslim-world.

18. Trump's Islamophobia led him in 2015 to call for a ban on Muslim immigration to the United States, an idea that outraged the international community and was later revised in the form of a select ban on seven Muslim countries. See, "U.N. Rights Chief: Trump Call for Muslim Ban "Irresponsible," *Associated Press*, December 8, 2015, http://www.nexis.com/results/enhdocview.do? Behind Trump's Islamophobia was an attempt to knock down Obama as a closet Muslim, questioning Obama's legitimacy by raising suspicions about his American birth certificate, as a right-wing campaign strategy. For more on this see, Roger Stone, *The Making of the President 2016: How Donald Trump Orchestrated a Revolution* (New York: Skyhorse Publishing, 2017).

19. Stephen M. Walt, "Why Trump Is Getting Away with Foreign Policy Insanity," *Foreignpolicy.com*, July 18, 2018, https://foreignpolicy.com/2018/07/18/why-trump-is-getting-away-with-foreign-policy-insanity/.

20. Oystein Tunsjo, "Another Long Peace?" *The National Interest*, October 17, 2018, https://nationalinterest.org/feature/another-long-peace-33726. Tunsoj has summarized what Trump has done with respect to Russia: "Approved the deployment of NATO forces . . . delivered lethal weapons, including anti-tank weapons to the Kiev government . . . expelled dozens of Russian diplomats and closed the Russian consulate in Seattle; maintained sanctions on Russia for its invasion of Crimea . . . and killed over a hundred Russian mercenaries in Syria."

21. Quoted in Martin S. Indyk, "A Trump Doctrine for the Middle East," *Brookings Institution*, April 16, 2018, https://www.brookings.edu/blog/order-from-chaos/2018/04/16/a-trump-doctrine-for-the-middle-east/.

22. Michael Wolf, *Fire and Fury: Inside the Trump White House* (New York: Henry Holt and Company, 2018): 225. Wolf describes Trump's hostile Iran policy as a Trump's version of realpolitik by a president who conducted foreign policy out of "just pure opportunism" (226).

23. Robin Wright, "Trump's New, Confrontational Foreign Policy and the End of the Iran Deal," *New Yorker*, May 21, 2018, https://www.newyorker.com/magazine/2018/05/21/the-end-of-the-iran-deal-and-trumps-new-confrontational-foreign-policy. After losing the House of Representatives to the Democratic Party in November 2018 mid-term congressional elections, Trump's Iran policy faced a new challenge in

the form of congressional oversight. See, Brett Samuels and Rebecca Kheel, "Trump Faces New Hurdles on Foreign Policy," *The Hill*, November 13, 2018.

24. "Donald Trump: It's Time to Shake Rust Off America's Foreign Policy," *Bloomberg*, April 27, 2016, https://www.bloomberg.com/news/videos/2016-04-27/t rump-it-s-time-to-shake-the-rust-off-america-s-foreign-policy. To open a parenthesis here, it is tempting to use the Hegelian term *aufhebung* (sublation) to describe the contradictory nature of Trump's connection to Obama's legacy. Hegel described *aufhebung* as "a union which can only be stated as an unrest of incompatibles." See G.W.H. Hegel, *Science of Logic*, translated by A. V. Miller (Amherst, NY: Humanity Books, 1969): 106–107. The concept *aufhebung* conveys a perpetual oscillation between opposition and preservation, in contrast to a straightforward "overcoming" or negation. Despite the appearance of an outright destruction of the Obama legacy, our point her backed by empirical data is a more complex reality denoting a differentiated Trumpian pivot away from and toward his predecessor's foreign policy orientation particularly with respect to Iran, with the points of "suppression" and negation or discontinuity having the upper hands. A philosophical re-reading this subject has the merit of not only recasting what has transpired so far but also the potential release of "a back to the past" progression of Trump's Iran policy, that is, a new reconciliation with Obama's Iran legacy, instead of "tarrying with the negative," to paraphrase Hegel. The detection of traces of Obamaian thinking in Trump's foreign policy approach discussed here can also be studies through the Derridaian lens and, indeed recalls what Derrida wrote about Hegel, which applies *mutatis mutandis*, to relations between Trump and Obama: "Hegel . . . blinded himself to that which he had laid bare under the rubric of negativity." See Jacques Derrida, *Writing and Difference*, translated by Alan Bass (Chicago: Chicago University Press, 1978): 259. Hence, it can be said that the paradoxical, self-contradictory, and internally split *aufhebung* of Trump's post-Obama Iran policy was the crux of Trump's dilemma on Iran. Trump's "radical alterity" vis-à-vis Obama could evolve more pronounced, but it could also turn toward a new reconciliation at the policy level signifying mutations born by the limits of the confrontation approach or paradigm. It could of course move in the opposite direction of reflecting the lopsidedness of the points of discontinuity and the stabilization of the negative tension (with Obama's legacy).

25. Michael R. Pompeo, "Confronting Iran: The Trump Administration's Strategy," *Foreign Affairs*, November/December 2018, https://www.foreignaffairs.com /articles/middle-east/2018-10-15/michael-pompeo-secretary-of-state-on-confrontin g-iran.

26. Randal Schweller, "Three Cheers for Trump's Foreign Policy: What the Establishment Misses?" *Foreign Affairs*, September/October 2018, https://www.for eignaffairs.com/articles/world/2018-08-13/three-cheers-trumps-foreign-policy.

27. According to Michael Barnett, "For all his bluster, Trump acts cautiously and is respectful of constraints." In Michael N. Barnett, "What Is International Relations Theory Good For?" in Robert Jervis, et al., eds., *Chaos in the Liberal Order: The Trump Presidency and the International Order* (New York: Columbia University Press, 2018).

28. "Donald Trump's Demolition Theory of Foreign Policy Won't Work," *The Economist*, June 7, 2018, https://www.economist.com/leaders/2018/06/07/donald-trumps-demolition-theory-of-foreign-policy-wont-work.

29. Kaveh L. Afrasiabi, "Lessons from NAFTA for Iran, to Renegotiate the Nuclear Deal," *Iran Project*, December 9, 2018, https://theiranproject.com/blog/2018/12/09/lessons-from-nafta-for-iran-to-renegotiate-the-nuclear-deal/.

30. Charlie Laderman and Brendan Simms, *Donald Trump: The Making of a World View* (London: I.B. Tauris, 2017): 19.

31. Daniel Yergin, *The Prize: The Quest for Oil, Money, and Power* (New York: Simon and Schuster, 2008): 594, 616.

32. Daniel J. Sargent, *Superpower Transformed: The Remaking of America's Foreign Relations in the 1970s* (New York: Oxford University Press, 2015): 289.

33. David Farber, *Taken Hostage: The Iran Hostage Crisis and America's First Encounter with Radical Islam* (Princeton, NJ: Princeton University Press, 2006).

34. Victor Bulmer-Thomas, *Empire in Retreat: The Past, Present, and Future of the United States* (New Haven, CT: Yale University Press): 333.

35. Hal Brans, *Making the Unipolar Moment: U.S. Foreign Policy and the Rise of the Post-Cold War Order* (Syracuse, NY: Cornell University Press, 2016).

36. Max Weber, *Collected Methodological Writings*, translated and edited by Hans Henrick Braun and Sam Whimster (London: Routledge, 2012): 273–301. According to Weber, "The number and type of causes which have influenced any given event are always infinite and there is nothing in the things themselves to set some of these apart as alone meriting attentions."

37. We draw attention to Thomas Schelling, who has called for a "theory of interdependent decision" by making distinctions between "mixed games" of conflict and cooperation. See Thomas Schelling, *The Strategy of Conflict* (Cambridge, MA: Harvard University Press, 1960).

38. For a relevant work on the (inter) personal effect in foreign policy, see Lloyd S. Etheredge, "Personality Effects on American Foreign Policy, 1898–1968: A Test of Interpersonal Generalization Theory," *American Political Science Review* 72, no. 2 (1978), 434–451.

39. Here, we draw on the rich literature on "levels of analysis" linking the domestic and external dimensions of foreign policy-making. See for instance, Brian M. Pollins and Randall L. Schweller, "Linking the Levels: The Long Wave and Shifts in U.S. Foreign Policy, 1790–1993," *American Journal of Political Science* 43, no. 2 (1999), 431–464.

40. For more on Bannon see, Gwynn Guilford and Nikhil Sonnad, "What Bannon Really Wants?" *Quartz*, February 3, 2017, https://qz.com/898134/what-steve-bannon-really-wants/.

41. Michael T. Flynn and Michael Ledeen, *The Field of Fight: How We Can Win the War against Radical Islam and Its Allies* (New York: St. Martin's Press, 2016).

42. According to Peter Beinart, "Pompeo advances anti-Muslim bigots, and defames Muslims with almost as much gusto as Trump himself." See, Peter Beinart, "Mike Pompeo at State Would Enable Trump's Worst Instincts," *Atlantic Monthly*,

November 3, 2017, https://www.theatlantic.com/international/archive/2017/11/po mpeo-trump-tillerson/547217/.

43. "Part 1: U.S. Reimposes Sanctions on Iran," *United States Institute of Peace*, November 5, 2018.

44. "Remarks on the Creation of the Iran Action Group," *US Department of State*, August 2018, https://iranprimer.usip.org/blog/2018/nov/05/part-1-us-reimp oses-sanctions-iran https://www.state.gov/secretary/remarks/2018/08/285183.htm. According to Pompeo, "Our hope is that one day soon we can reach a new agreement with Iran. But we must see major changes in the regime's behavior both inside and outside of its borders. The Iranian people and the world are demanding that Iran finally act like a normal nation."

45. "Bolton Says More Sanctions on Iran Likely," *Radio Farda*, November 9, 2018, https://en.radiofarda.com/a/bolton-says-more-us-sanctions-will-come-for-ira n/29592150.html.

46. The MEK, once on the US State Department's terrorism list, was courted by various Trump administration officials as an alternative to the existing Iranian government. For more on this subject, see Barbara Slavin, "US Government No Longer Excludes MEK as Leadership Option for Iran," *Al-Monitor*, March 6, 2019, https:// www.al-monitor.com/pulse/originals/2019/03/us-government-no-longer-excludes-m ek-alternatives-iran.html.

47. "Latest U.S. Sanctions Show Disregard For Human Rights of All Iranians: Foreign Minister," *Reuters*, October 17, 2018, https://www.reuters.com/article/us-iran-nuclear-sanctions/latest-u-s-sanctions-show-disregard-for-human-rights-of-all-ir anians-foreign-minister-idUSKCN1MR2NC.

48. For more on this, see Sirwan Kajjo and Mehdi Jedinia, "Growing Concerns over Saudi Arabia's Rights Abuses," *VOA News*, April 30, 2019, https://www.voa news.com/united-states/extremism-watch/growing-concerns-over-saudi-arabias-right s-abuses. Also, Peter Wade, "Trump on Khashoggi Murder and Saudi Human Rights Abuses: We 'Take Their Money,'" *Rolling Stone*, June 23, 2019, https://www.rollings tone.com/politics/politics-news/trump-saudi-arabia-take-their-money-851524/.

49. A representative works is Palmer, Glenn; Morgan, T. Clifton. Princeton, *A Theory of Foreign Policy* (Princeton, NJ: Princeton University Press. 2006).

50. "Remarks by President Trump on the Joint Comprehensive Plan of Action," *The White House*, May 8, 2018, https://www.whitehouse.gov/briefings-statements/re marks-president-trump-joint-comprehensive-plan-action/

51. David M. Halbfinger, David E. Sanger and Ronen Bergman, "Israel Says Secret Files Detail Iran's Nuclear Subterfuge," New *York Times*, April 30, 2018, https ://www.nytimes.com/2018/04/30/world/middleeas t/israel-iran-nuclear-netanyahu. html.

52. See, "Remarks by President Trump on the Joint Comprehensive Plan of Action," *White House*, May 8, 2018, https://www.whitehouse.gov/briefingsstatement s/remarks-president-trump-jointcomprehensive-plan-action/.

53. According to some US pundits, on Iran Trump the president became the "prisoner" of his own hyperbole. See for instance, Peter Bergen, "On Iran, Trump Became the Prisoner of His Own Hyperbole," *CNN*, May 8, 2018, https://www.cnn

.com/2018/05/08/opinions/on-iran-trump-is-a-prisoner-of-his-own-hyperbole-bergen/index.html.

54. Katie Zezima, "Donald Trump, Ted Cruz Headline Capitol Rally against Nuclear Deal," *Washington Post*, September 9, 2015, https://www.washingtonpost.com/news/post-politics/wp/2015/09/09/donald-trump-ted-cruz-to-headline-capitol-rally-against-iran-nuclear-deal/. Also, Wayne Lesperance, "Foreign Policy and the 2016 Presidential Election," *Society* 53, no. 5 (October 2016), 498–502.

Both candidates portrayed the JCPOA as a "winner-loser" proposition, the winner, that is, Iran, arousing only their scorn. Between the two, however, Trump was better skilled as a demagogue, a bully, easily enraged, and deft at mockery and insults against his opponents. For more on this see, John Sides, Michael Tesler and Lynn Vavreck, *Identity Crisis: The 2016 Presidential Campaign and the Battle for the Meaning of America* (Princeton, NJ: Princeton University Press, 2018). Trump won a sold 304-227 majority in the Electoral College, even though his rival Hillary Clinton led in the popular vote, the gap between the two forming a legitimacy "deficit."

55. Eli Clifton, "Follow the Money: Three Billionaires Paved Way for Trump's Iran-Deal Withdrawal," *Lobelog*, May 8, 2018, https://lobelog.com/three-billionaires-paved-way-for-trumps-iran-deal-withdrawal/.

56. Adam Entous, "The Enemy of My Enemy: How Trump, Israel, and the Gulf States Plan to Fight Iran," *New Yorker*, June 18, 2018, https://www.newyorker.com/magazine/2018/06/18/donald-trumps-new-world-order.

57. Donette Murray, *US Foreign Policy and Iran: American-Iranian Relations since the Islamic Revolution* (UK: Routledge, 2010).

58. Joost R. Hiltermann, *A Poisonous Affair: America, Iraq, and the Gassing of Halabja* (New York: Cambridge University Press, 2007).

59. John Mearsheimer and Stephen M. Walt, *The Israel Lobby and U.S. Foreign Policy* (New York: Farrar, Straus and Giroux, 2007).

60. Murray, *US Foreign Policy and Iran*, 95. According to Murray, talking past one another—"dialogue of the duff"—is often a feature of US-Iran relations, attributing it to various factors such US policymakers being distracted by other priorities as well as ignorance or missed signals. Concerning the latter, in 2008, the Bush administration rejected the possibility of opening a consular office in Iran. See Kaveh L. Afrasiabi, "Bush's Final Blunder," *Asia Times*, October 7, 2008, http://www.atimes.com/atimes/Middle_East/JJ07Ak02.html.

61. Mearsheimer and Walt, *Israel Lobby*, 287.

62. Stephen Zunes, *Tinderbox: U.S. Foreign Policy and the Roots of Terrorism* (Monroe, ME: Common Courage Press, 2003).

63. For a revisionist re-thinking of the Islamic Revolution in Iran as containing the "traces" of a post-Cold War order, see Kaveh Afrasiabi, *After Khomeini: New Directions in Iran's Foreign Policy* (Boulder, CO: Westview Books, 1994).

64. For more on this, see Ralph B. Levering, *The Cold War: A Post-Cold War History* (West Sussex: Wiley & Son, 2016). Also, Melvyn Leffler, *A Preponderance of Power: National Security, The Truman Administration, and the Cold War* (Palo Alto, CA: Stanford University Press, 1992). According to Rashid Khalidi, the Soviet Union's reluctance to withdraw its forces from Iran after World War II

was "motivated by a desire to push its defensive perimeter as far south as possible." In Rashid Khalidi, *Sowing Crisis: The Cold War and American Dominance in the Middle East* (Boston: Beacon Press, 2009), 53.

65. See, Ervand Abrahamian, *The Coup: 1953, the CIA, and the Roots of Modern U.S.-Iranian Relations* (New York: The New Press, 1953).

66. Stephen Kinzer, *All the Shah's Men: The Coup and the Roots of a Middle Eastern Terror* (Hoboken, NJ: Wiley and Sons, Inc., 2008).

67. For an apt discussion of "twin pillar" policy of United States prior to the Islamic Revolution, see Sargent, *Superpower Transformed.*

68. For a discussion of how the Cold War calculus shaped the policy of the United States post World War II toward Iran, see Richard Cottam, *Iran and the United States: A Cold War Case Study* (Pittsburgh, PA: University of Pittsburgh Press, 1988); Nikki R. Keddie and Mark J. Gasiorowski, eds., *Neither East Nor West: Iran, the Soviet Union, and the United States* (New Haven, CT: Yale University Press, 1990).

69. Dilip Hiro, *After Empire: The Birth of a Multipolar World* (New York: Nation Books, 2010). Also, F. Gregory Gause III, "The Illogic of Dual Containment," *Foreign Affairs* 73, no. 2 (March–April 1994), 56–66. Barbara Conry, "America's Misguided Policy of Dual Containment in the Persian Gulf," *Cato Institute Foreign Policy Briefing 33* (November 10, 1994).Also, George Lenczowski, *American Presidents and the Middle East* (Durham, NC: Duke University Press, 1990); William O. Beeman, *The "Great Satan" vs. the "Mad Mullahs": How the United States and Iran Demonized Each Other* (Westport, CT: Praeger, 2005); James Bill, *The Eagle and the Lion: The Tragedy of American-Iranian Relations* (New Haven, CT: Yale University Press, 1989).

70. For more on the Iran-Contra affair, see Theodore Draper, *A Very Thin Line* (New York: HarperCollins, 1987).

71. Carol D. Leonning, "Iran Held Liable in Khobar Attack," *Washington Post*, December 22, 2006, http://www.washingtonpost.com/wp-dyn/content/artic le/2006/12/22/AR2006122200455.html?noredirect=on. For a discussion of US-Iran "hostage diplomacy," see Giandomenico Picco, *Man without a Gun: One Diplomat's Secret Struggle to Free the Hostage, Fight Terrorism, and End a War* (New York: Times/Holt Publication, 1999).

72. Kenneth Pollock, *The Case for Invading Iraq* (New York: Random House, 2003).

73. This approach was theorized by the National Security Adviser, Anthony Lake, in a seminal article called "Confronting Backlash States" in which Lake elaborated a detailed articulation of rogue states policy: "as the sole superpower, the United States has a special responsibility for developing a strategy to neutralize, contain and, through selective pressure, perhaps eventually transform these backlash states into constructive members of the international community". After the successful containment of USSR, the United States "now faces a less formidable challenge in containing the band of outlaws." See Anthony Lake, "Confronting Backlash States," *Foreign Affairs* 73, no. 2 (March–April 1994), https://www.foreignaffairs.com/articles/iran/ 1994-03-01/confronting-backlash-states.

74. Richard N. Haass, *War of Necessity, War of Choice: Memoir of Two Iraq Wars* (New York: Simon and Schuster, 2009).

75. Flynt Leverett, *Dealing with Tehran: Assessing US. Diplomatic Options toward Iran* (New York: Century Foundation, 2006).

76. Barbara Slavin, *Bitter Friends, Bosom Enemies: Iran, the US, and the Twisted Path to Confrontation* (New York: St. Martin's Press, 2009). Although rich in details, Slavin's book has all the limitations of a journalistic narrative that is bereft of a sound theoretical framework.

77. Mehran Kamrava, *Troubled Waters: Insecurity in the Persian Gulf* (Ithaca, NY: Cornell University Press, 2018).

78. Beeman, *The "Great Satan vs. the "Mad Mullahs."*

79. "Iran, Russia Can Cooperate to Contain U.S., Ayatollah Khamenei," *Press TV*, September 7, 2018, https://www.presstv.com/Detail/2018/09/07/573471/Khamen ei-Putin-Leader-US-Iran-Russia.

80. According to Obama, "We need to maintain a strategic force posture that allows us to manage threats posed by rogue nations like North Korea and Iran." In Barack Obama, *The Audacity of Hope: Thoughts on Reclaiming the American Dream* (New York: Random House, 2006): 307.

81. Thomas L. Friedman, "Not So-Strange-Bedfellow," *New York Times*, January 31, 2007, https://www.nytimes.com/2007/01/31/opinion/31friedman.html.

82. For more on these issues, see Afrasiabi, After Khomeini, the chapter on the Kuwait crisis. Also, Ali M. Ansari, *Confronting Iran: The Failure of American Foreign Policy and the Next Great Conflict in the Middle East* (New York: Basic Books, 2006).

83. This issue has been discussed in detail in Bledar Prifti, *US Foreign Policy in the Middle East: The Case for Continuity* (New York: Palgrave Macmillan, 2017). The problem with Prifti's analysis is that it assumes a strategic harmony between the United States and Iran, which is not warranted by empirical facts. As noted by Bob Woodward, Iran agreed to assist the US efforts in Afghanistan because both agreed on the post-Taliban leadership by Hamid Karzai, who had spent time in exile in Iran. This was tantamount to a tactical coincidence of interests at the time. See Bob Woodward, *Bush at War* (New York: Simon and Schuster, 2002): 314–315.

84. Helene Cooper, "U.S. Strategy in Iraq Increasingly Relies on Iran," *New York Times*, March 5, 2015, https://www.nytimes.com/2015/03/06/world/middleeast/us-strategy-in-iraq-increasingly-relies-on-iran.html?_r=0.

85. "Transcript of the Third Debate," *New York Times*, October 20, 2016, https://www.nytimes.com/2016/10/20/us/politics/third-debate-transcript.html.

86. Hillary Rodman Clinton, *Hard Choices* (New York: Simon and Schuster, 2014): 438.

87. Ibid., 446.

88. According to Clinton, the Obama administration presented Iran with a "clear choice," that is, "if they complied with their treaty obligations and addressed the international community's concerns about their nuclear program, they could benefit from improved relations." Ibid., 421.

89. The United States has imposed sanctions on Iranian officials alleged to have committed human rights abuses, and on firms that help Iranian authorities censor or monitor the Internet. For a summary of these human rights sanctions, see Kenneth Katzman, "Iran: Internal Politics and U.S. Policy and Options," *Congressional Research Service*, April 30, 2019, https://fas.org/sgp/crs/mideast/RL32048.pdf.

90. Bruce Laingen, *Yellow Ribbon: The Secret Journal* (McLean, VA: Brassey's, Inc., 1992): 10.

91. For more on the JCPOA and human rights in Iran, see Peter Beinart, "When a Nation Is Threatened, Democracy Is Impossible Dream," *Atlantic*, April 20, 2015, https://www.theatlantic.com/international/archive/2015/04/iran-nuclear-deal-demo cracy-akbar-ganji/390900/. Also, Akbar Ganji, "The Iran Nuclear Agreement: You Can't Expect People to Walk on Water," *Middle East Eye*, April 13, 2015, https://www.middleeasteye.net/opinion/iran-nuclear-agreement-you-cant-expect-people-w alk-water. According to Ganji, "When a nation such as Iran is threatened...and suffering from the most crippling sanctions in history, democracy becomes an impossible dream for its people."

92. For more on the Iranian debate of the nuclear diplomacy, see Saeid Ajorloo, "Internal Discourses in Iran's Nuclear Diplomacy." *Discourse: An Iranian Quarterly* 11, no. 3 (Winter 2017), 97–112.

93. "U.S. Comes Clean about the Coup in Iran," *CNN International*, April 19, 2000, http://transcripts.cnn.com/TRANSCRIPTS/0004/19/i_ins.00.html. It has been noted that "the Clinton administration dispensed with grand strategy because it was no longer needed." See, Walter A. McDougall, *The Tragedy of U.S. Foreign Policy* (New Haven, CT: Yale University Press, 2016).

94. "Iran Signs Oil Deal with Conoco: First Since 1980 Break with U.S.," *New York Times*, March, 7, 1995, https://www.nytimes.com/1995/03/07/world/iran-sign s-oil-deal-with-conoco-first-since-1980-break-with-us.html.

95. Derek Davison, "Bacevich and Mearsheimer on Obama's Legacy," *Lobelog*, January 17, 2017, https://lobelog.com/bacevich-and-mearsheimer-on-obamas-legacy/.

96. E. J. Dionne, Jr., "The Obama Doctrine in Action," *Washington Post*, April 16, 2009, http://www.washingtonpost.com/wp-dyn/content/article/2009/04/15/AR2009041502902.html.

97. Stephen M. Walt, "Obama Was Not a Realist President," *Foreign Policy*, April 7, 2016, https://foreignpolicy.com/2016/04/07/obama-was-not-a-realist-pres ident-jeffrey-goldberg-atlantic-obama-doctrine/.

98. "President Obama: Libya Aftermath 'Worst Mistake' of Presidency," *BBC News*, April 11, 2016), http://www.bbc.com/news/world-us-canada-3601370.

99. In the theoretical literature on foreign policy-making, steps are taken not to confuse foreign policy mistake from foreign policy failure or outcome, by integrating historical, game-theoretic, and psychological approaches, in order to deepen our understanding of how to avoid miscalculations. The difficulties of building support for Arab democratic transitions after the outbreak of Arab Spring, for example, were only partially attributable to the lack of preparation of the Obama administration and or its ambiguities. Even in the absence of American shortfall in supporting the Arab democratic movements, the internal difficulties of such transitions in non-democratic societies ill-prepared to deal with sudden changes were, and continue to be, important determining factors. On foreign policy error, see Stephen G. Walker and Akan Malici, *US Presidents and Foreign Policy Mistakes* (Palo Alto, CA: Stanford University Press, 2011).

100. Michael Dobbs, "Obama, Samantha Power, and the 'Problem from Hell,'" *Foreign Policy*, April 23, 2012, https://foreignpolicy.com/2012/04/23/obama-sa mantha-power-and-the-problem-from-hell/

101. For more on this see, Hooshang Amirahmadi and Kaveh L. Afrasiabi, "The West's Silence over Bahrain Smacks of Double Standards," *The Guardian*, April 29, 2011, https://www.theguardian.com/commentisfree/2011/apr/29/bahrain-saudi-ar abia-iran-west.

102. Bob Woodward, *Obama's Wars* (New York: Simon and Schuster, 2010).

103. Stephen L. Carter, *The Violence of Peace: America's Wars in the Age of Obama* (New Haven, CT: Yale University Press, 2011).

104. As a presidential candidate, Obama had vowed to meet, without precondi- tions, with the leaders of Iran, Syria, Venezuela, Cuba and North Korea, in order to bridge the gap that divided the United States from those countries. See, "Part I: CNN/ YouTube Democratic Presidential Debate Transcript," *CNN*, July 24, 2007, http:// www.cnn.com/2007/POLITICS/07/23/debate.transcript/.

105. Quoted in Brans, *Making the Unipolar Moment*, 227. Brzezinski's "balance of power" vacuum theory signified a major adjustment of his earlier "arch of crisis" alarm, according to which the area spanning from Aden to Chilagong—a crescent atop the Indian Ocean—was the source of America's "greatest vulnerability" requir- ing an augmentation of America's "military presence." This view essentially rede- fined the Middle East as a strategic priority of the first order.

106. Thomas L. Friedman, "U.S. To Counter Iran in Central Asia," *New York Times*, February 6, 1992, https://www.nytimes.com/1992/02/06/world/us-to-counter- iran-in-central-asia.html.

107. "Transcript of President Obama's Interview with Novaya-Gazeta," *White House*, 2009, https://www.whitehouse.gov/the_press_office/Transcript-of-Preside nt-Obamas-Interview-with-Novaya-Gazeta.

108. "Transcript: Bush Withdraws from ABM Treaty," *Washington Post*, Decem- ber 13, 2001, https://www.washingtonpost.com/wp-srv/onpolitics/transcripts/bush _text121301.html.

109. According to Kayhan Barzegar, the problem with the "Shia Crescent" theory is that Iran's presence in the region is a result of the need to make an alliance with friendly Shiite governments and groups in response to security threats caused after the arrival of U.S. troops in the region. It is therefore defensive, not expansionist. See, Kayhan Barzegar, "Iran and the Shiite Crescent: Myths and Realities," *Belfer Center. Org* (Fall/Winter, 2008), https://www.belfercenter.org/sites/default/files/files/publi cation/BRZ.BJWA.2008.pdf.

110. "Mapping the Global Muslim Population," *Pew Research Center*, October 7, 2009, http://www.pewforum.org/2009/10/07/mapping-the-global-muslim-popu lation/.

111. Fawaz A. Gerges, *Obama and the Middle East: The End of America's Moment?* (New York: Palgrave Macmillan, 2012).

112. Quoted in Helene Cooper and Mark Lander, "U.S. Eyes New Sanctions Over Iran Nuclear Program," *New York Times*, February 9, 2010. For more on this, see Nader Entessar and Kaveh L. Afrasiabi, *Iran Nuclear Negotiations: Accord and Détente since the Geneva Agreement of 2013* (Lanham, MD: Rowman and Littlefield, 2015).

113. "Remarks by President Obama and Prime Minister Netanyahu of Israel in Joint Press Conference," *The White House*, March 20, 2013, https://obamawhiteho

use.archives.gov/the-press-office/2013/03/20/remarks-president-obama-and-prime-m inister-netanyahu-israel-joint-press-

114. "Interview with Laura Ingraham of the Laura Ingraham Show," *US Department of State*, October, 2018, https://www.state.gov/secretary/remarks/2018/10/287031.htm.

115. "U.S. Gulf Cooperation Council Camp David Joint Statement," *Obamawhite-house.archives.gov*, May 14, 2015, https://obamawhitehouse.archives.gov/the-pres s-office/2015/05/14/us-gulf-cooperation-council-camp-david-joint-statement

116. David Andrew Weinberg, "No Show at Camp David: What the Saudi King's Snub Really Means," *National Interest*, May 13, 2015, https://nationalinterest.org/f eature/no-show-camp-david-what-the-saudi-kings-snub-really-means-12883.

117. Mortimer B. Zuckerman, "Something, but Not Enough: Appeasement Has Enabled Iran's Imperial Ambitions—Even without a Nuclear Bomb," *USA Today*, April 3, 2015, https://www.usnews.com/opinion/articles/2015/04/03/nuclear-agreem ent-with-imperial-iran-is-something-but-not-enough. Also, Joshua Keating, "What if the Iran Nuclear Deal Was a Mistake?" *Slate.com*, February 6, 2018, https://slate.c om/news-and-politics/2018/02/what-if-the-iran-deal-was-a-mistake.html.

118. For more on how the Obama administration's pursuit of the Iran nuclear deal translated into making the war in Yemen worse, see Nicolas Niarchos, "How the U.S. Is Making the War in Yemen Worse?" *New Yorker*, January 22, 2018, https://www.new yorker.com/magazine/2018/01/22/how-the-us-is-making-the-war-in-yemen-worse.

119. Jeffrey Goldberg, "The Obama Doctrine," *The Atlantic*, April, 2016, https:// www.theatlantic.com/magazine/archive/2016/04/the-obama-doctrine/471525/. Peter Feaver has argued that in the Middle East during the second Obama administration, the US shift to an offshore balancing strategy "proved disastrous for American inter-ests and paved the way for the rise of the Islamic State, forcing Obama to shift back once again to an onshore balancing in the region." Peter Feaver, "A Grand Strategy Challenge Awaits Trump," *Foreign Policy*, November 29, 2016, https://foreignpolic y.com/2016/11/29/a-grand-strategy-challenge-awaits-trump/

120. "A Conversation with Valiollah Seif on the Future of the Iranian Economy," *Council on Foreign Relations*, April 15, 2016, https://www.cfr.org/event/conversat ion-valiollah-seif-future-iranian-economy.

121. Ben Rhodes, *The World as It Is: A Memoir of the Obama White House* (New York: Random House, 2018).

122. Rebecca Kheel, "Top General: Countering Iran in Syria Is Not a U.S. Military Mission," *The Hill*, February 27, 2018, https://thehill.com/policy/defense/375789-top -general-countering-iran-in-syria-not-a-us-military-mission.

123. John Kerry, *Every Day Is Extra* (New York: Simon and Schuster, 2018). The destruction of Syrian government's chemical weapons arsenal was achieved by a US-Russian agreement under the supervision of the Organization for the Prohibition of Chemical Weapons (OPCW), which confirmed in January 2016 that the destruction of the stockpile was completed. See, "OPCW: Destruction of Declared Syrian Chemical Weapons," *OPCW.Org*, January 4, 2016, https://www.opcw.org/media-centre/news/2 016/01/destruction-declared-syrian-chemical-weapons-completed.

124. "Letter from the Senate Republicans to the Leaders of Iran," *New York Times*, March, 9, 2015, https://www.nytimes.com/interactive/2015/03/09/world/middleeast/ document-the-letter-senate-republicans-addressed-to-the-leaders-of-iran.html.

125. "Treaty Affairs," *U.S. Department of State*, No Date, https://www.state. gov/s/l/treaty/.

126. "Resolution 2231 (2015)," *UN Security Council*, July 20, 2015, http://www. un.org/en/sc/2231/. For the initial "brief" by the Resolution 2231 Facilitator, see "Implementation of UN Security Council Resolution 2231 (2015)," *United Nations*, March, 2016, http://www.un.org/en/sc/2231/pdf/Facilitator-presentation-Implementati on-of-resolution-2231(2015).pdf. For the report of the Secretary General, see "Report of the Secretary General on the Implementation of Resolution 2231 (2015)," *United Nations*, March 2016, http://www.un.org/en/ga/search/view_doc.asp?symbol=S/20 16/589&Lang=E. Both reports confirm Iran's fulfillment of its JCPOA obligations.

127. See Oscar Schachter, "United Nations Law," *American Journal of International Law* 88, no. 1 (1988), https://www.cambridge.org/core/journals/american-j ournal-of-international-law/article/united-nations-law/6227E9193C689C8E79C5 719E107BFD7F. Also, Gaetano Arrangio-Ruiz, "On the Security Council's 'Law-Making,'" *Rivista di Diritto Internazionale* 83, no. 1 (2000). Eric Rosand, "The Security Council as "Global Legislator," *Fordham International Law Journal* 28, no. 3 (2004). Also, Armin Von Bogdandy and Ingo Venzke, "Beyond Dispute: International Institutions as Lawmakers," *German Law Journal* 12, no. 5 (2011).

128. A relevant work is: Renata Sonnefeld, *Resolutions of the United Nations Security Council* (Leiden: Martinus Nijhoff Publishers, 1988). Also, A. *Pellet, "La formation du droit* international dans le cadre des Nations Unies," *Journal Europeen de Droit International* 6, no. 3 (1995).

129. A relevant work is: Renata Sonnefeld, "The Obligation of UN Member-States to Accept and Carry Out the Decisions of the Security Council," *Polish Yearbook of International Law* (1976), 129. Also, Hans Kelsen, *The Law of the United Nations: A Critical Analysis of the Fundamental Problems* (London: Steven & Sons, 1951).

130. See note number 6.

131. J. Castaneda, *Legal Effects of UN Resolutions* (Oxford: Oxford University Press, 1969). Also, Wilfried Bolewski, *Diplomacy and International Law in Globalized Relations* (Berlin: Springer-Verlag, 2007).

132. Eric Heinze and Malgosia Fitzmaurice, *Landmark Cases in Public International Law* (London: Kluwer Law International, 1998), 559.

133. According to President Rouhani, "The result of JCPOA is win-win and beneficial to all and I hope all countries witness its good results in coming years." Quoted from "President: Iran's Nuclear Activities to Continue with International Cooperation," *Ministry of Foreign Affairs, Islamic Republic of Iran*, January 1, 2017, http: //en.mfa.ir/index.aspx?siteid=3&fkeyid=&siteid=3&fkeyid=&siteid=3&pageid=19 97&newsview=432269.

134. John Carlson, "Iran and a New International Framework for Nuclear Energy," *Harvard University, Managing the Atom Project*, November, 2016, http://belferce nter.ksg.harvard.edu/files/Carlson%20-%20Iran%20and%20a%20New%20Int%20 Framework%20for%20Nuc%20Energy.pdf.

135. Kaveh Afrasiabi, "Nuclear Deal-Making in Vienna and Tehran," *Iranian Diplomacy*, July 2015, http://www.irdiplomacy.ir/en/page/1949559/Nuclear+DealM aking+in+Vienna+and+Tehran.html.

136. For a complete text of the JCPOA, see "Iran Deal—An Historic Day," *European Union External Action,* July 17, 2015, http://collections.internetmemory.o rg/haeu/content/20160313172652/http://eeas.europa.eu/top_stories/2015/150714_ira n_nuclear_deal_en.htm.

137. During the first seven months of JCPOA's implementation, Iran sold heavy water to both the United States and Russia and was considering selling to the Europeans as well. See "AEOI Spokesman: Europeans New Customers for Iran's Heavy Water," *Iran Project*, December 26, 2016, http://theiranproject.com/blog/2016/12/2 6/aeoi-spokesman-europeans-new-customers-irans-heavy-water/.

138. From 2003 until 2006, Iran voluntarily implemented, though it never ratified, the Additional Protocol and then stopped in protest against the UN Security Council resolutions against Iran.

139. It has been observed that the JCPOA's Joint Commission can "modify, as necessary, procedures to govern its activities" and that "Using this forum could be an opening to address some US concerns," in Corentin Brustlein, James Dobbins, Dalia Dassa Kaye, Oliver Meier, Marco Overhaus, Neil Quilliam, Charles Ries, Dorothée Schmid, Sanam Vakil, and Azadeh Zamirirad, "Saving Transatlantic Cooperation and the Iran Nuclear Deal: A View from Europe and the United States," Rand Corporation, *SWP Comment 9*, February 2018, https://www.rand.org/pubs/external_publi cations/EP67500.html.

140. For more on this, see Sahand Moarefi, "Partially Unwinding Sanctions: The Problematic Construct of Sanctions Relief under the JCPOA," *Harvard Law School National Security Journal*, July 2016, http://harvardnsj.org/2016/07/partially-unwin ding-sanctions-the-problematic-construct-of-sanctions-relief-in-the-jcpoa/.

141. For a useful summary of "post-JCPOA" US sanctions that remained in place against Iran, see: Kenneth Katzman, "Iran Sanctions," *Congressional Research Service*, May 18, 2016, http://www.fas.org/sgp/mideast/RS20871.pdf.

142. "JCPOA—Annex III Civil Nuclear Cooperation," *EU External Action*, July 14, 2015, https://eeas.europa.eu/statements-eeas/docs/iran_agreement/annex_3_civ il_nuclear_cooperation_en.pdf.

143. "U.S. to Buy Nuclear Material from Iran," *CNN*, April 22, 2016, https://ww w.cnn.com/2016/04/22/politics/us-nuclear-iran-purchase/index.html.

144. "UN Security Council Resolution 2231," *UN Security Council*, July 20, 2015, http://www.securitycouncilreport.org/atf/cf/%7B65BFCF9B-6D27-4E9C -8CD3-CF6E4FF96FF9%7D/s_res_2231.pdf.

Chapter 2

Trump and Iran Nuclear Program

In this chapter, we seek to provide an objective assessment of Trump's discourse on the JCPOA, drawing on the insights learned from deconstruction in political science. This means that our focus has a methodological point of departure in the deconstructive research—that focus on the potential juxtapositions and dichotomies of a discourse, the coherence and incoherence, the visible and the invisible silences, the operations of power and ideology often hidden in a political text, and the like. According to Hansen, "Policy discourse is seen as relying upon particular constructions of problems and subjectivities, but it is also through discourse that these problems and subjectivities are constructed in the first place."[1] With the help of deconstruction, it is possible to decode how a political discourse reveals particular versions of reality and what, sometimes hidden, assumptions underlie it. The value of deconstruction is that by posing relevant questions—such as how hegemony is exercised through a particular discourse or how contradictions of a discourse disrupt its intentions—it problematizes a political given and subjects it to rigorous scrutiny. We hasten to add that by invoking deconstruction, we do not convey dismissal of a discourse, but rather a critical reflection. To quote an adage from the *Federalist Papers:* "When men exert their reason coolly and freely on a variety of distinct questions, they inevitably fall into different opinions on some of them."[2]

Our primary material in this endeavor are the public statements of Donald Trump both as a candidate and president, as well as the related statements and policy announcements by other officials of the Trump administration, taking into consideration the administration's evolution during the first two years of Trump's presidency; between the two, Trump's own words form the centerpiece of the discourse on the JCPOA. Following Foucault and others, discourse produces and reproduces power structures, hierarchies, and

55

categories that define the relationship among subjects and form a part of
social reality.[3] A political discourse contains themes and central concepts that
are important for the overall discourse that informs an official policy decision, in this case, exit of United States from the JCPOA, which transpired
within a broader discourse of antagonism vis-a-vis Iran. One such concept
is "outlaw" or "rogue state" connected to the Islamic Republic of Iran as
part of a security narrative that is reflected in the US national security documents, including the new National Security Strategy (December, 2017): "The
scourge of the world today is a small group of rogue regimes that violate all
principles of free and civilized states. The Iranian regime sponsors terrorism
around the world. It is developing more capable ballistic missiles and has
the potential to resume its work on nuclear weapons that could threaten the
United States and our partners."[4] It goes without saying, however, that the
appellation "rogue" has also been used against US government, for example,
according to political scientist Robert Jervis, "in the eyes of much of the
world, in fact, the prime rogue state today is the United States."[5] In Trump's
discursive narrative, Iran's rogue behavior was related to its connections with
terrorist groups and organizations that, in turn, made Iran into an inherently
untrustworthy "terrorist state." To quote Trump, "The Iranian regime is the
leading state sponsor of terror. It exports dangerous missiles, fuels conflicts
across the Middle East, and supports terrorist proxies and militias such as
Hezbollah, Hamas, the Taliban, and al-Qaeda."[6] This was meant to reverse
the JCPOA-based improvement of Iran's image, as a rule-abiding country
allowed to normalize its trade with the West, that is, a legitimacy boon for the
Islamic Republic. Trump's perception of Iran fundamentally militated against
the very notion that Iran could be trusted on its nuclear declarations. This was
reflected in Trump's criticism that at the heart of the nuclear deal was a "giant
fiction...that a murderous regime desired only a peaceful nuclear energy program. Today, we have definitive proof that this Iranian promise was a lie.
Last week, Israel published intelligence documents long concealed by Iran,
conclusively showing the Iranian regime and its history of pursuing nuclear
weapons."[7] Trump could then jump with ease from the past to the future,
by arguing that the nuclear deal was not containing Iran's nuclear threat but
rather paving to it, thus accusing Tehran of violating both the "spirit" and the
letter of the agreement.

In fact, despite repeated certificates of Iran's compliance by both the IAEA
and UN officials, as well as admission by his own officials such as Tillerson
that Iran was in "technical compliance," Trump never conceded the point and
consistently refused to admit that Iran had given up substantial nuclear capabilities by agreeing to the onerous terms of the JCPOA; the latter included the
number and types of centrifuges, the amount of enriched uranium on hand,
and the maximum level of uranium enrichment, as well as a fundamental

redesign of its heavy-water reactor at Arak, making it essentially incapable of producing plutonium for bombs. For Trump to have acknowledged these would have created a "discursive dissonance" that, in turn, would have disturbed the internal unity of a discourse of suspicion and distrust, premised on a cynical notion of a nuclearizing pariah state, which stood in sharp contrast with the optimism exuded by the JCPOA (conveying a spirit of cooperation and verified trust). An important part of Trump's discourse on Iran was his effort on "politicizing intelligence on Iran" by insisting on "intelligence to support his policy preference to withdraw from the Iran nuclear deal," to paraphrase David Cohen, a former CIA deputy director.[8]

Another central theme of Trump's Iran discourse was the linkage between the JCPOA on the one hand and, on the other, Iran's rogue regional behavior that fed off the deal's financial relief fueling Iran's expansionism, the argument being that without the JCPOA the Iranian regime may have collapsed, for example, "But the previous administration lifted these sanctions, just before what would have been the total collapse of the Iranian regime, through the deeply controversial 2015 nuclear deal with Iran."[9] The notion of a weak or collapsing regime, of course, stood in sharp contrast to the powerful and expansionist Iran conveyed by the administration simultaneously, for example, JCPOA "boosted the economic fortunes of a regime that remains bent on exporting its revolution abroad."[10] In political discourses, there is often an expressed need for "proof" and here the narrative pointed at the post-JCPOA increase in Iran's defense budget, Iran's financial support of its regional proxies, and Iran's "nuclear-capable" missile tests that defied the UN Security Council and, from Trump's vantage, also pointed at one of the "disastrous flaws" of the JCAPOA, namely, its silence on Iran's missile arsenal. The other perceived flaws were with respect to the restricted timeline of JCPOA limitations on Iran's nuclear program and the absence of any provision for IAEA "inspections anytime, anywhere." The latter begged the question of a legal framework within which outside inspections of Iran's (secret) military facilities would transpire without due cause. In essence, the Trump administration operated in a legal vacuum by advancing nuclear demands from Iran that were not justifiable from the normative standards of the IAEA.

The question of legality aside, over time within the first year of his presidency, Trump's oppositional discourse on the JCPOA assumed a badge of legitimacy after an inter-agency review of the Iran policy of the United States that officially resulted in a new and bellicose approach unveiled in December 2017. Geared to address all of Iran's "rogue behavior" instead of focusing on a "small aspect" of it dealing with the nuclear issue, the new Iran policy was clearly informed by the logic of compellence, yet did so without completely shutting the door to a renegotiated JCPOA. During Tillerson's tenure, Trump's urge to terminate the JCPOA was contained by discussions of a "second" or "supplementary" agreement that could grow out of "working with our European friends and allies within the agreement," to paraphrase Tillerson.[11] This required some tactical maneuvering on the part of Tillerson, who was considered a policy dove in a sea of administration hawks, by echoing Trump's criticisms of JCPOA: "The [deal's] most glaring flaw is the sunset provision. . . . We all know that this is merely a kick-the-can-down-the-road agreement."[12] Another Trump official, US nonproliferation envoy Christopher Ford, weighed in and stated: "We are seeking a supplemental agreement that would in some fashion layer upon it a series of additional rules— restrictions, terms, parameters, whatever you want to call it — that help answer these challenges more effectively."[13] European governments were not unresponsive and the French President Emmanuel Macron in his White House visit in April 2018 sounded the need for a "new nuclear agreement" with Iran.[14] At the same time, Macron and other European leaders remained adamant about the importance of keeping the JCPOA, which they viewed from the prism of European national security as a major accomplishment, instead of scuttling it. To this effect, the European powers formed a "working group" with Trump administration, which initially made some progress in tackling the perceived flaws of the JCPOA. Leaders from the three European countries that the United States called on to negotiate the "supplemental" agreement with the United States—France, England, and Germany—offered in October 2017 to work with the administration to address Iran's ballistic missile program but rejected any renegotiation of the nuclear deal. In turn, the administration officials openly gave up on the idea of renegotiating JCPOA and focused on "fixing" the deal through an "add-on" brokered with their European allies: "We are not aiming to renegotiate the [Joint Comprehensive Plan of Action] or reopen it or change its terms." This was reflected in the US "talking points" circulated by Tillerson in his liaison with European diplomats that, according to a New York Times report, carried the warning that the United States would suspend lifting the Iran sanctions in the absence of any progress. The report also claimed that Tillerson's talking points called upon the Europeans to consent to three fundamental changes in the JCPOA: "A commitment to renegotiate limits on missile testing by Iran; an assurance that inspectors have unfettered access to Iranian military bases; and an extension of the deal's expiration dates to prevent Iran from resuming the production of nuclear fuel long after the current restrictions expire in 2030."[15]

Trump was required by law to decide every 120 days whether to extend the suspension of US economic sanctions against Iran, which Washington was obligated to lift according to the terms of the deal, discussed in detail in the previous chapter. He was also required by law to send a letter to US Congress every ninety days to certify Iran's compliance with the JCPOA. In April 2017, Tillerson sent such a letter to House Speaker Paul Ryan stating that the administration had undertaken a full review of the agreement and found Iran in compliance with its obligations, adding that "Iran remains a leading state sponsor of terror, through many platforms and methods."[16] Tillerson also stated that he had ordered a National Security Council-led interagency review of the agreement to determine whether it "is vital to the national security interests of the United States."[17] Three months later, Trump again certified Iran's compliance to Congress, but did so "reluctantly" and according to *New York Times* only because "all of the president's major security advisers recommended to preserve the Iran deal for now."[18] At the same time, through the White House spokesperson, Trump let it known that he persisted in the thought that the Iran nuclear deal was "very bad for the United States." The announcement on the second certification was accompanied by the news that the administration planned to toughen enforcement of the JCPOA, apply new sanctions on Iran over its "destabilizing" activities, and negotiate with the Europeans to craft a "broader strategy" on Iran. Three months later in October, Trump announced his refusal to certify Iran's compliance and, while refraining from scrapping the deal, hurled the matter to Congress to decide whether to re-impose sanctions on Iran and to discard the nuclear agreement. He warned that "in the event we are not able to reach a solution working with Congress and our allies, then the agreement will be terminated."[19] He also suggested that Iran would never change its rogue behavior: "Given the regime's murderous past and present, we should not take lightly its sinister vision for the future."

Trump had also claimed that Iran had violated the terms of the JCPOA, citing as an example reports that Iran had exceeded the inventory of heavy water it was allowed to keep, yet two days later Tillerson contradicted him by admitting that Iran was in "technical compliance" with the deal. When asked to square this with Trump's claim to the contrary, Tillerson clarified that Iran had committed technical violations of the deal, but that the agreement was structured in a way to give Iran significant time to remedy its violations. "They have remedied the violations, which then brings them back into technical compliance," Tillerson said, adding meaningfully that "US is trying to stay in" the JCPOA.[20] Then, in a subsequent statement in January 2018, Trump announced that he was waiving sanctions on Iran, coupling that with an ultimatum that this was the last time and he would not reissue the waivers again unless the deal was fixed; the next sanctions waivers were due in August 2018. This was presented as a gesture to America's European allies. "I am waiving the application of certain nuclear sanctions, but only in order to secure our European allies' agreement to fix the terrible flaws of the Iran nuclear deal," Trump stated.[21] Tillerson then embarked on quiet diplomacy with members of Congress, particularly with key Republican senators Bob Corker and Tom Cotton, to craft a bill that would amend the Iran Nuclear

Agreement Review Act.[22] The act recognized that a president might determine that Iran was in non-compliance with the nuclear deal. In that case, the
act stipulated that Congress would have sixty days to introduce legislation
to reintroduce US sanctions on Iran. The Corker-Cotton proposal would
effectively change the terms of the nuclear deal by imposing new sanctions
"triggers" if Iran got close to nuclear weapons capability and negated the
"sunset" provisions easing restrictions on Iran's nuclear activities. Tillerson
framed this as the last chance to save the deal. He said the United States must
"either put more teeth into this obligation that Iran has undertaken ... or let's
just forget the whole thing. We'll walk away and start all over."[23]

The decision to hurl the Iran ball in Congress' lap requires scrutiny from
the prism of deconstruction. It showed the traces of a tactical ploy to lay the
groundwork for the administration's fatal blow at JCPOA come August, by
the near certainty that fixing an international agreement was beyond the pale
of US Congress and required an international effort. This tactic, tantamount
to a politics of deflection, raised the suspicion that the administration was
deliberately putting the burden on Congress to avoid a withdrawal for the
moment and that, betting that Congress would fail, Trump would then make
good on his threat to withdraw—with added legitimacy. Without any surprise,
the Corker-Cotton proposal did not go far in Congress and in the end proved
to be a straw man in Trumpian oppositional discourse on Iran, that is, a
Habermasian "distorted communication." It was criticized by some lawmakers such as Senator Van Hollen (Demoract-Maryland) because the proposed
legislation "will essentially be calling for the violation of the agreement
because they would be calling for number one, imposing the Iran sanctions
on non-nuclear related conduct, and number two, they would be extending the
sunset provisions that had been negotiated in the bill."[24] With the Republican
leaders distracted with a tax reform bill and the Democratic leaders opposed
to re-writing the JCPOA, the sixty-day window mentioned earlier passed on
December 13, 2017, without leaders on either side of the aisle introducing
any new Iran legislation. The Cotton-Corker bill just remained "a fact sheet"
on the senators' website.[25] Congressional inaction, in essence, meant that the
administration's pro-JCPOA advocates, including Tillerson, Defense Secretary James Mattis, and National Security Adviser H.R. McMaster, would
be left out of options to convince Trump to stay with the deal. Between the
three, two of them, Tillerson and McMaster were ousted, leaving Mattis as
the "last bastion" of support for the JCPOA, who was repeatedly threatened
with dismissal months before he eventually resigned over policy differences
on Syria in December 2018.[26] When Trump spoke about Tillerson's departure in March 2018, he mentioned only one specific point of contention with
his deposed diplomat. "We disagreed on things. When you look at the Iran
deal—I think it's terrible; I guess he thought it was OK. I wanted to either

break it or do something, and he felt a little bit differently. So we were not really thinking the same."[27] According to Richard Haass, the president of Council on Foreign Relations, the former Exxon Mobil CEO Tillerson had "lost his effectiveness," had been dealt a "bad hand" by the president, and had "played it badly."[28] In comparison, Tillerson's replacement, CIA director Michael Pompeo, had a track record that was completely in sync with Trump vis-à-vis the JCPOA, even though during his nomination hearing Pompeo conceded that Iran was in compliance with the agreement.[29] Haass's criticisms of Tillerson were in retrospect overstated and somewhat unfair. With respect to Iran, Tillerson's attempt to salvage the JCPOA from the fury of the White House was perhaps doomed from the start. He brought a measure of stability to US foreign policy rocked by a protectionist and unpredictable president in the age of global "complex interdependence," and was also in the process of making progress on a multilateral effort with the European nations as stated above, which was essentially nipped in the bud by the combination of his dismissal and Pompeo's lack of interest to pursue that path. We will never know the answer to the question of what if Tillerson had remained in office and been allowed to pursue his diplomatic track with the Europeans to find a formula to fix the perceived flaws of the JCPOA. Tillerson had participated in one session of the JCPOA's joint commission in a face-to-face meeting with the Iranian diplomats in New York, In September 2017, subsequently described by Iran's Foreign Minister Javad Zarif to these authors as "productive."[30] Chances are that if permitted, Tillerson would have been able to open a channel of bilateral diplomacy with Iran, in parallel to the on-going efforts with the Europeans, exploring the options. His inability to achieve any success on the issue of Iran nuclear deal stemmed from a combination of internal and external factors, such as Iran's objection to discussing its missile capability and Trump White House's relentless vilification of Iran and the nuclear deal, setting the stage for Tillerson's failed gambit.

Thus, with Tillerson's and McMaster's departures and the rise of a new White House "war party" featuring hawkish Bolton and Pompeo and a new CIA Director Gina Haspell, accused of administering CIA rendition camps overseas, the administration's Iran discourse centered on compellence was elevated to a higher gear.[31] The administration had jettisoned the cacophony of voices on Iran, bringing new officials in harmony with Trump's vision and "doctrine" on Iran and thus ending the administration's initial phase of Iran policy featuring a mix of policy "doves" and "hawks." Both Bolton and Pompeo were on record opposing the JCPOA instead of "fixing' it and had previously favored military action against Iran.[32] Referring to the JCPOA as Obama's "diplomatic Waterloo," Bolton had openly advocated that the administration's declared policy on Iran should be "ending Iran's 1979 Islamic Revolution before its 40th anniversary."[33] This was based on his assessment that "regime change [in Iran] was within reach."[34] In January 2019, Bolton, without proffering any evidence and contrary to the assessment of the US intelligence community,[35] stated, "We have little doubt that Iran's leadership is still strategically committed to achieving deliverable nuclear weapons."[36] Pompeo echoed this assessment and prior to his selection as the director of CIA in Trump administration had stated in November 2016: "I look forward to rolling back this disastrous deal with the world's largest state sponsor of terrorism."[37]

In terms of periodization of Trump's Iran policy, it therefore makes sense to distinguish between two phases, the first stretching throughout 2017 until early Spring, 2018 and then evolving to a second phase after Tillerson's and McMaster's dismissals and replacements with ardently anti-Iran hawks at the helms of the State Department and National Security Council, marking a full-fledged shift to implement the administration's grand strategy with respect to Iran. Compared with the first phase, there would be little or no sign of internal fissure in the Trump administration on the principal pillars of the strategy targeting Iran as America's *bete noire* in the Middle East. But, as we discuss in this book, the expectation of complete unity of thought on Iran was to some extent chimerical and in the face of challenges confronting the hostile Iran policy, it was inevitable that new policy debates and even fissures would soon appear, bedeviling the administration. The strategy of compellence did not succeed in bringing Iran back to the table in the short-run, nor did it lead to Iran's implosion and, importantly, did not culminate in the formation of a new international coalition against Iran, as predicted by Bolton in his policy prescriptions for the Trump administration. Instead, it triggered a vocal European counter-move in defense of the JCPOA, indicating a new transatlantic rift, which had the potential to adversely impact the domination of the United States on the global financial system. Indeed, the compellence strategy ran into trouble almost from the beginning, its "maximum pressure" ethos compromised by the decision to grant oil exemptions to most of Iran's oil importers in November 2018, out of concern for rising oil prices in the absence of such exemptions. We discuss these issues in great details in the next chapter, suffice to say here that as a result of such exemptions, that included certain nuclear exemptions and exempting India's investment in Iran's Chah Bahar as well as for Iran-Iraq trade, there were important attrition of "maximum pressure" that lowered the temperature of punitive sanctions and, in effect, degraded it to medium pressures, as a result of which Iran's economy could survive the American onslaught and stay afloat for the foreseeable future. What was less certain, however, was the fate of the JCPOA after the exit of United States and the future of the its non-proliferation policy toward Iran; that policy was a sub-set of Trump's grand strategy on Iran and wrapped in a discourse that constantly conflated non-nuclear and specifically nuclear, that is, non-proliferation, standards, or parameters. Still, we disagree with those critics of the Trump administration, who have rushed to dismiss the administration's anti-JCPOA positions as a tissue of illogical warmongering and or imposition of completely nuclear-unrelated criteria on the part of an administration intent on sabotaging the deal. From a Habermasian theoretical vantage,[38] the Trumpian discourse operated by the logic of a "strategic" or instrumentalist rationality that reified the normative non-proliferation norms or concerns, which is invoked both directly and indirectly as part of a purportedly "clear-eyed" Iran policy that identified Iran as a nuclear threat. This was essentially a "monological" exercise that rebelled at the very "notion that allies' interests should be taken into account," to paraphrase a report in Los Angeles Time in July 2017.[39] The new policy was in sharp contrast to the previous multilateral diplomacy and was hotly contested in the nuclear expert community as well as policy circles, with many former officials, experts, and pundits questioning the administration's stance on the JCPOA as counterproductive to national security interests of United States as well as to global non-proliferation. In the section below, we appraise Trump's discourse on the JCPOA from the prism of non-proliferation standards.

DECONSTRUCTING TRUMP'S NORMATIVE STANDPOINT ON THE JCPOA

In this section, we seek to "compartmentalize" our deconstruction of Trump's discourse on Iran nuclear deal by separating his criticisms of the deal's short-comings or flaws (from the standpoint of disarmament) from the related criticisms of the deal's non-nuclear ramifications, such as affecting the regional balance of power. The two types of criticisms, of course, went hand in hand in the overall Trumpian narrative on Iran that with the help of concepts such as rogue state underscored the administration's pursuit of an ambitious compellence strategy vis-a-vis Iran. For purely analytical purposes, we may subdivide the Trumpian disarmament argument against the JCPOA into five components, which are as follows:

(a) The deal did not end Iran's nuclear fuel cycle and allowed Iran "to continue developing certain elements of its programs;"

(b) The deal's restrictions were limited in duration and "in just a few years, as key restrictions disappear, Iran can sprint towards a rapid nuclear weapons breakout What is the purpose of a deal that, at best, only delays Iran's nuclear capability for a short period of time?"

(c) Iran had violated the non-proliferation "spirit" of the deal by conducting missile tests and keeping a growing arsenal of missiles that could be fitted to carry nuclear warheads in the future.

(d) The deal created a "weak inspection system" and did so only for the sake of "weak inspections in exchange for no more than a purely short-term and temporary delay in Iran's path to nuclear weapons."

(e) As a result of the above, not only the JCPOA did not contain Iran's nuclear threat, it also destabilized the region by augmenting the proliferation threats in the Middle East.

Critics of the Trump administration have already provided ample arguments in defense of the JCPOA, highlighting the questionable assumptions of the anti-JCPOA stance aforementioned. Robert Einhorn, a senior adviser to the US negotiation team, has defended the JCPOA by asserting that the deal meets the "threshold test for the nuclear deal," which is that "it achieves its essential goal of preventing Iran from acquiring nuclear weapons" by blocking all Iran's paths to a nuclear weapon.[40] This view has been shared by many nuclear experts in the United States and around the world, who have criticized Trump's withdrawal of the United States from the JCPOA as a major setback for nonproliferation agenda. Commonly viewed by these experts as a "nonproliferation net plus," the JCPOA has been praised as a landmark achievement that "rolls back" Iran's nuclear program, which had advanced to the point where Iran could rapidly produce enough fissile material to build a bomb. The JCPOA "put a lid" on Iran's so-called nuclear breakout capacity as Iran removed two-thirds of its centrifuges, eliminated 97 percent of its stockpile of enriched uranium, and also destroyed the core of one its reactors that could have produced weapons-grade plutonium.[41] UN Secretary-General, Antonio Guterres, has also spoken in defense of the JCPOA as important for global disarmament and security.[42] Per the request of the Security Council, Guterres was required to present a bi-annual report to the Council on Iran's implementation of its JCPOA-related responsibilities. In all these reports, beginning in July 2016, Iran's full compliance with the terms of the JCPOA has been confirmed. In the aftermath of the US exit from the JCPOA, however, Guterres interjected his personal opinion by expressing his "deep regret" at the setback for international peace and security caused by Trump's decision.[43] Many former Israeli officials and security experts have concurred with this assessment.[44] In October 2017, more than ninety top American nuclear scientists wrote a letter urging US Congress to protect the JCPOA. "Since the JCPOA imposes strict restrictions and strong verification on Iran's nuclear program, Congress should act to ensure that the United States remains a party to the agreement," the scientists argued.[45] Their views were shared by dozens of retired US generals and admirals who signed an open letter to Trump in July 2017, urging him to preserve the JCPOA as it was beneficial to US national security interests, urging Trump to open diplomatic channels of communication with Iran.[46] Earlier, a bipartisan group of sixty former top US officials, including former secretary of state Madeleine Albright and former national security advisors Samuel Berger, Zbigniew Brzezinski, and Brent Scowcroft, had similarly urged Congress to approve the nuclear deal on the ground that it meets "all of the key objectives."[47]

But, perhaps the biggest defenders of the JCPOA were the officials of the Obama administration, beginning with Obama himself, who issued a statement after Trump's announcement on withdrawal from the JCPOA. It read in parts: "The JCPOA is working—that is a view shared by our European allies, independent experts, and the current U.S. Secretary of Defense. The JCPOA is in America's interest—it has significantly rolled back Iran's nuclear program."[48] According to Gary Samore, Obama White House's Coordinator for Arms Control and weapons of mass destruction, one of the most significant achievements of the JCPOA was that it significantly lengthened the breakout period from one to two months to eleven to twelve months in case Iran decided to build nuclear weapons.[49] This view was shared by various members of the US negotiation team, headed by then-secretary of state John Kerry. Both Kerry, Wendy Sherman, Ernest Moniz, and a number of other Obama-era negotiators were on record defending the JCPOA and criticizing Trump's anti-JCPOA decision. "This is the toughest agreement in terms of inspection, accountability—no country has had to do what Iran did in order to live up to this," Kerry wrote, lambasting Trump's claim—that the JCPOA was weak and harmful to the United States—as "false and disruptive to the international nuclear policy."[50] Kerry's view resonated with that of Yukiya Amano, the Director-General of IAEA, who described the JCPOA-led Iran nuclear inspections as the "strongest verification regime" in existence anywhere in the world.[51] Amano's predecessor, Mohammad El-Baradei, who had questioned the US pretext for the invasion of Iraq in 2003, tweeted that Trump's decision "brings to mind run-up to Iraq war."[52] The IAEA consistently defended the JCPOA as a "clear gain for verification." The agency's inspectors conducted 402 site visits and 25 snap inspections during the first year of the JCPOA. Since January 2016, the atomic agency has monitored and verified Iran's implementation of its nuclear-related commitments under the JCPOA, pursuant to UN Security Council Resolution 2231, which instructs the IAEA Director-General to "undertake the necessary verification and monitoring of Iran's nuclear-related commitments for the full duration of those commitments under the JCPOA." By the time of this writing, the agency had issued thirteen reports confirming Iran's faithful implementation of its responsibilities under the JCPOA. Thus, for example, the November 2018 IAEA report stated that the agency "continues to have regular access to relevant buildings" in Iran, that Iran has "provided all information necessary to enable" the agency to confirm Iran's compliance, and that the agency continued to use surveillance measures to verify "the non-diversion of declared nuclear material at the facilities.[53] Financially, the IAEA's JCPOA burden has been cumbersome and the agency has complained of being "underfunded."[54]

Citing the JCPOA's "robust" inspection and verification regime imposed on Iran's nuclear program, some former US officials raised their concern that with the US exit the whole deal may collapse and Iran would no longer feel obligated by the JCPOA's restrictions, as a result of which Iran may restart its curbed nuclear activities without the benefit of international inspections.[55] To the Congressional critics of the JCPOA who wanted a complete shutdown of Iran's nuclear fuel cycle, the Obama officials responded that Iran has acquired "extensive experience with nuclear fuel cycle technology" and "we can't bomb that knowledge away."[56] In his memoir, *A Day Extra*, Kerry reiterated these arguments, defending the JCPOA as an alternative to war and simultaneously representing a successful case of US-led multilateral diplomacy in resolving a vexing international crisis.[57] Kerry's views stood in sharp contrast to two other former secretaries of state, Henry Kissinger and George Shulz, who argued on the contrary that the United States had merely "traded temporary nuclear cooperation for acquiescence to Iranian hegemony."[58] In response, the Obama officials pointed out that (a) Iran in the JCPOA has categorically stated its nonproliferation commitments to steer clear of nuclear weapons, (b) while some of the nuclear restrictions are time-bound, some others, such as Iran's adherence to the IAEA's intrusive Additional Protocol have no time limit and Iran will continue to be subjected to rigorous outside inspections indefinitely.[59] To elaborate, the Additional Protocol substantially expands the IAEA's access to Iran's nuclear facilities under the Iran-IAEA Safeguards Agreement. Although considered a "voluntary agreement," the world powers insisted on Iran's compliance with the Additional Protocol, which was initially constructed between Iran and the IAEA in 2003 and implemented by Iran until 2006, when Iran in protest against outside sanctions ceased its adherence to the Protocol. Under the JCPOA, Iran has agreed to implement and legislate the Additional Protocol, which has no sunset clauses and will continue in perpetuity. Iran has repeatedly provided declarations under the terms of Additional Protocol to the IAEA. According to the IAEA, these declarations "provide broader information about Iran's nuclear nuclear-related activities and will facilitate the IAEA's assessment of the correctness and completeness of the information already provided by Iran on its past and present nuclear activities."[60] Under the JCPOA, Iran has twenty-four days to comply with an IAEA request to inspect a suspected undeclared nuclear facility; this includes military sites suspected of nuclear-related activities. However, Section 74 of the JCPOA's Annex I does not allow inspections that are not "in good faith," in other words, the IAEA's suspicions must be based on credible information, notwithstanding the Iranian concerns regarding Israeli and or American "disinformation campaign." According to US negotiator, former Energy Secretary Moniz, the JCPOA imposes a "strong nonproliferation regime" on Iran and "it is essentially impossible" for Iran to "clean up" and hide its nuclear activities in such a short period of time as the IAEA is likely to detect even small traces of nuclear material.[61] The JCPOA is referred to as "Additional Protocol plus" precisely because it provides greater leeway for IAEA inspections than that provided by the Additional Protocol. It includes monitoring of uranium mining and milling, centrifuge manufacturing, R & D, storage, and spent fuel. The agreement is also referred to as NPT plus because it enables verification of four nuclear weaponization activities which do not involve nuclear material (JCPOA, Annex I, para 82 through 82.4). Under the agreement, Iran will seek ratification of the Additional Protocol eight years after the Adoption Day, which will be in Fall, 2023. One of the significant achievements of the JCPOA is that Iran has agreed to implement the IAEA's modified Code 3.1 of the Subsidiary Arrangements to its safeguards agreement, according to which Iran is duty-bound to inform the IAEA of any new nuclear facility as soon as the decision to build it is taken, rather than six months prior to the introduction of nuclear material into the facility under the safeguard agreement.

With respect to Trump's allegations of flaws in the JCPOA's sunset clauses, Iran's counter-argument has been that "there is no sunset clause." According to Abbas Araghchi, one of the members of Iran negotiation team, the "sun never sets on Iran-IAEA safeguards and although the U.S. administration and Trump are talking about sunset clause and that JCPOA is just for 10 years, that is not true. Iran's commitment in the JCPOA not to go for the nuclear weapon is permanent."[62] Needless to say, for the critics of the JCPOA, Iran's verbal and official nonproliferation commitments were neither sufficient nor to be trusted, which was why these critics within and outside the Trump administration constantly hammered the alarm about the JCPOA's ten-year restrictions on Iran's nuclear fuel cycle which, once expired in 2025, could spell Iran's return to "industrial-scale enrichment activities." Even defenders of JCPOA such as Einhorn mentioned earlier raised concerns about this matter and advanced proposals to "fix" the problem, essentially by convincing Iran to meet its "legitimate" nuclear fuel requirements from the outside, instead of embarking on an industrial-scale uranium enrichment program that, in turn, raised the risk of "nuclearization."[63] It is noteworthy, however, that earlier during the negotiation process Einhorn had explicitly (in his open letter to Iran's negotiation team) assured Iran that "with the expiration of the CJPOA, Iran would be free—if it continues to see benefit in producing enriched uranium for power reactors—to ramp up its enrichment capacity, including by mass producing, installing, and operating advanced centrifuges that had been developed and tested while the CJPOA was in effect."[64] Richard Nephew, another Obama-era official, has acknowledged that the JCPOA-imposed restrictions on Iran's uranium enrichment activities represent a compromise of Iran's NPT rights, adding that Iran would not consent to be a second class NPT member permanently—by agreeing to extend those limitations indefinitely. As an NPT signatory, Iran was entitled to the full enjoyment of its nuclear rights under the articles of NPT, which included the right to possess a peaceful nuclear fuel cycle, much like so many other countries. There was, in other words, no viable non-proliferation standard with which to insist on Iran's total dispossession of its nuclear fuel cycle, as the Trump administration had done, for example, in Pompeo's 12-point demand that included "stop enrichment" and "close" the heavy-water reactor.[65] Veteran foreign policy expert Anthony Cordesman has characterized these Trump administration demands as "more ideological than practical."[66]

Even a less ambitious demand to simply extend the timeline for the JCPOA's restrictions on Iran's centrifuges, while more realistic, would likely entail arduous negotiations.[67] Nuclear negotiator Sherman raised skepticism on the Trump administration's ability to reach such a "new agreement" that would revise the terms of the JCPOA: "I'd like them to sit for nearly two years with a Rubik's cube of literally hundreds of details and see if they could get a better deal."[68]

Indeed, the Trumpian quest for a better nuclear deal with Iran faced a number of challenges. First, it was rejected by Iran, following the argument that the JCPOA is a multilateral agreement that cannot be unilaterally or even bilaterally renegotiated. Besides, as Iran's foreign minister Javad Zarif told these authors in September 2018, another problem was the "credibility issue. If we renegotiate the deal, we open a Pandora's Box since there is no guarantee that the next administration will not want to also renegotiate or that even this administration will abide by its own agreement."[69] As an example of Trump administration's untrustworthy character, Zarif cited Trump's turnabout on a G-7 communique that was initially agreed upon by all parties. Concerning the latter, citing his differences with Canada, in June 2018, Trump pulled the United States out of a joint G-7 statement after initially approving it.[70] The trust and credibility gaps on both sides notwithstanding, the prospect for a new round of nuclear talks between the United States and Iran remained suspended under a thick cloud of mutual hostility. The only way forward to break the impasse and explore the possibility of re-tracking the US-Iran diplomacy on a healthy and productive path was to re-open channels of communication between Tehran and Washington, both openly and secretly, and in the process set into motion the necessary groundwork for another round of negotiations either bilaterally or multilaterally. At the moment of this writing, however, diplomacy had taken a back seat to outright hostility, representing a widening gap between United States and Iran. There were offers by Trump's White House for Iran "negotiations without preconditions" amid the hail of punitive sanctions and demonization of Iran, leading Zarif to conclude that the United States was insincere in its offer and was merely engaging in a "public relations stunt."[71] While Rouhani repeatedly urged Trump to "return to JCPOA," Zarif, on the other hand, insisted that the US administration was in need of a "new approach" toward Iran if it were serious on negotiating with Iran. In December 2018, Rouhani claimed that the Trump administration had requested a meeting with representatives of the Iranian government "11 times." The White House did not deny this. The administration's infusion of an offer to talk concurrent with the blistering hammer of punitive sanctions, discussed in the next chapter, appeared to muddle the message to Iran and contributed to the confusion in the diplomatic community regarding Trump's intentions toward Iran. Was the maximalist stance taken by Trump and his foreign policy officials meant to represent the long-term objective of US government vis-a-vis Iran, rather than an actual expectation of an immediate Iranian surrender to US demands? Staking out a maximalist position on Iran's nuclear program, by demanding a complete shutdown of Iran's nuclear fuel cycle, that is, the "zero centrifuges" scenario, was a deliberate strategy that would offset the JCPOA-based argument that enough progress on the nuclear dimension had been achieved that warranted not only sustained adherence to the agreement but also a step-by-step strategy to telescope that progress to non-nuclear related issues and thus achieve a real and meaningful breakthrough in the stalemated US-Iran relations. Yet, the Trump administration's articulation of extreme nuclear demands aforementioned did not signal a serious negotiation position and was, rightly or wrongly, perceived by Iran as a "regime change" hostile maneuver that used the nuclear excuse to settle scores with Iran. With the validity of Trump's criticisms of Iran's nuclear agreement seriously questioned in the international community, it was hardly surprising that the pre-JCPOA context of a US-led international coalition against Iran did not materialize. There was a consensus among the other signatories of the JCPOA that Trump had essentially made a foreign policy misjudgment and or error by pulling the United States out of the nuclear agreement. Iran, despite its vocal criticisms of the unilateral action of United States, continued to abide by the JCPOA, as did the other parties, thus raising the prospects for a "JCPOA minus United States." In his address to the UN General Assembly in September 2017, Rouhani alluded to Trump as a "rogue newcomer to world politics" and declared that "the Islamic Republic of Iran will not be the first country to violate the agreement, but it will respond decisively and resolutely to its violation by any party."[72] A "JCPOA minus United States" entailed the emergence of new and creative measures to safeguard the JCPOA and thus to disallow Washington to torpedo the European ship of nuclear diplomacy with Iran. The final verdict on those measures had yet to be written and, yet, it was amply obvious that those measures faced formidable challenges coming from a hostile US administration that had vested a good deal of its power and credibility on a new Iran policy that relied extensively on the debilitating consequences for the Iranian economy by the arrows of a potent economic warfare.

NOTES

1. Lene Hansen, *Security as Practice: Discourse Analysis and the Bosnian War* (London: Rutledge, 2006): 17.

2. Quoted in Hannah Arendt, *On Revolution* (London: Faber, 1963): 227.

3. Michel Foucault, *Power/Knowledge* (New York: Pantheon Books, 1972) Foucault's insights on the disciplinary and "normalizing" operation of power in modern societies applies, *mutatis mutandis*, to Trump administration's quests to make revolutionary Iran into a "normal" state.

4. "National Security Strategy of the United States of America," *White House*, December 2017, https://www.whitehouse.gov/wp-content/uploads/2017/12/NSS-Final-12-18-2017-0905.pdf.

5. Robert Jervis, "Weapons Without Purpose? Nuclear Strategy in the Post-Cold War Era," *Foreign Affairs* 80, no. 4 (July/August 2001), 143.

6. "Remarks by President Trump on the Joint Comprehensive Plan of Action," *White House*, May 8, 2018, https://www.whitehouse.gov/briefings-statements/remarks-president-trump-joint-comprehensive-plan-action/.

7. Ibid.

8. David S. Cohen, "Trump Is Trying to Politicize Intelligence to Support His Iran Policy. That's Dangerous," *Washington Post*, August 4, 2017, https://www.washingtonpost.com/opinions/trump-is-trying-to-politicize-intelligence-to-support-his-iran-policy-thats-dangerous/2017/08/04/ffb192e0-77b6-11e7-8f39-eeb7d3a2d304_story.html?utm_term=.11cc3d884f85.

9. "Remarks by President Trump on Iran Strategy," *White House*, October 13, 2017, https://www.whitehouse.gov/briefings-statements/remarks-president-trump-iran-strategy/.

10. Michael R. Pompeo, "Confronting Iran: The Trump Administration's Strategy," *Foreign Affairs*, November/December 2018, https://www.foreignaffairs.com/articles/middle-east/2018-10-15/michael-pompeo-secretary-of-state-on-confronting-iran. Pompeo characterized Obama's Iran policy as one of "leading from behind," an accommodationist strategy that incorrectly signaled diminished American power and influence.

11. "Tillerson Says Washington, Europe Start Work on Iran Nuclear Deal," *Reuters*, January 27, 2018, https://www.reuters.com/article/us-mideast-crisis-syria-tillerson/tillerson-says-washington-europe-start-work-on-iran-nuclear-deal-idUSKBN1FG0CF.

12. Ibid.

13. "State Department Officials Says US Not Looking to Renegotiate the Iran Nuclear Deal," *The Hill*, April 25, 2018, https://thehill.com/homenews/administrat ion/384795-state-dept-official-says-us-not-looking-to-renegotiate-iran-deal.

14. Afshin Kumar Sen, "Macron Pitches a New Iran Nuclear Deal," *Atlantic Council*, April 24, 2018, https://www.atlanticcouncil.org/blogs/new-atlanticist/m acron-pitches-a-new-iran-deal.

15. Mark Lander, David E. Sanger, and Gardiner Harris, "Rewrite Iran Deal? Europeans Offer a Different Solution: A New Chapter," *New York Times*, February 26, 2018, https://www.nytimes.com/2018/02/26/us/politics/trump-europe-iran-deal. html.

16. "Letter to House Speaker Paul Ryan from Secretary of State Rex Tillerson Certifying Iran's Compliance with the JCPOA and Announcing Interagency Review," *Iran Watch*, April 18, 2017, https://www.iranwatch.org/library/governments/unit ed-states/executive-branch/department-state/letter-house-speaker-paul-ryan-secre tary-state-rex-tillerson-certifying-irans.

17. " 'Iran Nuclear Deal' Administration Approves but Review Looms," The *Guardian*, April 19, 2017, https://www.theguardian.com/world/2017/apr/19/iran-nucl ear-deal-trump-administration-approves-agreement-but-review-looms.

18. "Trump Recertifies Iran Nuclear Deal, Only Reluctantly," *New York Times*, July 17, 2017, https://www.nytimes.com/2017/07/17/us/politics/trump-iran-nuclear -deal-recertify.html.

19. "Trump Disavows Nuclear Deal, but Doesn't Scrap It," *New York Times*, October 13, 2017, https://www.nytimes.com/2017/10/13/us/politics/trump-iran-nu clear-deal.html.

20. "Tillerson: US Trying to Stay in Iran Deal," *CNN*, October 16, 2017, https:// www.cnn.com/2017/10/15/politics/rex-tillerson-iran-nuclear-agreement-cnntv/index. html.

21. "Trump Issues Warning, but Continues to Honor Iran Deal," *CNN*, January 12, 2018, https://www.cnn.com/2018/01/12/politics/president-donald-trump-iran-de al-waiver/index.html.

22. "H.R. 1191—Iran Nuclear Agreement Review Act of 2015," *Congress.gov*, May 22, 2015, https://www.congress.gov/bill/114th-congress/house-bill/1191/text.

23. Quoted in Josh Rogin, "Commentary: Trump Leaves to Congress to Clean His Iran Nuclear Deal Mess," *Chicago Tribune*, October 16, 2017, https://www.chicagot ribune.com/news/opinion/commentary/ct-trump-iran-deal-mess-20171016-story.html.

24. Quoted in "Cotton-Corker Bill Still Up in the Air," *National Iranian American Council*, November 3, 2017, https://www.niacouncil.org/cotton-corker-bill-still-air/.

25. James M. Lindsay, "The Iran Nuclear Deal Saga Continues," *Council on Foreign Relations*, December 10, 2017, https://www.cfr.org/blog/iran-deal-saga-conti nues.

26. Mark Perry, "Mattis's Last Stand Is Iran," *Foreign Policy*, June 28, 2018, https ://foreignpolicy.com/2018/06/28/mattiss-last-stand-is-iran/.

27. "Trump Fires Rex Tillerson as Secretary of State," *BBC News*, March 13, 2018, https://www.bbc.com/news/world-us-canada-43388723.

28. "Tillerson Should Resign, Haass Says," *Bloomberg*, October 7, 2017, https://www.bloomberg.com/news/audio/2017-10-04/tillerson-should-resign-haass-says.

29. Oren Dorrell, "Mike Pompeo Hearing: Key Takeaways on Russia, North Korea, Iran," *USA Today*, April 12, 2018, https://www.usatoday.com/story/news/world/2018/04/12/mike-pompeo-trump-pick-secretary-state-feels-russia-north-korea-and-syria/510924002/.

30. This information is based on the authors' interview with Foreign Minister Zarif in New York on September 26, 2018.

31. Democratic Senator Chris Murphy has raised the alarm that "Trump and his most radical advisers are begging for a war with Iran. This would be a disaster of epic scale, perhaps eclipsing the nightmare of the Iraq war." Chris Murphy, "Trump's Reckless Path toward War with Iran," *Hartford Courant*, February 3, 2017, http://www.courant.com/opinion/op-ed/hc-op-murphy-trumps-reckless-iran-policy-0206-20170203-story.html.

32. John R. Bolton, "Trump Must Withdraw from Iran Nuclear Deal-Now," *TheHill.com*, July 16, 2017, http://thehill.com/blogs/pundits-blog/foreign-policy/342237-opinion-trump-must-withdraw-from-iran-nuclear-deal-now. "Rep. Mike Pompeo (R-Kan.): One Year Later, Obama's Iran Nuclear Deal Puts Us at Increased Risk," *Fox News*, July 14, 2016, http://www.foxnews.com/opinion/2016/07/14/rep-mike-pompeo-one-year-later-obama-s-iran-nuclear-deal-puts-us-at-increased-risk.html.

33. John Bolton, "Beyond the Iran Nuclear Deal," *Wall Street Journal*, January 18, 2018, https://www.wsj.com/articles/beyond-the-iran-nuclear-deal-1516044178. In this article, Bolton criticized the Europeans for being more interested in a strong trade with Iran than a strong nuclear agreement.

34. John R. Bolton, "Iran: Regime Change Is Within Reach," *Gatestone Institute*, July 3, 2017, https://www.gatestoneinstitute.org/10620/iran-regime-change.

35. Joseph Cirincione, "Bolton's Big Con," *Defense One*, January 12, 2019, https://www.defenseone.com/ideas/2019/01/boltons-big-iran-con/154109/?oref=d-river.

36. Quoted in Hugh Hewitt, "Trump's Sledgehammer Tactics Are Fit for the Middle East," *Washington Post*, January 7, 2019, https://www.washingtonpost.com/opinions/trumps-sledgehammer-tactics-are-fit-for-the-middle-east/2019/01/07/27703fe6-129f-11e9-b6ad-9cfd62dbb0a8_story.html?noredirect=on&utm_term=.7ff4732a84d8.

37. Quoted in Shashank Bengali and Ramin Mostaghim, "Iran reacts to Pompeo as Trump's Secretary of State Pick: 'Cowboyish' and 'Eager to Start a War,'" *Los Angeles Times*, March14, 2018, https://www.latimes.com/world/middleeast/la-fg-iran-pompeo-20180314-story.html.

38. For more on this see, Jurgen Habermas, "On Systematically Distorted Communication," *Inquiry* 13, nos. 1–4 (1970), 205–218.

39. Quoted in David Frum, *Trumpocracy: The Corruption of the American Republic* (New York: Harper Collings, 2018): 152.

40. Robert Einhorn, "Debating the Iran Nuclear Deal: A Former American Negotiator Outlines the Issues," *Brookings Institution*, August 12, 2015, http://www.brookings.edu/research/debating-the-iran-nuclear-deal-a-former-american-negotiator-outlines-the-background-issues/.

41. "Remarks: Quitting the Iran Nuclear Deal: A Serious Mistake," *Arms Control Association*, June 2018, https://www.armscontrol.org/act/2018-06/features/remark s-quitting-iran-nuclear-deal-%E2%80%98-serious-mistake%E2%80%99.

42. "Preserving the JCPOA Key to Global Security: UN Chief," *Press TV*, June 20, 2018, https://www.presstv.com/Detail/2018/06/20/565501/Iran-JCPOA-UN-Al i-Akbar-Salehi.

43. "Implementation of Security Council Resolution 2231 (2015): Fifth Report of the Secretary-General," *UNDOCs.org*, June 12, 2018, https://undocs.org/S/2018/602.

44. "Israeli Experts Defend the Iran Nuclear Deal," *Boston Globe*, October 13, 2017, https://www.bostonglobe.com/opinion/2017/10/13/israeli-experts-defend-iran-nuclear-deal/Ayy654bqx8ZWTJXmPNAfrM/story.html. Also, Carmi Gillon, "The Iran Nuclear Deal Has Been a Blessing for Israel," *Foreign Policy*, July 13, 2017, http://foreignpolicy.com/2017/07/13/the-iran-nuclear-deal-has-been-a-blessing-fo r-israel-jcpoa/.

45. "Scientists' Letter on the Iran Nuclear Accord," *New York Times*, October 30, 2017, https://www.nytimes.com/interactive/2017/10/30/world/middleeast/iran-n uclear-deal-letter.html.

46. "An Open Letter from Retired Generals and Admirals," *American Security Project*, July 12, 2017, https://www.americansecurityproject.org/asp-retired-flag-off icers-sign-letter-supporting-iran-nuclear-agreement/. The letter urged Trump to "weigh the risks to our troops of escalating tensions with Iran."

47. "Former Top Officials Urge Congress to Back the Iran Deal," *The Hill*, July 25, 2015, https://thehill.com/policy/defense/248483-former-top-us-officials-iran-deal -meets-key-objectives.

48. "A Serious Mistake: Read Obama's Statement on Trump's Decision to Pull Out of Iran Nuclear Deal," *CNBC*, August 9, 2018, https://www.cnbc.com/2018/05/0 8/a-serious-mistake-read-obamas-statement-on-trumps-decision-to-pull-out-of-iran -deal.html.

49. Gary Samore, ed., "Iran Nuclear Deal: A Definitive Guide," *Belfer Center*, August 2015, p. 29, https://www.belfercenter.org/sites/default/files/legacy/files/Ira nDealDefinitiveGuide.pdf.

50. "John Kerry: Trump Really Just Doesn't Really Know What He Is Talking About: He Makes Things Up," *Business Insider*, September 2, 2018, https://www.bus inessinsider.com/john-kerry-trump-makes-things-up-iran-nuclear-deal-2018-9.

51. Quoted in Shashank Bengali, "World's Most Robust Nuclear Inspection under Fire as Trump Tries to Rewrite the Iran Deal," *Los Angeles Times*, October 4, 2017, https://www.businessinsider.com/john-kerry-trump-makes-things-up-iran-nuclear-de al-2018-9.

52. Quoted in "Trump's Iran Stance Reminds run-up to Iraq War," *Financial Tri-bune*, October 15, 2017, https://financialtribune.com/articles/national/74252/trump-s -iran-stance-reminds-run-up-to-iraq-war.

53. "Verification and Monitoring in the Islamic Republic of Iran: In Light of United Nations Security Council Resolution 2231 (2015), *IAEA*, November 22, 2018, https://www.iaea.org/sites/default/files/18/11/gov2018-47.pdf.

54. Mark Leon Goldberg, "The Cash Strapped Agency at the Heart of the Iran Deal," *The Atlantic*, July 18, 2015. The May 2015 IAEA report notes that while the IAEA member-states had pledged 6.13 million euros in support of JPOA verification activities, the agency had received 6.06 million euros, almost half of the amount that Amano stated was required. The United States provided close to Euros 1.5 million for the JPOA verification, while other big contributors included Norway with a pledge of Euro 1 million.

55. Wendy Sherman, "How We Got the Iran Deal. And Why We'll Miss It," *Foreign Affairs*, September/October 2018, https://www.foreignaffairs.com/articles/2018-08-13/how-we-got-iran-deal. According to Sherman, "The most important facet of the Iran deal was the higher principles we sought and the reimagining of the world that it took to make the deal happen." See, Wendy Sherman, *Not for the Faint of Heart: Lessons in Courage, Power, and Persistence* (New York: Hachette Books, 2018): xix.

56. "Sec. Kerry Fiercely Defends Iran Nuclear Deal to Congress," *NBC*, July 23, 2015, https://www.nbcnews.com/storyline/iran-nuclear-talks/sec-kerry-fiercely-defends-iran-nuclear-deal-congress-n397201.

57. John Kerry, *Every Day Is Extra* (New York: Simon and Schuster, 2018). In this book, Kerry writes of secret talks in 2011 with the government of Oman as a US Senator that helped launch negotiations with Tehran. He portrays Hillary Clinton, then secretary of state, as initially doubtful but finally coming around. Kerry also describes tensions that periodically emerged between Iran and Russia during the final rounds of nuclear negotiations. According to Kerry, Sergei Lavrov, Russia's foreign minister, at one point snapped at Javad Zarif, his Iranian counterpart, over his reluctance to close the deal.

58. Henry Kissinger and George P. Schulz, "The Iran Deal and Its Consequences," *Wall Street Journal*, April 7, 2015, http://www.wsj.com/articles/the-iran-deal-and-its-consequences-1428447582.

59. For more on this see Ali Vaez, "The Iranian Nuclear Deal's Sunset Clauses," *Foreign Affairs*, October 3, 2017, https://www.foreignaffairs.com/articles/iran/2017-10-03/iranian-nuclear-deals-sunset-clauses.

60. "Iran Submits Declaration under the Additional Protocol," *IAEA News Center*, 2004/2008, https://www.iaea.org/newscenter/mediaadvisories/iran-submits-declaration-under-additional-protocol.

61. Ernest Moniz, "Commentary: Ernest Moniz Why the Iran Deal Will Work," *Chicago Tribune*, August 6, 2015, https://www.chicagotribune.com/news/opinion/commentary/ct-iran-nuclear-deal-moniz-obama-perspec-0807-20150806-story.html. A former nuclear physicist at Massachusetts Institute of Technology, Moniz had also worked for decades in the Department of Energy's laboratories and was highly respected as a nuclear expert. His statement denouncing Trump's stance on JCPOA reads in part: "The agreement put an ironclad straitjacket on Iran's ability to develop or obtain a nuclear weapon. Under the agreement, Iran has dismantled key aspects of its nuclear program, and it has and must continue to allow international inspectors continuous monitoring and verification, with the ability to access any site—including military sites—where the nuclear activity is suspected. The most important aspects

of the agreement are permanent—a prohibition on Iran ever having a nuclear weapon or a nuclear weapons program and the most comprehensive verification and transparency measures that currently exist. Those who argue that the agreement permits Iran to become a nuclear weapon state after 10 or 15 years are flat out wrong." In "Statement by Ernest J. Moniz on President Trump's Decision not to Certify Iran's Compliance with the Nuclear Deal," *NTI.org*, October 15, 2017, https://www.nti.org/newsroom/news/statement-ernest-j-moniz-president-trumps-decision-not-certify-irans-compliance-nuclear-agreement/.

62. "Iran Says We Do Not Want Nuclear Weapons—There Is No Sunset Clause in the Nuclear Deal," *Reuters*, February 22, 2018, https://www.reuters.com/article/us-iran-usa-nuclear-deal/iran-says-w e-do-not-want-nuclear-weapons-there-is-no-sunset-clause-in-nuclear-deal-idUSKCN1G60Y4.

63. Robert Einhorn, "Fix the Iran Deal, But Don't Move the Goalposts," *Brookings Institution*, January 18, 2018, https://www.brookings.edu/blog/markaz/2018/01/18/fix-the-iran-deal-but-dont-move-the-goalposts/.

64. Robert Einhorn, "An Open Letter to the Iranian Nuclear Negotiation Team," *IRDIPLOMACY*, August 16, 2014, http://irdiplomacy.ir/en/news/1937125/an-open-letter-to-the-iranian-negotiating-team.

65. "Mike Pompeo Speech: What Are the 12 Demands Given to Iran?" *Al-Jazeera*, May 21, 2018, https://www.aljazeera.com/news/2018/05/mike-pompeo-speech-12-demands-iran-180521151737787.html.

66. Anthony H. Cordesman, "U.S. Strategy, the JCPOA Iranian Nuclear Arms Agreement, and the Gulf: Playing the Long Game," *Center for Strategic and International Studies*, March 28, 2018, https://www.csis.org/analysis/us-strategy-jcpoa-iranian-nuclear-arms-agreement-and-gulf-playing-long-game.

67. "5 Questions: Richard Nephew on Iran Sanctions," *Columbia News*, January 18, 2018, https://news.columbia.edu/content/1815.

68. "Ask an Expert: Iran Nuclear Deal Two Years Later," *Center for Arms Control and Non-Proliferation*, July 20, 2017, https://armscontrolcenter.org/ask-expert-iran-deal-two-years-later/.

69. This information is based on the interview of the authors with Iran's Foreign Minister Mohammad Javad Zarif in New York, September 25, 2018.

70. "Trump Pulls US Out of G-7 Statement, Accuses Trudeau of Being 'Dishonest'," *NBC News*, June 9, 2018, https://www.nbcnews.com/politics/white-house/trump-pulls-u-s-out-g-7-communique-accuses-trudeau-n881761.

71. "Zarif: Trump's Offer of Negotiation with Iran, Only a PR Stunt," *MSN.com*, June 8, 2018, https://www.msn.com/en-xl/middleeast/top-stories/zarif-trumps-offer-of-negotiations-with-iran-only-pr-stunt/ar-BBLAAta.

72. Nicole Gaouette, "Iran's Rouhani Pushes Back on Trump," *CNN*, September 20, 2017, https://www.cnn.com/2017/09/20/politics/iran-rouhani-trump-nuclear/index.html.

Chapter 3

Maximum Pressure Strategy
and Iran's Response

This chapter has been divided into three sections. In the first section, a comprehensive examination of the ravaging economic assault waged by the Trump administration against Iran will be presented, demonstrating the huge blows to the Iranian economy that wiped out the positive momentum for normalizing Iran's external trade following the signing of the nuclear deal in 2015. In the scholarly debate on US-Iran relations, there is a lively debate on the effectiveness of Trump-imposed sanctions on Iran, not to mention their appropriateness as a tool of US foreign policy vis-à-vis not only Iran but also a host of other nations including North Korea, Russia, and Venezuela. For example, Mark Fitzpatrick has raised interesting questions about the wisdom and ultimate purpose of new US sanctions on Iran.[1] Our position is that there was little evidence to support the Trump administration's optimism that the Iran sanctions could realize its ambitious foreign policy goals with respect to Iran. This issue becomes clearer as we then turn (in the second section) to the geopolitics of exemptions from new US sanctions covering both some of Iran's neighbors as well as the important Chabahar project in southern Iran, overlapping with the strategies of United States for South Asia and Iraq, with consequential implications for all these policies. The net effect of these sanctions waivers was to undercut the maximalist (rollback) strategy and to lower the prospects for the success of that strategy's aim of instigating sea changes in Iran's domestic and foreign behavior. As a result, the Trump administration could at best count on sub-optimal "mixed results" from its economic warfare on Iran, thus putting its Iran policy at a crossroad: either continue with the oil and non-oil sanctions waivers that appeased America's friends and allies, or risk alienating them by insisting on a complete halt to Iran's oil exports, which could also affect the world oil market and trigger an Iran hard power response in the Persian Gulf. How the Trump administration responded to the conflicting priorities (reflected in the sanctions waivers) would reveal a great deal about the future direction of US foreign policy for the remainder of Trump's presidency. In the third section of this chapter, we examine Iran's counter-strategy to safeguard its economy from the impact of the US economic onslaught, focusing on Iran's regional approach and the resilience of Iran's post-revolutionary "economic populism" that underscored its will to survive and was also an important aspect of the country's "resistant economy," creating legitimacy and undermining the US policy of tapping into mass discontent and inciting a domestic revolt in Iran.

Undoubtedly, the economic dimension of Trump's new Iran strategy formed the centerpiece of that strategy—that was part of a broader US Middle East policy targeting Iran and its regional allies. The new coercive economic measures adopted by US government were nothing short of economic warfare, explicitly aimed at "busting up" Iran's economy as a prelude to a thinly veiled, much-hoped for regime-change in Iran.[2] These measures had, however, both intended and unintended consequences and also faced formidable challenges, particularly those stemming from the absence of a global consensus on Iran threat, the reluctance of other nations to bandwagon with US against Iran, and the paradoxes of the US policy for South Asia that (indirectly) counted on Iran's contribute to the stability of Afghanistan in collaboration with India. Taking stock of Trump administration's rapid-fire economic warfare on Iran and these challenges, this chapter seeks to enhance our knowledge of the scope of downward spiral impacting the US-Iran relations during the Trump era, affecting not only Iran but also the economy and security of Iran's neighbors. A clue to the latter, in September 2018, addressing the UN General Assembly, President Trump vehemently criticized the "ideology of globalism," lashed out at Iran's "corrupt dictatorship" and accused Iran's leaders of "sowing chaos, death, and destruction" across the Middle East. Claiming that Iran's rulers "do not respect their neighbors or borders," Trump cited Syria as an example and blamed Iran for the humanitarian crisis in Syria: "Every solution to the humanitarian crisis in Syria must also include a strategy to address the brutal regime that has fueled and financed it: the corrupt dictatorship in Iran."[3] In response, Iran's President Hassan Rouhani used the UN podium to denounce Trump's unilateralism and "bullying" and accused his administration of harboring "Nazi dispositions."[4] Simultaneously, two main architects of Trump's Iran policy, namely, National Security Adviser John Bolton and Secretary of State Mike Pompeo, addressed a separate gathering in New York and repeated the administration's long list of complaints against Iran, branded by the US Department of State as "the leading state sponsor of terrorism." Thus, while Bolton warned Iran that it would have "hell to pay" if "you cross us, our allies, or our partners,"[5] Pompeo on the other hand went one step further by citing a concrete threat by Iran's proxies in Iraq: "Iranian-supported militias in Iraq launched life-threatening rocket attacks against the U.S. embassy compound in Baghdad and at the U.S. consulate in Basra. Iran did not stop these attacks, which were carried out by proxies it has supported and funded and trained, and with which—and militias with which it has provided weapons." Pompeo then went on to warn that "the United States will hold the regime in Tehran accountable for any attack that results in injury to our personnel or damage to our facilities. America will respond swiftly and decisively in [defense of] American lives, and we will respond against the source of the attack on American interests."[6] In preparation for this contingency, according to a report in the *Wall Street Journal*, Bolton asked the Pentagon officials to draw up a plan of attack on Iran.[7] A few days later, Pompeo ordered the closure of US consulate in the Southern Iraqi city of Basra, citing "security threats from Iran."[8] Hardly surprising, such vehement anti-Iran rhetoric was in fact consistently heard loud and clear ever since President Trump's first foreign visits to Saudi Arabia in May 2017, where he refrained from any criticisms of his hosts and, instead, lashed out at Iran, accusing it of fueling "the fires of sectarian conflict and terror" and calling for its international isolation "until the Iranian regime is willing to be a partner for peace." That refrain echoed the Saudis' self-serving description of the Iranian government as "the tip of the spear of global terrorism."[9]

A clue to the worsening tensions between US and Iran played out in the region, Iran blamed United States and Israel for an attack on Iranian consulate in Basra on September 7, 2018 and, similarly, pointed at the United States and its Arab regional allies for the terrorist attack at a military parade in Iranian city of Ahvaz that claimed the lives of dozens of civilians and military personnel on September 22, 2018.[10] Iran's revolutionary guards fired missiles at "terrorists" responsible for the Ahvaz attack in their sanctuary inside Syria within a few miles of US forces stationed in Syria, meant as a warning "signal" to the United States.[11] In Persian Gulf, tensions were also simmering with Iran playing brinksmanship by threatening to close the strategic Strait of Hormuz as a countermeasure to oil embargo of the United States,[12] eliciting the US warning that it "stands ready" to "keep the Persian Gulf waterway open" despite Iran's threat.[13] The mere proximity of US and Iranian navies in Persian Gulf risked an accidental warfare in the tense security environment—that spelled greater and greater insecurity for Iran under siege of a unilateral economic warfare waged by the US superpower. Although Iran's leaders publicly downplayed the extent of damages to Iran by American measures, the tsunami of these new pressures was devastating Iran's post-JCPOA economic rebound. Iran's economy in 2018 had turned recessionary, with double-digit inflation and unemployment rates and a depressing negative rate of growth, attributed to the acidic combination of economic mismanagement, corruption and, above all, the vicissitude of the economic war of the United

States on Iran geared to instigate a "collapse" of the Iranian economy. Rudy Giuliani, White House's legal adviser, thus boasted: "When the greatest economic power stops doing business with you, then you collapse." But, as the US did not entirely stop others from doing business with Iran, as discussed later in this chapter, Giuliani's view appeared to be overly optimistic and undermined by the opposing evidence that for a variety of economic reasons, Iran's economy did not melt down under US pressure and could conceivably survive for the foreseeable future.[14] The contrary assessment that "Trump's economic war on Iran is doomed to failure" had the upper hands in some Western policy circles, exemplified by an opinion column by a former British ambassador to Iran, Sir Richard Dalton, who characterized the administration's claim of Iranian threat to America as "transparently exaggerated."[15]

ECONOMIC FALLOUT OF COMPELLENCE STRATEGY

In fact, Trump's economic pressures on Iran preceded the administration's actual re-imposition of sanctions by a full year, with the combined threat of exiting the JCPOA and actively lobbying foreign governments and banks against doing business with Iran yielding some intended results, essentially by casting a cloud of uncertainty over the Iran business environment. As a result, major European and Asian banks avoided dealing with Iran, in light of the multi-billion dollar fines that banks such as HSBC and PNB Paribas had paid to the US during the Obama era.[16] The British banks in particular avoided normalization of relations with Iran even prior to Trump's presidency despite a plea by both the British prime minister and the US Secretary of State John Kerry with their executives, pointing out that while Washington and Europe had lifted some sanctions, there was still a ban on the use of dollars in the US banking system to finance Iranian trade; this is not to mention that some US local states had defied the federal government on Iran sanctions relief.[17] Subsequently, these banks proved more receptive to Trump's Treasury Secretary, who traveled to Europe and warned the banks to stay away from Iran—in violation of the terms of the JCPOA according to Iran—months before Trump pulled out of the deal.[18] Moreover, the Financial Action Task Force (FATF), an inter-governmental body combating money laundering and terrorist financing, still viewed Iran as a non-compliant jurisdiction of money laundering, thus adding to the outside banks' concerns about Iran.[19] Trump himself played a key role in fanning the flames of these concerns, for example, by lobbying the G-7 leaders against doing business with Iran at the G-7 summit, while ironically endorsing a statement that praised the JCPOA,[20] thus bringing an air of "uncertainty and risk" toward Iran; the latter increasingly thickened as time went on and the administration escalated its action and rhetoric, particularly when Trump announced his refusal to "re-certify" the JCPOA to US Congress in October, 2017;[21] initially, on two occasions in April and July 2017, the administration sent Congress a letter confirming that Iran was in compliance with the JCPOA and that the US was therefore abiding with its obligations under the agreement.

Yet, despite the absence of any evidence that Iran had violated the JCPOA, a fact confirmed by several reports of the IAEA as well as by Pompeo himself at his nomination hearing in May, 2018,[22] the US government issued a "National Security Presidential Memorandum" directing immediate preparations for the re-imposition of all US sanctions lifted by that country since 2015, with the aim of "reinstating U.S. nuclear sanctions on the Iranian regime at the highest level."[23] This was followed by the US Executive Order 13846, issued on August 6, 2018, that prohibited any person from "materially assisting, sponsoring, or providing financial, material, or technological support for, or goods or services in support of, among others, the National Iranian Oil Company and the Central Bank of Iran after November 5, 2018."[24] By imposing what the Secretary of State Pompeo called the "strongest sanctions in history," the Trump administration had made it abundantly clear that its aim was to bring down Iran's oil exports to "close to zero" and thus to deprive the Iranian government of a bulk of its revenue while, simultaneously, targeting the Iranian financial and banking, automotive, and other sectors. Senior White House officials bragged about an early success by noticing that "the rial is tanking, unemployment in Iran is rising, and there are widespread protests over social issues and labor unrest . . . in the last 90 days we have seen company after company announce that they are getting out, so there's no question that this pressure is already working... We're very pleased that nearly 100 international firms have announced their intent to leave the Iranian market, particularly in the energy and the finance sectors"[25] In August, 2018, Trump tweeted: "The Iran sanctions have been officially cast. They are the most biting sanctions ever imposed. Anyone doing business with Iran will NOT be doing business with the United States."[26]

Initially, Iran was dismissive of the hostile actions of the United States, which was often couched in a discourse of "failed revolution" in Iran.[27] Case in point, Foreign Minister Mohammad Javad Zarif asserted that since the JCPOA's adoption, Iran had attracted a huge amount of foreign investment and was able to sell its oil and receive its money, explaining that "we now sell more than 2.5 million barrels of oil."[28] Bahman Zanganeh, Iran's oil minister, also dismissed US attempt to halt Iran's oil exports as "unrealistic."[29] Other Iranian officials, however, including Jaafar Mehdizadeh, an executive of Iran's Central Bank, readily admitted that "the U.S. sanctions . . . are currently having many negative effects on various macroeconomic indicators such as GDP growth, employment, inflation and various welfare indicators of households."[30] This view was shared in the international community by, among others, Idriss Jazairy, the United Nations Special Rapporteur, who in his report to the UN Human Rights Council (August, 2018) lambasted the US's unilateral measures as "unjust" and "harmful" by virtue of "destroying the economy and currency of Iran, driving millions of people into poverty and making imported goods unaffordable." With respect to "humanitarian commodities" such as food and medicine, Jazairy stated: "The current system creates doubt and ambiguity which makes it all but impossible for Iran to import these urgently needed humanitarian goods. This ambiguity causes a 'chilling effect' which is likely to lead to silent deaths in hospitals as medicines run out, while the international media fail to notice."[31] This was subsequently corroborated by the news that "Cargill, Bunge and other global traders have halted food supply deals with Iran because new U.S. sanctions have paralyzed banking systems."[32] Under US pressure, SWIFT (Society for Worldwide Interbank Financial Telecommunication), the world's biggest interbank-transfer network, announced in November 2018 that it was suspending some Iranian banks' access to its messaging system "in the interest of the stability and integrity of the wider global financial system."[33]

One key aspect of the dramatic impact of US sanctions was the plummeting of Iran's currency, the rial. According to the Director of Economic Research and Planning at the Central Bank of Iran: "From May 1 to August 20, 2018, the rial depreciated against the US dollar and the euro by 78.5% and 68.6% in parallel exchange market." Tehran's grand bazaar went on strike in June 2018, protesting the rial's alarming devaluation that had resulted in a significant increase in the price of imported goods and increased the inflation rate.[34] Another big blow was capital flight from Iran, notwithstanding the fact that prior to JCPOA exit of the United States, foreign direct investment was increasing and the Iranian government reported a growth of 55 percent compared to the previous year; in effect, this meant the cancellation of numerous major foreign contracts sealed in the aftermath of the nuclear agreement. These included: 5 billion euro investment agreement between Italy's Invitalia and Bank of Industry and Mine and Middle East Bank; 660 million euro joint-venture deal between Renault and Iran's state-run Industrial Development and Renovation Organization, Bpifrance's consent to finance investment projects of French companies in Iran as of 2018, granting up to 500 million euros, and other French agreements worth 400 million euro and 300 million euro with Iranian car makers Iran Khodro and Saipa, and with Iran Air worth 350 million dollars, and with Petropars worth 5 billion dollars; South Korea's 1.8-billion-dollar deal with National Iranian Oil Engineering and Construction Company, 831-million-dollar deal for passenger rail cars production, Export-Import Bank's 9.6-billion-dollar deal; Austrian Oesterreichische Kontrollbank's agreement to increase its export guarantees for deals with

Iran to roughly 1 billion euros; British Quercus's deal with Iran's Ministry of Energy to build a 500 million euro solar power farm; Norway's 2.5-billion-euro deal with Iran's Ministry of Energy; Danish Danske Bank's 500 million euro credit line deal with ten Iranian banks. Other deals potentially impacted were: Chinese Sinopec's 1.2 billion dollar agreement with National Iranian Oil Refining and Distribution Company and a 10 billion dollar credit line deal with Iranian banks; and Russia's Transmashholding's 3 billion dollar deal with the Industrial Development and Renovation Organization of Iran, a 3 billion euro agreement between Russian Export Center (REC) and Iran Railway Company, and a 742 million dollar deal with National Iranian Oil Company (NIOC).

Previously, with the oil sanctions lifted as a result of the JCPOA, Iran had been able to resume its oil exports to Europe for the first time since Europe's oil embargo of 2012 and the French energy giant Total became the first Western energy company to sign a deal with Iran when it agreed as part of a twenty-year contract to develop phase 11 of the country's South Pars field, the world's largest gas field that is shares with Qatar. The project was targeted to a production capacity of two billion cubic feet per day or 400,000 barrels of oil equivalent per day including condensate. The produced gas was scheduled to supply the Iranian domestic market starting in 2021. But, this project and numerous other (both energy and non-energy) projects mentioned earlier were canceled as a direct result of the (threat of) new US sanctions. Case in point, the British oil company BP halted work on a gas field in the North Sea which it co-owns with NIOC, citing US sanctions.[35] According to Total's chairman, Patrick Pouyanné, "There's not a single international company like Total who can work in any country with secondary sanctions . . . It's impossible, let me be clear, to run an international company like Total without having access to U.S. financing or to U.S. shareholding." Pouyanné further explained that American banks were involved in over 90 percent of the company's financing and that the company had a large number of shareholders in the United States.[36] This was echoed by a number of other European corporate executives, many of them lamenting that the US sanctions left them with little choice but to abandon the Iran market.[37] Thus, the CEO of German giant Siemens, Joe Kaeser, in an interview with CNN announced that Trump's decision on re-imposing sanctions on Iran meant that his company could not do any new business in Iran. Similarly, the Italian steel manufacturer, Danieli, announced in May 2018 that it had halted work on finding financial coverage for orders in Iran worth 1.5 billion euro, with the CEO explaining that "the banks are no longer ready to fund Iranian projects for fear of secondary sanctions."[38] South Korea's Hyundai Engineering & Construction also scrapped a 521 million dollar deal to build a petrochemicals complex in Iran, citing the inability to raise the fund due to US sanctions.[39] Similarly, Austria's

Oberbank announced in June, 2018, its withdrawal from financing business in Iran, including a September 2017 agreement to provide project finance to Iran worth 1 billion euros, stating that "the threat to European companies by US secondary sanctions is forcing us to retreat."[40] Other examples were: the Swiss bank, Banque de Commerce et de Placements, announced that it will not accept any new transactions with Iran, including payments for medical raw materials supplied by the healthcare company Sanofi—and this was despite the Iranian bank concerned, Bank Pasargad, protesting that medical products are meant to be exempt from the US measures.[41] As an example of impacts to food imports into Iran, cattle in the thousands ready for export from northern France were reported in August 2018 as staying put because of a bank's refusal to process payment, and also due to the withdrawal of the insurer.[42] The world's two largest container companies, MAERSK and MSC, also withdrew from business with Iran. According to the Maersk chief executive, "with the sanctions the Americans are to impose, you can't do business in Iran if you also have business in the U.S., and we have that on a large scale."[43]

The US's sanctions on Iran's energy sector translated in the loss of certain key oil markets for Iran as a whole or in parts, such as India, South Korea and Japan, due to difficulties in making payments or obtaining insurance for shipments of Iranian oil.[44] In Japan, "refiners were told that the banks won't handle transactions for Iran-related deals that were signed on or after May 8, and that those signed before that period will be dealt with "on a case-by-case basis."[45] With international insurers such as the German Allianz deciding to "wind down" business with Iran due to US sanctions, it became harder and harder for Iran to export its oil, for example, India's HPCL was reported in July, 2018 to have canceled Iran oil shipment after insurer excluded coverage.[46] Similarly, a number of European refineries were winding down purchases of Iranian oil prior to US imposition of oil sanctions in November 2018.[47] Another potential casualty was the lucrative thirty billion-dollar deal between Iran and Russia's oil giant Rosnet to produce up to fifty-five million tonnes of oil per year.[48] In December 2018, the Russian media reported that Rosneft had quit the Iran market, a claim disputed by Iran.[49] If confirmed, this was a big blow to Iran and also an embarrassment to Ali Akbar Velayati, a key adviser to Iran's supreme leader, who met Putin in Moscow in July, 2018 and then confidently asserted that "Russia is ready to invest $50bn in Iran's oil and gas sectors."[50]

The US sanctions also severely impacted Iran's own tanker fleets on which the country was forced to rely. For example, the National Iranian Tanker Company (NITC), a privatized subsidiary of NIOC, was unable to obtain vessels, spare parts, fuel, technical and other services, because multiple foreign insurers refused coverage for NITC's fleet due to US sanctions. Another company, the Islamic Republic of Iran Shipping Lines (the IRISL) had an agreement with Hyundai Heavy Industries worth around 760 million dollars for the building of four container ships and six 49,000-ton tankers for petrochemical products. The vessels were supposed to be delivered in the second quarter of 2018 and although some of those ships were finished, there were no deliveries and the Hyundai officials admitted that not a single ship had been delivered to IRISL. Furthermore, the Hyundai officials acknowledged the impossibility of delivering the ships with U.S. sanctions back in full force. Targeting Iran's oil tankers, Brian Hook, the head of State Department's "Iran Action Group," warned other nations that Iran's oil tankers were "floating liability . . . . If Iranian takers make calls to your ports or transit through your waterways, this comes at great risk. Countries, ports, and canal operators, and private firms should know they will be likely responsible for the cost of an accident involving a self-insured Iranian tanker."[51]

As to the rail and automotive sectors, a large number of foreign companies decided to leave the Iran market in reaction to US sanctions. For instance, the French manufacturer Peugeot-Citroen announced their withdrawal from Iran—a huge loss to Iran as more than 230,000 of their cars were manufactured under license in Iran since 2016, following the opening of a new plant.[52] Mazda and Hyundai also withdrew from Iran, alongside further withdrawals or suspensions by Renault, Scania, Daimler, and the German automotive supplier, Duerr.[53] With respect to civil aviation, the new US sanctions meant the loss of substantial transactions with Boeing and ATR and the loss of the 30 billion dollar Airbus deal,[54] thus frustrating the post-JCPOA plan of Iran's airline companies to renew their fleets—after a decade of external sanctions that had left Iran with one of the oldest fleets in the world.[55] Adding to Iran's predicament, a number of European airlines such as KLM, British Airways, and Air France, suspended their direct flights to Iran.[56] Also, the US sanctions triggered the departure of renewable energy companies from Iran, including the UK solar company Quercus, which had intended to build the sixth-largest solar plant in the world in line with Iran's commitments under the Paris Climate Agreement to reduce pollution.[57]

In light of the aforementioned impacts of US sanctions, there was a growing fear in Iran that the country was at the beginning stages of an economic slump that may prove worse than the period 2012–2015 when the previous sanctions were at their peak.[58] Concerning the latter, the economist Djavad Salehi-Isfahani has estimated the costs of sanctions for the period 2012–2017 to be more than one trillion dollars.[59] Similar figures were on Iran's future horizon due to new US sanctions, assuming that the maximalist US pressure campaign could choke off the "core areas" of Iran's economy, above all its energy sector, responsible for some 80 percent of the country's export earnings. Despite temporary waivers issued to some nations to continue importing oil from Iran, discussed further, the Trump administration did not officially retreat from the stated objective of bringing Iran's oil exports to zero. According to Mark Menezes, a principal adviser to the Trump administration on energy policy, "Our goal remains zero export of Iranian oil and we are absolutely clear about that."[60] Indeed, the fate of Trump's Iran policy and its central axis of compellence revolved to a large extent around the key question of whether or not the OPEC's third largest oil producer would be effectively marginalized and its energy sector crippled? On this question, the verdict was still out, first and foremost due to the sizable exemptions issued by the administration in November 2018.

The Politics of Oil Exemptions

The Trump administration's Iran oil embargo was initially premised on the confident assertion that the world oil market was sufficiently supplied and could readily absorb the absence of Iranian oil. This was reflected in an official statement in October, 2018, ahead of the second wave of Iran sanctions in November: "There is a sufficient supply of petroleum and petroleum products from countries other than Iran to permit a significant reduction in the volume of petroleum and petroleum products purchased from Iran or through foreign financial institutions." At the time, Iran produced about 3.8 million barrels per day (bpd), accounting for about 4 percent of world supply; Iran's oil exports in October 2018 were estimated at between 1.5 million bpd and 1.85 million bpd, including about 450,000 bpd of crude to Europe. But, during the months preceding the November announcement, the OPEC oil supply had fallen from a two-year high largely due to market anxieties over Iran sanctions, with Saudi Arabia and the UAE able to plug only some of the output gap left by Iran—in response to Trump's explicit messages to OPEC—with only modest success as the OPEC cartel largely ignored Trump's request to boost production in order to lower the rising prices. The latter was reflected at a crucial OPEC meeting in June, 2018 when the rival powerhouses Saudi Arabia and Iran reached an agreement that called for only a modest increase in oil supply—well below the expectations of United States.[61] Hence, in the context of a crisis-torn Venezuela lowering its exports and fresh reports of Saudi "shrinking capacity" indicating that the Saudi ability to produce more oil was more limited than previously estimated, the Trump administration was forced to retreat.[62] By then the administration's Iran announcements on coming Iran sanctions compliance had already shaken oil markets, which were already tightening from a deal between the OPEC and Russia to limit supply to boost the price of oil. In turn, this introduced a major headache for India, among other US allies, openly raising fear of heightened oil prices in the absence of US exemptions: "The impact on world oil prices will be the immediately visible impact of the U.S. decision. Iran is presently India's third biggest supplier (after Iraq and Saudi Arabia), and any increase in prices will hit both inflation levels as well as the Indian rupee." Fearing a price spike that would adversely impact not only friendly countries such as India and South Korea but also the "rebounded" US economy itself, the Trump administration opted to grant Iran's biggest buyers - China, India, South Korea, Japan, Italy, Greece, Taiwan, and Turkey - sanctions waivers. The first four were Iran's top Asia's oil buyers and received waivers allowing them to purchase a combined 960,000 bpd. India was exempted at the allowed rate of some 300,000 bpd, slightly lower than China, which was allowed to continue buying Iranian crude at a rate of 360,000 bpd but it also had rights to production from fields in Iran where Chinese companies were shareholders. However, these exemptions would allow these countries to import Iran's oil at "greatly reduced levels," with the ultimate goal of "zero" purchase from Tehran. "We have the toughest sanctions ever imposed. But on oil, we want to go a little bit slow because I don't want to drive the oil prices in the world up . . . . This would send a shock to the market," Trump stated. Trump had also granted some countries exemptions from global steel and aluminum tariffs, so these oil exemptions seemed to fit a pattern of flexible response But, in Iran's case, these exemptions were cast in terms of a gradualist total oil embargo that " accelerate towards zero," to paraphrase Pompeo. Attaching tough conditions to these exemptions, the administration stipulated that payments for the Iranian oil must go into escrow accounts in their local currencies and could only be used by Iran to purchase certain non-sanctioned goods from its crude export clients. The US sanctions had a 180-day period during which buyers were to "wind down" Iran oil purchases.

Although the United States granted exemptions to eight buyers of Iranian oil, US officials expected that number would soon shrink to five and that oversupplied market in 2019 would help cut Iranian oil sales further—in his November announcement of oil exemptions, Pompeo took credit for the fact that "over 20 importing nations had zeroed out their imports of [Iran] crude oil already, taking more than 1 million barrels of crude per day off the market." The administration confidently predicted that "many more barrels will be coming off very soon." Consequently, some energy experts had predicted that "Iranian exports will average 1.4–1.5 million barrels bpd during the exemption period." In Tehran, on the other hand, the decision on waivers was interpreted as "a victory," as Tehran was able to sustain its energy exports "after months of US threats that oil sales would be pushed down to zero." Some in the US concurred and interpreted the exemptions as being tantamount to "snatching defeat from the jaws of victory" and "calling into question the ultimate effectiveness of the Trump Iranian sanctions project overall." As of April 2019, the granted exemptions were due for review on a case by case basis, and it was unclear at the time of this writing whether or not they would be extended or curtailed. Even with the exemptions, it was still unclear if exempted countries such as South Korea, which had lobbied Washington for "maximum flexibility" on Iran oil sanctions, would continue to take advantage of the temporary waiver or switch to other alternative buyers due to uncertainties regarding Iran. With respect to China, embroiled in a trade war with Trump administration, the government's proclivity was to continue business-as-usual with Iran yet this was a risky proposition brought to full light in the high-profile of arrest of a Chinese high-tech executive accused of bypassing US sanctions on Iran.[63] An even more ominous news, however, was regarding the announcement by China's state-owned Bank of Kunlun at the heart of China's trade with Iran, that it had made a dramatic change in its policies, informing clients that it will no longer process payments that contravened US secondary sanctions on Iran. Kunlun's change in policy cut a longstanding financial lifeline for Iran's automotive, shipping, petrochemical, and steel industries. This decision, representing a huge blow to Iran's counter-sanctions strategy, stemmed from the need for Chinese state energy group CNPC, the majority shareholder in Bank of Kunlun, to protect its interests in the US market.[64] Unwilling to take on the US over Iran by itself, the Chinese government had vested hope in Europe's delivery of its much-promised financial mechanism, which had not materialized despite repeated assurances by the EU officials (discussed in the next chapter).[65] Europe's failure, in other words, had a cascading effect on other countries, above all China, that was pressured by Trump on trade and other non-trade issues and did not appear as determined as in the past to assist Iran as the price was growing prohibitively too high.[66]

With respect to India, a big question was if New Delhi would be able to sustain its Iran oil imports at a time when the country's privately owned refineries were bulking at the idea in light of the specter of non-renewal of US exemptions? In 2018, India's crude oil imports from Iran had dropped from 690,000 bpd in May to around 400,000 bpd in August. Citing difficulties in finding substitute sources, India's officials were engaged in a difficult balancing act between the US and Iran, two rival countries with whom India maintained healthy relations, yet this did not prevent India from ordering new Iran oil shipments even before the onset of US sanctions in early November, 2018, betting that Trump would avoid confronting them due to strategic calculations.[67] Those calculations were reflected in the US's South Asia policy that counted on India as a reliable partner in regional stabilization and, in turn, motivated the administration's willingness to make a non-oil exemption—for the Iranian port of Chabahar developed by India and considered vital for Afghanistan's economy. Both the oil and Chabahar exemptions discussed below reinforced the impression that the "maximum pressure" policy had been compromised by the parameters of a pragmatic consideration of US priorities, thus lowering the temperature of economic warfare on Iran. For New Delhi, however, keen on keeping a healthy relation with Trump's White House, the Indian authorities had turned down Iran's quest for permission for the Indian refineries to use Iranian crude over and above the ceilings set by Washington. Not only that, they also consented to Iran's investment of around 15 billion rupees in the expansion of a state-owned refinery in southern India.[68]

THE CHABAHAR EXEMPTION AND CLASH OF STRATEGIES

Located on the Gulf of Oman, the port of Chabahar has been slated for regional expansion by the government of India. The port project is the subject of a multi-project connectivity agenda on the part of Iran, India, and Afghanistan, involving an elaborate scheme for a free-trade zone and a 1.6 billion dollar rail way linking Iran and Afghanistan. Considered as a new regional hub serving India's ambition to compete with China and its development of a China-Pakistan corridor centered on the Pakistani port of Gwadar, the Chabahar project is equally important to the government of Afghanistan as an alternative trade route to lessen its dependence on Pakistan. The project is also important to the land-locked Central Asian states and presents a viable, relatively accessible venue to open sea for them. From the vantage of US strategic interests, Chabahar project dovetailed with the Afghanistan and South Asia policy, announced by President Trump in August 2017, accenting Afghan stabilization, with India as a valuable partner, worth quoting at length:

> Another critical part of the South Asia strategy for America is to further develop its strategic partnership with India—the world's largest democracy and a key security and economic partner of the United States. We appreciate India's important contributions to stability in Afghanistan, but India makes billions of dollars in trade with the United States, and we want them to help us more with Afghanistan, especially in the area of economic assistance and development. We are committed to pursuing our shared objectives for peace and security in South Asia and the broader Indo-Pacific region.[69]

Despite reservations about Iran, the Trump administration opted to exempt the Chabahar project from its list of sanctions after a number of high-level US official visits to New Delhi, including one by the US ambassador to UN, Nikki Haley, aiming to "solidify partnership" between US and India.[70] "We know the port has to happen and the US is going to work with India to do that.

We know that they're [India] being a great partner with us in Afghanistan and really trying to assist the US and trying to do more. The port is vital in trying to do that," Haley admitted, adding meaningfully "We realize we're threading a needle when we do that," describing the balancing act of ensuring Indian use of the Iranian port while the US simultaneously attempted to scuttle Iran's economy.[71] Five months later, this became the official US policy in conjunction with the oil exemptions above-mentioned. This was justified within the framework of the South Asia policy: "South Asia strategy underscores our ongoing support of Afghanistan's economic growth and development as well as our close partnership with India."[72] By all indications, the decision to exclude a segment of Iran's economic activities involving Chabahar was a wise move born of the administration's self-professed "principled realism" since not to have done so would have adversely affected both India and Afghanistan. Afghan President Ashraf Ghani immediately took credit for convincing the White House to exempt Chabahar;[73] the administration granted this in part as a symbolic gesture to give India a larger role in Afghanistan—much to the chagrin of Pakistan, which had fallen out of favor with the Trump administration.[74]

The trouble however was that the Chabahar and India oil exemptions did not match up with the Trump administration's stated policy of "maximum economic pressure" to "cripple" the Iranian economy. The clash of Iran and South Asia strategies weakened both strategies, notably in the form of lessening the temperature of maximalist Iran strategy and in effect reducing it to medium-level pressures that, in turn, lessened the chance of short-term success for the administration's thinly veiled regime change approach. The two strategies overlapped and led to (unacknowledged) policy incoherence, impelling a partial step back from the Iran strategy—premised on the notion of a purely destructive regional behavior on Iran's part, vividly belied by the details of the Chabahar project, which potentially served as a source of policy learning by an administration that was otherwise hellbent on neutralizing all aspects of Iran's foreign behavior, even though some aspects of that behavior such as with respect to Afghanistan, countering terrorism, and cooperating with India, resonated with the description of a regional power pivotal for regional stability, permeating even the Pentagon's assessment that admitted Iran's role in restoring "clam" to troubled Afghanistan.[75] In addition to being a source of revenue for Iran given the millions of dollars India was paying to use the port's berths, Chabahar was also seen as a potentially elaborate free-trade zone, to attract foreign investment and become a regional hub, particularly for the land-locked Central Asian states. Already, by late 2018, over 400 companies from 15 countries had gotten involved in Chabahar free-trade zone and the Iranian officials expected the number to grow to 3000 in near future.[76] Over time, Chabahar could be linked to the parallel north-south transportation corridor that Russia, Iran, and India were creating to expand regional connectivity.[77] The Chabahar project had experienced costly delays due to India's slow fulfillment of its investment promises, which was partly blamed on sanctions-based banking restrictions on doing business with Iran.[78] Had Trump opted to include Chabahar in its long list of Iran sanctions, then it would have alienated not only Iran, India, and Afghanistan but also Tajikistan and other Central Asian states. The Chabahar exemption was thus a product of pragmatic realism, similar to the oil exemptions, which as stated earlier the United States had explicitly linked to its desire to avoid an oil shock to the world economy. The same logic was likely to prevail once the 180-day exemptions were up for renewal in April 2019, barring unforeseen developments. Still, since the Chabahar project allowed Iran to some extent to dodge the bullet of US sanctions, the exemption had generated some ambivalence in the Trump administration. National Security Advisor John Bolton, who was adamant about not allowing anyone to evade sanctions, was reportedly opposed to the Chabahar exemption. In December, 2018, Chabahar was the target of a terrorist attack, which the Iranian officials interpreted as intended to "inflict economic damage" in implicit reference to the Chabahar project—and its long-term significance for Iran's counter-strategy vis-a-vis a fierce economic war waged by a Western superpower against a "regional fulcrum"— confronted in a dire situation not unlike the Melians in the Peloponnesian War, recalling Thucydides' famous declaration that the "strong do what they can, and the weak endure what they must."[79] Calling for national unity in the face of US pressures, Iranian president Rouhani evoked the memory of Iran-Iraq war (1980–1988), thus reminding the nation that Iran was subjected to an "unjust" economic warfare by the Western superpower—that had invaded Iraq under false WMD pretexts incurring a huge 1.3 trillion dollar bill and still kept thousands of troops on Iraqi soil after a decade of nation-building in Iraq. Inevitably, this meant another clashing strategy, between the policies of the United States for Iran and Iraq.

THE IRAQ EXEMPTIONS: TEMPORARY OR LONG TERM?

Initially, prior to the imposition of new sanctions on Iran, US officials visited Baghdad and warned its officials that the US would sanction any Iraqi bank that conducted financial transactions with Iran. The Iraqi government held bank accounts with the US Federal Reserve, where its assets in dollar were kept—and could be frozen if Iraq was found violating the Iran sanctions. After the onset of the second wave of US sanctions in early November 2018, US Energy Secretary Rick Perry visited Iraq along with a trade delegation of over fifty US energy and security firms. During the visit, Perry urged Bagh-dad to wean itself off Tehran and pave the way for American investment in its energy sector. "The time has come for Iraq to break its dependence . . . on less reliable nations seeking domination and control," Perry urged the Iraqis.[80] That was indeed a tough request given Iraq's heavy dependence on trade with its eastern neighbor with which it shares a long 1,458-km border. In fact, by then, US had already granted a sanctions waiver to Iraq in response to direct appeal by the Iraqi government that sent its officials to Washington seeking a waiver.

"A waiver was granted to allow Iraq to continue to pay for electricity imports from Iran. We are confident this will help Iraq limit electricity short-ages in the South," the administration officials informed the media.[81] At the time, Iraq was experiencing chronic power shortage particularly in southern Iraq that often experienced blackout as much as 20 hours a day and was a key driving factor behind mass protests in summer of 2018. To cope with those shortages, Iraq imported up to 28 million cubic meters of Iranian gas per day and also directly imported up to 1,300 megawatts of Iranian electric-ity. In early August, the then Iraqi prime minister Haider al-Abadi expressed disagreement with reinstated US sanctions against Iran "as a matter of prin-ciple," but stressed that his government would abide by them to protect Iraq's national interests.[82] The remarks provoked the ire of Tehran and its powerful allies in Iraq, forcing Abadi to recant: "I did not say we [would] abide by the sanctions, I said we [would] abide by not using dollars in transactions. We have no other choice."[83] Indeed, post-war Iraq had little choice but to con-tinue its trade relations with Iran, which was beneficial to both sides. Iran was Iraq's third largest trade partner in 2018 and the two countries were hoping to increase their total trade from twelve billion a year to twenty billion a year. Iraq received from Iran approximately 20 percent of the electricity it needed, swapping oil for electricity. Despite efforts to produce natural gas of its own, Iraqi officials in 2017 had admitted that Iraq would be reliant on Iranian gas to generate electricity for at least seven years. Two weeks after the second wave of US sanctions in November, 2018, Iraq's new president Bahram Salih was in Iran agreeing with his hosts that improving Iran-Iraq trade was a "fixed principle" that was "rooted in shared history, faith and geography" and raised the prospects for a free-trade zone along the Iran-Iraq border.[84] Iran had extended a three billion-dollar credit line to Iraq's reconstruction and was also involved in trade with the semi-autonomous Kurdish administration in northern Iraq. The economic ties had grown also as a result of Iraqis investing in Iran's stock exchange market and buying (undetermined) shares of various banks and transportation companies. Tourism was another major factor, with millions of Iranian and Iraqi pilgrims crossing the borders each year and the number of Iraqi passenger flights to Iran quintupled since 2015.[85]

Credited for its vital assistance in defeating the menace of ISIS terrorism, Tehran enjoyed broad support among the majority Iraqi Shiites, who had set up popular mobilization militias to fight foreign-induced terrorism with much support from Iran. Despite the US effort to dismantle these (pro-Iran) militias after the liberation of Mosul from ISIS's control, Tehran succeeded in convincing the Iraqi leaders to resist the US pressure and maintain the armed militias—which served as Iran's leverages over Baghdad. Another leverage was Iran's control of the shared waterway, which could result in a chronic water shortage for Iraq in case Baghdad went along with US sanctions on Iran as Iran could easily cut the flows of water, as it already had done in the northern Kurdistan area in Sulaymaniyah province, according to the Kurdistan regional government's Ministry of Agriculture.[86] According to some Tehran foreign policy experts interviewed by the authors, Iran was fairly confident that the temporary waivers granted to Iraq would be extended based on the calculation of the United States of the massive harms to its Iraq strategy if it decides to end the waivers—that were crucial for Iraq's economic well-being and, by implication, Iraq's security.[87] Given the proximity of (over 5000) US military personnel in Iraq to Iran and its Iraq proxies, this was yet another leverage for Iran, whose military leaders openly hinted at their "access" to US forces in the region in the event of a US-Iran confrontation. Such a confrontation bode ill for Iran's neighbors, above all Iraq, whose leadership dreaded the negative fallout of US sanctions and desperately sought a healthy balancing act between the two rival powers. For Iran, on the other hand, its Iraq policy was part of a broader counter-sanction strategy that focused on regional cooperation and inter-regional trade as an important antidote to US sanctions. With both the United States and Iran supporting the Iraqi government, there was however a "zone of agreement" between Tehran and Washington that belied the perception of a zero-sum struggle between US and Iran and was ultimately responsible for the waivers that Trump administration granted to prevent chaos and instability in Iraq, even though this had the unwanted consequence of bringing its Iraq policy in conflict with its maximalist Iran strategy, similar to the Chabahar exemption and its South Strategy and, to a lesser extent, its policy toward Turkey, another Iran's neighbor enjoying the benefits of a sanctions waiver.

THE TURKEY EXEMPTIONS REVISITED

Iran and Turkey share a 560-km long border, unchanged for almost 400 years. Both are founding members (along with Pakistan) of the regional organization, Economic Cooperation Organization (ECO), as well as the D-8 group of countries, comprising Malaysia, Indonesia, Egypt, Bangladesh, Pakistan and

Nigeria. Relations between Iran and Turkey have been on a positive trend ever since Turkey's Justice and Development Party came to power in 2002, albeit with certain fluctuations dictated by changing regional circumstances. Some Iranian officials have viewed Turkey as the most important country for Iran among countries that received exemption from US sanctions—for good reasons. Turkey and Iran have deep economic ties and are bound by long-term trade agreements. Iran has been a major source of energy for Turkey since 1996, when the then Turkish president Erbakan visited Iran and signed a twenty-three-billion-dollar gas deal with a timeline of over twenty-five years.[88] In August 2007, Turkey and Iran signed an important energy agreement despite the sanctions on the latter. According to this, the Turkish Petroleum Corporation (TPAO) was allowed to explore for oil and gas in the South Pars fields of Iran and deliver Iranian as well as Turkmen gas to Europe via Turkey, but also supply the Turkish market.[89] In January 2014, Turkey and Iran signed a comprehensive trade agreement, which aims the bilateral trade to reach to thirty billion dollars by the end of 2015.[90] At the time of Trump's new sanctions against Iran, Turkey relied on Iran for the import of 16 percent of its natural gas imports and 20 percent of the oil imports. A sudden elimination of Iran's energy source would have had a profound negative effect on the Turkish economy because Turkish utilities and refineries will face unforeseen costs and possible shortages.[91] As a result, Turkish officials actively pressured the Trump administration to extend the six months waiver granted to Turkey; these officials were counting on the improved climate between Washington and Ankara following months of mutual hostility at the outset of Trump's presidency—Trump had authorized the doubling of tariffs on steel and aluminum imports from Turkey, praising "the strong dollar" and drawing attention to the plummeting Turkish lira; The exchange rate of the Turkish lira plummeted more than 16 percent against the US dollar, reaching an all-time low following Trump's announcement. The Turkish government, in turn, had vowed to retaliate against restrictive US measures, stressing that Washington will not obtain any tangible results from slapping sanctions on Turkey.

The timing of Trump's anti-Turkey measures proved particularly disadvantageous to his Iran policy and may have incentivized Turkey to stand firm against the US sanctions on Iran. President Erdogan thus repeatedly stated his opposition to Trump's Iran policy, for example, "The US withdrawal from the nuclear deal is not considered as the right one. This decision increases the risks of the situation in the region, we do not support it. We will continue to be close to Iran at a time when unjust decisions are being taken against it,"[92] In the previous rounds of sanctions before Trump, Turkey had assisted Iran and the state-run Halkbank was implicated in the largest sanctions-evasion scheme in history, with a US court sentencing a Turkish bank executive for his involvement in the multi-billion dollar gold-for-oil scheme.[93]

As in the past, Turkey was increasingly caught between the demands of its US NATO ally and its own national interests, which dictated close economic cooperation with Iran.[94] The Turkish-Iranian High-Level Cooperation Council that was established in 2014 provided a structured basis to this cooperation. The fifth gathering of this council in December 2018 was jointly chaired by Erdogan and Rouhani, who stressed the importance of turning "sanctions into an opportunity for interweaving the economies of Iran and Turkey with proper management."[95] The two countries were exploring venues to trade in their local currencies or in euro to bypass dollar, to expand banking ties, and to continue their cooperation together with Russia through the so-called Astana process for peace in Syria, which had resulted in the establishment of "de-escalation zones." In addition to shared economic interests, Tehran and Ankara had similar misgivings about Kurdish separatism and were wary of the prospect of an independent Kurdish state that could spell irredentist troubles with respect to their Kurdish minorities. In December, 2018, Trump's abrupt decision to withdraw the US forces from Syria after consultation with Erdogan represented a new challenge to Iran-Turkey relations, particularly if Turkey tried to fill the vacuum of US power in eastern Syria, where a bulk of Syria's oil and gas fields are located.[96] Some Iran experts speculated that Turkey may enter into a "grand bargain" with the United States, by cooperating with the US sanctions on Iran in exchange for Turkey's free hand in US-controlled areas in Syria.[97] After all, Turkey during the Obama era had agreed to cease its role as financial intermediary for Iran's oil transactions with India, and had also lowered its Iran oil imports in a nod to US sanctions, so it was not entirely far-fetched to believe that history would repeat itself and Turkey could be persuaded by Washington to cooperate with the new Iran sanctions regime. Not everyone agreed with this assessment however, and other Iran experts argued that the depth of Turkish-Iran interdependence and Turkey's reliance on Iran for its energy security prevented such a scenario. Despite their differences on Syria, Tehran and Ankara were careful to insulate their bilateral relations from other regional issues. The US exemptions for Turkey were likely to extend in the future in light of the potential damages to Turkey's economy if that were not the case—Ankara would almost certainly resort to sanctions-busting trade with Iran in order to secure its own interests, thus complicating Turkey-US relations. For all these reasons, the geopolitical considerations behind the Turkey exemptions were grounded in a complex regional reality that forced selective retreat by the Trump administration from its declared economic warfare on Iran, which was not at any rate accompanied with a verbal adjustment as the rhetoric of "strongest sanctions in history" continued from Trump's mouthpieces even though such exemptions clearly reduced the severity of those sanctions and allowed Iran a respite crucial for its economic survival.

IRAN'S ECONOMIC COUNTER-STRATEGY

In order to survive the economic tsunami of the coercive sanctions of the United States, Iran resorted to a litany of diplomatic, political, economic, and security counter-measures with the stated objective of neutralizing the unilateral sanctions that, unlike in the past, did not enjoy broad international support but nevertheless inflicted painful economic damages. The latter was reflected in the government's budget for the calendar year beginning in March 2019, which showed a 28 percent decline in oil revenue compared to the previous year—sales of more than one million bpd of crude oil was envisaged in the national budget bill, that is, a good indicator of the mounting pressure of US oil embargo coinciding with declining oil prices; the latter was attributed by energy experts to the emerging signs of a global economic slowdown, partially attributed to US-China trade war, as well as to the ability of the oil market to absorb the shocks of Iran export decline due to sanctions. Anticipating an oil glut in 2019, OPEC had agreed to cut production by 1.2 million bpd By December 2018, the latter had succeeded to reduce Iran's oil exports by roughly 1.5 million bpd, excluding Iran's skillful use of "informal market." A clue to the latter, US sanctioned a Russian company accused of transporting Iranian oil to Syria to sell off as Syrian oil. In the previous round of sanctions, there were unconfirmed reports of Russia's role in channeling banned Iranian oil to the world market, which could likely resurface in the new milieu. Russia was not alone, however, and thanks to Iran's active regionalism resulting in largely healthy relations with the majority of its fifteen neighboring states particularly in Central Asia-Caucasus, there were multiple venues for smuggling Iranian oil and thus generating additional, off the book oil income for the beleaguered government. The "informal" oil market had (according to one estimate) allowed Iran to continue exporting at around 2 million bpd, using evasive measures such as ship-to-ship transfers as well as turning off transponders to hide the destination of cargoes.[98] Drawing on decades of accumulating experience in sanctions-busting, the government was optimistic that compared with the past more countries in the region and beyond will be willing to accommodate Iran. In fact, Iranian officials openly boasted that Iran had perfected the "art of evading sanctions" and was even willing to educate other countries about it.[99] In a bid to keep customers, the state-run NIOC began offering record discounts on its crude in order to sweeten the appetite of its potential customers.[100] Another strategy was to privatize the sale of Iranian oil by NIOC allowing the private sector a growing role in marketing the country's energy products. Iran began selling oil to private buyers on its energy exchange (bourse) first in October and then November, 2018.[101] A related measure was a deal with Russia known as oil-for-goods program, reached in 2017, whereby Russia agreed to buy 100,000 bpd of Iran's crude oil and sell Iran forty-five billion dollars' worth of goods.[102] Indeed, Russia played a prominent role in Iran's sanctions-busting efforts, for example, in November 2018, US imposed sanctions on an Iranian-Russian network for smuggling Iranian oil to Syria.[103] Several months earlier, Iran had inked an agreement establishing a free-trade zone between the Russia-led Eurasian Economic Union (EEU) and Iran, hoping to trigger further trade and investment with the EEU countries. The EEU, which is based on the Customs Union of Russia, Kazakhstan and Belarus, was established in 2015. It was later joined by Armenia, Kyrgyzstan, and Vietnam.[104]

On the whole, these counter-measures helped Iran's economy to remain afloat, given the fact that an estimated 100 billion dollars of Iran's oil assets had been released to the country after the JCPOA and Iran had a large foreign exchange reserve, valued at around 100 billion dollars, that could be used as a war chest to take care of economic issues for at least three years without any oil revenues, according to a former deputy governor of Iran's Central Bank.[105] In addition, Iran had an undetermined sum in its "National Development Fund," also known as "future generation fund," that it could tap into and thus avoid a complete crash as hoped for by Trump administration.[106] Still, these were insufficient in preventing an economic slide, in light of gloomy forecasts about a declining economy in 2019. President Rouhani blamed the country's economic woes on both the US sanctions and "structural problems" such as retarded privatization. Another problem was tax extraction, as the government officials openly admitted that some 40 percent of the economy was "off taxation" and despite increased taxes, there were serious shortfalls with collecting them. Another major problem was that Iran's sanctions-hit energy sector was in dire need of tens of billions of dollars of investment in equipment and infrastructure, now blocked off due to resumed sanctions, thus complicating the country's future energy policy. Further complicating Iran's oil counter-strategy was the depressing oil prices—that had declined from over 80 dollar per barrel at the time of announcement of US sanctions to over 40 dollar per barrel in December, 2018, instead of shooting up to 100 dollars or more, as predicted by some analysts. Had the latter been the case, it would have compensated for the loss of oil income due to the deep reduction in Iran's oil exports. The oil exemptions effectively prevented an oil price hike hoped for by Tehran, at least for a while, and thus much depended on both the volatile oil market and the extension or non-extension of those exemptions in 2019 and beyond. Several countries, such as Japan and South Korea, had already started looking for alternative supply, casting a question mark on their future availability as oil importers from Iran. These countries had difficulty acquiring insurance for the Iran oil cargoes, only some of which were loaded into Iran-owned tankers.

In contrast, to reiterate China, Iran's number one importer, was almost guaranteed to continue its extensive energy relations with Iran in the Trump era marked with increasing tensions between Washington and Beijing. This was communicated to Iran by the head of the international office of the China Petroleum and Chemical Industry Federation (CPCIF), Andrey Yu, who told the Iranian media that "China doesn't pay attention to the US sanctions on Iran" and would continue to buy oil and gas from Tehran. It is a routine between Iran and China and "has nothing to do with the US. Oil, gas, and trade shouldn't be influenced by the US anymore."[107] Iranian traders had the option of trading in Chinese yuan-denominated crude oil futures on the Shanghai International Energy Exchange—circumventing any restrictions on dollar-denominated trade and US banks.[108] But, most likely this was not immediate as Shanghai oil futures trade was still a largely domestic affair and Beijing "also would not want to be seen to be openly pushing back on US sanctions" as it negotiated bilateral trade with the Trump administration.

India too was determined to retain its energy ties with Iran, parallel to its involvement with the Chabahar project, which had no specific timeline. From Iran's vantage, there was a "soft linkage" between the two issues, resulting in Iran's decision to press India to continue its Iran economic connections undisturbed by US sanctions. Another oil client was Greece, which had gone from the 19th country in the EU's list of trading countries with Iran to the sixth, thanks to a whopping 3500 percent increase in trade with Iran over a two-year (2016–2018) period. In early 2016, Greece's biggest oil refiner, Hellenic Petroleum, was the first European company to resume Iran oil import since the EU oil embargo of 2012. As of November, 2018, Iran's oil officials were engaged in oil negotiations with Greece and other EU countries, initially reporting some "progress."[109] Yet, by late 2018, it was apparent that Greece and other European recipients of US sanctions waivers were threading the path of caution and had ceased their oil trade with Iran, thus adding to Iran's "European problem."[110] A key question, discussed in the next chapter in greater detail, revolved around the special financial mechanism, introduced by the EU to salvage the European trade with Iran: Would it cover oil or be limited to humanitarian goods? As of this writing, that mechanism had not yet been operationalized and there were several unanswered questions about its scope and effectiveness. Iran's economic policies at the macro and micro levels were patently obvious and, increasingly, tied to the preeminent agenda of sustaining economic well-being and, with it, the government's mass constituency—first and foremost through the channels of mass mobilization and economic populism.

Iran's Economic Populism, Antidote to US Pressure

In the Iranian context, the concept populism draws together various strands: the pattern of post-revolutionary mass mobilization, the role of charismatic leadership, multiple patron-client ties between the state and civil society, the mushrooming of quasi-state foundations, and the frozen context of anti-American hegemony. The gist of "economic populism" is a redistributive polity that seeks to gain political legitimacy by resorting to populist measures, that is, a hallmark of post-revolutionary identity. Despite the passage of time and the onset of a technocratic-managerial state under President Hassan Rouhani (2013-present), Iran remained wedded to this enduring populism. The previous pattern of state-making stretching back to the Khomeini era remained remarkably consistent, featuring a part-theocratic, part-republican hybrid electoral system that emerged from the ashes of a U.S.-dependent monarchy. A proud legacy of this political order is the nation's endurance during the 1980–1988 Iran-Iraq war—commonly referred to as the "imposed war"—through popular mobilizations and a "coupon economy" that was later reintroduced as rations for fuel and food staples in response to the US-led international sanctions over Iran's nuclear program. Thirty years later, faced with the debilitating consequences of Trumpian sanctions, Iran was once again on the verge reintroducing the ration system.[111]

The Trump administration assumed that the Iranian regime lacks legitimacy at home and was ruled simply by repression from above. This view overlooked the integrative role of regular (local and national) elections in Iran, the multifaceted welfare state that provided a safety net for millions of Iranians and also allocated the lion's share of the budget to public education, healthcare, subsidies, transportation, and the like. The latter is reflected in the chart below, compiled from the latest statistics on Iran (figure 3.1).

These figures show, contrary to some misleading analyses, the Rouhani administration had not ended Iran's economic populism. Rather he had sought to trim and adjust it, for instance by ending cash subsidies to well-to-do Iranians while maintaining basic government expenditures on goods and services such as wages for government employees, employer contributions to social security and pensions, and all the payments connected to government functions such as military, health, education, cultural, and social activities, for example, the 2018–2019 budget called for 20 percent increase in public sector wages. Also, the government invests in infrastructure services and public goods through capital or development expenditures. Today as a result, about 90 percent of Iranians have some form of health insurance, which ranks, according to a 2016 US media report, above even the United States and Brazil.[112] Two-thirds of Iranians, meanwhile, are covered by social security. Additionally, a vast network of parastatal foundations, such as the martyrs'

2018-2019 PERCENTAGE OF MAJOR BUDGET CATEGORIES

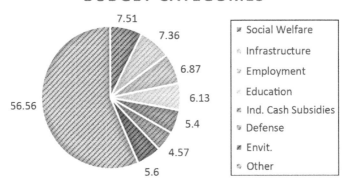

- Social Welfare
- Infrastructure
- Employment
- Education
- Ind. Cash Subsidies
- Defense
- Envit.
- Other

Figure 3.1 Percentage of Budget Categories. *Source*: Author-Generated. Data compiled from Iran's 2018–2019 Budget, http://media.dolat.ir/uploads/org/151289010503749600.pdf.

foundation, complements the government's economic populism by providing crucial aid to millions of their constituents. Confronted by an emerging gap between the government's populist priorities and the shrinking revenues due to sanctions, the Rouhani administration had resorted to higher taxes, borrowing, and issuing public bonds—all with mixed results so far. It was a daunting task to keep pace with the burgeoning demands of a growing population—nearly one million people enter the job market each year—and to prevent Trump's economic war from derailing post-JCPOA economic growth. Rouhani's government sought to reshape consumption patterns, expand the cooperative sector, combat corruption, and devise the elements of a smart "resistance economy." The sixth Five-Year Plan (2016–2021), on which such a resistance economy was based, forecast 8 percent annual growth. According to the IMF, however, Iran's economy was expected to contract by 1.4 percent between 2018 and 2021.[113] Iran was also an ecological basket case, although some of the problems such as dried-up rivers, desertification, and dust storms can't be solved by Tehran alone and require regional solutions.

Ironically, Trump's economic war on Iran could have the opposite result in enhancing the Iranian government's legitimacy, by virtue of the fact that many (nationalistic) Iranians blamed the United States for their economic woes. Deflecting attention from the domestic sources of the economic problems, the US sanctions were meant to heighten popular discontent and ultimately trigger a mass rebellion to dislodge the Islamic Republic, yet had the unintended consequences of reducing the government's "legitimacy deficits" to borrow a term from the German philosopher, Jurgen Habermas. US nuclear negotiator, Wendy Sherman, alluded to this fact when she criticized

Trump administration's ignorance of Iran's "culture of resistance." To add to Sherman's insight, the Trump administration was also ignorant of the elections-based sources of legitimacy in Iran. Concerning the latter, it is worth quoting Iran specialist James Bill: "Although there is an important element of authoritarianism in Iran's internal political system, the Islamic Republic, unlike many of its neighbors, has developed important mechanisms of participatory democracy. Iran's elections have been generally fair and free. Robust debate takes place in the Islamic Majls."[114] Trump officials' blanket dismissal of the Iranian presidential elections as "unfree" and illegitimate was patently wrong and recalled the late Harvard professor Samuel Huntington's admission that in Persian Gulf, "the most democratic government is the greatest antagonist of the United States while the least democratic is America's closest ally."[115] Despite its shortcomings, Iran's competitive, albeit restricted, elections presented the 50 million or so eligible Iranian voters with alternative choices among candidates, who openly clashed with each other on important domestic and foreign issues, including the nuclear issue.[116] This aside, as the shocks of the sanctions rippled through the economy, Iran could be forced to impose some budgetary discipline. Mitigating the impact of coercive sanctions required a Herculean effort that needed to also address the growth-sapping features of the Iranian economy, such as the obliteration of boundaries between private and public interests, factional politics that favor the status quo and stymie change, and the impact of import-based market liberalization. The Rouhani administration had vowed to continue its social-welfare policies to shelter millions from the poverty induced by US sanctions.[117]

IRAN RESORTS TO INTERNATIONAL COURT OF JUSTICE

In response to Trump administration's hostile economic activities against Iran, Iran filed complaints against the US government in the International Court of Justice (ICJ), asking that the United States be restrained from continuing to engage in the harmful acts that clearly violate the two countries' 1955 Treaty of Amity. That treaty, ratified by the US Senate in 1956, is aimed at promoting "mutually beneficial trade and investments and closer economic intercourse generally."[118] In a nutshell, the treaty guarantees three sets of rights with respect to Iranian nationals and companies. First, it requires the United States to accord fair and equitable treatment to Iranian nationals and companies and to their property and enterprises. Second, it prohibits unreasonable or discriminatory measures that would impair the legally acquired rights and interests of Iranian nationals and companies. Third, it requires the United States to ensure that the lawful contractual rights of Iranian nationals and companies will be effectively enforced. Article IX of the Treaty also requires Washington to accord to Iranian nationals and companies' treatment no less favorable than that accorded to nationals and companies of any other state with respect to all matters relating to the import and export of goods.

On October 3, 2018, the justices of ICJ delivered a stinging setback to the Trump administration's bellicose policy toward Iran. The ICJ ordered the United States to respect humanitarian norms by suspending its sanctions on Iran in a number of key areas, including food, medicine, and aircraft spare parts. Although this "provisional" or "interim" ruling fell short of meeting all of Iran's demands in its complaint against Washington in the ICJ based on the 1955 US-Iran Treaty of Amity, it nonetheless delivers enough (both direct and indirect) benefits to Iran to enable it to legitimately declare victory.[119] Pompeo immediately announced the United States pulling out of the Treaty of Amity in response to the adverse ruling.[120]

In its "Interim Order," the ICJ assumed jurisdiction and noted that "the measures adopted by the United States have the potential to endanger civil aviation safety in Iran and the lives of its users to the extent that they prevent Iranian airlines from acquiring spare parts and other necessary equipment." It also noted that the "restrictions on the importation and purchase of goods required for humanitarian needs, such as foodstuffs and medicines, including life-saving medicines, treatment for chronic disease or preventive care, and medical equipment, may have a serious detrimental impact on the health and lives of individuals on the territory of Iran."[121] It ruled that the United States "must remove any impediments" to Iran's import of medicines and medical devices, foodstuffs and agricultural commodities, and spare parts, equipment, and related services needed by the civil aviation industry. Finally, it ordered Washington to ensure that licenses and payments covering these goods and services are not restricted. The Treaty's unilateral demise by the US did not, however, translate into a fatal blow to Iran's complaint. The retrospective withdrawal was immaterial to the legal context of new US sanctions on Iran. Following a long tradition in international law, the court decides the merits of a case according to existing agreements or treaties at the time of the dispute and not the subsequent, post-litigation, developments.[122] In other words, the treaty will likely continue to be relevant to the court's future proceedings on the case, particularly since the initial ruling favored Iran on some issues. Per the court's tradition, it is sufficient that the rights asserted be "grounded in a possible interpretation" of the treaty invoked. The injunction issued against the United States centers on Article 41 of the statute: "when irreparable prejudice could be caused to rights." The ICJ ruling was also significant because the court explicitly cited UN Security Council Resolution 2231, which endorses the Iran nuclear accord (the JCPOA) abandoned unilaterally by the United States. In paragraph 18 of its order, the court took note of Resolution

2231 without, however, clarifying the legal consequences of Washington's violation of the resolution, which was binding on all UN member states. Although theoretically "binding," the court's order sadly lacked the necessary teeth to compel US compliance. At the same time, however, it offered compelling moral and ethical authority that added to the isolation that Washington faced on its Iran policy. Still, According to Djamchid Momtaz, the ad hoc judge for Iran, the ICJ ruling was insufficient since, among other things, it had failed to instruct the United States to end its sanctions on sales of civilian aircraft to Iran. Contrary to Pompeo's claim that the United States was not blocking Iran's access to "humanitarian" goods, the sanctions have effectively blocked the purchase of aircraft spare parts—the sorry state of Iran's aging aircraft has resulted in numerous plane crashes—as well as the delivery and availability of life-saving medical supplies.[123] In early spring 2019, this issue assumed a new significance as a result of massive flooding throughout Iran affecting hundreds of towns and villages and causing the displacement of tens of thousands. International relief organizations admitted that US sanctions had impeded assistance to Iran.[124] The United States, on the other hand, remained adamant that there was no bar to humanitarian assistance to Iran and that Iran had invoked the Treaty of Amity in an effort to force the United States to implement an entirely separate, non-binding arrangement—the JCPOA—which contains its own dispute resolution mechanism that purposefully excludes recourse to the ICJ.[125] The ICJ provisionally accepted jurisdiction in this case based on the Treaty of Amity potentially complicated the US position in another pending ICJ case brought by Iran against the United States, that is, titled *Certain Iranian Assets*, under the same treaty. In that case, Iran asserted that the United States violated the international law of state immunity by allowing the execution of judgments issued under the terrorism exception to the Foreign Sovereign Immunities Act against property of Iran's Central Bank. The United States had previously raised jurisdictional objections in *Certain Iranian Assets* based in part on its interpretation of certain terms in the Treaty of Amity.[126]

In bringing this chapter to a close, our analysis has demonstrated the effectiveness of US economic warfare in terms of inflicting serious damages to the Iranian economy, yet failing to cripple it as a result of a combination of factors ranging from the self-imposed limits of this warfare reflected in the sanctions waivers, to the structural limits imposed by the world (oil) market, to the exigencies of Iran's counter-measures as well as Iran's "economic populism" that was a well-spring of mass support. In a word, the Trump administration had succeeded in bleeding Iran and causing some macro-hemorrhage that was at any rate below the level of catastrophic blows devastating the entire economy. Despite causing tremendous hardship, Trump's economic war against Iran was not mortifying and was unlikely to prevent it from keeping afloat as a result of Iran's counter-measures. Still, there was a chance Iran's economic woes could be worsened due to the stream of new US sanctions and US designation of (economically powerful) revolutionary guards as "terrorists," thus throwing more hurdles against Europeans and others who wished to maintain normal trade with Iran. As we discuss in the next chapter, much depended on Europe and how the European governments would respond to the avalanche of US moves against Iran? Would it be that while Uncle Sam was plotting to dislodge the ruling clergy in Iran the Europeans would somehow prove as their "saviors"?

NOTES

1. Mark Fitzpatrick, "More Iranian Sanctions for What Purpose?" *Warontherocks.com*, April 10, 2019, https://warontherocks.com/2019/04/more-iranian-sanctions-for-what-purpose/. According to Fitzpatrick, in the past, sanctions were used as multilateral leverages to gain nuclear concessions from Iran. This strategy worked because both sides made compromises and the United States agreed to some of Iran's key demands. With the end of that political bargain reached, even the most stringent sanctions the United States could impose remained aspirational in intent, designed only to inflict pain and to cause a regime change. Absent any acceptance that sanctions only create leverage when they can be removed, the room for compromise is so tiny that no Iranian government could ever submit to the excessive demands of the United States.

2. Some critics of Trump's Iran policy argued that Trump had overused the tool of sanctions and presented only the stick, that is, coercive approach, to Iran, without any "carrots." See, for example, Gardiner Harris, "Trump Has Only Sticks, No Carrots," *New York Times*, November 9, 2018, https://www.nytimes.com/2018/11/09/sunday-review/trump-sanctions-iran-foreign-policy.html.

3. "Full Text: Trump's 2018 UN Speech Transcript," *Politico*, September 25, 2018, https://www.politico.com/story/2018/09/25/trump-un-speech-2018-full-text-transcript-840043.

4. "President Addressing UNGA 73," *President.ir*, September 25, 2018, http://www.president.ir/en/106243.

5. "Bolton Turns Up Anti-Iran Rhetoric in Speech: 'We Will Coe after You," *The Daily Caller*, September 25, 2018, https://dailycaller.com/2018/09/25/bolton-iran-speech-united-nations/.

6. "Remarks at the United against Nuclear Iran Summit," *U.S. Department of State*, September 25, 2018, https://www.state.gov/secretary/remarks/2018/09/286216. htm. The International Crisis Group has argued that "if true, these attacks [in Iraq attributed by the US to Iran—authors] would constitute an escalation unseen in Iraq since 2011 and indicate that tightening the noose of sanctions has made Iran more, not less, aggressive." In "The Illogic of U.S. Sanctions Snapback on Iran," *International Crisis Group*, November 2, 2018, https://www.crisisgroup.org/middle-east-north-africa/gulf-and-arabian-peninsula/iran/b64-illogic-us-sanctions-snapback-iran.

7. Dion Nieesenbaum, "White House Sought Options to Strike Iran," *Wall Street Journal*, January 13, 2019, https://www.wsj.com/articles/white-house-soug ht-options-to-strike-iran-11547375404.

8. "US Pulls Staff from Iraq, Citing Security Threat from Iran," *CNN*, September 29, 2018, https://www.cnn.com/2018/09/28/politics/us-consulate-basra-evacua tion/index.html.

9. "Donald Trump Focuses Fire on Iran's Support for Terrorists and Militias," *The Guardian*, May 22, 2017, https://www.theguardian.com/us-news/2017/may/22/ir an-donald-trump-hassan-rouhani-israel.

10. "Iran Blames US Policies for Attack on Its Basra Consulate," *Iran Front Page*, September 12, 2018, https://ifpnews.com/exclusive/iran-blames-us-policies-f or-attack-on-its-basra-consulate/. Also, "Rouhani Fumes at US after Ahvaz Parade Attack," *BBC News*, September 23, 2018, https://www.bbc.com/news/world-midd le-east-45617800.

11. "Tehran: Iran's Missile Strike Near U.S. Troops in Syria Sent Washington a 'Signal,'" *Sputnik News*, October 3, 2018: https://sputniknews.com/middleeast/20181 0031068549075-iran-missile-us-troops-syria-signal/.

12. Nader Entessar and Kaveh L. Afrasiabi, "Strait of Hormuz: Iran's Potential Countermeasure to U.S. Hostility," *Lobelog*, August 14, 2018, https://lobelog.com/ the-strait-of-hormuz-irans-potential-countermeasure-to-us-hostility/.

13. "U.S. to Keep Persian Gulf Waterway Open despite Iran's Threat," *Associated Press*, July 8, 2018, https://apnews.com/9b919a29d05741a996f3e97cc6fe808f.

14. In its October 2018 report, the International Monetary Fund (IMF) stated that Iran's economy had entered in a recession and estimated that the economy would shrink by 1.5 percent in 2019, that is, a negative turnaround from the projected 4 percent growth before the onset of US sanctions. See, "IMF Says U.S. Sanctions Have Pushed Iran's Economy into a Recession," *Radio Free Europe*, October 8, 2018, https://www.rferl.org/a/imf-says-us-sanctions-pushed-iran-economy-into-rece ssion-cut-oil-exports/29533226.html.

15. Richard Dalton, "Trump's Economic War on Iran Is Doomed to Failure," *The Guardian*, November 6, 2018, https://www.theguardian.com/commentisfree/201 8/nov/16/trump-economic-war-iran-oil-sanctions-us.

16. "BNP Paribas Sentenced in $8.9 Billion Accord over Sanctions Violations," *Reuters*, May 1, 2015, https://www.reuters.com/article/us-bnp-paribas-settlement-se ntencing-idUSKBN0NM41K20150501.

17. "US and UK Urge Banks to Do Business with Iran," *The Guardian*, May 12, 2016, https://www.theguardian.com/world/2016/may/12/us-and-uk-urge-banks-to-do-business-with-iran.

18. "Major European Banks Wary of Doing Business with Iran," *The Guardian*, January 24, 2016, https://www.theguardian.com/world/2016/jan/24/europes-big-ba nks-remain-wary-doing-business-with-iran.

19. In its February 2016 statement on Iran, the FATF expressed concerns about Iran's failure to apply measures to address the "risks of terrorist financing." See, "FATF Public Statement," *FATF*, February 19, 2016, http://www.fatf-gafi.org/publi cations/high-riskandnon-cooperativejurisdictions/documents/public-statement-febr uary-2016.html.

20. "Joint Communique," G7's Foreign Ministers' Meeting, Lucca Italy, April 10, 2017, http://www.esteri.it/mae/resource/doc/2017/04/g7_-_joint_communiqu_final.pdf.

21. "Trump Disavows Nuclear Deal but Doesn't Scrap It," *New York Times*, October 13, 2017, https://www.nytimes.com/2017/10/13/us/politics/trump-iran-nu clear-deal.html.

22. At his nomination hearing in Pompeo was asked whether he had seen any evidence that Iran had not complied with its commitments under the JCPOA. Pompeo responded: "With the information I have been provided, I have seen no evidence they are not in compliance today." See "Secretary of State Nominee Mike Pompeo Hearing," *C-Span*, April 12, 2018, https://www.c-span.org/video/?443693-1/secretary-s tate-nominee-mike-pompeo-testifies-confirmation-hearing&live.

23. "Remarks by President Trump on the Joint Comprehensive Plan of Action," *White House*, May, 8, 2018, www.whitehouse.gov/briefings-statements/remarks-pr esident-trump-joint-comprehensive-plan-action/. Presidential Memorandum, May 8, 2018, "Ceasing U.S. Participation in the JCPOA and Taking Additional Action to Counter Iran's Malign Influence and Deny Iran All Paths to a Nuclear Weapon," https://www.whitehouse.gov/presidential-actions/ceasing-u-s-participation-jcpoa-taking-add itional-action-counter-irans-malign-influence-deny-iran-paths-nuclear-weapon/.

24. "US Executive Order 13846 of 6 Aug. 2018," *White House*, August 6, 2018, https://www.gpo.gov/fdsys/pkg/FR-2018-08-07/pdf/2018-17068.pdf. Also, "Frequently Asked Questions Regarding the Re-Imposition of Sanctions Pursuant to the May 8, 2018 National Security Presidential Memorandum Relating to the Joint Comprehensive Plan of Action (JCPOA)", *US Treasury*, May 8, 2018 (updated August 6, 2018), para. 2.7, https://www.treasury.gov/resource-center/sanctions/Programs/Documents/jcpoa_winddown_faqs.pdf.

25. "Senior Administration Officials Previewing Iran Sanctions," *Special Briefing*, August 6, 2018, https://www.state.gov/r/pa/prs/ps/2018/08/284955.htm.

26. https://twitter.com/realDonaldTrump/status/1026762818773757955. Also, "Iran Sanctions: Trump Warns Trading Partners", *BBC News*, August 7, 2018, https://www.bbc.com/news/world-us-canada-45098031.

27. For more on the "failed revolution" assumptions, see Kaveh Afrasiabi, "Discourses of the Failed Revolution Revisited," *uni.muenster.de*, February 17, 2003, https://www.uni-muenster.de/PeaCon/global-texte/g-a/g-ss/WS0304%20American%20Empire%F8/Iran/02-03%20Discourses%20of%20the%20%27Failed%20Revo lution%27%20Revisited%20(Dr.Afrasiabi).htm.

28. "Foreign Minister: US Declines to Abide by JCPOA from Very Beginning," *Mehr News*, February 6, 2018, https://en.mehrnews.com/news/131941/US-declin es-to-abide-by-commitments-under-JCPOA-from-very-beginning. According to the Foreign Ministry's fifth report to the Parliament on the status of implementation of the JCPOA, as of early 2017, the country had attracted more than sixty billion dollars foreign contracts (minus energy). See, "The Fourth Quarterly Report of the Ministry of Foreign Affairs to the Foreign Policy and National Security Commission of the Islamic Assembly," (in Farsi), *Ministry of Foreign Affairs*, January 2017, 18.

29. "US Dream of Zero Iranian Oil Won't Come True: Zanganeh," *Tehran Times*, September 24, 2018, https://newstral.com/en/article/en/1107269746/u-s-dream-of-zero-iranian-oil-won-t-come-true-zanganeh.

30. https://www.icj-cij.org/files/case-related/175/175-20180827-ORA- HYPER-LINK "https://www.icj-cij.org/files/case-related/175/175-20180827-ORA-01-00-BI. pdf" 0 HYPERLINK "https://www.icj-cij.org/files/case-related/175/175-20180827 -ORA-01-00-BI.pdf" 1-00-BI.pdf.

31. "Iran Sanctions Are Unjust and Harmful, Says UN Expert Warning against Generalized Economic War," *United Nations Human Rights Special Procedures*, August 20, 2018, https://www.ohchr.org/EN/NewsEvents/Pages/DisplayNews.a spx?NewsID=23469&LangID=E.

32. Johnathan Saul and Parisa Hafezi, "Global Traders Halt New Iran Food Deals, as U.S. Sanctions Bite – Sources," *Reuters*, December 1, 2018, https:// www.reuters.com/article/us-iran-nuclear-food/global-traders-halt-new-iran-food-dea ls-as-u-s-sanctions-bite-sources-idUSKCN1OK1OR.

33. "SWIFT Suspends Iranian Banks' Use of Interbank Transfers," *INTEL-LINEWS*, November 5, 2018, http://www.intellinews.com/swift-suspends-iranian-banks-use-of-interbank-transfer-network-151310/?source=bne-credit.

34. "Strike in Tehran's Grand Bazaar over Rial Devaluation," *Aljazeera*, June 26, 2018, https://www.aljazeera.com/news/2018/06/strike-tehran-grand-bazaar-rial-deva luation-180625180010879.html.

35. "BP Halts Work on Gas Field over US Sanctions on Iran," *Press TV*, May 23, 2018, https://www.presstv.com/Detail/2018/05/23/562643/Iran-UK-BP-gas-field-sanctions-OMV.

36. "US Sanctions Mean No Big Oil Company Can Risk Doing Business with Iran, Total CEO Says", *CNBC*, June 20, 2018, https://www.cnbc.com/2018/06/20/ no-big-oil-company-can-risk-doing-business-with-iran-total-ceo-says.html.

37. "US Sanctions on Iran Leave European Companies with Difficult Choice," *Arab Weekly*, June 25, 2018, https://thearabweekly.com/us-sanctions-iran-leave-european-companies-difficult-choice.

38. "Italy's Danieli Iranian Orders Blocked after U.S. Decision on Nuclear Deal," *Reuters*, May 17, 2018, https://www.reuters.com/article/us-danieli-iran-sanctions/it alys-danieli-iranian-orders-blocked-after-u-s-decision-on-nuclear-deal-idUSKCN1I I1NL.

39. "South Korea's Hyundai E&C Cancels $521 Million Petrochemicals Deal, Cites Iran Financing Failure," *Reuters*, October 29, 2018, https://www.reuters.com/ article/us-hyundaie-c-iran/south-koreas-hyundai-ec-cancels-521-million-petrochemi cals-deal-cites-iran-financing-failure-idUSKCN1N30U9.

40. "Austria's Oberbank Withdraws from Iran', *Reuters*, June 13, 2018, https ://www.reuters.com/article/us-oberbank-iran/austrias-oberbank-withdraws-from-ira n-idUSKBN1J926D.

41. "Swiss Bank BCP Halts All New Business with Iran," *Reuters*, May 29, 2018, https://www.reuters.com/article/us-switzerland-iran-bcp/swiss-bank-bcp-halt s-all-new-business-with-iran-idUSKCN1IU19Q.

42. "Iran Sanctions Hurt French Cattle Farmers," *RFI*, August 9, 2018, http://en. rfi.fr/france/20180809-iran-sanctions-hurt-french-livestock-exports.

43. "Maersk Latest Company to Shun Iran as EU Scrambles to Save Nuclear Deal," *Reuters*, May 17, 2018, https://www.reuters.com/article/us-iran-nuclear-ma

ersk/maersk-says-u-s-sanctions-make-doing-business-in-iran-impossible-idUSK
CN1II0YR.

44. "Scor Says Will Not Sign or Renew Iran Contracts," *Reuters*, July 13, 2018,
https://www.reuters.com/article/scor-iran/scor-says-will-not-sign-or-renew-iran-
contracts-idUSP6N1TU005.

45. "Iran's Oil-Market Realities: How Buyers Are Positioning for U.S. Sanctions," *Bloomberg*, August 6, 2018, https://www.bloomberg.com/news/articles/2018-
08-06/iran-s-oil-market-realities-how-buyers-are-positioning-for-u-s-sanctions.

46. "India's HPCL Cancels Iran Oil Shipment after Insurer Excludes Coverage,"
Reuters, July 26, 2018, https://www.reuters.com/article/us-india-iran-oil-exclusive/
exclusive-indias-hpcl-cancels-iran-oil-shipment-after-insurer-excludes-coverage-
sources-idUSKBN1KG1BO.

47. "European Refiners Winding Down Purchases of Iranian Oil," *Reuters*, June
6, 2018, https://www.reuters.com/article/us-iran-oil-europe/european-refiners-windin
g-down-purchases-of-iranian-oil-idUSKCN1J21F0.

48. "Rosneft Decides to Leave Iran Market—Media," *VESNIK*, December 13, 2018,
http://vestnikkavkaza.net/news/Rosneft-decides-to-leave-Iranian-market-media.html.

49. "Iran National Oil Company Rejects Rumor of Rosneft Leaving," *Trend
News Agency*, December 18, 2018, https://en.trend.az/business/energy/2995179.html.

50. "Tsvetana Paraskova, "Russia Plans $50 Billion Investment in Iran's Oil, Gas
Industry," *Oil Price*, July 13, 2018, https://oilprice.com/Latest-Energy-News/World
-News/Russia-Plans-50-Billion-Investment-In-Irans-Oil-Gas-Industry.html.

51. Joel Gehrke, "State Department Warns the World: Iranian Oil Tankers Are
a 'Floating Liability,'" *Washington Examiner*, November 7, 2018, https://www.was
hingtonexaminer.com/policy/defense-national-security/state-department-warns-the-
world-iranian-oil-tankers-are-a-floating-liability.

52. "French Car Giants Peugeot and Citroen to Exit Iran over US Sanction Risk,"
The Local, June 5, 2018, https://www.thelocal.fr/20180605/french-car-giants-peug
eot-and-citroen-to-exit-iran-over-us-sanction-risk.

"French Carmaker Likely to Halt Iran Operations as Other Companies Leave",
Radio Farda, July 28, 2018, https://en.radiofarda.com/a/french-carmaker-likely-to-h
alt-iran-operations-as-other-companies-leave/-29395780.html.

53. "France's PSA Suspends Joint Ventures in Iran to Avoid U.S. Sanctions",
Reuters, June 4, 2018, https://www.reuters.com/article/us-iran-nuclear-peugeot/
frances-psa-suspends-joint-ventures-in-iran-to-avoid-u-s-sanctions-idUSKCN1J026
R. Also, "Daimler Abandons Iran Expansion Plans as Sanctions Bite," *Reuters*,
August 7, 2018, https://www.reuters.com/article/us-iran-nuclear-daimler/daimler-a
bandons-iran-expansion-plans-as-sanctions-bite-idUSKBN1KS0N8.

54. "Boeing Confirms Passing $20B Iran Deal," *AeroTime News*, June 7, 2018,
www.aerotime.aero/clement.charpentreau/21390-boeing-confirms-passing-20b-iran-de
al. Also, "FACTBOX-Iran's $38 Billion Airplane Purchases under Nuclear Deal,"
Reuters, May 8, 2018, https://www.uk.reuters.com/article/iran-nuclear-aircraft-deals/fa
ctbox-irans-38-billion-airplane-purchases-under-nuclear-deal-idUL8N1SE75Z.

55. "Iran Aseman Airlines Crash: Years of Sanctions Have Left Passengers with One of Oldest Air Fleets in the World," *The Independent*, February 18, 2018, https://www.independent.co.uk/news/world/middle-east/iran-aviation-crash-aseman-airlines-oldest-fleet-boeing-727-a8216221.html.

56. "KLM to Suspend Direct Flights to Ian," *KLM News*, July 7, 2018, https://news.klm.com/klm-to-suspend-direct-flights-to-tehran/. "BA and Air France to Stop Flights to Iran Next Month," *BBC News*, August 28, 2018, https://www.bbc.com/news/business-45288659.

57. "Exclusive: UK's Quercus Pulls Plug on $570 Million Iran Solar Plant as Sanctions Bite," *Reuters*, August 14, 2018, https://www.reuters.com/article/us-iran-sanctions-quercus-exclusive/exclusive-uks-quercus-pulls-plug-on-570-million-iran-solar-plant-as-sanctions-bite-idUSKBN1KZ0ZR.

58. For more on this and the rising consumer goods in Iran due to the US sanctions, see "Tomato Squeez: U.S. Sanctions Begin to Distort Iran's Economy," *Reuters*, October 11, 2018, https://www.reuters.com/article/us-iran-economy-life/tomato-squeeze-u-s-sanctions-begin-to-distort-irans-economy-idUSKCN1ML0EV.

59. Djavad Salehi-Isfahani, "The Tyranny of Numbers: The Costs of Sanctions for Iran's Economy," *Djavadsalehi.com*, July 23, 2018, https://djavadsalehi.com/2018/07/23/the-cost-of-sanctions-for-irans-economy.

60. "US to Review Waiver for India on Iran Oil Exports," *Iran News*, December 9, 2018.

61. "OPEC Agrees to Modest Hike in Oil Supply after Saudi and Iran Compromise," *Reuters*, June 22, 2018, https://www.reuters.com/article/us-oil-opec/opec-agrees-modest-hike-in-oil-supply-after-saudi-and-iran-compromise-idUSKBN1JI0OG.

62. "Petroleum Intelligence Weekly: Saudi Conduct Review of Shrinking Spare Capacity," *Energy Intelligence*, November 5, 2018, http://www.energyintel.com/pages/login.aspx?fid=art&DocId=1016064&ts=1.

63. "Fresh Tensions Between America and China as Huwaei CFO Is Arrested in Canada for Violating Sanctions on Iran," *Daily Mail*, December 5, 2018, https://www.dailymail.co.uk/news/article-6465203/UPDATE-1-Huawei-CFO-arrested-Canada-violating-U-S-sanctions-Iran-report.html.

64. "Policy Change at China's Bank of Kunlun Cuts Iran Sanctions Lifeline," *Bourse & Bazaar*, January 2, 2019, https://www.bourseandbazaar.com/articles/2019/1/2/policy-change-at-chinas-bank-of-kunlun-cuts-sanctions-lifeline-for-iranian-industry.

65. "China Unexpectedly Gambles on European Mechanism to Sustain Iran Trade," *Bourse & Bazaar*, October 13, 2018, https://www.bourseandbazaar.com/articles/2018/10/31/china-unexpectedly-gambles-on-european-spv-to-sustain-iran-trade.

66. For more on this see, Esfandyar Batmanghelidj, "Why Isn't China Standing by Iran?" *Bloomberg*, March 27, 2019, https://www.bloomberg.com/opinion/articles/2019-03-27/spooked-by-u-s-sanctions-china-isn-t-standing-by-iran.

67. "India to Continue with Iran Oil Imports Despite U.S. Sanctions," *Tehran Times*, October 9, 2018, https://www.tehrantimes.com/news/428310/India-to-contin ue-with-Iranian-oil-imports-despite-U-S-sanctions.

68. "Indian Oil Says Iran May Still Invest in Chennai Petroleum Expansion," *Energy World*, January 2, 2019, https://energy.economictimes.indiatimes.com/news/ oil-and-gas/indian-oil-says-iran-may-still-invest-in-chennai-petroleum-expansion/ 673.

69. "Remarks by President Trump on the Strategy in Afghanistan and South Asia," *White House*, August 21, 2017, https://www.whitehouse.gov/briefings-sta tements/remarks-president-trump-strategy-afghanistan-south-asia/. In this important policy speech, Trump advised against "hasty withdrawal" from Afghanistan, warned of the dangerous vacuum benefiting ISIS terrorists as a result of hasty US withdrawal from Iraq, and vowed that US is not "nation-building again."

70. "India Visit Aimed at Solidifying Partnership: Nikki Haley," *The Hindu*, June 27, 2017, https://www.thehindu.com/news/national/india-visit-aimed-at-solidifyin g-partnership-nikki-haley/article24271676.ece.

71. "US Says It Won't Impede India's Chabahar Project," *Financial Tribune*, June 30, 2018, https://financialtribune.com/articles/economy-business-and-market s/88954/us-says-it-won-t-impede-india-s-chabahar-project.

72. "U.S. Exempts Iran's Chabahar Port from Sanctions in Nod to Afghanistan," *Radio Free Europe*, November 7, 2018, https://www.rferl.org/a/us-exempts-iran-chabahar-port-project-from-sanction-in-nod-to-afghanistan-india/29586874.html.

73. "Afghans Hail Exemption of Iran Port From US Sanctions," *VOA*, November 7, 2018, https://www.voanews.com/a/afghans-hail-exemption-of-iran-port-from-us-sanctions-/4648348.html.

74. "Islamabad Summons US Envoy in Protest to Trump's Pakistan Criticism," *Radio Free Europe*, November 30, 2018, https://www.rferl.org/a/islamabad-summon s-u-s-envoy-in-protest-to-trump-s-pakistan-criticism/29610592.html.

75. "Pentagon Admits Iran's Key Role in Bringing Calm to Afghanistan," *Press TV*, December 27, 2018, https://www.presstv.com/Detail/2018/12/27/584088/Iran-A fghanistan-US-Pentagon-Taliban-Shamkhani.

76. "Over 400 Companies from 15 Countries Registered in Chabahar," *Iran Proj-ect*, January 1, 2019, https://theiranproject.com/blog/2019/01/08/over-400-companie s-from-15-countries-registered-in-chabahar/.

77. "Iran, Russia, and India to Meet on International North-South Corridor," *Financial Tribune*, October 30, 2018, https://financialtribune.com/articles/domesti c-economy/94802/iran-russia-india-to-meet-on-international-north-south-corridor. Russia extended a 3-billion-dollar credit line to finance the corridor, planned as a 720-km, multimodal corridor stretching from India to northern Europe, via Iran, Azerbaijan and Russia. See, "Iran Says Russia to Open 3-bln-USD Credit Line for Transport Corridor," *Xinhua*, November 21, 2018, http://www.xinhuanet.com/engli sh/2018-11/21/c_137620406.htm.

78. "Iran Slams India for Not Making Promised Investments in Chabahar Port, Warns of Ending Oil 'Privileges,'" *India TV*, July 11, 2018, https://www.indiatvnews.

com/news/world-india-iran-oil-supply-chabahar-port-us-sanctions-iran-nuclear-deal
-452111.

79. Thucydides, *History of the Peloponnesian War*, translated by Rex Warner
(London: Penguin Books, 1972).

80. "US Energy Secretary Urges Iraq to Quit Dependency on Iran," *VOA NEWS*,
December 11, 2018, https://www.voanews.com/a/us-energy-secretary-urges-iraq-to-
quit-dependency-on-iran/4696542.html.

81. "Iraq Receives 90-Day Extension to Iran Sanctions," *Associated Press*,
December 21, 2018, https://www.apnews.com/86c2c5730adb4696aedfda1bc55
5d15c.

82. "Iraqi Leader Says Disagrees with US Sanctions on Iran, But Will Honor
Them," *Radio Free Europe*, August 8, 2018, https://www.rferl.org/a/iraqi-leader-aba
di-says-disagrees-us-sanctions-iran-will-honor-them/29418380.html.

83. "Iraq PM Walks Back on Commitment to US Sanctions on Iran," *Aljazeera*,
August 13, 2018, https://www.aljazeera.com/news/2018/08/iraqi-pm-walks-commit
ment-sanctions-iran-180813180322399.html.

84. "Iraqi President Calls for Closer Energy Coop. With Iran," *Mehr News*,
December 28, 2018, https://en.mehrnews.com/news/140964/Iraqi-president-calls-fo
r-closer-energy-coop-with-Iran.

85. "Flights from Iraq to Iran Quintuple Over Past 3 Years," *Mehr News*, December 29, 2018, https://en.mehrnews.com/news/141001/Flights-from-Iraq-to-Iran-qui
ntuple-over-past-3-years.

86. "Iraq on Brink of Water Crisis as Neighboring Countries Decrease Water
Supply," *Kurdistan 24*, June 2, 2018, http://www.kurdistan24.net/en/news/6376f
a97-d458-4c7e-a083-201ed2294c05.

87. According to Philip Gordon and Robert Malley, "If the administration forces
Iraq to wind down its gas imports from Iran, more such protests are likely, seriously
threatening otherwise promising political developments. That would be a further
unintended consequence of a policy designed to promote regional stability." In Philip
Gordon and Robert Malley, "Trump's Magical thinking on Iran Sanctions Won't
Advance U.S. Interests," *Foreign Policy*, November 14, 2018, https://foreignpolic
y.com/2018/11/14/trumps-iran-sanctions-are-built-on-magical-thinking-yemen-saudi
-arabia-nuclear-foreign-policy/.

88. Abdullah Bozkurt, 'Erbakan's Legacy and Gas Deal with Iran,' *Today's
Zaman*, May 18, 2012.

89. Elin Kinnander, "The Turkish-Iranian Gas Relationship: Politically Successful, Commercially Problematic," *Oxford Institute for Energy Studies* (January 2010),
p. 11.

90. "Iran, Turkey to Boost Economic Trade Level to $30 billion," *Al-Alam*, May
16, 2014, http://en.alalam.ir/news/1594619.

91. For more on this see, Ellen R. Wald, "Turkey and Iran: Energy, Economy,
and Politics in the Face of Sanctions," *Turkish Policy* 17, no. 3 (2018), http://turkishp
olicy.com/files/articlepdf/turkey-iran-energy-economy-and-politics-in-the-face-o
f-sanctions_en_4628.pdf.

92. Quoted in "Iran, Turkey Pledge to Promote Economic Ties to $30 billion Trade," *Press TV*, December 20, 2018, https://www.presstv.com/Detail/2018/12/2 0/583461/Iran-Turkey-Rouhani-Erdogan.

93. Eli Lake, "Despite Everything, Turkey and US Are Getting Closer," *Bloomberg*, November 5, 2018, https://www.bloomberg.com/opinion/articles/2018-11-05/u -s-sanctions-on-iran-why-is-turkey-exempt/

94. Arshin Adib-Moghadam, "After the "Middle East": Turkey and Iran in a New Region," *JETRO-IDE ME-Review* 6, no. 1 (2018–2019), https://www.ide.go.jp/lib rary/Japanese/Publish/Periodicals/Me_review/pdf/201808_01.pdf.

95. "Iran Poised to Supply Energy to Turkey in Long-Term," *Mehr News*, December 21, 2018, https://en.mehrnews.com/news/140720/Iran-poised-to-supp ly-energy-to-Turkey-in-long-term.

96. Kilic Burga Kanat, "Trump's Withdrawal Decision May Boost Ties with Ankara," *Setadc.org*, December 26, 2018, https://setadc.org/trumps-withdrawal-dec ision-may-boost-ties-with-ankara/.

97. For more on this see, Kaveh Afrasiabi, "Syria Partition: The 'Next Phase' of US Campaign," *Iran Duplomacy*, December 20, 2018, http://www.irdiplomacy.ir/en/ news/1980724/syria-partition-the-next-phase-of-us-campaign.

98. Robert Bolego, "Crude Oil Stampede from 'Iran Sanction' Trade," *Seeking Alpha*, October 23, 2018, https://seekingalpha.com/article/4213538-crude-oil-bull s-stampede-iran-sanctions-trade. According to the author, "Iran's oil exports are much higher than previously reported due to the use of "ghost ships."

99. Patrick Goodenough, "Iran's Zarif Boasts About Regime's Ability to Evade Sanctions – And We Can Teach It to Others for a Price," *CNS News*, December 17, 2018, https://www.cnsnews.com/news/article/patrick-goodenough/irans-zarif-boasts- about-regimes-ability-evade-sanctions-and-we-can.

100. "Iran Offers Oil Discounts to Keep Its Asian Customers," *Radio Farda*, August 14, 2018, https://en.radiofarda.com/a/iran-oil-exports-discount-asian-buyer s/29433197.html.

101. "Iran Plans 3 Million Barrels of Oil Sales to Private Sectors," *Press TV*, December 26, 2018, https://www.presstv.com/Detail/2018/12/26/584009/Iran-oil-ex ports-energy-bourse-private-US-sanctions.

102. "Russia & Iran Drop Dollar Trade by Extending Oil-for-Goods Supply Agreement," *Russia Today*, August 19, 2018, https://www.rt.com/business/424541- russia-iran-oil-supplies/.

103. "US Imposed Sanctions on Iranian-Russian Network on Oil Shipment to Syria," *Middle East Eye*, November 20, 2018, https://www.rt.com/business/424541- russia-iran-oil-supplies/.

104. "Iran Joins Russia-led Free Trade Zone," *Russia Today*, April 24, 2018, https ://www.rt.com/business/424943-iran-eeu-free-trade-russia/.

105. "Iran's Economy Could Survive for Years Without Oil, Ex Official," *Tasnim News*, October 3, 2018, https://www.tasnimnews.com/en/news/2018/10/03/1843318/ iran-s-economy-could-survive-for-years-without-oil-ex-official.

106. "National Development Fund of Iran," *Ifswf.org* (No Date), http://www. ifswf.org/members/iran. This fund was established in 2011 to direct a portion of oil

and gas revenues toward "sustainable investment" as well as preserving the funds for future generation of Iranians.

107. "China to Buy Iran Oil Regardless of US Sanctions," *Islamic Republic News Agency*, August 13, 2018, http://www.irna.ir/en/News/82999852.

108. "China Aims to Shake up Oil-Futures Market with Own Contract," *Market Watch*, March 25, 2018, https://www.marketwatch.com/story/china-aims-to-shake-up-oil-futures-market-with-own-contract-2018-03-26.

109. "Iran: Oil Deal Negotiations with Europe Proceeding Well," *Press TV*, October 2, 2018, https://www.presstv.com/Detail/2018/10/02/575839/Iran-oil-exports-Europe-US-sanctions-Russia-China.

110. "Referring to Greece, Iran Says Europeans Aren't Buying Oil Despite US Waivers," *Associated Press*, February 5, 2019, https://www.thenationalherald.com/229463/referring-to-greece-iran-says-europeans-arent-buying-oil-despite-us-waivers/.

111. "Zanganeh: Gasoline Ration System May Be Revived," *Financial Tribune*, October 24, 2018, https://financialtribune.com/articles/energy/94688/zanganeh-gasoline-rationing-system-may-be-revived?utm_source=email&utm_medium=mail&utm_campaign=newsletter.

112. For more on this, see Jafar Sadegh Tabrizi, Faramarz Pourasghar, and Raana Gholamzadeh Nikjoo, "Status of Iran's Primary Health Care System in Terms of Health System Control Knobs: A Review Article," *Iranian Journal of Public Health* 46, no. 9 (September 2017), https://www.ncbi.nlm.nih.gov/pmc/articles/PMC5632316/pdf/IJPH-46-1156.pdf.

113. "IMF Says US Sanctions Have Pushed Iran's Economy into Recession," *Radio Free Europe*, October 9, 2018, https://www.rferl.org/a/imf-says-us-sanctions-pushed-iran-economy-into-recession-cut-oil-exports/29533226.html.

114. James A. Bill, "The Politics of Hegemony: The United States and Iran," *Middle East Policy* 8, no. 3 (Fall 2001), https://www.mepc.org/journal/politics-hegemony-united-states-and-iran. Also, Kaveh Afrasiabi, "Iran: Elections and the Evolution of Islamist deliberative Democracy," *Eurasia Review*, February 24, 2016, http://www.eurasiareview.com/24022016-iran-elections-and-the-evolution-of-islamist-deliberative-democracy-analysis/.

115. Samuel P. Huntington, "The Erosion of American National Interests," *Foreign Affairs*, September/October 1997, https://www.foreignaffairs.com/articles/1997-09-01/erosion-american-national-interests.

116. Kaveh L. Afrasiabi, "Iran's Islamic Democracy," *New York Times*, June 14, 2013, https://www.nytimes.com/2013/06/15/opinion/global/irans-islamic-democracy.html.

117. Aresu Egbali and Asa Fitch, "Iran Moves to Shelter Millions as US Sanctions Bite," *Wall Street Journal*, October 25, 2018, https://www.wsj.com/articles/iran-moves-to-shelter-millions-as-u-s-sanctions-bite-1540459800.

118. "Treaty of Amity, Economic Relations, and Consular Rights Between the United States of America and Iran, Signed at Tehran, on 15 August 1955," *iilj.org*, http://www.iilj.org/wp-content/uploads/2016/08/Provisions-of-the-1955-Treaty-of-Amity-Economic-Relations-and-Consular-Rights.pdf.

119. "Zarif: ICJ Ruling Is Victory for Rule of Law," *Tehran Times*, October 3, 2018, https://www.tehrantimes.com/news/428151/Zarif-ICJ-ruling-is-a-victory-for-r ule-of-law.

120. "Pompeo Pulls Out of Treaty with Iran in Response to UN Court Ruling," *Fox News*, October 3, 2018, https://www.foxnews.com/politics/pompeo-pulls-out-of-treaty-with-iran-in-response-to-un-court-ruling.

121. "Document: ICJ Order in Iran Deal Case," *Lawfare*, October 3, 2018, https://www.lawfareblog.com/document-icj-order-iran-deal-case.

122. For more on this see, Kaveh L. Afrasiabi, "Trump and the Iran Nuclear Accord: The Legal Hurdle," *Columbia Journal of International Affairs*, February 28, 2018, https://jia.sipa.columbia.edu/online-articles/trump-and-iran-nuclear-accord -legal-hurdles.

123. "Declaration de M. Le Judge ad Hoc Momtaz," *ICJ* (2018), https://www.icj -cij.org/files/case-related/175/175-20181003-ORD-01-02-FR.pdf.

124. "Iran Floods: US Sanctions Impede Rescue Efforts," *Aljazeera*, April 6, 2019, https://www.aljazeera.com/news/2019/04/iran-floods-sanctions-impede-re scue-efforts-190406172112425.html. Also, "Iranian Red Crescent Says US Sanctions Impeding Flood Relief," *Al-Monitor*, April 1, 2019, https://www.al-monitor.com/ pulse/originals/2019/04/iran-floods-rouhani-irgc-red-crescent-sanctions-aid-impact. html. Read more: https://www.al-monitor.com/pulse/originals/2019/04/iran-floods-ro uhani-irgc-red-crescent-sanctions-aid-impact.html#ixzz5lIY03V37.

125. For more on this, see the proceedings in the ICJ's Iran case available on the ICJ's website: https://www.icj-cij.org/files/case-related/175/175-20180828-ORA-0 1-00-BI.pdf.

126. "Iran Files Complaint in ICJ to Recover $2 Billion Frozen Assets in U.S.," *Reuters*, June 15, 2016, https://www.reuters.com/article/us-iran-politics-court-idUSK CN0Z12EU.

Chapter 4

Extended Compellence and
European Diplomacy

"They view it as the linchpin, I view it as a disaster." These words by the US Secretary of State Pompeo describing the divergence of views between Europe and Washington on the Iran nuclear deal epitomized the emerging Western divide on a major foreign policy issue, affecting Europe's economic interests.[1] The resumption of US sanctions on Iran translated into a tremendous loss of economic opportunity for Europe, freezing the blossoming of trade and investment with Iran. Within the first two years of the JCPOA, EU's trade with Iran had increased from 7.7 billion euro to 21 billion euro, thus turning the bloc into Iran's third largest trade partner after China and the United Arab Emirates.[2] In contrast, the combined total of American imports and exports with Iran was only 170 million dollars in 2017. As a result, some European commentators compared the "secondary sanctions" of the United States to a set of "sophisticated tools" that had become "a bludgeon with which to threaten allies."[3] From a European perspective, the new dynamic set by the American sanctions reversed not only the impressive economic gains wrought by the JCPOA, but it also impacted the continent's "shared" security interests.[4] Concerning the latter, Europe was concerned that the escalation of tensions between the United States and Iran threatened a military confrontation that could directly impact Europe by triggering an inflow of war refugees.[5] Even short of war, a collapse of the JCPOA could trigger Iran's resumption of nuclear fuel cycle "on an industrial scale" and, with it, a new Iran nuclear crisis amid growing non-proliferation concerns in the Middle East.[6] Confronted by a US administration that was openly disdainful of the EU as an international institution and threatened trade war,[7] EU policymakers found themselves in a "collision course" with the United States and, increasingly, in league with Iran driven by a common concern, that is, the need to salvage the JCPOA and thereby protect their vested economic interests.[8] This was reflected in the EU's Global Strategy, adopted in October 2017:

> As regards Iran, the EU, through the High Representative, has continued to play a key role in the implementation of the Joint Comprehensive Plan of Action (JCPOA) as coordinator of the Joint Commission. In addition to that, and in line with the Foreign Affairs Council conclusions of November 2016, the EU has also stepped up its strategy of gradual engagement with Iran, following the joint statement agreed by the HRVP and Iranian Foreign Minister Zarif in April 2016.[9]

But, compared to the EU representatives, some European government leaders, such as the German Chancellor Angela Merkel, were more cautious and sounded skeptical about the possibility of recuperating the US-imposed European losses in Iran.[10] Nonetheless, as of late 2018, a tentative conclusion was inescapable: the pre-JCPOA nexus between the United States and Europe vis-a-vis Iran nuclear crisis was definitely over and the JCPOA was still standing, that is, a huge blow to American diplomacy, partly due to Iran's own maneuvers. To elaborate, Iran's leaders had repeatedly warned Trump against axing the JCPOA, warning of their "strong response" if he pulled out of the deal, consequently raising the expectation in Washington that Tehran would pull out of the agreement in retaliation.[11] Yet, contrary to the American expectation, which included some of Obama-era officials who had negotiated with the Iranians, Iran did not follow Trump's footsteps on JCPOA exit and nor did it quit the IAEA and or the NPT as hinted by some officials; instead, Iran stubbornly clung to the agreement and urged other parties to do the same.

Despite the lack of sufficient data regarding the internal debates and discussions on JCPOA at the White House prior to the August 2018 decision, circumstantial evidence suggests that Trump himself was surprised by the fact that not one European ally stood by him on this matter. According to Bob Woodward, in his book titled *Fear, Trump in the White House*, at one point Trump repeatedly asked his advisers if there were any European country that supported him on Iran and the response was negative. But, Trump may have had ample reasons to believe that Europeans' shared threat perception on Iran's missile activities and regional behavior would temper their opposition to his Iran policy. After all, for several months, Tillerson had engaged with the Europeans on ways to "fix" the JCPOA (as demanded by Trump) making some progress, and various European leaders and officials often seemed to appease the White House in its criticisms of the JCPOA's "egregious flaws" to the point of even invoking the idea of a "new nuclear agreement." Intent on bridging their differences with the United States on Iran, the linchpin of European strategy was to approximate Trump's position on Iran's non-nuclear matters as a means of securing his preservation of the JCPOA, albeit with certain "add-on" presented as a "supplementary" agreement. Then with Tillerson's dismissal in March 2018, attributed in part to his disagreement with his boss on Iran, it became abundantly clear to the European diplomats that Trump was on the verge of delivering a final blow to the JCPOA, prompting several last-ditch efforts, including by the British Foreign Secretary Boris Johnson, to save the JCPOA—to no avail. In an opinion article in *New York Times*, Johnson compared the JCPOA to "handcuffs" on Iran's nuclear program and warned the White House that it would be risking the removal of those handcuffs by scuttling the deal.[12] "It has weaknesses, certainly, but I am convinced they can be remedied. Indeed at this moment, Britain is working alongside the Trump administration and our French and German allies to ensure that they are," Johnson wrote. After all, a few weeks earlier Trump in his joint press conference with his first state visitor, French President Emmanuel Macron, had boasted of his "special relationship" with Macron and had reassuringly stated: "We can change, we can be flexible." For his part, Macron reported that the French and US officials were working "intensively" together to fashion a common approach toward Iran, citing progress in "overcoming" their differences: "Regarding Iran, we have a disagreement regarding the JCPOA but I think we are overcoming it by deciding to work towards a deal, an overall deal."[13] The latter was based on "four pillars," which Macron identified as the JCPOA, extending the freeze on Iran's nuclear weapons program beyond 2025, ending Iran's ballistic missiles program, and curtailing its influence in the Middle East, especially Yemen, Syria, Iraq, and Lebanon.

In retrospect, there were multiple problems with Macron's approach to the subject. First, Macron had not coordinated his White House move with other European leaders and was quickly rebuffed, for example, Mogherini, EU's High Representative for Foreign Policy and Security Affairs, responded firmly by questioning Macron and stating that "there is one deal. It is working. It needs to be preserved."[14] One of the main arguments against Macron's approach was that a potential side agreement between Europe and the United States on Iran risked a tit-for-tat exchange between Tehran and Washington that could alter and muddy their respective commitments under the nuclear agreement and cumulatively cause it to unravel. Second, Iran was equally unhappy with Macron's "Trump appeasement" and both Rouhani and Zarif immediately rejected it. "We have an agreement called the JCPOA," said Rouhani in a speech in Tehran. "It will either last or not. If the JCPOA stays, it stays in full."[15] Third, Macron's solo initiative did not go well in France either and he was labeled a "Trump whisperer" in a country where the public opinion was solidly against Trump due to his stance on the Paris Climate Accord, among other things. Finally, perhaps the biggest con side of Macron's attempt to meet Trump half-way on Iran was that it gave the impression that Macron was indeed "Trump's biggest asset," to paraphrase a CNN headline,[16] and would not put up a big fight once the JCPOA had been scuttled by the White House (presenting Europe with a *fait accompli*). Having accommodated Trump in a tripartite US-UK-French missile attack on Syria over its alleged use of chemical weapons in April 2018,[17] Macron had also echoed the American alarm on Iran's "hegemonic ambitions" and thus seemed poised to appease Trump on Iran. Yet, faced with the strong backlashes against his Iran approach at home and elsewhere in Europe, Marcon quickly shelved the idea of a "new nuclear agreement" and put the accent on preserving the JCPOA with or without the United States, this while seeking to minimize any damage to US-France relations by insisting "we are not going to be the allies of Iran against the United States of America."[18] Still, this, together with Macron's increasingly vocal criticisms of Trump's anti-globalist ideology, eroded the initial special bond between him and Trump;[19] this new bond had come at the expense of Britain's traditional closeness to the United States, in light of Trump's criticisms of Prime Minister Theresa May over the Brexit deal.[20] But with Macron's France exerting its independence from American "tutelage" and criticizing Trump's bid to "become the world's policeman," the relationship between Trump and Macron soured and, predictably, Trump tapped into the old British reservoir of American sympathy in order to enlist London's support for its anti-JCPOA position; this was reflected in an opinion article in a London daily by US ambassador Robert Wood Johnson.

"Back us not Brussels," Johnson wrote in the *Telegraph* challenging the UK to abandon its European neighbors who were still sticking with the JCPOA and its trade terms and to join forces with the United States in renouncing the defective Iran deal. Johnson also delivered an explicit ultimatum to British companies, telling them to stop doing business with Iran or face "serious consequences" for their trade with America.[21] It was not to be, and Johnson's call on "global Britain to stand with us" fell on deaf ears as UK officials remained steadfast in their support for the JCPOA and backed the EU-led efforts to create the necessary mechanisms to maintain trade with Iran and bypassing the onslaught of new American sanctions on Iran, altogether representing a new transatlantic rift that was unlikely to evaporate as long as Trump was in the office. This was vividly demonstrated at the 2019 Munich Security Conference, where Vice President Pence and German Chancellor Merkel clashed over it.[22] Interpreting the JCPOA withdrawal as a major policy blunder on Trump's part, the European powers acted in concert to safeguard their interests in a nuclear deal that they (rightly) viewed as a product of their intense diplomatic labor stretching back to 2003, when the EU-3 (i.e., France, England, and Germany) started negotiating with Iran, resulting in some initial tangible progress, that is, Iran's agreement in the so-called Paris Agreement to suspend its uranium enrichment program and to adopt the IAEA's Additional Protocol.

To elaborate, Iran had agreed to the European demands as a "voluntary" and "legally non-binding" confidence-building measure, in exchange for European promises of loans and trade cooperation. Although it was commonly understood that Iran's adopted measures were temporary, the EU-3 raised Iran's ire when it sought to turn those restrictions "permanent" and also failed to deliver on some of its promises, causing a conservative backlash in Iran in the form of presidency of Mahmoud Ahmadinejad, who ordered the IAEA seals on Iranian equipment to be broken and the enrichment program reinstated, boasting of the country's rapid advance in nuclear technology. At the same time, Ahmadinejad was not averse toward negotiation and during his era (2005–2013) the United States joined the nuclear talks alongside the European powers; those early rounds did not lead to any breakthrough but laid the groundwork for the subsequent achievements during the first administration of Hassan Rouhani. Concerning the latter, in fact, Rouhani was surprised to learn, as a newly installed moderate president keen on ending the nuclear crisis, that secret bilateral talks with the United States had been initiated by his (hard-line) predecessor. For the Europeans, on the other hand, when they learned about the Tehran-Washington secret talks, they reacted negatively and France, in particular, played the "bad cop" by adopting the most hard-line positions among the Western parties during the final negotiation rounds.[23] The resulting "French malfeasance" was responsible for certain delays in reaching the final nuclear agreement, according to the US and Iranian negotiators.[24] But, once the JCPOA was reached, the French and other European defense of the historic agreement became almost unshakable. By April 2018, the appointments of hawkish Bolton and Pompeo should have triggered the European policymakers to step up contingency planning to salvage the deal, yet little was done in this regard until after the deal had been officially broken by the United States. A combination of inaction, distraction with other issues, and mixed messaging that partially appeased the Trump administration on Iran's non-nuclear behavior, proved conducive to the unilateral US exit from the Iran deal, which did not face a firestorm of big power opposition in the UN Security Council—that would have certainly been the case had it been Iran that had unilaterally scuttled a UN-backed agreement. The absence of a European contingency plan was tantamount to the absence of an effective European deterrence to prevent Trump from tearing the JCPOA. Long before Trump dismantled the JCPOA, the Western media was awash with reports of the United States and Europe being on "collision course" over Iran and, yet, because of the perceived need to maintain healthy relations with the United States, the preeminent guardian of post–World War II liberal international order, the Europeans did not draw a line in the sand with Trump administration on JCPOA. Their last-ditch efforts mentioned earlier proved to be too late and too little, rebuffed by an American administration that openly questioned Europe's political will. "You know the European Union is strong on rhetoric and weak on follow through," National Security Adviser Bolton said, chiding Europe as a "paper tiger" and warning of "terrible consequences" if "Europe or anybody else" tried to "evade" US sanctions.[25] Conceptually, this pattern of US behavior fits the description of "extended compellence," that is, a type of coercive diplomacy that extended its tentacles beyond Iran to America's (recalcitrant) allies in Europe and Asia, seeking their conformity with the US guidelines vis-à-vis Iran. Another example of this was a twitter message by US ambassador to Germany, Richard Grenell that urged the German companies to "wind down" their business in Iran. It read: "As @realdonaldtrump said, US sanctions will target critical sectors of Iran's economy. German companies doing business in Iran should wind down operations immediately."[26] That tweet and the subsequent behavior of ambassador Grenel, such as urging the German auto manufacturer Volkswagen to quit Iran or to stop transferring Iran's money in German banks, were met with strong German disapproval and resentment, for example, Wolfgang Ischinger, a former German ambassador to the United States, tweeted that "Germans are eager to listen, but they will resent instructions."[27] Despite the vocal criticisms of Grendel's "meddling" in German affairs, he did not quiet down and successfully pressured his host government to freeze Iranian assets. Concerning the latter, according to the German Finance Ministry, ahead of the US sanctions due in November, 2018, Iran had requested the transfer of some 300 million euros it had held in the Iranian-owned European-Iranian trade bank (EIH) operating in Hamburg; the Europäisch-Iranische Handelsbank is established specifically to engage in trade finance with Iran. Grenell adamantly opposed that request and told the German daily newspaper "We encourage the highest levels of the German government to intervene and stop the plan.[28] The American pressure proved successful and subsequently in August 2018 the Deutsche Bundesbank– the country's central bank– imposed a rule stopping the cash transfer to Iran, hailed as a victory for the Trump administration.[29]

Despite such episodic successes, the principal problem with the "extended compellence" strategy as applied to Europe was that it treated the European powerhouse, a pillar of the post-Cold War multipolar world order, with disrespect, undermining European autonomy. Inversely, Europe's assertion of its independence over the fate of the JCPOA related to a broader global reality and, indeed, traversed the mere issue of Iran—a point hammered by Iran's president Rouhani in his call on multilateral Europe to join hands with Iran against American unilateralism.[30] Rouhani's call on Europe was in sync with the views of some EU officials, including the European Commission

President Jean-Claude Juncker, who vigorously opposed Trump's stance on Iran: "At this point, we have to replace the United States, which as an international actor has lost vigor, and influence."[31] Indeed, the European rift with the United States on Iran increasingly became an "identity" issue and acted as a catalyst for broader strategies that would cement pan-European independence from the American power, such as by contemplating the application of new financial mechanisms for Iran trade for larger goals addressing US domination of global financial systems.[32] The French economy minister Bruno Le Maire underscored a growing sentiment in Europe for greater independence from the US-dominated financial systems by stating that the European leaders were asking themselves "what can we do to give Europe more financial tools allowing it to be independent from the United States?"[33] But, of course, Europe had a lot of other issues to worry about, roiled as it was by far-right populism, reassertion of Russian power, spill-over Middle East conflicts, mass refugees, Brexit, authoritarianism in Eastern Europe, and rising popular discontent, as vividly demonstrated in the huge outbreak of economic protests throughout France in late 2018. These developments were not conducive to a united front against America over Iran, highlighted by a joint US-Poland conference on the Middle East in February 2019, which was denounced by Tehran as "anti-Iran" and received a lukewarm response from the EU officials, who feared a repetition of the Iraq-war scenario.[34] But, while the Warsaw conference did not yield an anti-Iran consensus, it was nonetheless a minor success for the Iran policy of the United States; a bigger blow to Iran came in the form European complaints of Tehran's attacks on its dissidents in Europe.[35] Such accusations, vigorously denied by Iran claiming "false flag" hatched by Iran's regional opponents, came at an inopportune time when Europe was seriously contemplating remedial actions vis-a-vis the sanctions of the United States.[36] An example of the latter was an eighteen million euro allocated by the European Commission in August 2018 "in support of sustainable economic and social development in the Islamic Republic of Iran."[37] A largely symbolic gesture, this amount was of course too little for a meaningful aid for Iran's troubled economy. Other measures were as follows:

EUROPEAN COUNTER-MEASURE:
THE BLOCKING STATUTE

The "blocking statute," a 1996 regulation originally created to get around Washington's trade embargo on Cuba, prohibits EU companies and courts from complying with specific foreign sanctions laws. It decrees that no foreign legal judgments based on these laws have any jurisdiction within the European Union. Various European policymakers, pundits, and scholars have

interpreted it as an act of European "sovereignty" against the encroachment
of adverse US laws and regulations.[38] In the words of EU's foreign policy
chief, Mogherini, "it is true that this situation has triggered a conversation on
European economic sovereignty. We Europeans cannot accept that a foreign
power —even our closest friend and ally—makes decisions over our legitimate trade with another country."[39]

According to the "updated" regulation, adopted by the European Commission in August 2018, "The Blocking Statute allows EU operators to recover
damages arising from US extraterritorial sanctions from the persons causing
them and nullifies the effect in the EU of any foreign court rulings based on
them. It also forbids EU persons from complying with those sanctions, unless
exceptionally authorized to do so by the Commission in case non-compliance
seriously damages their interests or the interests of the Union."[40] But, the
twenty-two-year-old statute had not yet been tested, save as passing political leverage with the Clinton administration. In other words, it represented
untested waters and its effectiveness in blocking the US efforts to thwart
EU trade with Iran particularly in the energy sector was an open question,
depending on a number of factors such as enforcement and the comple-
mentary role of other remedial EU measures, including the promotion of
government-financed trade with Iran, direct investment through the European
Investment Bank (EIB), and bypassing US dollar by making special Euro-
denominated oil and gas transactions with Iran's Central Bank. With respect
to the Blocking Statute, it is important to keep in mind that it can pose an
empty threat to the United States if it lacks the necessary tooth to bite the US
interests. There is no EU court where these damages can be claimed. Rather,
the regulation explains that "the action can be brought before the courts of
the Member States and the recovery can take the form of seizure and sale of
the assets of the person causing the damage, its representatives or interme-
diaries. As in any litigation for damages, it will be for the judge to assess
the merits of the case or the causal link." This leaves it up to the national
courts to rule as they please, namely determining what the damage is, who
has caused the damage, and what the duties of the plaintiffs are to mitigate
the damage. Moreover, European companies must inform the Commission
"within 30 days since they obtain the information—of any events arising
from listed extra-territorial legislation that would affect their economic or
financial interests." This provision has led to some uncertainties, such as what
must be reported by whom and when. The regulation was somewhat vague
and failed to make clear whether it applied to any transactions. For instance,
it specified that only in the event of "serious damage" incurred as a result of
non-compliance with US sanctions, remedial action can be authorized. The
German government had set up an "Iran hotline" to provide clarification on

such matters, following a European Commission "fact sheet" released to provide Q & A for European firms.⁴¹ Since compliance with the Regulation was at the national level, there needed to be a uniformed behavior in strict enforcement, otherwise some countries might seek to take advantage of the Regulation's loophole, for example, Article 5(2) provides for the possibility of obtaining an authorization to comply with the US sanctions to the extent that non-compliance would seriously damage the interests of the companies involved or those of the European Community. The European Commission may grant such authorization according to the procedure set out in Article 8 of the Statute. In addition, the road ahead is strewn with important procedural implications that can delay adoption of the Iran-related Blocking Statute by months. It was unclear as of this writing if the new regulation will require a co-decision by the European Parliament, following the EU Treaty's Article 100A, or simply a cooperative procedure with the Parliament (per Article 57)?⁴² Also, recalling how in 1996 the Blocking Statute was reinforced by a similar "Joint Action" that directly covered the persons or firms affected by the anti-Iran D'Amato Act, an integrated legal initiative that invokes the Joint Action was necessary for Europe since the Statute was too narrow by itself to provide an adequate legal response to US sanctions. At any rate, the Trump administration publicly dismissed the blocking regulation as "not something that we're publicly concerned by."⁴³

One option for the EU was to utilize the dispute resolution mechanism of the World Trade Organization in conjunction with the updated Blocking Statute, just as the EU did in 1996, when the EU sought the formation of a panel under WTO Dispute Settlement Understanding concerning the alleged US violations under the General Agreement on Tariffs and Trade (GATT) rules. The United States raised the "national defense" exception contained in GATT Article XXI.⁴⁴ Similarly, the EU can cite the secondary boycott of the United States of Iran as a violation of GATT, for example, Article XI prohibits restrictions on the importation of the products of contracting parties and Article V on freedom of transit requires the United States to permit goods to transit through US territory, to or from the territory of other contracting parties, without regard to the place of origin of the goods, or of the place of departure. Conceivably, these provisions can be utilized vis-a-vis US restrictions on financial goods involving Iran, as well as other restrictions promulgated in new US sanctions, notwithstanding the fact that the EU has had some successes through the WTO against US extraterritorial actions deemed against both the GAA and customary international law.⁴⁵ In case in the future the EU undertakes such an initiative and prevails, then it would have the right under the WTO rules to impose countervailing duties on US goods commensurate with the damages.

EUROPEAN COUNTER-MEASURE:
EUROPEAN INVESTMENT BANK (EIB)

Following a unanimous decision by the EU heads of states at the EU summit in Sofia, Bulgaria, in mid-May, 2018, another initiative launched to preserve the JCPOA was "to remove obstacles for the European Investment Bank to support EU investment in Iran"—deemed as "useful in particular for small and medium-sized companies." Additionally, according to the President of the European Council Donald Tusk, at the EU summit, the Commission "was given a green light to be ready to act whenever European interests were affected."[46] The EIB provides long-term funding, guarantees, and advice to support economic and infrastructure development projects, primarily inside the EU Member States, which are the Bank's shareholders, but also outside the EU, in pursuit of the EU's external objectives. The European Commission added Iran to the EIB's list of "eligible regions and countries" in order to facilitate the bank's future investment in Iran.[47] But, the final decision on this rested with the EIB's Board of Governors, which is made up of government ministers from the 28 EU Member States. This explains why an EU spokesperson clarified that while the EU had added Iran to the list of countries the EIB could do business with, the change "does not force the EIB to begin lending."[48] The EIB also raises funds on US markets, and there were reportedly concerns within the bank that US sanctions may scare off EIB bond buyers—the EIB was indebted in 2018 by 500 million euros in bond issues. As one of the world's largest borrowers, the EIB had raised 56.4 billion euros ($66 billion) in 2017 on international capital markets. Even if it wanted to proceed with Iran investment, there would be a cap on the total amount that the EIB could invest in Iran within the overall ceiling of the EU budget-backed of 32.3 billion euros for the 2014–2020 period.[49] Werner Hoyer, the president of EIB, ruled out any investment in Iran as it would put to risk the bank's US market. Iran is a place "where we cannot play an active role," Hoyer informed the media in July 2018, and, several months later, there was no sign of any change of mind on his part. Thus, in an interview in October 2018, Hoyer characterized the EIB as "probably the worst instrument" to push for European investment in Iran, the reason being that the bank was "financed exclusively on the international capital markets" and its Iran investments "would be easily attackable by the Americans."[50] Having backed away from the European plans to support European businesses in Iran, the EIB's decision was unlikely to be impacted by the political decisions at the EU level, which had launched the idea with so much fan-fare without however producing any tangible results (except an embarrassing rebuff by the bank). More than anything else, the EIB's refusal to toe the EU's line on Iran reflected one of the fundamental problems of EU, namely, a growing chasm between the political decisions and the economic decisions. The former centered on neutralizing the extraterritorial effects of US sanctions on Iran, yet the success of EU's political and legal decisions ultimately rested on the decisions of corporate Europe, a fact acknowledged by Macron at the EU Sofia summit when he pointed out that "the president of the French Republic is not the CEO of Total" and therefore he was not going to "pressure French businesses to stay in Iran."[51] Still, Macron risked the American ire by agreeing to join Germany to co-sponsor a special financial mechanism to foster trade with Iran, considered the linchpin of European effort to save the JCPOA.

EUROPEAN COUNTER-MEASURE: SPECIAL PURPOSE VEHICLE

The Special Purpose Vehicle (SPV) was initially announced on the sideline of UN General Assembly summit in September 2018, after a meeting of representatives of other signatories of the JCPOA minus United States.[52] It was immediately denounced by US officials as "one of the most counterproductive measures imaginable for regional and global peace and security."[53] The SPV aim was to allow European companies to continue to trade with Iran in accordance with EU law and could be open to other partners. The vehicle would operate as a barter system allowing Iran to supply, for instance, oil and, in return, to purchase the goods or technology it needs, using a credit account. To carry out payment processing between trade partners, so as to balance out different amounts and varying payment periods, the mechanism may require a banking license.[54] Moreover, the EU had reportedly planned to ensure that the SPV would be able to provide export loans to facilitate significant economic projects.

The SPV was conceived as an alternative to the Belgium-based SWIFT financial network, on which the United States interfered almost at will. The Trump administration had put some fifty Iranian banks on its blacklist and SWIFT had agreed to comply with the US demand to steer clear of those banks.[55] Some experts had predicted that the SPV might lead to the creation of an alternative to the dollar-dominated financial architecture extending beyond the case of Iran.[56] Jean-Claude Juncker, president of the European Commission, in his 2018 State of the Union speech, had stressed the need for the EU to reinforce the international role of the euro, the second most used currency worldwide.[57] After an initial delay due to the hesitation of some European countries such as Austria and Luxembourg to host the SPV, France and Germany had agreed to join hands in sponsoring it, a move described as "strength in number" tactic to minimize the risk of American retribution against the European powerhouses." In the European political discourse, the

SPV's initiative was considered a potentially significant turning point transcending Iran, often articulated in the name of Europe's "economic sovereignty."[58] A common European refrain was that the SPV had a high political value and "it is important for us to defend the interests of our companies and to underpin our economic independence from the US."[59]

Accordingly, if EU prevailed in preserving the JCPOA through the SPV and other similar initiatives designed to protect European businesses in Iran from the extraterritorial sanctions of United States, this would be a net plus for global multipolarism as well as rule-based EU multilateralism. The stakes were, indeed, very high and, by the same token, if Europe ultimately failed in its bid to keep the JCPOA, then this could disproportionate ramifications in terms of the reassertion of American global power and loss of EU's credibility.[60] In a word, the battle over the JCPOA was the microcosm of a broader global reality at the crosscurrent of divergent potentials.

As expected, the Trump administration was adamantly opposed to the SPV initiative by Europe and threw many verbal volleys at it. Case in point, Gordon Sondland, US ambassador to EU, belittled its importance by calling the SPV a "paper tiger."[61] The irony was, however, that while denigrating the SPV as ineffective and "doomed to failure," United States was using the coercive tactics (in line with the extended compellence strategy) to scare European banks and companies away from daring to bypass US sanctions through the SPV. Thus, Brian Hook, the head of State Department's Iran Action Group, made it abundantly clear that those that defy the United States will incur severe punishment: "European banks and European companies know that we will vigorously enforce sanctions."[62]

But, the SPV was tailored primarily for small and medium-size companies, particularly those that with little or no connection to US banks or US markets. Without the participation of big companies, such as the auto manufacturers including Mercedes Benz and Renault, who had pulled out of Iran due to US sanctions, the SPV was unlikely to generate more than marginal impacts in terms of sanctions-busting and maintaining "normalized trade" with Iran as called for by the JCPOA. Financial Times referred to it as "humanitarian SPV" designed to facilitate the import of medicine, food, and other basic necessities to Iran—already waived by US Treasury yet still facing banking hurdles due to US restrictions.[63] A US media report had quoted unnamed EU officials expressing doubt that the SPV will cover oil trade.[64] Foreign Minister Zarif flatly denied that report and insisted that oil trade was "the focus" of Iran's negotiations with Europe, which remained confidential due to the opposition of United States. "If no money is deposited in an account for our oil sales, it is clear that no money will be available for trade. On the other hand, oil forms the main part of Iran's exports, therefore, it seems that certain propaganda and fabrications are being formed to disappoint people," Zarif insisted.[65]

This corresponded with the news from Iran's deputy oil minister Amir Hossein Zamaninia that "oil and gas agreements between Iran and Europe have good momentum and are proceeding well."[66] From an Iranian perspective, there was ample ground for this optimism. First, this optimism was fueled by a European Commission's proposal that the EU government should make direct money transfers to Iran's Central Bank in order to avoid US penalties.[67] Second, after all, three European countries, namely, Italy, Greece, and Turkey, were on the US list of oil exemptions from Iran sanctions and, third, the EU statement on SPV clearly mentioned oil trade: "Mindful of the urgency and the need for tangible results, the participants welcomed practical proposals to maintain and develop payment channels, notably the initiative to establish a Special Purpose Vehicle (SPV) to facilitate payments related to Iran's exports, including oil." The oil inclusion was significant and appeared to meet the conditions set by Iran's Supreme Leader Ayatollah Khamenei for Europe to meet or face Iran's withdrawal from the JCPOA and resumption of banned nuclear activities. "Europe should fully guarantee Iran's oil sales. In case Americans can damage our oil sales . . . Europeans should make up for that and buy Iranian oil," Khamenei insisted in May 2018.[68] Several months later, Ali Akbar Salehi, the head of Iran's atomic energy organization, traveled to Europe and openly complained of Europe's tardiness in delivering the promised goods to Iran, warning that "if words are not turned into deeds, then . . . it is very ominous, the situation would be unpredictable." In addition to oil, there were a number of other issues regarding the SPV that needed clarification as the time went on. The principal issues were as follows:

(a) Sectorization of SPV: it is not practical to have specific classification criteria, such as "humanitarian" goods, applicable to this SPV. SPV must outline its operational guidelines and it is better to use general sector classification guidelines to determine the scope of its activities.

(b) Legal protection: Whereas EU has lauded the SPV as a means to protect European business with Iran, in the event of US reprisal against participating companies, how are these companies protected? Without an adequate answer to this question, the sponsors actually run the risk of legal liabilities. Also, there are reputational risks, as a European company's reputation may be blemished by taking part in this scheme, opposed by the United States and its regional allies.

(c) Dispute resolution: In the event of a transactional dispute, how is it resolved? Will the SPV have a corresponding dispute resolution mechanism? How will it tackle the issue of legal enforceability of trade agreement channeled through the SPV?

(d) Government credit support: Will it possibly has dual structure and carries an additional "funding agreement" to facilitate Iran trade and also provide coverage in the event of a default by the participating parties? Closely connected to this question is, of course, the issue of SPV's legal status, whether or not it will be an "ancillary unit" or an "institutional unit"?[69]

(e) Control: Who actually controls the SPV and what is its level of autonomy? What role if any the banks will play and should be viewed as a public/private partnership in case it acquires a banking license?

(f) Transparency: will the SPV resemble the private SPVs that typically operate as off-balance sheet entities, in order to hide the identity of European companies and thus shield them from potential US backlash? If so, then how will the SPV handle the accounting reports and will it improvise special guidance for the companies, such as exemptions of import/export duties?

Unfortunately for Iran, the European situation had also turned more unpredictable as a result of delays and uncertainties over British exit from the Union known as the Brexit, popular protests in France, political transition toward a post-Merkel Germany, and rise of far-right populist movements across the continent, casting a dark shadow on the EU's future.[70] In a word, political turmoil and increasing political fragmentation was poison for the JCPOA and its future prospects, heightening the need for apt European leadership to protect its Iran interests. Despite such challenges, the EU's "global strategy" that in part reiterated steadfast commitment to the JCPOA was an important compass pointing at EU's resolve on the matter.[71] Coupled with on-going Iran-EU dialogue on such matters as nuclear and agricultural cooperation, peace in Yemen, and human rights, the European counter-measured aforementioned were important policy expressions that fueled an Iranian hope about the future prospect of JCPOA (minus the United States).[72] One Iranian thinking was that the SPV may start small yet had a bright future and its purview could expand to include a growing array of commodities including energy commodities. The important point was to kick start the process no matter how limited and then seek to persuade potential donors, banks, and corporations to participate in it under the cover of legal protection. The big unknown was how Europe would react if the United States acted on its threats and began punishing some of those companies engaged with Iran through the SPV? Would Europe retaliate in kind, or prefer not to agitate the US administration that wielded the leverage of trade war similar to the one waged against China? The fact that United States and Europe partially converged on the subject of Iran's regional behavior and missile proliferation was also an important consideration, which was aptly used by Pompeo and other Trump administration officials to hammer the need for a united front against Iran. As of late 2018, European policy-makers had successfully shielded their pro-JCPOA approach from American influence, but the overall context of European politics that showed disconcerting signs of erosion of unity and growing fragmentation was not entirely conducive to that approach and, indeed, bespoke of internal and external challenges that could pile up as time went on. Much depended on the resolve and (in)flexible attitude of the Trump administration with respect to Iran. If Trump remained consistently hostile against Iran during the second half of his presidency and turned up the heat, for example, by actively seeking to halt Iran's oil exports, this had an excellent chance of hardening the European resolve to pursue its independent approach toward Iran, instead of caving to Washington's pressure and joining its crusade against Iran. At the same time, developments inside Iran were also key, as the hard-liners, political fortune seemed to gain as a result of "unjust" US sanctions and other threatening measures that served to undermine the cause of political moderation in Iran. Moreover, European capitals were constantly lobbied by the Arab and Israeli governments to adopt a tougher line against Iran, with some members of European Parliament sharing that sentiment and highlighting the absence of a European consensus on Iran. Altogether, the highly fluid nature of European external and internal politics had grown more complicated during the Trump era and the new transatlantic fissures over Iran were only one aspect of a greater, disconcerting reality. That reality was to some extent dictated by structures and also to some extent by the agency, the particular individuals occupying positions of power at EU and individual European states. EU figures such as Mogherini and Junker were enthusiastic supporters of the JCPOA and favored European detente with the Islamic Republic of Iran, yet it was unclear if their future replacements would have the same kind of candid commitments to this cause, just as it was unclear if a more inward-looking Macron, shaken by domestic turmoil, would continue the rest of his presidency along the same projected image of globalism and multilateralism, which had put him increasingly at odds with Trump? In Britain too, Prime Minister Theresa May's political capital appeared to be dwindling over the Brexit complications, adversely affecting the British government's ability to focus on other external matters, this while in Germany the decision by Merkel to step down as the leader of her party against the backdrop of rising anti-immigrant far-right political parties was also vexing from the prism of European external relations. European counter-diplomacy on Iran had as stated earlier put it on a collision course with the United States, its military protectorate NATO partner, and this, in turn, had triggered the need for damage control, which could conceivably manifest itself in European self-reversals on its bold Iran policy, given the disproportionate value of doing business with the United States compared with doing business with Iran. Still, sacrificing the latter for the sake of the former was not an optimal option and many European politicians did not subscribe to a

Manichean either or choice and, instead, relied on the European soft power to orchestrate a delicate balancing act whereby sustaining their Iran ties would run in parallel, as opposed to conflict with, their (much more substantial) American ties. The prerogative of war-avoidance for Europe partly depended on Europe's ability to exert some influence on Washington, which would not be forthcoming if Europe projected the impression that it had sided with Tehran against Washington. In essence, this meant that Europe's Iran policy was to some extent destined to be coordinated with Washington, irrespective of how the America-First Trump's Washington constantly trashed the European institutions and undermined their political and economic sovereignty. For the foreseeable future, no matter what the outcome of European countermeasures to safeguard the JCPOA, there would be no realignment of NATO Europe with Iran. On the whole, Europe remained within the American sphere of influence and there were structural limitations on how far Europe would go to assert an independent Iran policy; those limitations were bound to grow more formidable over time if the illiberal forces of right-wing populism continued to grow and capture sites of power around Europe. European integration and rule-based multilateralism could be overturned in the future, and a European failure in maintaining the JCPOA, a likely possibility as of this writing, was sure to augment EU's credibility problems, highlighting an impotent multilateral institution. Cognizant of such risks, EU leaders were determined to go the extra mile to preserve one of their salient diplomatic achievements, and the main question was of course if their efforts were ultimately in vain?

From Iran's perspective, the EU was embroiled in internal problems and did not seem to possess the necessary political will or the determination to "pay a price" to defend the JCPOA, resulting in a growing pessimism in Tehran over the JCPOA's future prospects. The latter was reflected in an opinion column of Iran's representative to the EU in Euronews stating that Iran's patience was wearing thin and that the price Iran was paying for one-sided compliance with the JCPOA "does not support its restraint." This was yet another clear warning to Europe that unless the "much-hyped PSV" arrived soon, "things might move towards hanging by a thread."[73] Europe's tardiness backfired against the Rouhani government and emboldened the hard-liner critics of the administration, who became increasingly vocal in their apt question of what benefit was accrued by Iran with its one-sided implementation of the JCPOA? Chief among the latter was Saeed Jalili, former Iran negotiator and the representative of the supreme leader at the Supreme National Security Council, who championed an alternative policy option of playing hardball with the West.[74] A main criticism of Jalili and other like-minded politicians in Iran was that Europe had failed to forcefully condemn the JCPOA exit of United States while insisting on Iran's full compliance with the nuclear deal and continuing to push for more concessions from Iran on its missile program and other issues without, however, meeting their own minimum obligations under the deal, for example, the British government had reneged on the JCPOA-based arrangement to sell "yellow cake" to Iran's atomic energy organization.[75] These criticisms were bound to grow louder in the event of EU's failure to deliver the "deliverables" to Iran in the future, portending a political shift in Iran to the detriment of political moderates in Iran. The fate of the JCPOA and the political fortunes of the Rouhani government were clearly intertwined, which is why Zarif and other government officials had a sigh of relief when in late January 2019, Europeans finally came through with their promise to launch an SPV—known as "Instrument for Supporting Trade Exchanges" (INSTEX).[76] INSTEX will be based in Paris and will be managed by German banking expert Per Fischer, a former manager at Commerzbank. The UK will head the supervisory board. It is fully supported by EU, which has vowed to make this channel operational as soon as possible in close coordination with Iranian counterparts and also to support the EU-3's commitment to expand INSTEX to other European countries and open it, in due course, to economic operators from third countries.[77] Initially, INSTEX would be intended primarily for the sale of "humanitarian" commodities to Iran, with an eye to expand it in the future. However, it will be possible to expand it in the future. That said, the future operation of INSTEX was subject to certain conditions. The E3 announcement stated that Iran will need to continue to fully implement its nuclear-related commitments under the JCPOA. It also stated the E3's expectation that Iran swiftly implement all elements of its Financial Action Task Force ("FATF") action plan, in view of the fact that INSTEX will need to operate under the "highest international standards" in relation to anti-money laundering, combating terrorism financing (AML/CFT) and EU and UN sanctions compliance. Iran, on the other hand, rejected the notion that there was any linkage between INSTEX and FATF.[78] In February, the FATF applauded Iran's adoption of an anti-money laundry bill but regretted that the "action plan" on the bill was still outstanding, requiring further legislation, and extended prior sanctions waivers granted to Iran until June 2019. It warned that Iran's failure to act by then will result "increased supervisory examination for branches and subsidiaries of financial institutions based in Iran."[79] As expected, the US government seized on the FATF concerns to press the European countries on the "significant risks" of providing Iran with a special facility for trade.[80] Inside Iran, the fate of pending FATF legislation rested on the balance of political power between the moderates/reformists and the hard-liners, who controlled the powerful Guardian Council and enjoyed support from the Supreme Leader, who was increasingly critical of Europe's "inaction."[81] As a result, there was a distinct possibility that Iran would not meet FATF's demands and consciously assume the cost of FATF's future backlash, which would in turn potentially imperil European trade with Iran.

NOTES

1. Carol Morello, "Pompeo Asks UN to Bar Iran Ballistic Missile Testing," *Washington Post*, December 12, 2018, https://www.washingtonpost.com/world/national-security/pompeo-asks-un-to-bar-iran-from-ballistic-missile-testing/2018/12/12/3c853ef8-fe2d-11e8-83c0-b06139e540e5_story.html?noredirect=on&utm_term=.1d19ad3ce9da.

2. "European Union, Trade in Goods to Iran," *European Commission*, 2017, http://trade.ec.europa.eu/doclib/docs/2006/september/tradoc_113392.pdf.

3. Mark Leonard, "The New Tyranny of the Dollar," *European Council on Foreign Relations*, October 31, 2018, https://www.ecfr.eu/article/commentary_the_new_tyranny_of_the_dollar.

4. According to Boris Johnson, "the UK and our European partners continue to view the nuclear deal as vital for our shared security, and remain fully committed to upholding it." Quoted in "Europe, Iran Seek to Save Nuclear Deal after US Pull Out," *VOA News*, May 15, 2018, https://www.voanews.com/a/europe-iran-seek-to-save-nuclear-deal-after-us-pullout/4394548.html.

5. Christiane Hoffmann, "What If Iran Becomes the Next Syria?" *Der Spiegel Online*, August 14, 2018, http://www.spiegel.de/international/world/editorial-what-if-iran-becomes-the-next-syria-a-1223167.html.

6. "We are working, as a union of 28 member states and with the rest of the international community, to preserve a nuclear agreement that has so far been implemented in full, as certified by the International Atomic Energy Agency in 13 consecutive reports. We do this because of our collective security: we do not want to see Iran developing a nuclear weapon, and the JCPOA is delivering precisely on that purpose. I start by saying this because I often hear that, on this issue, Europe is motivated mainly by economic or trade considerations. That is not the case: we do this to prevent a nuclear non-proliferation agreement that is working from being dismantled, and to prevent a major security crisis in the Middle East." Quoted in Mark Leonard, "Federica Mogherini: Shaping Europe's Present and Future," *Livemint.com*, January 1, 2019, https://www.livemint.com/Opinion/RdCS4qYMsXV0ZS7i0mKz9K/Federica-Mogherini--Shaping-Europes-present-and-future.html.

7. "Pompeo Questions the Value of International Groups like UN and EU," *New York Times*, December 4, 2018, https://www.nytimes.com/2018/12/04/world/europe/pompeo-brussels-speech.html.

8. Sascha Lohmann, Oliver Meier, and Azadeh Zamirirad, "Irans Atomprogramm: Washington und Brussel auf Kollisionkurs," *SWP Commentary*, July 2017, https://www.swp-berlin.org/fileadmin/contents/products/aktuell/2017A53_lom_mro_zmd.pdf.

9. The EU's Global Strategy—Year 1," *European External Action Service*, October 1, 2017, https://eeas.europa.eu/topics/eu-global-strategy/49750/eu-global-strategy---year-1_en.

10. "Iran Deal: Merkel Cautious on Compensation after US Pullout," *Associated Press*, May 17, 2018, https://www.apnews.com/04e7f9db24e345bea607eb bf9b045b16.

11. David Brennan, "Iran Threatens Trump with Strong Response if Nuclear Deal Fails as Arch-Hawk Bolton Begins National Security Tenure," *Newsweek*, April 9, 2018, https://www.newsweek.com/iran-threatens-trump-strong-response-john-bol ton-877306.

12. Boris Johnson, "Don't Scuttle the Iran Nuclear Deal," *New York Times*, August 6, 2018, https://www.nytimes.com/2018/05/06/opinion/boris-johnson-trump-iran-nu clear-deal.html.

13. "Macron Pitches New Iran Deal to Sweeten Existing Agreement for Iran," *Guardian*, April 24, 2018, https://www.theguardian.com/world/2018/apr/24/trum p-iran-deal-macron-new-agreement-white-house-visit.

14. "EU Leader Says Current Iran Nuclear Deal Should Be Kept," *Fox News*, April 25, 2018, https://www.foxnews.com/world/eu-leader-says-current-iran-nuclear -deal-should-be-kept.

15. "EU, Iran Oppose Macron's Offer of a New Deal to Trump," *Hindustan Times*, April 26, 2018, https://www.hindustantimes.com/world-news/eu-iran-oppose-mac ron-s-offer-of-new-deal-to-trump/story-XLcVfvPYXCnBRYMOS76Z0K.html.

16. David A. Andelman, "Macron Could Become One of Trump's Greatest Assets," *CNN*, September 28, 2017, https://www.hindustantimes.com/world-news/ eu-iran-oppose-macron-s-offer-of-new-deal-to-trump/story-XLcVfvPYXCnBRYMO S76Z0K.html.

17. "Syria: US, UK, and France Launch Strikes in Response to Chemical Attack," *Guardian*, April 14, 2018, https://www.theguardian.com/world/2018/apr/14/syria-air -strikes-us-uk-and-france-launch-attack-on-assad-regime.

18. Quoted in "EU Vows to Keep Iran Nuclear Deal, Protect European Businesses," *France 24*, May 17, 2018, https://www.france24.com/en/20180517-eu-vows-keep-iran-nuclear-deal-protect-european-businesses-macron-sofia.

19. Both Macron and the German Chancellor Merkel were at the forefront of a more independent Europe that would not be "waiting for solutions to their problems from the other side of the Atlantic," to paraphrase Macron. According to Merkel, "the days when Europe could depend on the US are to some extent over" and "we Europeans must really take our destiny into our hands." See "Merkel Tells Macron She Wants to See Europe Be More Independent," *Bloomberg*, September 27, 2018, https ://www.bloomberg.com/news/articles/2018-09-07/merkel-tells-macron-she-wants -to-see-europe-be-more-independent. Also, "Macron and Merkel Seek Independence for Europe as Rift with Trump Deepens," *Express*, August 30, 2018, https://www.exp ress.co.uk/news/world/1010892/angela-merkel-emmanuel-macron-news-donald-tru mp-nato-latest.

20. "Trump Criticizes PM Theresa May Over Brexit Deal," *CNN*, July 12, 2018, https://www.cnn.com/2018/07/12/politics/donald-trump-theresa-may-interview/ index.html.

21. Robert Wood Johnson, "America Is Turning Up the Pressure on Iran and We Want Global Britain to Stand with Us," *Telegraph*, August 11, 2018, https://www.tel

egraph.co.uk/politics/2018/08/11/america-turning-pressure-iran-want-global-brita
in-stand-us/.

22. "Merkel, Pence Clash on Iran Deal at Munich Conference," *Aljazeera*, February 16, 2019, https://www.aljazeera.com/news/2019/02/merkel-pence-clash-iran-de
al-munich-conference-190216115506690.html.

23. This information is based on the authors' interview with Iran's Foreign Minister Javad Zarif in New York on September 26, 2018.

24. For more on this see, Kaveh L. Afrasiabi, "French Malfeasance in Geneva,"
Iran Review, November 13, 2013, http://www.iranreview.org/content/Documents/F
rench-Malfeasance-in-Geneva.htm.

25. Quoted in "US Warns Europe of 'Terrible Consequences' if Iran Link Maintained," *Irish Times*, September 26, 2018, https://www.irishtimes.com/news/world/us
/us-warns-europe-of-terrible-consequences-if-iran-links-maintained-1.3641914.

26. https://twitter.com/richardgrenell/status/993924107212394496?s=21.

27. https://twitter.com/ischinger/status/994113518604636160.

28. "German Envoy Calls for Germany to Block Iran Cash Withdrawal," *Channel NewsAsia*, July 10, 2018, https://www.channelnewsasia.com/news/world/us-envo
y-calls-for-germany-to-block-iran-cash-withdrawal-10516782.

29. "Bundesbank andert nach Streit uber Iran-millionen Reglen fur Zahlungs-
verkehr," *Der Spiegel Online*, August 1, 2018, http://www.spiegel.de/wirtschaft/so
ziales/iranischer-bargeldtransfer-bundesbank-aendert-geschaeftsbedingungen-a-122
1283.html. Also, "German Central Bank Blocks 400 Million Cash Delivery to Iran
Ahead of Crippling US Sanctions," *Fox News*, August 7, 2018, https://www.fox
news.com/politics/german-central-bank-blocks-400-million-cash-delivery-to-iran-a
head-of-crippling-us-sanctions.

30. Hassan Rouhani, "Europe Should Work with Iran to Counter US Unilateralism," *Financial Times*, November 1, 2018, https://www.ft.com/content/3ecaed5e
-dcfc-11e8-b173-ebef6ab1374a.

31. Quoted in Kim Sengupta, "How the Rest of the World Is Trying to Save Iran
Nuclear Deal from Trump's Attempts to Sabotage It," *Independent*, 9 May 2018,
https://www.independent.co.uk/news/world/middle-east/trump-iran-nuclear-deal-lat
est-russia-china-europe-us-response-a8343891.html.

32. A previous example of transatlantic rift transpired in June 2000, when the EU
challenged a US law, "Section 211," that prohibited US courts from considering or
enforcing certain trademark claims of Cuban nationals. The WTO Appellate Body
found that Section 211 violates WTO national treatment and most-favored-nation
requirements. To date, the United States has not brought Section 211 into compliance with the WTO ruling, and the EU retains the right to retaliate against the United
States for its failure to do so. For more on this, see Henry L. Clark and Lisa W. Wang,
"Foreign Sanctions Countermeasures," *NFTC.org*, August 2007, http://nftc.org/defa
ult/usa%20engage/Foreign%20Sanctions%20Countermeasures%20Study.pdf.

33. "France Urges Europe to Push Back against 'Unacceptable' US Sanctions on
Iran," *France 24*, May 12, 2018, http://www.france24.com/en/20180511iran-franc
e-usa-europe-business-push-back-againstunacceptable-sanctions-nuclear-trump.

34. Eldar Mamedov, "Warsaw and the Limits of Anti-Iran Alliance," *Lobelog*, February 18, 2019, https://lobelog.com/warsaw-and-the-limits-of-the-anti-iran-allian ce/. Poland's willingness to echo some of the concerns of the United States regarding Iran and its perceived "proxy" role in hosting the conference helped the US campaign to ramp up pressure on Iran to some extent despite the conference's shortcomings, above all the boycott of key European officials.

35. "Denmark Accuses Iran of Activist Murder Plot," *BBC News*, October 30, 2018, https://www.bbc.com/news/world-europe-46029981. Also, "France blames Iran for Foiled Bomb Attack Near Paris," *The Guardian*, October 2, 2018, https://ww w.theguardian.com/world/2018/oct/02/france-blames-iran-for-foiled-bombtack-near-paris-at.

36. "Iran Accuses Mossad of Running 'False Flag' Ops to Frame Tehran," *Times of Israel*, October 17, 2018, https://www.timesofisrael.com/iran-accuses-mossad-of-running-false-flag-ops-to-frame-tehran/

37. "European Commission Adopts Support Package for Iran, with a Focus on the Private Sector," *European Council*, August 23, 2018, http://europa.eu/rapid/ press-release.

38. A representative work is by Joachim Bertele, *Souveränität und Verfahren-srecht: eine Untersuchung der aus dem Völkerrecht ableitbaren Grenzen staatlicher extraterritorialer Jurisdiktion im Verfahrensrecht* (Tubingen: Mohr Siebeck, 1998).

39. Mark Leonard, "Federica Mogherini: Shaping Europe's Present and Future," *Livemint.com*, January 1, 2019, https://www.livemint.com/Opinion/RdCS4qYMsXV0 ZS7i0mKz9K/Federica-Mogherini--Shaping-Europes-present-and-future.html.

40. Updated Blocking Statute in Support of Iran Nuclear Deal Enters into Force," *European Commission*, August 6, 2018, http://europa.eu/rapid/press-release_IP-18-4805_en.htm.

41. "Questions and Answers: Entry into Force of the Updated Blocking Statute," *European Commission*, August 6, 2018, http://europa.eu/rapid/press-release_MEM O-18-4786_en.htm. Despite such clarifications, many answers remained, and it has been argued that for German companies, in particular, the situation was especially vexing. See, Axel Spies, "EU Blocking Statute and US Sanctions: Difficult Choices for German Companies," *aicgs.org*, August 20, 2018, https://www.aicgs.org/201 8/08/eu-blocking-statute-and-u-s-sanctions-difficult-choices-for-german-companies/.

42. A useful background book on this subject is by Nicholas Moussis, *Access to the European Union: Law, Economics, Politics* (Cambridge: Intersentia Publishers, 2016).

43. "American Dismisses EU 'Blocking Statute' as Iran Sanctions Finally Bite," *The Telegraph*, August 6, 2018, https://www.telegraph.co.uk/news/2018/08/06/a merica-dismisses-eu-blocking-statute-iran-sanctions-finally/.

44. "The United States—The Cuba Liberty and Democratic Solidarity Act," *World Trade Organization*, 1998, https://www.wto.org/english/tratop_e/dispu_e/cases_e/ds 38_e.htm.

45. "WTO Sides with EU in Rum Dispute," *ADWEEK.com*, August 6, 2001, https ://www.adweek.com/brand-marketing/wto-sides-eu-rum-dispute-51245/.

46. "Remarks by President Donald Tusk after the EU Western Balkans Summit," *European Council*, May 17, 2018, https://www.consilium.europa.eu/en/press/press-releases/2018/05/17/remarks-by-president-donald-tusk-after-the-eu-western-balkans-summit/?utm_source=dsms-auto&utm_medium=email&utm_campaign=Remarks+by+President+Donald+Tusk+after+the+EU-Western+Balkans+summit#.

47. "Extending the European Investment Bank's Mandate to Iran," *European Parliamentary Research Service*, June 2018, http://www.europarl.europa.eu/RegData/etudes/ATAG/2018/623544/EPRS_ATA(2018)623544_EN.pdf.

48. Quoted in "European Investment Bank Casts Doubt on EU Plan to Save Nuclear Deal," *Reuters*, July 18, 2018, https://www.reuters.com/article/us-iran-nuclear-eu/european-investment-bank-casts-doubt-on-eu-plan-to-salvage-nuclear-deal-idUSKBN1K81BD.

49. Ibid.

50. Adva Salinger, "Q & A EIB President Werner Hoyer on European Turf War, Iran, and More," *devex.com*, October 2, 2018, https://www.devex.com/news/q-a-eib-president-werner-hoyer-on-european-aid-turf-war-iran-and-more-93566.

51. "The Latest: Macron Won't Take Sides over Trade with Iran," *Financial Post*, May 17, 2018, https://business.financialpost.com/pmn/business-pmn/the-latest-macron-wont-take-sides-over-trade-with-iran.

52. "Remarks by HR/VP Mogherini Following a Ministerial Meeting of E3/EU + 2 and Iran," *European Union External Action Service*, September 24, 2018, https://eeas.europa.eu/headquarters/headquarters-homepage/51040/remarks-hrvp-mogherini-following-ministerial-meeting-e3eu-2-and-iran_en.

53. Natasha Turak, " 'Disturbed' and 'Disappointed' Pompeo Slams EU Plan to Bypass Iran Sanctions," *CNBC*, September 27, 2018, https://www.cnbc.com/2018/09/27/pompeo-slams-eu-plan-to-avoid-iran-sanctions-disturbed-disappointed.html.

54. "Special Purpose Vehicle for Trade with Iran," *European Parliament*, 2018, http://www.europarl.europa.eu/RegData/etudes/ATAG/2018/630273/EPRS_ATA(2018)630273_EN.pdf.

55. "SWIFT System to Disconnect Some Iranian Banks This Weekend," *Reuters*, November 9, 2018, https://www.reuters.com/article/usa-iran-sanctions-swift/swift-system-to-disconnect-some-iranian-banks-this-weekend-idUSFWN1XK0YW.

56. Leonid Bershidsky, "Europe Finally Has an Excuse to Challenge the Dollar," *Bloomberg*, September 25, 2018, https://www.bloomberg.com/amp/opinion/articles/2018-09-25/europe-finally-has-an-excuse-to-challenge-the-dollar?__twitter_impression=true.

57. "It is time Europe developed what I coined "Weltpolitikfähigkeit"— the capacity to play a role, as a Union, in shaping global affairs. Europe has to become a more sovereign actor in international relations." In "State of the Union 2018: The Hour of European Sovereignty," *European Commission*, 2018, https://ec.europa.eu/commission/sites/beta-political/files/soteu2018-speech_en_0.pdf#page=106.

58. See, for example, Daniel Daianu, "Can Europe Strengthen Its "Economic Sovereignty?" *European Council on Foreign Affairs*, November 5, 2018, https://www.ecfr.eu/article/commentary_can_europe_strengthen_its_economic_sovereignty.

59. Quoted in "Deutschland und Frankreich wollen Zweckgesellschaft für Iran-Handel," *Wirtschafts Woche*, December 6, 2018, https://www.wiwo.de/politik/au sland/diplomatenkreise-deutschland-und-frankreich-wollen-zweckgesellschaft-fuer-iran-handel/23723910.html. According to this report, the SPV was intended to start as a "small entity" geared toward humanitarian goods and to acquire a banking license "over time."

60. For a representative US argument that Europe was losing credibility since it had the means but not the political will to stand up to the US, see Leonid Bershidsky, "Europe's Losing Credibility on Iran Sanctions," *Bloomberg*, November 16, 2018, https://www.bloomberg.com/opinion/articles/2018-11-16/europe-s-losing-credibilit y-on-trump-iran-sanctions.

61. Richard Bravo, "U.S. Lambasts Europe's 'Paper Tiger' Response to Iran Sanctions," *Bloomberg*, November 5, 2018, https://www.bloomberg.com/news/articles/ 2018-11-05/u-s-lambasts-europe-s-paper-tiger-response-to-iran-sanctions.

62. "U.S. Envoy for Iran Warns EU Banks, Firms against Non-Dollar Iran Trade," *Reuters*, November 5, 2018, https://www.reuters.com/article/us-usa-iran-sanctions-e u/u-s-envoy-for-iran-warns-eu-banks-firms-against-non-dollar-iran-trade-idUSKCN1 NK1RD.

63. "Europe Struggles to Protect Iran Trade as US Reimposes Sanctions," *Financial Times*, November 5, 2018, https://www.ft.com/content/644d3400-e045-11e8 -a6e5-792428919cee.

64. "France, Germany Taking Charge of EU-Iran Trade Mover but Oil Sales in Doubt," *Reuters*, November 28, 2018, https://www.reuters.com/article/us-iran-nucle ar-eu/france-germany-taking-charge-of-eu-iran-trade-move-but-oil-sales-in-doubt-idUSKCN1NX2C1.

65. "Zarif: Oil Axis of Europe's Financial Channel to Iran," *Persia Digest*, December 4, 2018, https://persiadigest.com/Zarif-Oil-sale-axis-of-Europe%E2%80 %99s-financial-channel-with-Iran.

66. Quoted in "Iran: Oil Negotiations with EU Proceeding Well," *Press TV*, October 2, 2018, https://www.presstv.com/Detail/2018/10/02/575839/Iran-oil-exports -Europe-US-sanctions-Russia-China.

67. "EU Considers Central Bank Transfers to Beat US Sanctions," *Reuters*, May 18, 2018, https://www.reuters.com/article/us-iran-nuclear-europe/eu-considers-ir an-central-bank-transfers-to-beat-u-s-sanctions-idUSKCN1IJ100.

68. "Iran's Top Leader Sets Conditions for Europe to Save Nuclear Deal," May 28, 2018, https://www.reuters.com/article/us-iran-nuclear-khamenei-conditions/ir ans-top-leader-sets-conditions-for-europe-to-save-nuclear-deal-idUSKCN1IO331.

69. For more on the legal distinction between "institutional units" and "ancillary units" in the European context, see Sagé De Clerck, "Special Purpose Entities in the Public Sector," *International Monetary Fund*, September 2005, https://www.imf.org/ external/NP/sta/tfhpsa/2005/09/SPEsdc.pdf.

70. Kaveh L. Afrasiabi, "Turmoil in Europe Is Poison for JCPOA," *IRDIPLO-MACY*, December 12, 2018, http://www.irdiplomacy.ir/en/news/1980591/turmoil-in-europe-is-poison-for-jcpoa.

71. "Shared Vision, Common Action: A Stronger Europe—A Global Strategy for the European Union's Foreign and Security Policy," *European Union External Action Service*, June 2016, https://eeas.europa.eu/archives/docs/top_stories/pdf/eu gs_review_web.pdf. Juncker's ambitious plans for the EU affecting the EU-Iran trade were, however, toned down by other EU officials, who favored a more limited SPV confined to humanitarian goods. See footnote number 47.

72. "Iran, EU to Hold Nuclear Meeting, High-Level Talks in Brussels," *Press TV*, November 25, 2018, https://www.presstv.com/Detail/2018/11/25/581114/Araqch i-Iran-EU-Brussels-seminar-nuclear.

73. "In 2019, the Iran Nuclear Deal Is Hanging by a Thread," *Euronews*, January 1, 2019, https://www.euronews.com/2019/01/01/the-iran-nuclear-deal-under-life-s upport-view.

74. Jalili accused the Rouhani government of "political amnesia" and blamed it for changing the language on the JCPOA by claiming that the purpose of nuclear negotiations was not to remove the sanctions, contrary to the earlier statements to the contrary. See "Jalili's Response to Zarif's New Claims," (in Farsi) *Rajanews*, January 1, 2019, http://www.rajanews.com/news/303073.

75. "Iran Nuclear Chief Lambasts UK Conduct in Yellow Cake Contract," *Tasnim News*, March 10, 2017, https://www.tasnimnews.com/en/news/2017/03/10/1350995/i ran-nuclear-chief-lambasts-uk-conduct-in-yellowcake-contract.

76. "Joint Statement on the Creation of INSTEX, the Special Purpose Vehicle Aimed at Facilitating Legitimate Trade with Iran in the Framework of the Efforts to Preserve the Joint Comprehensive Plan of Action (JCPOA)," *Foreign and Commonwealth Office*, January 31, 2019, https://www.diplomatie.gouv.fr/IMG/pdf/19_01_ 31_joint_statement_e3_cle0d129c.pdf.

77. "Statement by High Representative/Vice-President Federica Mogherini on the Creation of INSTEX, Instrument for Supporting Trade Exchanges," *European Union External Action*, January 31, 2019, https://eeas.europa.eu/headquarters/headquart ers-homepage/57475/statement-high-representativevice-president-federica-mogherin i-creation-instex-instrument_en.

78. "Zarif Says No Linkage between INSTEX, FATF," *Azernews*, April 19, 2019, https://www.azernews.az/region/145100.html.

79. "FATF Extends Suspension of Its Measures against Tehran," *Press TV*, February 22, 2019, https://www.presstv.com/Detail/2019/02/22/589227/FATF-Iran-Tehran -JCPOA.

80. "Top Official Says US Has Cautioned Europe on 'Risks' with Iran Trade," *VOA*, March 13, 2019, https://www.voanews.com/a/top-official-says-us-has-caut ioned-europe-on-risks-with-iran-trade-/4827373.html.

81. Tahereh Hadian-Jazy, "FATF Legislation Reflects Continuing Political Divide in Iran," *Atlantic Council*, October 16, 2018, https://www.atlanticcouncil.org/blogs/ir ansource/fatf-legislation-reflects-continuing-political-divide-in-iran.

Chapter 5

The Regional Dimension

The proponents of Trump's aggressive Iran policy have often used the word *rollback* to describe that policy. A Cold-War concept judiciously used by several US administrations against the Soviet Union, rollback in the Iranian context has an offensive connotation conveying a strategy not merely to contain Iranian power but rather to significantly reduce it and to reverse the momentum for Iran's "expansionism" presumably generated by the nuclear accord. To reiterate, during the Obama era, rollback was used in a limited language that focused on rolling back Iran's nuclear program that was perceived to be steadily progressing toward a nuclear bomb. A nuclear Iran, it was feared, would be able to project power and dominate its region, perhaps triggering a regional nuclear arms race destabilizing the oil-rich Persian Gulf region. The nuclear prioritization of the Obama administration was met with approval by the regional allies of the United States, above all Israel and Saudi Arabia, albeit with a growing apprehension that the final deal was sub-optimal and, worse, created new opportunities for Iran's "hegemonic aspirations" throughout the Middle East. Obama was faulted, rightly or wrongly, for facilitating Iran's hegemony by inking a defective nuclear arms agreement that failed to cover the non-nuclear issues of concern to the United States and its allies in the Middle East. This perceived defect was corrected in the new US National Security Strategy of 2017 that defined counter-hegemony as a top priority: "The United States must prevent the emergence of a hegemon in Europe, Northeast Asia, or the Middle East. A rival could utilize the region's power potential to endanger U.S. territory or block U.S. commerce. A hegemon in the Middle East, for example, could endanger energy flows, raising the global price of key commodities, which would, in turn, harm the U.S. Economy."[1] Attaching this label to Iran, the Trump administration identified Iran as "the single most enduring threat to stability and peace in the Middle

East."[2] This (Iran-centric) threat assessment jettisoned the hopeful expectations that with the signing of the JCPOA Iran's "rogue" external behavior
would improve in parallel to the economic reintegration of the country in the
world economy. In his 2014 interview with the *New Yorker*, Obama had
fueled those expectations by raising the prospect of an "equilibrium" between
the Sunni Saudi-led bloc and the Shiite Iran-led bloc "if we were able to get
Iran to cooperate in a responsible fashion."[3] US intelligence agencies' assessment was that in the post-JCPOA context, Iran continued its "sphere of influence" politics tightly connected to the proliferation of its missile program in
places such as Lebanon and Yemen. In Yemen, Iran was accused of facilitating the Houthi missile strikes at Saudi targets.[4] A December 8, 2017, report
by the UN Secretary-General on implementation of Resolution 2231 generally supported those allegations as well as allegations that Iran had shipped
other weapons to the Houthis. US Ambassador to the United Nations, Nikki
Haley, cited that report in a December 14, 2017, presentation to the Security
Council that asserted definitively that Iran had given the Houthis the missiles
fired on Riyadh.[5] A report by a UN panel of experts in January 2018 reportedly found that two missiles fired on Saudi Arabia by the Houthis, on July 22
and November 4, 2017, were consistent with the design of Iranian missiles,
but the panel did not state definitively who supplied the missiles or how they
were transported to Yemen.[6] In late February 2018, Russia blocked a UN
Security Council resolution from identifying Iran directly as a violator of the
UN ban on weapons shipments to Yemen (Resolution 2216). Another UN
report in January 2019 discovered that Iran was using front companies to load
fuel at Iran ports for Yemen and "the revenue from the sale of fuel was then
used to finance the Houthi war effort."[7] Iran denied providing the Houthis
with missiles and asserted that they were from a government arsenal assem-
bled before the 2011 civil strife.[8] Iran's argument went unheeded in the Arab
capitals of Persian Gulf as well as the Western capitals, both dominated by
the narrative that evidence of Iranian intervention was irrefutable, for example, in January 2013, the US Navy, in cooperation with the Yemeni Navy,
seized an Iranian dhow, the Jihan I, carrying some forty tons of military supplies intended for the Houthis. The cargo included Katyusha rockets, surface-
to-air missiles, rocket-propelled grenades, explosives, and ammunition.[9] The
United States also tracked Iranian Revolutionary Guards providing training
and assistance to the Houthis in the Saadah governorate and accused Lebanon's Hizbollah of supplying arms and personnel into Yemen.[10] To counter
Iranian influence in Yemen, Pompeo stipulated as one US demand on Iran
that the country "must also end its military support for the Houthi militia and
work towards a peaceful political settlement in Yemen."[11] The rollback strategy of the United States thus focused on Iran's missile technology and the
regional portfolio that appeared to "entrench" Iran's influence beyond its

borders and grow in a seemingly zero-sum, that is, win-lose, fashion to the detriment of America's allies. Financially starving Iran so that it could no longer bankroll its subversive activities beyond its borders both directly and through its proxies was a leitmotif of orchestration of the United States of new sanctions. In the words of Pompeo, these sanctions intended to confront Iran with a stark choice: "Either fight to keep its economy off life support at home or keep squandering precious wealth on fights abroad. It won't have the resources to do both."[12] Within months of re-imposing the Iran sanctions, Trump was, however, close to declaring an interim victory by claiming that Iran "is a much different country now" and the Iranians were "pulling out of Syria" and Yemen.[13] Iran's response was that its military presence in Syria was defensive in nature and at the request of its regional ally to assist it with fighting the menace of ISIS and other terrorists and that it was recalling its military forces since the fighting was mostly over and the battle won. In other words, Tehran adamantly denied that its regional calculations were in any way influenced by the US pressure campaign. Irrespective, Trump's point about the departing Iranian forces, hotly contested by the Israelis, undermined the urgency of building an anti-Iran alliance, which the administration had pursued through the idea of creating the Middle East Strategic Alliance—an "Arab NATO"—centered on fostering security cooperation among the conservative Arab states, including a regional anti-missile defense shield following the conviction that deterring Iran's aggression formed a central purpose of the new regional alliance. An Arab NATO would consist of six Gulf states (Saudi Arabia, the UAE, Kuwait, Bahrain, Oman, and Qatar) plus Egypt and Jordan.[14] This was an old Saudi proposal that was embraced wholeheartedly by Trump administration as part of a *carte blanche* to Riyadh's plans for the architecture of a Saudi-centered security environment in the Persian Gulf and the adjacent regions including the Red Sea and the Gulf of Oman. US military commanders in the region accused Iran of seeking "to disrupt the balance of force" in the region thus necessitating the adoption of lessons from NATO's experience in Europe. Case in point, Commander of US Air Forces Central Command, Lieutenant General Joseph Guastella, mentioned Iran specifically as a threat to stability in the Gulf region and argued that "when the Iranian military exercises are aimed at the blocking at the Strait of Hormuz, the potential of miscalculation of military intent has strategic consequences. Their actions are directly aimed to threaten all of our economies."[15] Some experts have interpreted this initiative along the sectarian Sunni-Shiite divide, arguing that Trump was abandoning Obama's balancing approach and trying to create a "Sunni axis" against Iran.[16] Others saw it as a result of "threat inflation," whereby from Iraq to Syria to Lebanon, Iran's "threat was overstated."[17] "Threat inflation" in the scholarly literature is defined as "the attempt . . . to create concern for a threat that goes beyond the scope and urgency that a disinterested analysis would justify."[18] Rather than being a tissue of personal "obsession" with Iran and or any other subjective variable, some analysts have traced the huge American arms sales to the region to the economic logic of the military-industrial complex.[19] Trump inked huge arms sales agreements with Saudi Arabia and other GCC states such as Bahrain;[20] these sales augmented the regional arms race and made it less likely that Iran, which was still under a UN conventional arms embargo, would agree to any curbs on its missile program. Also, these arms sales fueled Iranian criticism that the United States and other Western powers were following the false narrative that the influx of more arms into the volatile region translated into greater security.[21] Certainly, there was a grain of truth in the Iranian criticism, just as there was some truthfulness to the accusations against Iran. Data published by the Stockholm International Peace Research Institute (SIPRI) showed that the scope of weapons exports to the Middle East increased in monetary terms by 103 percent in the period 2013–2017, compared to 2008–2012. According to SIPRI, in 2013–2017, Saudi Arabia was the world's second-largest arms importer, with arms imports increasing by 225 percent compared with 2008–2012. The UAE was the fourth largest importer in 2013–2017, while Qatar (the twentieth largest arms importer) increased its arms imports and signed several major deals in that period.[22] Outspent by the Saudi-led GCC bloc by a margin of more than ten to one, Iran was in an unenviable military position in a competitive regional context, wherein the GCC states have "an overwhelming advantage over Iran in both military spending and access to modern arms," an imbalance stretching back decades.[23] Inevitably, the missile program served Iran's deterrence purposes and compensated for the loss of Iran's regional prestige as a result of the nuclear deal, which removed the Iranian nuclear threat under Western pressure. Hence, US objective of compelling Iran to roll back its missile program had practically no chance of success short of an outright war by virtue of the fact that Iran's national security dictated a heavy reliance on its missile arsenal for defense and deterrence in an unstable and risk-prone regional environment where Iran faced the predicament of arms race imbalances favoring its rivals, who were able to purchase cutting-edge military hardware from United States, United Kingdom, France, and other countries.

Siding with Riyadh against Tehran and continuing the traditional US military protection, Trump's Persian Gulf policy can be summed up in one word: Saudi primacy. We label this policy as "Saudi primacy" because primacy is a material condition that coalesces the various actors around one pole, consolidating its regional clout through a combination of direct action and external support. Viewed as the only logical alternative to rising Iranian hegemony, Saudi primacy was the hallmark of Trump's Persian Gulf policy, bolstered by the additional argument that the wealthy Saudis invested billions of dollars in US economy and thus contributed to creating jobs in the United States. Preserving the Gulf's security through a Saudi-centered unipolar moment was Trump's ambition, which required a substantial offensive United States against Iran in order to diminish Iranian power while beefing up the Saudi power and endorsing Riyadh's increasingly aggressive regional policy—that had resulted in a protracted war in Yemen since early 2015, military intervention in Bahrain, blockade of neighboring Qatar (accused of getting too close to Iran), interfering in Lebanon's politics, and bankrolling the extremist groups operating in Syria. Led by a young and ambitious crown price, Mohammad Bin Salman, who established cordial relations with Trump's son-in-law Jarred Kushner, Saudi Arabia was able to bully its neighbors and dictate terms to them while enjoying an unconditional US support that continued unabated even after the scandalous murder of a Saudi dissident, Jamal Khashoggi, at the Saudi consulate in Istanbul in October 2018.

Initially, the Khashoggi issue rocked the boat of US-Saudi diplomacy and had the potential to act as a game-changer, particularly after the US Senate passed a resolution condemning Khashoggi's murder and blamed it on the de facto ruler of Saudi Arabia.[24] This, together with another resolution calling for an end to US involvement in the Yemen war, reflected an unprecedented foreign policy intervention by Congress during the first two years of Trump's presidency.[25] The Republican-dominated Congress had undergone a makeover after the mid-term elections in November 2018, which brought a democratic majority in the House of Representatives, thus delivering an indirect electoral defeat to Trump administration. Trump could no longer take for granted a docile Congress with respect to foreign affairs and the last two years of his presidency was fated to feature a more muscular congressional input in US foreign policy, already demonstrated by Senate's resolutions on Khashoggi and Yemen aforementioned.[26] In the aftermath of the Khashoggi incident, there was a widely held belief in Washington that Trump had emboldened Saudi "adventurism" and a more critical approach toward Saudi Arabia "gone too far" was needed.[27]

To some extent, Trump appeared responsive to such criticisms of his Saudi policy and his administration made a number of adjustments, such as by calling for a cease-fire in Yemen conflict, ending the logistical support of the United States for Saudi bombing campaign in Yemen, urging Saudi Arabia and UAE to lift their blockade of Qatar, and openly questioning the Saudis' capability to maintain their hold on power without US support; concerning the latter, during a joint news conference with French President Emmanuel Macron, Trump said that Western allies in the Middle East wouldn't "last a week" without the protection of the United States.[28] This was in contrast to the image of independence projected by Iran. These adjustments reflected a more nuanced US approach toward Saudi Arabia and Persian Gulf affairs, compared with the initial fury of wholehearted support of Riyadh's regional approach, marking a tiny step back toward a more balanced US policy. The Saudis responded by making their own adjustments, by adopting a more restrained regional facade, a cabinet turnover and the replacement of key foreign policy officials. These policy adjustments by Riyadh, in turn, made it easier for Trump administration to retain the strategic priority given to the Saudis while slapping them on the wrist by imposing sanctions on the seventeen Saudi operatives who carried out Khashoggi's gruesome murder.

Then, in a major policy statement in November 2018, Trump listed the principal reasons for the pro-Saudi approach of the United States, including the economic ones: "The Kingdom agreed to spend and invest $450 billion in the United States. This is a record amount of money. It will create hundreds of thousands of jobs, tremendous economic development, and much additional wealth for the United States. Of the $450 billion, $110 billion will be spent on the purchase of military equipment from Boeing, Lockheed Martin, Raytheon, and many other great U.S. defense contractors." Another reason was oil: "Saudi Arabia is the largest oil producing nation in the world. They have worked closely with us and have been very responsive to my requests for keeping oil prices at reasonable levels—so important for the world." A third reason was strategic: The Saudis "have been a great ally in our very important fight against Iran." Trump claimed that Iran "is responsible for a bloody proxy war against Saudi Arabia in Yemen" and that Saudi Arabia "would gladly withdraw from Yemen if the Iranians would agree to leave." But, such assertions have been contested by various Middle East experts, who have pointed at the complex socio-economic and political dynamic in Yemen, the historical and territorial feud between Saudi Arabia and Yemen, as well as the "new assertiveness" in Saudi foreign behavior.[29] Some scholars have traced this assertiveness to the 1991 Kuwait War, when Saudi Arabia set aside its traditional restraint and permitted a huge influx of Western forces on its soil who were able to roll back Iraq's invasion of Kuwait.[30] A fourth reason given by Trump was Israel's security, connected to Iran's attempt to establish a presence in the Red Sea: "The United States intends to remain a steadfast partner of Saudi Arabia to ensure the interests of our country, Israel and all other partners in the region."[31] We may characterize this reason as a "balance of relationships," one that favored a growing Saudi-Israeli concert against Iran and also sought to elicit Riyadh's support for White House's plans for a new "Middle East peace process." This Saudi-Israeli concert, stemming from shared threat perceptions regarding Iran and its proxies, increasingly entailed diplomatic openings, intelligence-sharing, and low-level security cooperation including in Yemen. It has been observed that "wider Saudi efforts to build an anti-Iran Sunni axis had hit obstacles, as seen most notably in Egypt's repeated refusal to provide active support."[32] Another reason, mentioned in

Trump's other speeches, was the concern that Saudi Arabia would turn to China and Russia in the event that the United States curbed its arms sales to the kingdom—an issue of worry seeded by Saudi rejection of the Senate resolutions aforementioned and their growing ties to Russia.[33] Pompeo, on the other hand, praised Saudi Arabi as a "force for stability in the Middle East" that was working to "secure Iraq's fragile democracy and keep Baghdad tethered to the West's interests, not Tehran's."[34] Consequently, whereas the critics of Trump's Saudi policy blamed it as "amoral" and driven by human rights-unrelated standards, Trump's supporters praised it for its "strategic clarity" and its "clear-eyed" focus on Iran threat.[35] In the Persian Gulf, on the other hand, not all of the GCC states were of the same mind toward Iran, thus complicating Trump's Iran strategy.

THE CHALLENGES OF BUILDING ANTI-IRAN ALLIANCE IN FRACTIOUS GULF

In January 2019, in a major policy speech at the American University in Cairo—intended as a clear repudiation of Obama's Middle East policy—Pompeo claimed that "countries increasingly understand that we must confront the ayatollahs not coddle them." Earlier he had warned Iran against launching three communication satellites, describing them as a pretext for testing long-range nuclear-capable missiles, and had been quickly rebuffed by Tehran. His Iranian counterpart, Javad Zarif, was in India around the same time, meeting with India's foreign minister, who had sent a clear message that India did not recognize any unilateral sanctions on Iran and would only respect UN sanctions. Yet, irrespective of signs to the contrary, Pompeo asserted that "nations are rallying to our side to confront Iran in the region like never before." Following the speech, Pompeo toured the Persian Gulf region and consistently raised the centrality of confronting Iran. A major challenge facing him, however, was the politics of disunity in the region.

To elaborate, GCC unity had suffered a long-term setback as a result of the rift between Saudi Arabia and Qatar, which opted to move closer to Iran and Turkey in response to the Saudi-led blockade.[36] Kuwait too maintained positive relations with Iran and wisely decided not to antagonize Iran by echoing Riyadh's propaganda that blamed Iran as the source of all instabilities in the region. The Emir of Kuwait, Sheikh Sabah Al Ahmad, had underlined his country's interest in promoting collaboration with Iran, that is, "We consider Iran as our neighbor and we are interested in developing our beneficial cooperation with Tehran."[37] Another GCC state Oman was considered uniquely close to Iran as it had played a key role in secret US-Iran negotiations and it had been largely successful in maintaining a healthy balance in relations with Riyadh and Tehran. Oman and Iran were planning a gas pipeline, which would cement their diplomatic closeness with economic interdependence. UAE, on the other hand, although aligned with Riyadh on regional affairs, had its own set of economic and security calculations with respect to Iran, in light of the huge trade with Iran totaling more than seventeen billion dollars in 2017, compared to the paltry Iran-Saudi trade.[38] Dubai was the regional hub for re-exporting Iranian businesses, often relying on boats ferrying goods to Iran only 150 km away. In the previous round of sanctions, Dubai's trade with Iran actually grew, serving as a venue for global companies to deal with Iran. Despite official statements assuring the United States of their compliance with the new sanctions, UAE leaders were apt to let history repeat itself and reap the economic benefits of Iran trade as much as possible, that is, without incurring Washington's wrath.[39] Bahrain among the GCC states was closest to the Saudi stance against Iran as its ruling elite was contested by a dissident movement among the majority Shiites drawing sympathy from Iran. As a result of their policy differences and their different "threat perceptions," the GCC had not been able to determine any roadmap in future relations with Iran. Rising tensions between United States and Iran and the possibility of their showdown in Persian Gulf affecting the flow of oil had was a cause of worry and had moved some of the GCC oil states like Kuwait to seek to defuse the crisis by reaching out to Iran just as they tried to bolster their own defense by procuring more arms and entering into new military arrangements. Their quest for security was mortgaged, however, to the intricacies of Iran-Saudi relations and the fate of their bitter rivalry. By all accounts, in the Persian Gulf, the road from Washington to Tehran traveled through Riyadh and it was inconceivable that US-Iran relations could be normalized in an atmosphere of hostility between Iran and Saudi Arabia. Therefore, it was incumbent to understand the dynamics of power relations between the Gulf's two biggest powerhouses, whose rivalry cut across all religious, ideological, geopolitical, geoeconomic, and strategic dimensions.

IRAN-SAUDI RELATIONS REVISITED

Iran and Saudi Arabia established diplomatic relations in 1928. In 1966, King Faisal visited Iran and the (second) Pahlavi Shah returned the visit in 1968. These visits resulted in an amicable resolution of their disputes over the islands of Farsi and Arabia in the Persian Gulf, by agreeing on Iran's possession of the former and Saudi ownership of the latter, designating the territorial waters for each island. During the Cold War, Iran and Saudi Arabia shared concerns about the threat of communism and the Soviet expansion in the Persian Gulf. Both countries were also opposed to the radical Arab nationalism epitomized by Egypt's Gamal Abdul Nasser. The pan-Arab nationalists tried to sow divisions between Tehran and Riyadh by labeling the Persian Gulf as "the Arabian Gulf" and the southern Iranian province of Khuzestan as "Arabestan." In 1968, Britain's announcement of its decision to vacate its forces from the Persian Gulf culminated a few years later in a new geostrategic situation known as the "twin pillar," whereby Iran and Saudi Arabia assumed the primary responsibility for peace and security in the region, in conformity with the foreign policy approach of the Nixon administration, which came to be known as the "Nixon doctrine." Both countries played a leading role in the OPEC cartel's price revolution and shared similar energy policies. Yet, despite their common security concerns and similar monarchical systems, prior to the Islamic revolution of 1979 relations between Iran and Saudi Arabia were not always harmonious. Saudis were concerned about the rapid pace of Iran's military modernization and military dominance in the region, and the issue of Bahrain's independence and Iran's reluctant forfeiture of its historical claim to Bahrain was also a sour point for some time. Another source of tension was Iran's takeover of the three islands of Abu Moussa, Little Tunb and Big Tunb in 1971, also claimed by the UAE.

The 1979 Islamic revolution in Iran proved a watershed in Iran-Saudi relations, effectively sounding the death knell for decades of amicable ties between the two countries by setting into motion a long period of mutual recriminations. Tehran's revolutionary government led by Ayatollah Ruhollah Khomeini castigated the "corrupt" Saudis as "American puppets" and the Saudis accused it of seeking to subvert their political system through "exporting the revolution" ethos. The Iran-Iraq war of the 1980s worsened these relations as the Saudis threw their weight behind Iraq's Baathist regime that marketed itself among the conservative GCC states as a "bulwark" against revolutionary Iran. These states led by Saudi Arabia played a key role in keeping Iraq's economy afloat by providing generous financial assistance while whipping up support for Saddam Hussain's war efforts in the Arab world. At the end of the Iran-Iraq war and the implementation of the UN cease-fire resolution 598, Saudi Arabia adjusted its policy by welcoming the new developments, for example, King Fahd openly asked the Saudi interior minister to take steps toward resolving problems related to Iranians making the annual pilgrimage to Saudi Arabia. Soon after, diplomatic relations were restored, respective embassies re-opened and bilateral ties improved after the Iraqi invasion of Kuwait and the subsequent 1991 Gulf war as Iran backed Kuwait's sovereignty and proved its "goodwill" to its southern Gulf Arab neighbors.[40]

Iran's constructive behavior in the first Gulf war put Tehran and Riyadh on a friendlier path, reflected in the exchanges of high-ranking delegates between the two countries in the 1990s. Case in point, Iran's foreign minister

Ali Akbar Velayati visited Riyadh in March 1997 and the Saudis reciprocated by sending a high-level delegation to the 1997 summit of the Organization of Islamic Conference (OIC) in Tehran. Iran's then-president Mohammad Khatami, a known moderate, spoke at the conference, hammering the need for a "dialogue among civilizations" and stating that Islamic nations and the West were "not necessarily in conflict and contradiction in all their manifestations and consequences." Khatami's discourse also focused on "inter-civilizational" dialogue and was considered an important gesture from Iran with respect to Sunni-Shiite dialogue, resonating with improvement in relations between Sunni Saudis and Shiite Iranians, deemed important by the Saudis in light of their own Shiite minority.

During Khatami's presidency, Iran-Saudi relations were put on a stable and friendly path as bilateral relations encompassing various fields including economic, educational, and security, grew at a steady pace. Tehran and Riyadh coordinated their OPEC moves over such issues as oil pricing and production quotas for the member states, reflecting the depth of their closeness. A major indicator of warming relations was their cooperation on security affairs, reflected in a "low-security" agreement in 1997 aimed at criminal maritime activities in the Persian Gulf and combating terrorist organizations endangering the region's stability. The latter was, however, deeply impacted by the seismic shocks of post-9/11 wreaking havoc in Iraq and Afghanistan.

With respect to Afghanistan, the Taliban during their rule (1996–2001) enjoyed cordial diplomatic relations with Saudi Arabia and UAE (as well as Pakistan) while opposing Iran and murdering Iranian diplomats (at the Iranian consulate in Mazar Sharif), which brought Iran to the precipice of a military invasion. Iran welcomed the fall of anti-Iran Taliban in 2001 and engaged in direct diplomacy with the United States over the shape of the post-Taliban political order in Afghanistan. Iran was wary of a Saudi-Pakistan concert that sought to create protected zones for Taliban inside Afghanistan, as well as of a new Saudi assertiveness with respect to Lebanon, where Iran's protege, the Hizbollah, grew more and more powerful and became a political force in Lebanese national politics in no small measure due to Iran's backing, viewed with alarm by Saudi leadership. In February 2016, the kingdom withheld a four-billion-dollar aid package to Lebanon in retaliation for Lebanon's "official neutrality" in Saudi-Iranian rivalry. Saudi Arabia also spearheaded a campaign to have the GCC and the Arab League declared the Hezbollah a terrorist organization. Thus, Lebanon became a theater of Iran-Saudi competition threatening the nightmare scenario of spiraling into a civil war with sharpened Shiite-Sunni hostilities. Lebanon's fragile democracy, featuring a plethora of confessional groups as well as secular parties and political organizations, glued the multi-religious nation together and as of this writing that scenario has not materialized, yet it would be far-fetched to argue that the threat had passed, given Lebanon's vulnerability to foreign meddling.

But, more than Lebanon, it was the post-invasion developments in Iraq, heralding the rise of a Shiite-dominated polity in league with Tehran that raised the fears of a "Shiite Crescent" spelling trouble for the Sunni-Wahhabist Saudi Arabia. Initially unwilling to reconcile themselves with the idea of a Shiite-run Iraq, the Saudis initially antagonized the Iraqi Shiites by pushing for the release of Saddam Hussain and the resurrection of Iraq's Baath Party (to act as an anti-Iran influence bulwark). Faced with a realignment of regional powers benefiting Iran, widely viewed as a "winner" of America's invasions of Iraq and Afghanistan, the Saudis then responded by backing the Sunni insurgents in Iraq and the armed opposition in "post-Arab Spring" Syria as of 2011. Both the Saudi government and private Saudi donors were important foreign backers of militant jihadist groups that would ultimately extend far beyond Syria. Saudi Arabia and Qatar backed different groups in Syria and by 2013 Riyadh had sought to displace Qatar as the principal Arab supporter of the Syrian opposition. With Saudi Arabia and Iran backing opposing sides in Iraq and Syria, the stage was thus set for one of the bleakest chapters in the bilateral relations between the two countries, spilling over to a number of other countries including Lebanon and Yemen. This rivalry reached a new peak after the onset of a self-proclaimed Caliphate by the Sunni extremists of ISIS (also known as Daesh), after their successful takeover of a vast swath of Iraqi and Syrian territory in 2014.

From Iran's vantage, the Daesh phenomenon was an offshoot of Saudi Wahhabi extremism, which viewed Shiites as apostles befitting extermination, thus representing an existential threat. Countless evidence of ISIS atrocities against the Shiite population in various Iraqi and Syrian cities and town confirmed this Iranian perception, not to mention ISIS's own virulently anti-Shiite propaganda (echoing the position of some Saudi clerics broadcast on state-owned media). In addition to ISIS, other Sunni extremist groups such as the al-Nusra Front were on the US terrorism list and yet were backed by the Saudis in an effort to undermine the Iran-Syria-Hizbollah "axis of resistance." This occurred increasingly in tandem with the Israelis, who clandestinely provided military support to the jihadists fighting pro-Iran forces in Syria.[41] Coinciding with the on-going battles in Syria and Iraq was another regional crisis, in Yemen, which presented itself as an opportunity for Iran to hit back at Saudi Arabia and its GCC allies by backing the Houthi rebels sharing Shiite credentials with their brethren in Iran, Iraq, and Lebanon.[42] Although none of these crises should be reduced to the Iran-Saudi rivalry and each should be carefully studied in terms of their own political and historical root causes, there was nonetheless an organic connection between them stemming from the impact of religion-ideological and geopolitical competition between two opposed "power blocs," one led by Iran and the other by Saudi Arabia pitched against each other in an intense "proxy war" over regional dominance.[43] Parallel to these developments was yet another crisis, Iran nuclear crisis, which served the Saudi interest as it led to the imposition of international sanctions on Iran weakening the Iranian regime, particularly as the Saudis resorted to playing the "oil card" by boosting production in order to assist with the oil embargo on Iran. Accusing Iran of meddling in the internal affairs of Arab countries, the Saudis after an initial nod to the JCPOA reversed themselves under the conviction that the nuclear deal will exacerbate regional tensions by virtue of strengthening Iran and its protege forces fighting the Saudi-backed forces throughout the region. Tensions spiked in 2016, when a well-known Saudi Shia cleric, Nimr al-Nimr, was executed by Riyadh after being found guilty of supporting "terrorism." His death led to attacks on Saudi diplomatic compounds in Tehran, leading Riyadh to cut ties with Tehran. Later in the year, a Saudi court sentenced fifteen people to death for allegedly spying for Iran; most of them were members of the kingdom's Shia minority. In May 2016, Tehran banned Iranian citizens from traveling to Saudi Arabia to perform Hajj following disagreements regarding a stampede at the previous year's pilgrimage which cost the lives of 2,000 pilgrims—including 464 Iranians. From Iran's vantage, the incident cast doubt on the kingdom's efficiency in hosting the rituals. Some Western scholars such as Marc Lynch have interpreted Saudis' moves as a reaction to warming ties between the United States and Iran. According to Lynch, "Saudi Arabia views Iran's reintegration into the international order and its evolving relationship with Washington as a profound threat to its own regional position. Mobilizing anti-Shiite sectarianism is a familiar move in its effort to sustain Iranian containment and isolation."[44]

The new polarization between Tehran and Riyadh in effect froze Obama's tilt toward a "balanced" approach in the Persian Gulf at its infancy, thus forcing the White House to prioritize its traditional alliance with Saudi Arabia and to eschew any desire to telescope the JCPOA to a normalization of relations with Tehran. Together with Israel's incessant campaign against the JCPOA, vilified as a "historic mistake," the Saudi propaganda depicted Iran as a new "Reich" on the march determined to dominate its neighbors, and Obama's thaw with Tehran as "appeasement."[45] In the short run, two important factors assisted the Saudi aims on Iran. First, the impressive victories of pro-Iran forces in Iraq and Syria, increasingly routing the Saudi-backed groups and coalition of forces and, second, the post-JCPOA concert of Russia-Turkey-Iran in Syria, which marginalized the anti-Damascus front and, simultaneously, demonstrated a more assertive Russia in Middle East affairs and a less NATO-reliable Turkey throwing its lots with two of America's implacable rivals, altogether representing a strategic setback for the United States and its regional allies. All these (geo) strategic concerns and considerations were fully taken advantage of by Donald Trump, who questioned Obama's foreign priorities and accused his administration of turning its back on America's allies, particularly in the Middle East. Trump's focused anti-Iranian U-turn on the JCPOA (and potential detente with Iran) must therefore be understood in the context of Middle East realignment benefiting Iran and its allies, who declared victory in the battles for influence in Iraq and Syria, depicting Saudi Arabia as a losing party that made "the bad choices" and chose "the wrong partners" in the regional conflicts gone sourly for their side, to paraphrase Iran's foreign minister, Mohammad Javad Zarif. According to Zarif, Saudi Arabia continues to compound its own problems by repeating the past mistakes instead of drawing the right lessons from its debacle in the Syrian conflict. But, with Iraq's sovereignty restored and the bloody conflict in Syria nearly over after seven grueling years, from Iran's perspective, the Saudis were amenable to revise their approach, accept the status quo, patch up their differences with Baghdad and recognize the Syrian government, which they failed to dislodge after considerable investment in Syrian rebels and out of area jihadists who swarmed the country. A strong clue that this may indeed be the case was presented by the restoration of diplomatic relations between Damascus and a number of GCC states, as well as by attempts to re-admit Syria to the Arab League. With the possibility of Syria lapsing back to another round of vicious conflict practically non-existent, the stage was gradually set for a new chapter in Iran-Saudi relations, particularly if the conflict in Yemen, another flashing point, subsided as well, in light of a UN-brokered cease-fire and related peace negotiations in Sweden that held the promise of peaceful resolution of that particular conflict. If the fragile cease-fire in Yemen culminated in a veritable end to the catastrophic conflict affecting the lives of millions of civilians, then an important point of contention between Iran and Saudi Arabia, which like the United States accused Iran of giving arms and missiles to the Houthi rebels, would be removed. But, even under a power-sharing scheme, Yemen was bound to be vulnerable to Iranian influence, which, in turn, raised the question of Saudi "end-game" in Yemen, notwithstanding their stated apprehension about "another Hizbollah" at their doorsteps. For Iran, on the other hand, leveraging their influence in Yemen and elsewhere in the region vis-a-vis the United States and its sanctions regime on Iran was an important consideration that militated against the option of leaving Yemen, where Iran's influence extended to the Red Sea and its important Bab al-Mandab waterway. In a worst-case scenario, Iran contemplated the idea of closing not only the Strait of Hormuz but also other waterways including the narrow strait of Bab al-Mandab connecting the Gulf of Aden to the Red Sea—on which the Saudis relied for the shipment of a significant portion of their crude oil. In July 2018, after the Houthi rebels fired on two Saudi oil tankers, Riydah halted its oil shipments through the Red Sea and while it resumed them in August, nevertheless the fear of future attacks and insecurity of this shipping lane remained.

Yet, in the midst of their stormy relations, there was a glimmer of hope for a future thaw in Iran-Saudi bilateral ties. Previously, the Saudis had ruled out dialogue with Iran, due to its perceived ambitions "to control the Islamic world." The Rouhani government made a concerted effort to assure the Saudis of Iran's benign intentions, for example, "We don't have to fight; we don't need to fight. We don't need to try to exclude each other from the scene in the Middle East." Iran proposed the idea of a forum for security dialogue in the Persian Gulf and reiterated its long-standing proposal for a "collective security" framework. With respect to Yemen, Iran floated a "four-point plan" to end the conflict, prioritizing sustainable ceasefire, humanitarian assistance, intra-Yemeni dialogue, and "establishment of a broad-based government." In December 2018, Tehran announced support for the Yemen peace talks transpiring in Sweden. The foreign ministry urged "all Yemeni sides to adopt trust and confidence-building measures, preparing the ground for achieving a comprehensive agreement to put an end to the suffering of all Yemenis—including ending the brutal blockade that they are subjected to."

Slowly, with the winds of war in Syria abating and the quagmire in Yemen continuing, the Saudi made small adjustments, such as by allowing Switzerland to represent Iranian interests in Saudi Arabia then permitting an Iranian diplomat to function at the consular office, and by resolving the dispute over Iranian pilgrimage to Mecca. Another adjustment was replacing the outspoken Saudi Foreign Minister Adel al-Jubeir, who had repeatedly complained of Iran's "nefarious activities" and had also cast the Saudi rivalry with Iran in Manichean terms by asserting that the Kingdom was "a beacon of light" against the "dark" Iran. The new foreign minister, Ibrahim al-Assaf, was a former finance minister who had been detailed in 2017 during a crackdown on corruption, facing a complex regional scene marked with the growing role of Turkey, Russia, and Iran, the defeat of ISIS, and US withdrawal from Syria. A big question was whether Riyadh would follow UAE's footstep of resuming diplomatic relations with the government of Bashar al-Assad? Another important question was how to proceed with respect to Iran, that is, dialogue or confrontation?

Certainly, confidence-building steps were necessary in order to improve the climate for a thaw in Iran-Saudi relations. Iran could demonstrate its goodwill by using its influence with the Houthi-led government for a political and diplomatic solution to the deadly quagmire. Also, to assuage the Saudi and other GCC states' worries about Iran's "hegemonic intentions," Iran could revise its rhetoric favoring Iran's "primacy" which convinced the other side that Iran's ultimate intention was to become the "unchallenged power" (*ghodrat-e bela monaze*) in the region. To be sure, many Western, and even some US officials, have admittted the fact that Iran is a leading power in the region and they have to accept and get along with Iran as a significant regional power. The Iranian discourse often conflated "primacy" with "regional power" and undermined the assurances that Tehran was content with the Saudis as their "co-equal." The Iran primacy thesis had permeated Iranian official documents, such as the "20-Year Strategic Outlook (2005–2025) that spoke of the need for Iran to gain primacy in its region in economic and technological terms. Steeped in a traditional economic perspective, this document did not mention "interdependence" and was insufficiently in tune with the dictates of globalization and its regional context. In military terms, no single Persian Gulf power had the capability to dominate the region and the Iranian rhetoric of primacy was counterproductive and fueled the region's bifurcated security structure reflecting a polarized reality. For some Iranian authors, this rhetoric was connected by some authors to "Iranian 'exceptionalism' stemming from a cultural pre-disposition in the belief "in the inherent superiority of Iranian civilization."[46] For others, including some members of Iran's parliament, Iran's primacy was the result of exaggerated claims, for example, "three Arab capitals have today ended up in the hands of Iran and belong to the Islamic Iranian revolution."[47] Within the Iranian national security discourse, on the other hand, Iran's support for the "oppressed people of Yemen" was in tune with the post-revolutionary ethos reflected in Article 154 of the Islamic Constitution that emphasizes "while scrupulously refraining from all forms of interference in the internal affairs of other nations, it supports the just struggles of the *Mustazafin* against the *Mustakbirun* (the oppressed against the tyrants) in every corner of the globe." There is, however, a contradiction between the first and second part of this article, which needs to be resolved, for example, by putting the accent on self-restraint and respect for the sovereignty of other nations.

Mirror imaging each other to some extent, the assertive regional policies of Iran and Saudi Arabia posed a security dilemma for both countries, neither of whom could underwrite regional supremacy on their own, and who sought divergent means to overcome this dilemma, with Saudi Arabia relying on US protectorate power and Iran beefing up its maritime and other hard power.[48] A frank admission by Iran's foreign minister that no power can or should dominate the Persian Gulf was a step in the right direction—that had yet to be echoed by the country's military leaders, who prioritized "regional autonomy" and the expulsion of the United States and other foreign forces from the region, particularly after the onset of new US sanctions. "The US must leave the Persian Gulf" thus became a common refrain in Iran's military hierarchy, backed by the Supreme Leader who shared this sentiment. Increased tension with the United States had cemented Iran's soft power discourse that was framed epistemologically within a hierarchical paradigm which, implicitly if not explicitly, divided the region's countries and imagined them according to hierarchical categories. Still, there was a residual ambiguity here stemming from the fact that in Iraq Washington effectively cooperated with Iran. Although defeated, ISIS still represented a threat that had the potential for a "second comeback." The terrorist group had managed to carry an impressive attack on Iran's parliament in September 2018, reminding the nation that the emergence of a "post-ISIS" milieu was far from complete, mandating the continuation of Iran's counter-terrorism strategy that extended beyond Iran's borders. In the Persian Gulf, the Iranian and Saudi counter-terrorism efforts were not in conflict and in fact showed signs of a potential synergy that could become the basis for future security cooperation. This depended to some extent on the resolution of the outstanding conflicts in the region as well as on US policy in the region which, as stated above, revolved around the threat of Iran in the post-ISIS context and therefore by definition was opposed to a thaw in Iran-Saudi "cold war." In a word, Washington's rollback strategy moved along the track of "anti-diplomacy" whereas the Persian Gulf dynamic increasingly steered in the opposite direction of inter-state diplomacy and was in a sense incongruent with Trump's Iran policy even though that policy originated partly in response to heightened demand from the Arab states of the Persian Gulf for a more vigorous anti-Iran stance. The latter was thus put in the predicament of being forced to bandwagon with the United States against Iran at an inopportune time when the regional transition toward a post-conflict subsystem mandated the stability of their relations with their ancient Persian neighbor. Without an enduring peaceful relation between Iran and its Arab neighbors in the Persian Gulf, the region was destined to be in perpetual turmoil, even more so with the advent of Trump's presidency that had made it's Iran rollback strategy a defining characteristic of US foreign policy. Yet, the shifting sands in the Persian Gulf affecting the national security calculus of all littoral states posed a challenge to Trump's Iran policy that by all indications had little chance of success in causing a re-entrenchment of Iranian power within the confines of its national borders, simply as a result of the complex national security priorities of Iran. The rollback strategy was offensive in nature, conveyed a sense of urgency, and was potentially onerous, with uncertain results, as it could culminate in an ethnic implosion of Iran with spill-over effects on its neighbors. It also implied an enhanced US military presence in the region, highlighted in December 2018 by the return of US aircraft carriers to the Gulf, which, in turn, augmented the foreign dependence of the oil sheikhdoms and played into Iran's hands as Iran portrayed itself as the guardian of region's "sovereignty." Indeed, Iran's counter-compellence strategy in the Persian Gulf was to demonstrate the futility of that strategy in achieving either a regime change or wholesale policy change on the part of the Islamic Republic, a failure that many in Iran and the region hoped would propel Washington toward a less confrontational approach reminiscent of the past containment approach. A solid reason for this expectation was Trump's own antipathy to the idea of committing US resources for another Middle East war, which had resulted in the decision to pull out of Syria (discussed below), even to the point of compromising the very pillar of Iran containment by stating "Iran can do what it wants in Syria." In sharp contrast to the position of his hawkish advisers, Trump had never identified the role of US military in Syria in terms of containing Iran and, therefore, there was no flip flop, only a noticeable attenuation of the Iran-phobic prism through which Trump had designed the policy of the United States for the Middle East during the first two years of his presidency. "Russia, Iran and Syria have been the biggest beneficiaries of the long term U.S. Policy of destroying ISIS in Syria—natural enemies." This tweet by Trump in mid-January 2019 alone highlighted a built-in ambiguity of the rollback strategy. By hinting at a common interest with Iran and Russia inside Syria, Trump was in effect conceding that the Manichean enemy image of Iran was a candidate for reconsideration. In contrast, Trump's foreign policy team showed no sign of sharing his point of view on Iran in Syria and, Bolton, in particular, was faulted for his obstructionism and disloyalty to Trump. Conceptually, such developments called for the need to distinguish between Trump the president and Trump administration, instead of assuming that the latter is simply a predicate of the former. A policy tug-of-war over Syria could easily snowball to affect the whole edifice of Trump's Iran policy, particularly if Syria pull out somehow proved to be a prelude for a Trumpian re-thinking and re-consideration of the rollback strategy toward Tehran.

NOTES

1. "The National Security Strategy of the United States of America," *White House*, December 2017, https://www.whitehouse.gov/wp-content/uploads/2017/12/NSS-Final-12-18-2017-0905.pdf.

2. Jamie MacIntyre, "Mattis: Iran Is the Biggest Threat to Mideast Peace," *Washington Examiner*, April 22, 2016, https://www.washingtonexaminer.com/mattis-iran-is-the-biggest-threat-to-mideast-peace.

3. David Remnick, "Going the Distance: On and Off the Road with Barack Obama," *New Yorker*, January 27, 2014, https://www.newyorker.com/magazine/2014/01/27/going-the-distance-david-remnick.

4. "UN Panel of Experts report on Yemen," *United Nations*, January 2018, http://undocs.org/en/S/2018/68.

5. Missy Ryan and Kareem Fahim, "Trump Administration Is Showcasing Weapons to Allege Iran Is Increasing Its Role in Yemen," *Washington Post*, December

14, 2017, https://www.washingtonpost.com/world/national-security/trump-administr
ation-showcases-weapons-to-allege-iran-is-increasing-its-role-in-yemen/2017/12/14/
cf08d31a-e106-11e7-89e8-edec16379010_story.html?noredirect=on&utm_term=.7
1553bdcde1e.

6. Michelle Nichols, "Two Missile Launchers Found in Yemen Appear to Be
from Iran—U.N.," *Reuters*, December 11, 2018, https://www.reuters.com/article/us-
iran-nuclear-un/two-missile-launchers-found-in-yemen-appear-to-be-from-iran-u-n-
idUSKBN1OA225.

7. "Yemen's Houthis Finance War with Fuel from Iran," *Middle East Eye*, January 18, 2019, https://www.middleeasteye.net/news/yemen-houthis-finance-war-fuel
-iran-un-report-377829955.

8. "Iran's UN Envoy Dismisses Saudi Claims on Yemen Arms Transfer," *Tasnim News*, September 29, 2016, https://www.tasnimnews.com/en/news/2016/09/29
/1199518/iran-s-un-envoy-dismisses-saudi-claims-on-yemen-arms-transfer. For an
overview of Yemen's pre-conflict missile arsenal and the North Korea connection,
see "Yemeni Rebels Enhance Missile Campaign," *Jane's Intelligence Review*, 2017,
https://www.janes.com/images/assets/330/72330/Yemeni_rebels_enhance_ballist
ic_missile_campaign.pdf.

9. Thomas Shanker and Robert F. Worth, "Yemen Seizes Sailboat Filled with
Weapons, and U.S. Points to Iran," *New York Times*, January 28, 2013, https://ww
w.nytimes.com/2013/01/29/world/middleeast/29military.html. Also, "Third Illicit
Arms Shipment in Recent Weeks Seized in Arabian Sea," *US Navy*, April 4, 2016,
http://www.navy.mil/submit/display.asp?story_id=93990.

10. Jonathan Saul, "Exclusive: Iran Revolutionary Guards Find New Route to
Arm Yemen Rebels," *Reuters*, p. 6, August 1, 2017, https://www.reuters.com/article/
us-gulf-kuwait-iran-exclusive/exclusive-iran-revolutionary-guards-find-new-route-to
-arm-yemen-rebels-idUSKBN1AH4I4.

11. "Secretary Pompeo's Remarks to Members of the Senate," *US Department
of State*, November 28, 2018, https://www.state.gov/secretary/remarks/2018/11/
index.htm.

12. Quoted in "After the Deal, a New Iran Strategy," *The Heritage Foundation*,
May 21, 2018, https://www.heritage.org/defense/event/after-the-deal-new-iran-st
rategy?_ga=2.85216479.712759958.1548108226-131213565.1548108226.

13. Quoted in Mathew Lee, "Trump's Evolving Foreign Policy Challenges US
Top Diplomat," *Washington Post*, January 14, 2019, https://www.washingtonpos
t.com/world/middle_east/yemen-iran-khashoggi-murder-top-pompeos-talks-in-sa
udi/2019/01/14/0ccc754c-17c7-11e9-b8e6-567190c2fd08_story.html?utm_term=.a8
ad3af4248e.

14. Maria Abi-Habib, "U.S., Middle East Allies Explore Arab Military Coalition",
Wall Street Journal, February 15, 2017, https://www.wsj.com/articles/u-s-middle-
east-allies-explore-arab-military-coalition-1487154600.

15. Quoted in Agnes Helou, "What's Standing in the Way of an Arab NATO?"
Defense News, November 20, 2018, https://www.defensenews.com/global/mideast-af
rica/2018/11/20/whats-standing-in-the-way-of-an-arab-nato/.

16. Stephan M. Walt, "Making the Middle East Worse, Trump-Style," *Foreign Policy*, June 9, 2017, https://foreignpolicy.com/2017/06/09/making-the-middle-east-worse-trump-style-saudi-arabia-qatar-iran-israel/.

17. Steve Simon and Jonathan Stevenson, "Trump's Dangerous Obsession with Iran," *Foreign Affairs*, August 13, 2018, https://www.foreignaffairs.com/articles/iran/2018-08-13/trumps-dangerous-obsession-iran. Iranians concurred and Foreign Minister Zarif repeatedly sent tweet messages that attributed a psychological irrationality behind the American campaign against Iran, for example, "Pure obsession with Iran is more and more like the behavior of persistently failing psychotic stalkers." Javad Zarif, *Twitter Message*, January 8, 2019.

18. Trevor Thrall and Jane Cramer, *American Foreign Policy and the Politics of Fear: Threat Inflation since 9/11* (Abingdon: Routledge, 2009): 1.

19. See, for example, Michael T. Klare, *American Arms Supermarket* (Austin: University of Texas Press, 1985). A related work is by Clayton Thomas, "Arms Sales in the Middle East: Trends and Analytical Perspectives for U.S. Policy," *Congressional Research Service*, October 11, 2017, https://fas.org/sgp/crs/mideast/R44984.pdf.

20. Daniel Cebul, "New F-16s Are Headed to Bahrain," *Defensenews*, June 25, 2018, https://www.defensenews.com/air/2018/06/25/new-f-16s-are-headed-to-bahrain/.

21. Mohammad Javad Zarif, " 'Beautiful Military Equipment' Can't Buy Middle East Peace," *New York Times*, March 26, 2017, https://www.nytimes.com/2017/05/26/opinion/us-saudi-arabia-arms-deal-iran.html.

22. "Asia and the Middle East Lead Rising Trend in Arms Imports, US Exports Grow Substantially, Says SIPRI," *Stockholm International Peace Research Institute*, March 12, 2018, https://www.sipri.org/news/press-release/2018/asia-and-middle-east-lead-rising-trend-arms-imports-us-exports-grow-significantly-says-sipri.

23. Anthony H. Cordesman, "Military Spending and Arms Sales in the Gulf," *Center for Strategic and International Studies*, April 28, 2015, https://www.csis.org/analysis/military-spending-and-arms-sales-gulf.

24. Jordain Carney, "Senate Passes Resolution Naming Crown Prince 'Responsible' for Khashoggi Slaying," *The Hill*, December 13, 2018, https://thehill.com/homenews/senate/421287-senate-passes-resolution-naming-crown-prince-responsible-for-khashoggi. Some pundits in the West argued that the Khashoggi "event" had weakened Saudi Arabia and indirectly strengthened Iran. See, for example, Martin Chulov, "Middle East: Saudi Arabia Weakened as Iran Plans to Consolidate Gains," *The Guardian*, December 27, 2018, https://www.theguardian.com/world/2018/dec/27/middle-east-saudia-arabia-yemen-war-killing-jamal-khashoggi?fbclid=IwAR1iqR15T6hW3zAMEkIlc5m9xkOMaM1LHQax23axypGxuFYkbOBtdtmu07A. Also, Kaveh Afrasiabi, "Iran and the Khashoggi Crisis," *Lobelog*, October 22, 2018, https://lobelog.com/iran-and-the-khashoggi-crisis/.

25. "Senate Votes to End US Military Support for Saudis in Yemen," *The Guardian*, December 13, 2018, https://www.theguardian.com/us-news/2018/dec/13/senate-yemen-saudis-trump-resolution.

26. Deidre Shesgreen, "Trump's Foreign Policy Agenda Faces a Gauntlet of House Democrats Led by New York's Eliot Engel," *USA TODAY*, November 26, 2018.

27. Thomas W. Lippman, "Has Saudi Arabia Finally Gone Too Far?" *Lobelog*, October 9, 2019, https://lobelog.com/has-saudi-arabia-finally-gone-too-far/.

28. "Trump: Middle Eastern States 'Wouldn't Last a Week' Without U.S. Protection," *Washington Post*, April 25, 2018, https://www.washingtonpost.com/video/wor ld/trump-middle-east-states-wouldnt-last-a-week-without-us-protection/2018/04/26/ fa2f0a1a-4974-11e8-8082-105a446d19b8_video.html?noredirect=on&utm_term=.eb 487245b42a.

29. Zachary Laub, "Yemen in Crisis," *Council on Foreign Relations*, April 19, 2016, https://www.cfr.org/backgrounder/yemen-crisis. Also, Ginny Hill, *Yemen Endures: Civil War, Saudi Adventurism and the Future of Arabia* (New York: Oxford University Press, 2017).

30. Joseph Kechichian, "Trends in Saudi National Security," *The Middle East Journal* 53, no. 2 (Spring 1999), 232.

31. "Statement from President Donald J. Trump on Standing with Saudi Arabia," *White House*, November 20, 2018, https://www.whitehouse.gov/briefings-statements/ statement-president-donald-j-trump-standing-saudi-arabia/.

32. Jeffrey Heller and Stephen Kalin, "Israel Has Held Secret Talks with Saudi Arabia over Iran Threat, Says Minister", *Independent*, November 20, 2017, https:// www.independent.co.uk/news/world/middle-east/israel-saudi-arabia-secret-talks-iran -threat-middle-east-yuval-steinitz-benjamin-netanyahu-crown-a8064566.html.

33. "It's the best equipment in the world but if they don't buy it from us, they're going to buy it from Russia or they're going to buy it from China or they're going to buy it from other countries." Quoted in Alexander Bolton, "Trump Defends $110B Arms Sales to Saudi Arabia," *The Hill*, October 13, 2018, https://thehill.com/homen ews/administration/411271-trump-defends-110-billion-us-arms-sale-to-saudi-arabia. Nearly half the US arms exports went to the Middle East. See, Saeed Kamali Dehghan, "Nearly Half of US Arms Exports Go to the Middle East," *Guardian*, March 12, 2018, https://www.theguardian.com/world/2018/mar/12/nearly-half-of-us-arms-e xports-go-to-the-middle-east.

34. Mike Pompeo, "The U.S.-Saudi Partnership Is Vital," *Wall Street Journal*, November 27, 2018, https://www.wsj.com/articles/the-u-s-saudi-partnership-is-vi tal-1543362363.

35. See, for example, Tony Badran, "Standing with Saudi Arabia," *Tabletmag*, December 2, 2018, https://www.tabletmag.com/jewish-news-and-politics/middle-ea st/275697/trump-saudi-arabia. For an opposite view, see Daniel B. Shapiro, "Opinion: Trump's Saudi Statement is a Moral Abdication and Strategic Failure," *NPR*, November 21, 2018, https://www.npr.org/2018/11/21/669983971/opinion-trumps -saudi-statement-is-a-moral-abdication-and-strategic-failure.

36. "A Year Later, Iran Is the Big Winner of the Qatar Embargo," *Bloomberg*, June 5, 2018, https://www.bloomberg.com/news/articles/2018-06-06/a-year-later-i ran-is-the-big-winner-of-the-qatar-embargo.

37. "Kuwait Emir Welcomes Close Ties with Iran," *Tehran Times*, December 18, 2018, https://www.tehrantimes.com/news/430839/Kuwait-Emir-welcomes-close-tie s-with-Iran.

38. "Iran-Saudi Trade in Retrospect," *Financial Tribune*, June 9, 2016, https://fi nancialtribune.com/articles/economy-domestic-economy/33819/iran-saudi-trade-in-r etrospect.

39. "US Sanctions on Iran Affect Trade with UAE," *Financial Tribune*, August 14, 2018, https://financialtribune.com/articles/economy-business-and-markets/917 99/us-sanctions-on-iran-affect-trade-with-uae.

40. For more on this, see, Kaveh L. Afrasiabi, *After Khomeini: New Directions in Iran's Foreign Policy* (Boulder, CO: Westview, 1995).

41. "Israel Secretly Armed and Funded 12 Syrian Rebel Groups, Report Says," *Haaretz*, September 8, 2018, https://www.haaretz.com/middle-east-news/syria/in-syria-israel-secretly-armed-and-funded-12-rebel-groups-1.6462729.

42. Mareike Transfeld, "Iran's Small Hand in Yemen," *Carnegie Endowment for International Peace*, February 14, 2017, https://carnegieendowment.org/sada/67988.

43. Here, we follow the insights of Nicos Poulantzas on "power bloc" identi-fied as a "contradictory unity of dominant classes or fractions" whose interests are conjectural rather than monolithic. Following the Italian thinker Antonio Gramsci, Poulantzas maintains that the non-hegemonic elements of a power bloc are "incapable (through their own organizational means) of transforming their specific interests into the political interest which would polarize the interests of the other classes and frac-tions of the power bloc." See Nicos Poulantzas, *Classes in Contemporary Capitalism* (London: New Left Books, 1973), 297.

44. Marc Lynch, "Why Saudi Arabia Escalated Middle East's Sectarian Conflict," *Washington Post*, January 4, 2016, https://www.washingtonpost.com/news/monk ey-cage/wp/2016/01/04/why-saudi-arabia-escalated-the-middle-easts-sectarian-conf lict/?noredirect=on&utm_term=.65b7b82bf226.

45. Ahmed Al-Jarallah, "The 3rd Reich to Mullah Republic End Is Same," *Arab Times*, May 5, 2018, http://www.arabtimesonline.com/news/the-3rd-reich-to-mullah-republic-end-is-same/.

46. Sadegh Zibakalam, "Iranian Exceptionalism." In *The Middle East Institute Viewpoints: The Iranian Revolution at 30* (Washington, DC: The Middle East Insti-tute., 200).

47. Quoted in "Sana'a Is the Fourth Arab Capital to Join the Iranian Revolution," *Middle East Monitor*, September 27, 2014, https://www.middleeastmonitor.com/2 0140927-sanaa-is-the-fourth-arab-capital-to-join-the-iranian-revo.

48. "Iran's Foreign and Defense Policies," *Congressional Research Service Report*, January 16, 2019, https://www.everycrsreport.com/reports/R44017.html #fn125.

Chapter 6

War Scenarios and Iran's Defense Strategy

In early 2019, Trump administration's compellence strategy under the guise of a "maximum pressure" campaign against Iran reached a crescendo with the double whammy of officially designating the Islamic Revolutionary Guard Corps (IRGC)—an official branch of Iran's military—as a "Foreign Terrorist Organization" (FTO) and terminating all the exemptions from Iran oil sanctions. These two moves alone represented a substantial escalation of tensions with Iran and elevated the potential for a direct confrontation between the United States and Iran. As "non-declarations of war go, Trump's gauntlet comes very close to the edge," to paraphrase an editorial in *Financial Times*.[1] By reneging on its JCPOA obligations and re-sanctioning Iran in clear violation of the UN Security Council's directive, the Trump administration had effectively given Iran the right to complain of a *casus belli*, particularly since the attempted US oil embargo on Iran was tantamount to economic warfare and threatened the pivotal Middle Eastern country's economic survival. The IRGC's terrorist designation brought it within arm's reach of the 2001 Authorization for Use of Military Force, legislation originally written to provide a legal basis for the invasion of Afghanistan in the wake of 9/11. By claiming that Iran was responsible for the death of 608 American troops in Iraq and that Iran's connection to al-Qaeda "is very clear," to paraphrase Secretary of State Mike Pompeo, the Trump administration provided a further rationale to pile pressures on Iran and turn it into a legitimate military target.[2] However, even short of war, the IRGC's designation represented a deliberate effort to further isolate the Iranian economy by increasing the risks for foreign companies doing business with Iran, in light of the IRGC's heavy involvement in the Iranian economy. This designation entailed criminal penalties for anyone that provided "material support" to the IRGC including "financial services." Coinciding with European efforts to salvage the nuclear deal through a new financial mechanism known as INSTEX, discussed in chapter 4, the US move(s) undermined those efforts by increasing the extent of disincentives for European firms interested in Iran market, a point not lost on European officials who responded to the news on termination of waivers on oil exemptions by sounding upbeat about INSTEX.[3]

From Iran's vantage, these US moves against Iran represented its "endless hostility." Another overt sign of this hostility was the Trump administration's cold-hearted response to the massive flooding that hit Iran in April 2019 killing dozens and displacing tens of thousands. Pompeo faulted the Iranian government for "the mismanagement that has led to this disaster" and refused to make even a symbolic gesture toward the disaster victims in Iran, thus hampering the international efforts to assist Iran.[4] In turn, Iran's foreign minister Zarif lambasted the Trump administration's position as "economic terrorism." Iran's parliament, on the other hand, passed legislation in response to the IRGC designation by labeling the entire US military as "terrorist."[5] As expected, the leaders of revolutionary guards remained defiant and vowed to close the Strait of Hormuz if Iran were to be deprived of the ability to export its oil.[6] The IRGC played a pivotal role in Iran's navy protecting Iran's maritime interests such as patrolling Iran's territorial waters and their "fast boats" had particularly incensed Trump, who had reportedly sought a Pentagon plan to sink those boats that had been harassing the US ships.[7]

THE WAR SCENARIOS

In this section, we probe the various scenarios that splinter from the path of peace and diplomacy and could lead to a war between the United States and Iran. One scenario, as stated earlier, centered on the 2001 Authorization for Use of Military Force Act, whereby the Trump administration, citing the linking of Iran and al-Qaeda terrorists, would commence a war with Iran, bypassing US Congress and obviating the need to receive prior Congressional authorization for a war with Iran. With respect to this scenario, which was a matter of concern to some US lawmakers, Pompeo evaded a direct answer at a Senate hearing in April 2019 while remaining adamant that "there is no doubt there is a connection between the Islamic Republic of Iran and Al-Qaeda. Period, full stop."[8] Understandably, this evoked memories of the 2003 US invasion of Iraq, which was rationalized in part by the allegations of a secretive relationship between Saddam Hussain and al-Qaeda, proved to be false after the invasion. Many experts, as well as some US lawmakers, therefore saw the Iraq war *redux*, that is, a familiar logic of war-making that, in Iran's case, was all the more dubious in light of the longstanding hostilities between the Shiite Iran and the (virulently anti-Shiite) radical Sunni groups such as al-Qaeda and Islamic State. A definitive study by an American think tank poring over the so-called Bin Laden files had found no evidence that Iran collaborated with the 9/11 perpetrators.[9] The conclusions of this study belied Trump's claim that "Iran "supports terrorist proxies and militias such as . . . al Qaeda." Yet, despite widespread skepticism in the security expert community toward such insinuations, the Trump administration clung to them and (tacitly) threatened Iran by repeating them.

Preemptive strike at Iran formed another war scenario, stemming from the Trump administration's persistence in the accusation that Iran was actively pursuing nuclear weapons. Both Trump and his advisers repeatedly called on Iran to "end its pursuit of nuclear weapons" and dispensed with any ambiguity in this regard, for example, "we have little doubt that Iran's leadership is still strategically committed to achieving deliverable nuclear weapons."[10] To prove this allegation, Iran's missile tests were cited, by claiming that Iran's missiles were capable of carrying nuclear warheads and therefore those tests were in violation of UNSC Resolution 2231, which expressly bans such missile tests. Iran, of course, denied that its conventional missiles were for nuclear weapons purposes and insisted that it had already proved its noble nuclear intentions by agreeing to the terms of JCPOA, which by all accounts closed both the uranium and plutonium paths to nuclear weapons. But with Tehran threatening to resume full-scale nuclear work in response to US exit from the JCPOA and the resumption of sanctions, the specter of an American (and or Israeli) raid on Iran's nuclear facilities grew. Trump had repeatedly pledged to prevent the emergence of a "nuclear Iran" and he was pre-disposed toward the use of preemptive strike on Iran in a "worst case scenario" whereby Iran would end its cooperation under the terms of JCPOA and resume its banned programs. In this scenario, there was a direct linkage between the nuclear and the missile programs on the one hand and, on the other, the American and Israeli perception of Iran's nuclear behavior and the necessity of preemptive strike. To be effective, such a strike had to be comprehensive and devastate Iran's nuclear infrastructure, otherwise, it risked being a temporary respite as Iran would be able to rebuild and resurrect its nuclear program within a few years. Indeed, such was the conclusion of most nuclear experts, some pointing at the futility of harboring the illusion that Iran's nuclear weapons program could be effectively neutralized by a preemptive strike.[11] Not only that, the downside of such an action was that it risked angering Iranians to the point of putting aside all their hesitations and make them even more determined to provide the country with a nuclear deterrent similar to North Korea. As a result, a future "North Korea*ization*" of Iran as a direct result of sustained US hostility could not be precluded.[12]

Another potential war scenario centered on anti-Iran provocations by third parties "spoiling for war" to paraphrase Iran's foreign minister, Mohammad

Javad Zarif. According to Zarif, US allies in the region were plotting to provoke a US-Iran confrontation. Speaking at the Asia Society in April 2019,
Zarif pointed to Israeli Prime Minister Benjamin Netanyahu, National Security Adviser John Bolton, the crown prince of the United Arab Emirates
(UAE), Mohamed bin Zayed, and the crown prince of Saudi Arabia, Mohammed bin Salman—dubbing them "the B Team" and claiming that "The B
Team is pushing US policy toward a disaster."[13] Essentially, this would be a
"rent a superpower for proxy war" scenario—that could involve "false flag"
operations whereby, for example, foreign forces dressed as Iranian revolutionary guards would stage an attack on US forces in the region in order to
instigate a massive US military response against Iran. Such a clash could also
occur as a result of a "Gulf of Tonkin incident" in the Persian Gulf, stemming
from false alarms about an Iranian attack on US forces, who would then have
the desired rationale to retaliate against Iran with impunity.[14] According to
some commentators, a US attack on Iran could also come about as a result
of a beleaguered President Trump dealing with mounting domestic political
problems and seeking to boost his re-election chances, who would probably
look "presidential" in a "war of choice" with Iran.[15]

Iran's attempt to deliver on its threats to close the Strait of Hormuz could
also precipitate a war with the United States, which has vowed to keep the
Strait open to international maritime shipping. In case the United States
succeeded in halting the export of Iran's oil and or bringing the country's
exports to close to zero, thus depriving the Iranian government of a lion share
of its budget, then it is perfectly possible that with its back against the wall,
the Iranian government would resort to "brinksmanship" in Persian Gulf
waters, particularly if other regional states such as the UAE and Saudi Arabia
increased oil output in order to compensate for the market loss of Iranian oil
due to US sanctions. In this scenario, Iran retaliates by taking actions such as
mining the Persian Gulf waters, sinking ships, staging war games after war
games, and interdicting oil tankers in order to slow or completely halt their
passage through the Strait of Hormuz. Inviting a US military response, such
an escalatory move by Iran is bound to heighten tensions and lead to a spike
in oil prices, given the likelihood of a major US-Iran showdown—that would
eclipse the prior case of such a clash toward the end of the Iran-Iraq war,
when Iran was bogged down by another enemy, namely Iraq, and the United
States sunk nearly half the Iranian naval force while incurring minimal costs.
Iran now poses a much more formidable military challenge that ought to
make the anti-Iran hawks in the Trump administration think twice about their
military objectives.

Flexing its muscles, Iran's navy has conducted war games in the narrow
waters of the Strait of Hormuz, where up to 30 percent of world oil exports
travels each day. It has test-fired a Fateh 10 radar-guided anti-ship missile

over the Strait in what US military officials called a clear "message to the U.S."[16] With missile batteries on the mainland of the strategically important strait as well as on Iran's Persian Gulf islands, Iran's counter-force capability was certainly no match for US firepower, yet was still capable of inflicting severe pain. In addition to its (mobile) missile arsenal, Iran counted on its submarine fleet, including three Russian-made Kilo-class diesel submarines, several frigates, and corvettes, as well as several hundred missile-equipped boats designed to "swarm" the enemy as part of Iran's strategy of asymmetrical warfare; the latter refers to a military doctrine aimed at addressing the imbalances of power against a more powerful enemy, usually associated with irregular warfare making use of surprise, deception, speed, flexibility, adaptability, decentralization, and highly mobile and maneuverable units. The Iranian doctrine manifests itself "as hit-and-run style, surprise attacks, or the amassing of large numbers of unsophisticated weapons to overwhelm the enemies' defenses."[17]

An enhanced sea-mine capability and Russian sophisticated S-300 batteries also provided Iran much better protection from potential air strikes.[18] Iran's missile threat was the principal reason the US Navy kept a low profile in the Persian Gulf and preferred the relative safety of the Indian Ocean.[19] The United States risked losing a number of its naval assets, including aircraft carriers, in a showdown with Iran. A decade ago, an Oxford University study predicted that the United States would lose several naval vessels in such a scenario, and Iran's lethal power has much increased since then.[20] Thus, if the United States engages in mine-clearing efforts as a countermeasure to Iran's attempt to mine the shipping lanes in the Strait of Hormuz, then it is likely to set into motion an action-reaction dynamic in the theater of conflict. In other words, even a partial closure and an Iranian "harassment" strategy could culminate in complete closure of the strait for an uncertain period, given the unpredictability of modern warfare. Furthermore, Iran openly contemplated the option of disrupting Saudi and UAE oil shipments through the Red Sea and the *Bab al-Mandab* Strait, without interfering with shipping through the Strait of Hormuz, which was essential for Iran's own oil transits. In July 2018, Saudi Arabia temporarily suspended its oil shipments through the Red Sea after the Houthi rebels in Yemen attacked two Saudi ships in the *Bab al-Mandab* waterway.[21]

IRAN'S DEFENSE APPROACH

The Middle East has become one of the most militarized areas in the world in recent years. Between 2009–2013 and 2014–2018, the flow of arms to the Middle East increased by a staggering rate of 87 percent, while the other regions of the world experienced a decline in their arms flow during the same period.[22] In the period 2014–2018, four of the world's top-ten arms importers were countries in the Arab Middle East, with Saudi Arabia receiving 33 percent of all weapons transfers to the region. In the Persian Gulf, Saudi Arabia's arms imports increased by 192 percent between 2009–2013 and 2014–2018, with the United States accounting for 68 percent of Saudi arms imports. During the period 2014–2018, the UAE became the seventh largest arms importer in the world, with the United States accounting for 64 percent of that country's arms imports.[23] The Saudi-UAE axis has now become the most direct threat to Iran's security interests in the region with some of the world's most sophisticated weaponry in the world.[24]

Iran, on the other hand, has been under various sanctions regimes for decades and thus has been unable to match its adversaries' arms buildup in the region. Also, according to figures published by the International Institute for Strategic Studies (IISS) and the Stockholm International Peace Research Institute (SIPRI), Iran's defense spending for 2017 was $16,035 billion (IISS figure in 2017 US dollars) or $14,548 (SIPRI figure in 2017 US dollars), whereas the comparable figures for Saudi Arabia, Iran's principal regional competitor, amounted to $76,678 billion (IISS figure in 2017 US dollars) or $69,413 billion (SIPRI figure in 2017 US dollars).[25] The total military spending of the Gulf Cooperation Council (GCC) for 2017 amounted to $128,675 billion, dwarfing Iran's military expenditure.[26] The skewed arms buildup in the Persian Gulf by Iran's major adversaries has had a major impact on Iran's military strategy and defense posture. In fact, we can trace the Islamic Republic's current military thinking and war-fighting strategy to the Iran-Iraq war of 1980–1988. During this war, decentralization in military decision-making and allowing field commanders to improve tactics and strategies to confront a better organized, heavily armed with advanced modern weaponry, and larger Iraqi military forces were the most important transformation in Iranian military doctrine since the inception of the modern Iranian military in the late 1920s. Furthermore, strengthening the regular units of the Islamic Revolutionary Guard Corps (IRGC) and allowing them to function independent of, but in tandem with, the regular armed forces allowed tactical innovations and mobility that was lacking in Iraq's military formations. These lessons, of course, have been incorporated in Iran's war-fighting strategy; the latter are occasionally demonstrated via (days or week-long) war games mesmerizing foreign observers, who have described as "spectacular" the massive display of high-tech, mobile operations, including rapid-deployment forces relying on squadrons of helicopters, airlifts, missiles, as well as hundreds of tanks and tens of thousands of well-coordinated personnel using live munitions. Simultaneously, some 25,000 volunteers have signed up at newly established draft centers for "suicide attacks" against any potential intruders in what is commonly termed "asymmetrical warfare" (*jang-e ghayr-e motegharen*).[27] Behind these maneuvers is an Iranian war doctrine that is fashioned in direct opposition to the "limited war" objective attributed to US military strategy seeking to limit a potential conflict with Iran within a confined territory, that is, international waters and Iran's geographical space. On the contrary, Iran's military doctrine, cognizant of US firepower superiority combined with certain Iranian advantages in terms of ground forces, mobile forces, drone capability, cyber warfare capability, familiarity with the terrain, and high war-fighting motivation of its forces, is premised on the notion of "extending the theater of conflict" and a "follow-on" counter-strike capability; the latter refers to Iran's determination to not limit itself to defense if attacked, but rather to launch a counter-offensive vis-à-vis the points of origin of strikes against it. A key element of Iran's strategy would be to "increase the arc of crisis" in places such as Afghanistan and Iraq, where it has considerable influence, to undermine the United States' foothold in the region, hoping to create a counter-domino effect wherein instead of gaining inside Iran, the United States would actually lose territory partly as a result of thinning its forces, war fatigue, and military "overstretch." From Iran's vantage, one of the few advantages of a protracted, rather than quick, war with the United States is that it would likely force the United States to re-introduce the mandatory draft system, which, in turn, would fuel domestic opposition to US war efforts against Iran.[28] This aside, Iran's proliferation of a highly sophisticated and mobile ballistic-missile system plays a crucial role in its war strategy, again relying on lessons learned from the Iraq wars of 1991 and 2003: in the earlier war over Kuwait, Iraq's missiles played an important role in extending the warfare to Israel, notwithstanding the failure of America's Patriot missiles to deflect most of Iraq's incoming missiles raining in on Israel and, to a lesser extent, on the US forces in Saudi Arabia. Also, per the admission of the top US commander in the Kuwait conflict, General Norman Schwarzkopf, the hunt for Iraq's mobile Scud missiles consumed a bulk of the coalition's air strategy and was as difficult as searching for "needles in a haystack."[29] Missiles are after all weapons of confusion and possess a unique strike capability that can torpedo the best military plans, recalling how the Iraqi missile attacks in March 2003 at the US military formations assembled at the Iraq-Kuwait border forced a change of plan on the US part, thereby forfeiting the initial plan of sustained aerial strikes before engaging the ground forces, as was the case in the Kuwait war, when those forces entered the theater after some twenty-one days of heavy air strikes inside Iraq and Kuwait.

In terms of the history of Iran's deterrence strategy, the devastation of the Iran-Iraq war has created an indelible mark in the Iranian psyche that has affected all aspects of the Islamic Republic's approach to deterrence, missile policies, and its overall foreign and defense policies.[30] As Seyed Hossein Mousavian, a former Iranian diplomat and spokesperson for Iran's nuclear negotiators has observed, the Iraqi invasion of Iran in 1980 and the subsequent eight-year war resulted in hundreds of thousands of Iranian deaths. Iraq's war effort was bankrolled by Saudi Arabia and Kuwait and supported by major world powers, including the United States and France. One important lesson of the Iran-Iraq war was that Iran must always fight for its survival "at all costs."[31] Moreover, "Iraq's systematic use of Scud missiles to bombard defenseless Iranian cities gave Iran the incentive to invest in its ballistic missile program. Over the period of eight years, the Iraqi army launched 533 ballistic missiles on Iranian cities, resulting in 2,300 deaths and injuries to 11,600 Iranians. By the end of the war in 1988, Tehran had been attacked 118 times, resulting in 1,600 casualties."[32]

Moreover, "the traumatic experience of Saddam Hussein's systematic use of chemical weapons against Iran, and the international community's indifference to such violations, has convinced Iran that it cannot rely on international institutions to deter and punish such flagrant violations."[33] In addition, the current regional imbalance of conventional forces against Iran and the decades-old arms embargo against the Islamic Republic have played a major role in Iran's missile development program. Last, but not least, Iran is surrounded by several nuclear-weapon states and US military forces that present significant and even existential threats to Iran. The Iranian leadership continues to connect the county's experience in the Iran-Iraq war and the subsequent unabated hostilities and regional threats against the Islamic Republic to the country's defense policies, including its missile program.[34]

Also, in the Iranian leaders' view, the aggression against the Islamic Republic that the Iran-Iraq war embodied has not ended because "the country exists in an anarchical system without security guarantees and a region in which the inability to meet one's basic security needs can lead to the loss of sovereignty."[35] It is in this milieu that Iran has developed its theory of deterrence and its strategy to reduce its rivals' margin of maneuver.[36] More specifically, Iran's deterrence strategy of limiting its adversaries' maneuverability is based on all-around defense, strategic depth, and anti-access, anti-denial (A2/AD) capabilities.[37] Missiles play a key role in enhancing Iran's approach to defense and deterrence. As Kayhan Barzegar, one of Iran's leading international relations scholars has noted, Iran's reliance on its "massive missile power" allows the country to respond to attacks by hostile states and target their military bases in a cost-effective way.[38] Moreover, "the extension of economic sanctions has not limited Iran's missile program as the main source of the country's deterrence. In fact, sanctions make national missile production more attractive from an economic standpoint than buying foreign advanced fighter jets. Missiles are fast, precise and hit their targets effectively. Their mobility makes them less vulnerable to air defenses. Accordingly, an advanced missile strategy is institutionalized in Iran's defense policy."[39] As a recent quantitative study using data from 1960 to 2017 has also demonstrated, unilateral sanctions have had minimal impact on Iran's defense programs and spending and that the chances of success in altering Iran's defense approach via US sanctions policy are statistically insignificant.[40]

THE MISSILE CONUNDRUM

The Trump administration and Iran's regional adversaries, have focused their attention on pressuring Iran to abandon its defense posture and eliminate its ballistic missile program. Although the US intelligence community's 2019 worldwide threat assessment concluded that Iran has adhered to its obligations under the JCPOA and is not "currently undertaking the key nuclear-weapons development activities" but the country's "ballistic missile programs, which include the largest inventory of ballistic missiles in the region, continue to pose a threat to countries across the Middle East. Iran's work on a space launch vehicle (SLV)—including on its Simorgh—shortens the timeline to an ICBM because SLVs and ICBMs use similar technologies."[41] As we have stated earlier, missiles remain an important component of Iran's deterrence and defense posture. As Iran is woefully exposed to outside aggression and lacks the means to compete in acquiring advanced weapons that its adversaries possess, missiles remain the country's principal means to deter an aggressor; of course, Iran is not the only power in its neighborhood with an active missile program; almost all the Arab states possess one or another kind of advanced missile system, for example, Saudi Arabia's CSS-2/DF, Yemen's SS-21, Scud-B, Iraq's Frog-7. Without its missile program, Iran will face a serious existential threat to its territorial integrity and security. As the table 6.1 shows, Iran has indeed developed and tested an array of missiles. Chronologically speaking, Iran produced the 50-km range Oghab artillery rocket in 1985 and developed the 120-km- and 160-km-range Mushak artillery rockets in 1986–1987 and 1988, respectively. Iran began assembling Scud-Bs in 1988, and North Korean technical advisers in Iran converted a missile maintenance facility for missile manufacture in 1991. It does not seem, however, that Iran has embarked on Scud production. Instead, Iran has sought to build Shahab-3 and Shahab-4, having ranges of 1,300 km with a 1,600-pound warhead, and 2,000 km with a 2,200-pound warhead, respectively; the Shahab-3 was test-launched in July 1998 and may

Table 6.1   Iran's Missile Categories

Missile	Class	Range	Status
Dehlaviyeh	SRAAM	8 km	In development
Dezful	MRBM	1,000 km	Operational
Emad (Shahab-3 Variant)	MRBM	1,700 km	Operational
Fateh	SRBM	500 km	Operational
Ghadr (Shahab-3 Variant)	MRBM	1,950 km	In development
Heidar	SRAAM	8 km	In development
Khorramshahr	MRBM	2,000	In development
Koksan	Artillery	60 km	Operational
Qamar-e Bani Hashem	SRAAM	8 km	In development
Qiam	SRBM	800 km	Operational
Ra'ad	Cruise Missile	150 km	Operational
Safir	SLV	350 km altitude	Operational
Sejjil	MRBM	2,000 km	Operational
Shahab-1	SRBM	300–330 km	Operational
Shahab-2 (Scud-C Variant)	SRBM	500 km	Operational
Shahab-3	MRBM	1,300 km	Operational
Simorgh	SLV	500 km altitude	In development
Soumar	Cruise Missile	2,000–3,000 km	Operational
Tondar	SRBM	159 km	Operational
Zolfaghar	SRBM	800 km	Operational

Table is author-generated.
Source: Missile Defense Project, "Missiles of Iran," *Missile Threat*, Center for Strategic and International Studies, published June 14, 2018, last modified June 15, 2018, https://missilethreat.csis.org/country/iran/ and "Gozaresh: Vaziyat-e Sanat-e Mooshakiye Iran Baad az Shahadat-e Hassan Tehrani Moghadam" (Report: The Status of Iran's Missile Industry After the Martyrdom of Hassan Tehrani Moghadam), *Tasnim News Agency*, November 12, 2018, https://www.tasnimnews.com/fa/news/1397/08/21/1872494/
MRBM—Medium-Range Ballistic Missile; SRAAM—Short-Range Air-to-Air Missle; SRBM—Short-Range Ballistic Missile; SLV—Space Launch Vehicle.

soon be upgraded to more than 2,000 km, thus capable of reaching the middle of Europe.[42]

Notwithstanding Iran's missile capabilities, the country does not possess any ICBM missiles, nor has it violated the UN Security Council Resolution 2231, which was adopted in July 2015 after the signing of the JCPOA by Iran and the 5+1 countries. Contrary to Trump administrations claims, this resolution does not prevent Iran from developing missiles, including ballistic missiles. It only requests that Iran refrain from developing missiles that are capable of carrying nuclear warheads.[43] Iran's regional adversaries (i.e., Israel, Saudi Arabia, and, the UAE) rely on their Western-supplied air forces equipped with precision-guided bombs and cruise missiles to engage in long-range strikes. Lacking similar capabilities (Iran's aging and dying air force mostly relies on pre-1979 planes) Iran has sought to highlight its missiles. Also, in order to ensure an effective deterrence, Iran will most likely continue to test its missiles and improve their accuracy in order to overcome missile defense systems that are deployed by the country's regional adversaries.

Essentially, this is a "stealth" deterrence strategy because missiles are mostly mobile, can be relatively easily hidden, and also "on the cheap" because Iran's missiles are relatively cheap and manufactured domestically without much external dependency and the related pressure of "missile export control" exerted by the United States and other powers. Therefore, even under the most favorable political conditions, negotiating on eliminating or constraining Iran's missile programs will be a difficult task.

Iran, however, has shown a willingness to voluntary curtail its medium-range missile testing, with the last test conducted in 2017. In addition, Iran has limited the range of its ballistic missiles to 2,000 km to allay concerns about its missile programs, especially with respect to ICBMs. In other words, Iran "regards its existing ballistic missile arsenal as sufficient for regional deterrence. Iranian officials' repeated references to this policy appear to be supported by evidence."[44] This self-imposed limit can be a starting point to codify it in an agreement should the tense US-Iran relations improve. Based on a recent study by the International Institute for Strategic Studies (IISS), there is no verifiable evidence that Iran has an ICBM program.[45]

Iran does have a space program that can enable Tehran to "shorten a pathway to an ICBM because space launch vehicles use inherently similar technologies. Since 2008, Iran has conducted multiple successful launches of the two-stage Safir SLV. In 2010, Iran unveiled the larger Simorgh SLV."[46] But as missile experts Michael Elleman and Mark Fitzpatrick have observed:

> Iran's two space-launch rockets, the *Safir* and *Simorgh,* are optimized for launching satellites and are not well suited to perform as a ballistic missile, for which they have never been tested. The second-stage propulsion systems for both rockets rely on low-thrust, long-action time engines, which are ideal for accelerating a satellite on a path parallel to the earth's surface and into a sustainable orbit. But such engines are poorly suited for ballistic missile trajectories, which reach higher altitudes. Plus, the large and cumbersome *Simorgh*, which is prepared for launch over an extended time on a fixed launching pad, would be vulnerable to pre-launch attack.[47]

This may explain why no country has "converted a satellite launcher into a long-range ballistic missile."[48] Also, satellite launchers are not generally useful for warhead delivery because of "very different operational criteria and the requirement that a missile's payload must survive the stresses experienced during atmospheric re-entry."[49] The West and Iran's regional adversaries may have their concerns about Iran's missile program but conflating the "dangers" of Iran's space program with an ICBM threat or the unwillingness to place Iran's missile program in the context of regional threats to Iran's national security will not lead to an enduring peace and security in the region.

NOTES

1. Edward Luce, "Iran Left with Few Choices as Trump Steps up Pressure," *Financial Times*, April 25, 2019, https://www.ft.com/content/a40ec2e0-672a-11e9 -9adc-98bf1d35a056.

2. "Pompeo Says Iran Tied to Al-Qaeda, Declines to Say if War Legal," *France 24*, April 10, 2019, https://www.france24.com/en/20190410-pompeo-says-iran-tied-a l-qaeda-declines-say-war-legal.

3. "France Says E3 Moving INSTEX Forward," *Financial Tribune*, April 24, 2019, https://financialtribune.com/articles/business-and-markets/97597/france-say s-e3-moving-instex-forward.

4. "Iran Floods: Sanctions Hamper Relief Efforts," *Al-Jazeera*, April 12, 2019, https://www.aljazeera.com/news/2019/04/iran-floods-sanctions-hamper-relief-effor ts-190412174539077.html.

5. Nasser Karimi, "Iranian Military Labels Entire US Military as Terrorist," *ABC News*, April 23, 2019, https://abcnews.go.com/International/wireStory/iranian-parli ament-labels-entire-us-military-terrorist-62569423.

6. "Iran's Guards Navy Threats to Close Hormuz 'If Not Allowed to Use It'," *Radio Farda*, April 22, 2019, https://en.radiofarda.com/a/iran-guards-navy-threatens- to-close-hormuz-if-not-allowed-to-use-it-/29896686.html.

7. According to US media reports, before his resignation, Defense Secretary James Mattis ignored orders from the White House on Iran (as well as North Korea) that could have resulted in conflict. See Ellen Mitchell, "Mattis Ignored Orders from Trump White House on North Korea, Iran: Report," *The Hill*, April 29, 2019, https ://thehill.com/policy/defense/441240-mattis-ignored-orders-from-trump-white-hous e-on-north-korea-iran-report.

8. Lukas Mikelionis, "Paul to Pompeo: You Don't Have Authorization to Start War with Iran," *Fox News*, April 11, 2019, https://www.foxnews.com/politics/rand-paul-sl ams-pompeo-over-potential-war-against-iran-says-admin-doesnt-have-authority.

9. Warren Strobel, "Study Questions Iran-al-Qaeda Ties, Despite U.S. Allega- tions," *Reuters*, September 7, 2018, https://www.reuters.com/article/us-usa-iran-a lqaeda-idUSKCN1LN2LE. An earlier report in 2012 by the Combating Terrorism Center at the United States Military Academy at West Point found that the relation- ship between al-Qaeda, a Sunni terrorist group, and Iran, led by Shiite clerics, is "not one of alliance" but "highly antagonistic." See, "Letters from Abottabad," *Combat- ting Terrorism Center*, May 2012, https://ctc.usma.edu/app/uploads/2012/05/CTC_ LtrsFromAbottabad_WEB_v2.pdf.

10. Elise Labott, "Bolton Reassures a Nervous Israel about Trump's Syria Plan," *Politico*, January 6, 2019, https://www.politico.com/story/2019/01/06/john-bolton-i srael-syria-withdrawal-1083303.

11. See, for example, Michael E. O'Hanlon and Bruce Riedel, "Do Not Even Think of Bombing Iran," *Brookings Institution*, February 28, 2010, https://www.bro okings.edu/opinions/do-not-even-think-about-bombing-iran/.

12. Kaveh Afrasiabi, "Iran Nuclear Crisis II," *Bulletin of the Atomic Scientists*, September 6, 2018, https://thebulletin.org/2018/09/iran-nuclear-crisis-ii/.

13. "Zarif: B-Team, Not Trump, Wants War with Iran," *Asia News*, April 26, 2019, http://asianews.it/news-en/Zarif:-B-Team,-not-Trump,-wants-war-with-Iran-46 860.html.

14. In the Gulf of Tonkin incident in August 1964, United States falsely claimed that two US warships in international waters had come under "unprovoked attack" by North Vietnam, using this pretext to attack North Korea. See, Elisabeth Bumiller, "Records Show Doubt on 64 Vietnam Crisis," *New York Times*, July 14, 2010, https ://www.nytimes.com/2010/07/15/world/asia/15vietnam.html.

15. "Would Trump Start a War to Boost His 2020 Chances," *Washington Post*, April 29, 2019, https://www.washingtonpost.com/outlook/2019/04/29/would-trum p-start-war-boot-his-chances/?noredirect=on&utm_term=.450c9652de29.

16. "Iran Announces War Games in Gulf to 'Confront Possible Threats,'" *Independent*, August 5, 2018, https://www.independent.co.uk/news/world/middle-ea st/iran-war-games-revolutionary-guards-gulf-ramezan-sharif-us-trump-rouhani-a847 8081.html. Also, Lolita C. Baldor, "Iran Navy Exercise Was a Message to US on Sanctions, Says Top US Commander in Middle East," *Military Times*, August 8, 2018, https://www.militarytimes.com/flashpoints/2018/08/08/iran-navy-exercise-was -a-message-to-us-on-sanctions-says-top-us-commander-in-mideast/.

17. For more information on Iran's naval forces and strategy, see, "Iranian Naval Forces," *Office of Naval Intelligence*, February 2017, https://assets.documentcloud.o rg/documents/3512609/Iran-022217SP.pdf.

18. "Iran Gets First Missile Shipment for S-300 System," *Times of Israel*, July 18, 2016, https://www.timesofisrael.com/iran-gets-first-missile-shipment-for-s-300-sy stem/. Iran had also developed its own version of the S-300 system, which it claimed was even more precise than the Russian version. See, "Iran's Own Version More Precise than 300 Version, General," *Press TV*, September 9, 2018, https://www.pre sstv.com/Detail/2018/09/09/573635/Iran-S300-missile-system-Russia.

19. Dave Majumdar, "Navy Nightmare: Could Iran Sink a U.S. Aircraft Carrier?" *National Interest*, December 26, 2018, https://nationalinterest.org/blog/buzz/navy-n ightmare-could-iran-sink-us-aircraft-carrier-39787.

20. Paul F. Rogers, *Military Action Against Iran: Impact and Effects* (Oxford: Oxford Research Group Briefing Paper, July 2010).

21. Jeremy Vaughn and Simon Henderson, "Bab al-Mandab Shipping Chokepoint Under Threat," Washington Institute for Near East Policy, *PolicyWatch 2769*, March 1, 2017, https://www.washingtoninstitute.org/policy-analysis/view/bab-al-mandab -shipping-chokepoint-under-threat.

22. Pieter D. Wezeman, Aude Fleurant, Alexandria Kuimova, Nan Tian, and Siemon T. Wezeman, "Trends in International Arms Transfers, 2018," Stockholm International Peace Research Institute, *SIPRI Fact Sheet*, March 2019, https://ww w.sipri.org/sites/default/files/2019-03/fs_1903_at_2018_0.pdf.

23. Ibid.

24. For a detailed analysis of the US arms sales, see, William Hartung and Christina Arabia, "Trends in Major Arms Sales in 2018: The Trump Record—Rhetoric Versus Reality," Center for International Policy, *Security Assistance Monitor*, April 2019, pp. 1–27.

25. International Institute for Strategic Studies (IISS), *Military Balance 2018* (London: Routledge/IISS, 2018), ch. 7, Stockholm International Peace Research Institute, *SIPRI Military Expenditure Database*, 2017, https://www.sipri.org/databases.milex. Also, see Anthony H. Cordesman, with Assistance of Nicholas Harrington, *The Arab Gulf States and Iran: Military Spending, Modernization, and the Shifting Military Balance* (Washington, DC: Center for Strategic and International Studies, 2018): 45–48.

26. Cordesman, *The Arab Gulf States and Iran*, 4.

27. Kaveh Afrasiabi, "How Will Iran Fight Back," *Asia Times*, December 15, 2004, https://theshalomcenter.org/content/how-iran-will-fight-back.

28. Gil Barndollar, "If We're Headed for Regime Change in Iran, Get Ready for a Military Draft. We'll Need One," *USA Today*, May 31, 2018, https://www.usatoday.com/story/opinion/2018/05/31/iran-regime-change-american-troops-military-draft-column/656240002/.

29. H. Norman Schwarzkopf, *It Doesn't Take a Hero: The Autobiography of General H. Norman Schwarzkopf* (New York: Bantam Books, 1992).

30. Arian M. Tabatabai and Annie Tracy Samuel, "What the Iran-Iraq War Tells Us about the Future of the Iran Nuclear Deal," *International Security* 42, no. 1 (Summer 2017), 162–167.

31. Seyed Hossein Mousavian, "Six Factors Shaping Iran's Missile Decision-Making Calculus," *Al-Monitor*, December 12, 2018, https://www.al-monitor.com/pulse/originals/2018/12/iran-missiles-security-council-2231-wmd-free-zone-pompeo.html.

32. Ibid. Also, see Ali Khaji, Shoaodin Fallahdoost, and Mohammad Reza Soroush, "Civilian Casualties of Iranian Cities by Ballistic Missile Attacks during the Iran-Iraq War (1980–1988)," *Chinese Journal of Traumatology* 13, no. 2 (April 2010), 87–90, and Ali Khaji, Shoaodin Fallahdoost, Mohammad Reza Soroush, Vafa Rahimi Movaghar, and Song Shuand-ming, "Civilian Casualties of Iraqi Missile Attack to Tehran, Capital of Iran," *Chinese Journal of Traumatology* 15, no. 3 (June 2012), 162–165.

33. Mousavian, "Six Factors Shaping Iran's Missile Decision-Making Calculus."

34. See, for example, Foreign Minister Mohammad Javad Zarif's speech at the Munich Security Conference 2019, February 17, 2019, https://www.securityconference.de/en/media-library/munich-security-conference-2019/video/statement-by-mohammad-javad-zarif-followed-by-qa-1/filter/video/.

35. Tabatabai and Samuel, "What the Iran-Iraq War Tells Us about the Future of the Iran Nuclear Deal," 164–165.

36. For a discussion of the various components of Iran's deterrence strategy, see Guy Freedman, "Iranian Approach to Deterrence: Theory and Practice," *Comparative Strategy* 36, no. 5 (2017), 400–412. Also, see Walter Posch, "Ideology and Strategy in the Middle East: The Case of Iran," *Survival* 59, no. 5 (October–November 2017), 69–98, and Nikolay Kozhanov, *Iran's Strategic Thinking: The Evolution of Iran's Foreign Policy, 1979–2018* (Berlin: Gerlach Press, 2018): 19–37.

37. For a succinct discussion of these three strategies, see, Kayhan Barzegar and Abdolrasool Divsallar, "Political Rationality in Iranian Foreign Policy," *The Washington Quarterly* 40, no. 1 (Spring 2017), 48–49.

38. Kayhan Barzegar, "The Trump Administration's Terrorist Label Is Strengthening the IRGC," Atlantic Council, *IranSource*, April 15, 2019, https://www.atlantic council.org/blogs/iransource/the-trump-administration-s-terrorist-label-is-strengthen ing-the-irgc.

39. Ibid.

40. Sajjad F. Dizaji and Mohammad R. Farzanegan, "Do Sanctions Reduce the Military Spending in Iran?" University of Marburg, *Joint Discussion Paper Series in Economics*, no. 31 (2018), https://www.uni-marburg.de/fb02/makro/forschung/ma gkspapers/paper_2018/31-2018_dizaji.pdf.

41. Daniel R. Coats, Director of National Intelligence, Statement for the Record, *Worldwide Threat Assessment of the US Intelligence Community*, Senate Select Committee on Intelligence, January 29, 2019, p. 10.

42. Anthony Cordesman, *Iran's Rocket and Missile Forces and Strategic Options* (Washington, DC: CSIS, 2014).

43. Full Text of the UN Security Council Resolution 2231, July 20, 2015, https ://www.securitycouncilreport.org/atf/cf/%7B65BFCF9B-6D27-4E9C-8CD3-CF6 E4FF96FF9%7D/s_res_2231.pdf.

44. Tytti Erasto, "Dissecting International Concerns about Iran's Missiles," Stockholm International Peace Research Institute (SIPRI), *Commentary/ Backgrounders*, November 15, 2018, https://www.sipri.org/commentary/topical-backgrounder/2018/d issecting-international-concerns-about-irans-missiles.

45. Mark Fitzpatrick, Michael Elleman, and Paulina Izewicz, *Uncertain Future: The JCPOA and Iran's Nuclear and Missile Programmes*, Adelphi Series, vol. 57, nos. 466–467 (London: Routledge/IISS): 89–130.

46. Defense Intelligence Ballistic Missile Analysis Committee, *Ballistic and Cruise Missile Threat*, National Air and Space Intelligence Center (NASIC), Wright-Patterson AFB, OH, June 2017, p. 27.

47. Michael Elleman and Mark Fitzpatrick, "No, Iran Does Not Have an ICBM Program," *War on the Rocks*, March 5, 2018, https://warontherocks.com/2018/03/n o-iran-not-icbm-program/

48. Ibid.

49. Ibid.

Chapter 7

Paths to a New US-Iran Diplomacy

Our purpose in this concluding chapter is to examine the possibilities for a peaceful resolution of growing tensions between the United States and Iran that have peaked under the Trump administration. To reiterate, the latter's litany of provocative moves against the Islamic Republic of Iran, discussed in full in the preceding chapters, have set the stage for violent conflict between the two countries that could easily engulf the entire region and jeopardize global peace and security. Such a conflict in the oil hub of the Persian Gulf could result in the disruption of oil flows to the outside world and thus adversely impact the world economy by triggering a massive spike in oil prices; according to one estimate, if Iran carried out its threat to block the Strait of Hormuz, "Oil could hit $100 a barrel or more; about 0.6 percent could be wiped off global growth this year; and inflation could rise by 0.7 percentage points."[1] It could also spoil the impressive US economic growth, which in Spring 2019 boasted of reaching the lowest unemployment rate in decades, and thus adversely impact Trump's chances for a second term in office. A bloody, costly, and likely messy, conflict with Iran before the 2020 presidential elections was certainly unattractive from the prism of a Trump White House with its eyes set on an even better election results than in 2016 when Trump actually lost the popular votes and secured victory through (the arcane) electoral college. Nor did it sit well, and or was in harmony, with the "post-interventionist" streak in Trump's worldview, epitomized by his insistence that the United States is not "the world's policeman" as well as by his pledge that the it "will not be suckered" in another disastrous Middle East war.[2] Also important, in addition to Iran, the Trump administration grappled with a number of other foreign policy headaches, including the crisis in Venezuela and the nuclear standoff with North Korea, not to mention the post–Cold War competition with a "rising" China and a reasserted Russia. In

Venezuela, since early 2019, the Trump administration had willfully pushed for a regime change, by backing a young opposition leader and his quest for the presidency, threatening to militarily intervene while, just like Iran, subjecting the South American OPEC country to comprehensive sanctions.[3] Meanwhile, Trump's North Korean diplomacy had hit a tall wall with the collapse of direct talks and Pyongyang's resumption of nuclear tests.[4] Over time, the absence of progress in resolving these foreign policy challenges could come to haunt the Trump administration and provide fuel for his opponents in the upcoming presidential race. On the other hand, there was a connection among these discretely separate foreign policy issues that warranted careful attention by US policy-makers, for example, Iran and nuclear-armed North Korea could move closer to each other and enhance their trade and even military cooperation. Also, their common enmity toward the United States could spur closer cooperation between Tehran and Caracas, both slated for regime change from the without, reflected in Tehran's decision to raise Washington's ire by establishing direct flights to Caracas by one of its blacklisted airlines, Mahan Airline.[5] A big question at the time of this writing was: What would happen if the stalemated US tensions with these two OPEC nations lingered and or result in a pro-US outcome in one but not the other? This question owed its importance to the fact that a successful US bid for regime change in Venezuela could have profound ramifications for Iran. In all likelihood, such a development would be widely interpreted as a huge US foreign policy success and a big political and psychological blow to Iran, boosting the morale of Iranian political opposition and weakening Tehran's will to resist US demands. In other words, it was not far-fetched to think that there was a direct linkage between the policies of the United States for Iran and Venezuela, respectively, the former benefiting from a breakthrough in the latter and thus causing a major setback in the global alliance against US power, hypothetically speaking. But, by the same token, a successful US policy in Venezuela, in overturning the government of Nicolas Maduro one way or another, could also generate a concerted effort on the part of Iran to move closer to China and Russia, both wary of the domineering approach of the United States to global affairs. Moscow and Beijing were at odds with Washington with respect to various regional and global issues and they could conceivably show their displeasure by embracing Iran as a full member of the Shanghai Cooperation Organization (SCO), which had inducted Iran as an observer. A new "look East" Iranian orientation as a direct result of the unbounded animosity of the United States toward Iran was in the offing, despite the sentiments of Rouhani government to maintain a balanced relationship with both the West and the East, rebuffed by the West.[6] In essence, this meant that the Trump administration by virtue of its coercive approach was pushing Iran to new foreign policy directions away from the West as a survival strategy.[7] A walk back from the "maximum pressure" compellence strategy, which had brought United States and Iran to the brink of war in 2019, was the only antidote and, yet, it was unclear if the negative dynamic set into motion by that strategy was reversible? To answer this question, it is important to list the challenges confronting Trump's bellicose Iran policy, which are as follows:

(A) Well-entrenched Iran's resistance: post-revolutionary Iran has weathered decades of wars and foreign turmoil's and was adept at sanctions-busting. In the words of its foreign minister, Javad Zarif, Iran had a "Ph.D. in circumventing sanctions" and with so many neighbors as a maritime power was extremely averse toward a trade blockade;

(B) Absence of a viable political opposition: Aside from a token dissident group abroad, there was no internal dissident movement in Iran that the United States could count on and the US backing of the group known as the MEK (*Mojahedin-e Khalgh Organization*), favored by Bolton and a number of other Trump administration officials, was unlikely to yield much result as a direct result of that group's violent past and its history of collaboration with Iran's enemy, namely, Saddam Hussain, during the Iran-Iraq war.[8]

(C) Recalcitrant allies and failure to build a global alliance against Iran: Unlike the Iraq war, the United States had failed to build a viable global and even regional coalition against Iran, vividly reflected in the dismal attendance at the (anti-Iran) Warsaw conference on the Middle East, as well as by Egypt's refusal to join an "Arab NATO" against Iran;[9] Egypt's move contradicted Pompeo's claim at Cairo University a precious few months earlier that "nations are rallying to our side to confront Iran in the region like never before."[10] Even some of the GCC states, such as Qatar, Oman, and Kuwait, were reluctant to heed the marching of the United States order against Iran. Qatar had opted to move closer to Iran in response to the Saudi-led blockade, Oman and Iran were planning a gas pipeline that would cement their diplomatic closeness with economic interdependence, and Kuwait's Emir Sheikh Sabah Al-Ahmad was on record seeking close ties with Iran: "We consider Iran as our neighbor and we are interested in developing our beneficial cooperation with Tehran,"[11] In the absence of a regional and global consensus on Iran threat and the widespread perception of Trump administration as a menace to international norms, the policy of the United States for Iran relied principally on the unsavory method of allies arms-twisting interpreted in this book via the term of "extended compellence," which had complicated the relations of the United States with its European and Asian allies by virtue of its Iran "threat inflation." In the absence of any international ban on trade with Iran, the unilateral sanctions of United States faced the crucial test of implementation: to what extent and how long the Iran sanctions regime imposed by Washington could sustain itself in an inhospitable global environment? Indeed, a growing collateral damage to the relations of United States with other nations as a result of its robust Iran sanctions policy was a distinct possibility that, in turn, depended on how far was the administration willing to go to punish nations that deviated from its script on Iran and dared to evade the US-imposed prohibitions on oil and non-oil trade and investment with Iran? Was the United States willing to look the other way and ignore illicit (oil) trade between Iran and some friendly countries, or would it slap sanctions on those countries and thus risk alienating them and weakening its own global position? The Trump administration had failed to convince other nations to follow its lead on exiting the nuclear agreement and its subsequent decision to end the oil exemptions had prompted a strong denunciation by Europeans, who questioned that decision as yet another stab at JCPOA.[12]

(D) The war threat: By incubating the seeds of another major Middle East conflict that could turn into "mother of all wars," to paraphrase Iran's President Rouhani in his dire warning to the United States, Trump's Iran policy had implicated Trump's presidency in a basic dilemma: continue with the non-diplomatic path of confrontational policy led by comprehensive sanctions and prepare for a "war of choice," or retreat from that policy and make a U-turn toward diplomacy in order to avoid a costly conflict, that is, an expedient decision that was however politically risky at home and abroad. Basically, the nature of the challenge to Trump's Iran policy posed by the mere threat of war can be summarized as such: the specter of war itself could prove to be a new spur for peace and diplomacy.

(E) The proxy perception problem: Another key challenge to Trump's Iran policy was presented by the public perception of that policy as an issue of "Saudi Arabia first" and or "Israel first" instead of "America first" policy—that belied Trump's nationalist ethos and fueled the image of a "rent a superpower" for war with Iran on the part of Iran's regional rivals, who had cultivated close ties with President Trump and members of his family, who ran the Trump corporate conglomerate enhancing its Middle East portfolio since his presidency.[13] Trump had vetoed a congressional bill to stop US assistance to Saudi war campaign in Yemen and his administration was exposed to the charge of hypocrisy and double standards, by turning a blind eye to human rights abuses and authoritarian style of its Middle East allies while championing the cause of democracy in Iran, a country where regular albeit restricted elections set it apart from the closed polity of pro-US GCC states.

(F) Non-zero sum nature of relations: In addition, another challenge to Trump's Iran policy stemmed from the complex and non-zero sum nature of US-Iran relations that stood in sharp contrast to the opposite, that is, zero-sum, content of the one-dimensional confrontation policy scripted by a hostile White House harboring a pure Manichean enemy image of Iran. The problem with that image was rooted in its caricature of Iran's regional policy as purely destructive and subversive, when in fact the United States and Iran shared a rather sizable pool of parallel interests with respect to stability in Iraq and Afghanistan and anti-terrorism; even in Syria, the US government had endorsed the Russia-Turkey-Iran peace talks in Astana (by sending observers) as well as the "de-escalation" zones, despite Washington's misgivings about Iran's long-term intentions in Syria.[14] By stubbornly clinging to that purely negative image of Iran, the Trump administration ran the risk of inflicting severe harm to its own policies in Iraq and Afghanistan, where its Iran "obsession" could easily result in a major distraction from the war on terror and create a dangerous breathing space for ISIS and other terrorist groups. The flawed zero-sum approach toward Iran was, in other words, a risky proposition that not only wiped out the possibility of a war-averting diplomatic path with Iran, it also rubbed off on other dimensions of the policy of the United States for Middle East, to the detriment of US national security interests.

(G) Iran's unwanted nuclearization: Indeed, an unintended consequence of Trump's Iran policy was impelling Iran toward a new quest for a nuclear shield in response to the extreme national security threats posed by United States and its regional allies, that is, Israel and Saudi Arabia, instead of achieving a new nuclear agreement, whereby Iran would concede to the maximalist demands of the United States under pressure; those demands, reflected in Secretary of State Pompeo's laundry list, included the end of all uranium enrichment activities, which would deprive Iran of its nuclear fuel cycle.[15] But, having mastered the nuclear fuel cycle, Iran retained a Japan-style "proto-nuclear" weapons status (i.e., as a latent nuclear weapon state) that remained intact in the post-JCPOA milieu and could conceivably leapfrog to a full-blown nuclearization as Iran threatened to resume its banned nuclear activities and to even exit the NPT if the United States persisted with its "illegal pressures." At a minimum, faced with a vanishing JCPOA, where the United States had abandoned the deal and the Europeans were implementing "less than 1 percent of their commitments," to paraphrase Iran's foreign minister Zarif, Iran had the option of incrementally reducing its cooperation with the terms of the JCPOA without formally scrapping it.[16] Such a move had the advantage of minimizing the risk of "snap-back" UN sanctions, foreseen in JCPOA, principally as a result of the irrefutable evidence of compara- tive non-compliance by the Western nations to their agreed-upon JCPOA obligations.

Notwithstanding stated earlier, the totality of internal and external challenges facing Trump's confrontational Iran policy was potentially calculable in a new quest for diplomacy to replace the anti-diplomacy portfolio of the admin- istration vis-a-vis Iran. A cognitive remapping of the Trump administration in this direction was undoubtedly difficult to muster in a policy environment dominated by Iran hawks. Only a major compromise by the latteror decou- pling of President Trump from those hawks surrounding him from the within and the without, that is, in the form of lobbying by pro-Israel and pro-Saudi groups as well as hawkish members of US Congress, could facilitate such an outcome. Hoping for the latter, Iran's diplomacy was focused on splinter- ing Trump from his principal Iran advisers such as Bolton, by maintaining that "Trump wanted to talk" with Iran, while his advisers and his Israeli and Saudi partners were "spoiling for war."[17] Although denounced by Bolton as Iranian "propaganda," Iran's diplomatic overture was not necessarily a hopeless cause, counted as it did on "transactional Trump" self-glorifying in the "art of the deal" to give a new nod to diplomacy as an alternative to war or a frustrating Iran quagmire intensely disliked by many allies deprived of beneficial trade with Iran. A limited "humanitarian" dialogue on "exchange of prisoners" proposed by Iran in early 2019 could set the stage for this new path.[18] The United States and Iran had engaged in such an endeavor in prisoners' exchange on the sideline of the marathon nuclear talks, thus set- ting a precedent that could be used as a reference point for renewed US-Iran dialogue, starting off on a "humanitarian issue" and then telescoping the talks to broader issues. A preparatory and exploratory pre-dialogue with the help of third parties in a confidential environment away from the public limelight was necessary in this regard. Another exploratory venue was the so-called track II diplomacy, revolving around policy experts and former officials on both sides, which had yielded some positive results in the past, per a study by Suzanne DiMaggio at United States Institute of Peace.[19]

But, the problem with even a limited dialogue on prisoners' exchange was that it raised the suspicion of hardliners in Iran, as well as Iran hawks in Washington, that the seeds of a major policy shift could be planted and lead to uncalled for compromises by one or the other side. That is why Iran's hardlin- ers denounced any dialogue with Trump administration as a "surrender" even though the alternative of non-diplomacy and war-preparation was unattract- ive from the prism of Iran's national interests. Also, it was unattractive from the vantage of Iran's neighbors, such as Iraq and Afghanistan, whose political leadership were commonly backed by the United States and Iran and had a vested interest in US-Iran peace. Iraq's political leaders had offered to mediate between Tehran and Washington, knowing full well that their country could easily turn into a US-Iran battleground in light of the US military bases in Iraq, which Trump had explicitly connected to Iran containment.[20] A US-Iran conflict spillover would likely go beyond Iraq and engulf other Persian Gulf states, including UAE, which was at odds with Iran by bandwagoning with Saudi Arabia in the Yemen war and, yet, was apprehensive about the winds of war blowing in its direction. Oman, another GCC state that prided itself of a healthy and balanced relationship with both Iran and Saudi Arabia and of its past record in acting as interlocutor between Washington and Tehran, could be utilized as a fresh channel for US-Iran dialogue, particularly since Oman had made the fateful decision of accessing its ports to the US Navy and thus gaining a new prominence in the policy of the United States for Persian Gulf.[21] In a word, the United States could now relocate its naval assets from the Persian Gulf, vulnerable to Iran's firepower, to Sea of Oman, in turn, raising the clout of the Iran-friendly government of Oman.

In addition to the regional actors, there were undoubtedly a number of other extra-regional players, such as the UN Secretary General, Russian and Chinese presidents, and French and other European leaders, who could play a role in mediating the tensions between Tehran and Washington. French President Emmanuel Macron had played a go-between on the sideline of UN General Assembly gathering in September 2018, facilitating a potential Trump-Rouhani meeting in New York.[22] Although such a meeting did not take place for various reasons including Rouhani's cautious approach and concerns over backlashes at home by his hardliner critics, there was every expectation that Macron would renew his mediation efforts in the future, perhaps with even greater vigor in light of the growing risks of US-Iran war imperiling European security. Both France and other European powers such as Germany and England needed to demonstrate a greater zeal for Iran diplomacy, their impetus generated by their own national interests. These three European powers were the brains behind the new financial mechanism known as INSTEX to save the JCPOA, which had purposely self-limited to humanitarian commodities as the starter, raising the specter of allowing other countries such as China and Russia to participate, particularly if the Trump administration continued with its stubborn confrontational approach toward Iran without showing any signs of willingness to veer in the direction of diplomacy. In other words, the Europeans were not entirely without any leverage toward Trump when it came to Iran, but the question was if they could muster the necessary political will and unity of purpose in order to implement those leverages with Washington for the sake of a whole new chapter in European Middle East diplomacy? Unfortunately, at the time of this writing, prudent European conflict-management efforts were dreadfully lacking, reflecting a diplomatic hiatus that was unresponsive to Europe's own security needs and requiring an immediate upgrade. Whether or not Europe was able to wake up from its diplomatic slumber and to step in the void of US-Iran diplomacy was an open question that depended on the evolution of European politics and will power of specific leaders such as Macron, who was hampered by economic protests at home. Roiled by Britain's chaotic and uncertain Brexit plans, France's popular revolt, and the growing influence of far-right populist political forces, the European Union was in the midst of a political storm that clearly did not bode well for a "united and powerful" Europe.[23] Yet, as long as Iran remained in the JCPOA and did not act on its threat to tear up the nuclear agreement and resume its nuclear activities, Europe was likely to remain steadfast in its defense of the JCPOA and its rejection of US pressure to cancel the nuclear agreement. In this scenario, the JCPOA framework of cooperation with Iran put structural limits on how far Europe would be able to accommodate the Trump administration on Iran, particularly on the nuclear issue, on which the United States and Europe saw things with "parted eyes," like Hermia in Shakespeare's "A Midsummer Night's Dream." The saga, now over two years old, had the potential to grow into a deeper, and more complex, transatlantic division between the United States and Europe, if the present conflict spiral between United States and Iran continued and thus heightened European insecurity. In a sense, Europe was playing with fire by putting a major diplomatic effort on Iran to a backburner, limiting itself to feeble gestures and token actions that fell dreadfully below the bar of effective conflict management. A remedy too late, the European peace efforts could emerge after squandering precious time, with the window of US-Iran diplomacy closing by the hammering blows of US economic war-fare, which were "as bad as war," to paraphrase a US media commentary.[24] Indeed, the timing was of the essence and retarded European initiatives were disconcerting and antithetical to the cause of peace and stability in the Middle East. An important question here was, of course, if the Trump administra-tion was responsive to a new European conflict-management initiative on Iran, short of a closer US-Europe cooperation with respect to the perceived threat of Iran's ballistic missiles or its nuclear weapons potential? Another related question: Was Europe willing to honor the JCPOA and UNSC Resolution 2231 deadlines, such as with respect to the lifting of restrictions on the sale of conventional weapons to Iran, and thus defy Washington? How would a future negotiation with Iran on both nuclear and non-nuclear issues, look like?

TRUMP'S OFFER OF NEGOTIATIONS
WITHOUT PRECONDITIONS REVISITED

In July 2018, following the footsteps of his predecessor who spoke on the phone with President Rouhani in September 2013, Trump offered the olive branch of direct talks with Iran "without preconditions," which he presented as an open-ended invitation for fresh diplomacy with Iran that could take place "whenever they want to . . . . I would certainly meet with Iran if they Wanted to meet." Yet, Secretary of State Pompeo quickly nuanced Trump's offer by setting conditions for a dialogue with Tehran. Pompeo's insistence that Tehran had to meet certain "preconditions" before sitting at the table with Washington was at variance with Trump's stated sentiment and was subsequently utilized by Iran's top diplomat, who hammered the point that Trump and his foreign policy team did not see eye to eye on Iran. At the time however, Zarif categorically rejected Trump's overture as insincere and publicity stunt (as the midterm US congressional elections approached), in light of an earlier Bolton advice that "Iran is not likely to seek further negotiations once the JCPOA is abrogated, but the Administration may wish to consider rhetorically leaving that possibility open in order to demonstrate Iran's actual underlying intention to develop deliverable nuclear weapons, an intention that has never flagged."[25] Rouhani, on the other hand, welcomed Trump's overture and expressed his willingness to engage in talks with US president "right now," adding meaningfully "if there is sincerity, Iran has always welcomed dialogue and negotiations."[26] According to US author Robin Wright, Trump's own hesitations contributed to the failure of Macron-led mediation as mentioned earlier, with Trump insisting that the time for such talk was premature and Iranians had to "suffer" a bit more.[27] That was in Fall 2018 and, yet, chances were that by Fall 2019 and afterward, Trump may have reached the opposite conclusion that with Iran reeling under US sanctions, the timing was finally ripe and a new round of bilateral negotiations should commence with Iran. Of course, this was a risky proposition, assuming that punitive sanctions and exiting the JCPOA had not inflicted irreparable wounds of "no return" and the proud Iranians keen on saving face and maintaining their "dignity" would actually consent to a new negotiation with the United States from the position of weakness. With their backs "against the wall" metaphorically speaking, by virtue of being squeezed by United States and its allies on all fronts, Iran's leaders would have to swallow their pride and submit to a new nuclear negotiations, as well as broader talks on regional affairs, if they wanted a reprieve from the effective "maximum pressure" campaign. But, an important question was the "endgame" of the United States and the desired results from such a negotiation "under duress"?

Lest we forget, United States benefited from the non-proliferation dividend of the JCPOA and, despite its stated antipathy toward the nuclear deal, the latter actually served national security interests of the United States. This explained why the United States irrespective of the attempts to tighten the nuclear trade restrictions with Iran, which among other things banned Russia's plan to build new power reactors in Bushehr, nonetheless made certain nuclear exemptions for the sake of sustaining Iran's nuclear concessions under the JCPOA. These exemptions reflected a nuanced non-proliferation approach of the United States toward Iran that stemmed from a pragmatic realism noticeably absent in other ramparts of Trump's confrontational Iran policy. Also, it stemmed from an open US admission that Iran's new nuclear transparency under the JCPOA would make a future US military action "more effective." This was initially stated by US negotiators in the Obama administration, including the then secretary of state John Kerry, who stated: "Now, if Iran fails to comply, we will know it, and we will know it quickly, and we will be able to respond accordingly by reinstituting sanctions all the way up to the most draconian options that we have today. None of them are off the table at any point in time." By the same token, Iran had the option of reducing its nuclear transparency as part and parcel of a negotiation strategy, in order to elevate its "politics of leverage" and enhance its chips at the "nuclear poker" with the United States, in a word, try to "level the playing field." That Iran could potentially do so, instead of limiting itself to frequent "bluster" derived from the past lessons of prior negotiations, when the Western fear of a nuclearizing Iran acted as an impetus for a flexible approach yielding the historic agreement, which is essentially a complex exchange of rights and obligations among its seven signatories. In contrast, the Trump administration's approach was one of seeking Iran's complete surrender to the maximalist demands of the United States, which were unrealistic by virtue of presenting hardly any incentives for Iran to engage in new nuclear diplomacy with the United States. This "all sticks, no carrots" approach was clearly a non-starter and precluded the diplomatic path, in other words, was a major obstacle to the necessity of obviating the conflict spiral and re-tracking US-Iran diplomacy on the correct path toward de-confliction. The US requirement that Iran abandon its uranium enrichment program altogether was unrealistic and no Iranian political leader could consent to it short of committing political suicide. But this did not necessarily mean that Iran was completely closed to the option of considering future self-limitations in the realm of nuclear fuel cycle after the current JCPOA-imposed restrictions expire. Hypothetically speaking, in an altered environment, where Iran did not feel under siege by the United States and its allies and could thus shed some of its security "paranoia," it could be convinced to agree to extend and prolong those JCPOA restrictions for at least several years, provided that Tehran could receive robust guarantees that the United States would not renege again on its commitments. Such an agreement could come about as a result of new negotiations, which could contain new elements incorporated in the JCPOA, without the need for an entirely new agreement, which is opposed by Iran for various reasons, including its concern that the hard-gained JCPOA benefits, such as the Western consent to Iran's possession of a nuclear fuel cycle, may evaporate in the "fog" of new negotiations. On the whole, in a hypothetical Trump administration-Iran nuclear negotiations, the two sides have a realistic possibility to reach a common understanding on the following items:

1. Agreement on the various steps to ensure that Iran's "plutonium path" to nuclear weapons are blocked, by agreeing on constraints on heavy water reactors and reprocessing of spent nuclear fuel;
2. Agreement on Iran's nuclear transparency by Iran's agreement to continue the stringent IAEA inspection regime, its adoption of the intrusive Additional Protocol, and the related intrusive measures that even go beyond the Additional Protocol, in order to continue to provide objective guarantees of its peaceful nuclear intentions;
3. Agreement on a temporary extension of some of JCPOA deadlines, for example, a five to seven-year extension of the "sunset clauses" on uranium enrichment (and the type and number of centrifuges), as a voluntary "confidence-building measure" on Iran's part;
4. Agreement on US implementation of its JCPOA obligations, discussed in chapter 2 in this book, as well as the willingness of the United States to procure a full congressional authorization for the new agreement, which would, in turn, address Iran's concerns about another Trump turnaround from an agreement with Iran and or future US presidents' reneging on it as Trump had done with the JCPOA. In other words, a more legally robust nuclear agreement was needed that would not be so easily reversible because of its supposedly "non-binding" political nature as an "executive agreement," although the JCPOA was an international agreement and legally binding from the prism of international law as discussed in this book. Such a new agreement would need to be "global" in nature and tackle both the nuclear and non-nuclear issues on the US-Iran plate, in light of Trump's criticism of the Obama administration for engaging in a limited nuclear talk with Iran without addressing other instances of Iran's "maligned behavior." Case in point, the United States and Iran could engage in a dialogue on Persian Gulf security and or conflicts in Yemen and Syria and potentially reach some common understanding. With respect to Yemen, Iran had put forth a 4-point framework for peace, which could be the reference point by Iranian negotiators outlining to US negotiators their vision of how to end the bloody conflict in Yemen.

Trump himself did not seem completely opposed to an Iran talks on Yemen. In a press interview in November 2018, Trump was asked what he would do if the new Congress blocked arms sales to the Saudis or took other steps to end the Yemen War. The president replied: "I want to see [the] Yemen [war] end. But it takes two to tango. Iran has to end it also. Iran is a different country from when I took over, far weakened because of what I did with them . . . . Iran nuclear deal. I want to stop but I want Iran to stop also." On the surface, Trump seems to be offering a public rationalization of "business as usual US policy on Yemen, relying on the Saudis. But that policy was in fact in the throes of re-evaluation in light of the United States call for a ceasefire and, more importantly, the Pentagon's decision to cut off air refueling for the Saudi fighter jets, jolting Riyadh."[28] Similarly, it was not far-fetched to think that the United States and Iran could make tangible progress on the question of Syria's post-conflict situation, a new constitution, and general elections, provided that the United States was willing to put its military presence and support for the anti-Damascus forces on the table as well. Trump had shown little interest in getting the US forces heavily involved in Syria, a country of little geostrategic importance to United States, at one point declaring that Iran "can do whatever it wants" in Syria, that is, exhibiting a latent tendency to reach a *modus vivendi* with Iran with respect to Syria, which was held back by the combined pressure of his hawkish anti-Iran advisers as well as by pressures from Israel.[29]

5. Agreement on Hizbollah's hostility toward Israel: Iran's protege force in Lebanon, Hizbollah, was labeled as terrorist by the United States, even though Hizbollah participated in Lebanon's national politics and was fully integrated into Lebanese politics, with Hizbollah representatives in Lebanese Parliament as well as in the cabinet. Having demonstrated its military capability in the thirty-three-day war against mighty Israel in 2006 and then in Syria's bloody conflict, Hizbollah was a force to reckon with and, simultaneously, Iran's insurance policy vis-a-vis Israel, which menaced Iran both directly and indirectly through the United States. Having assisted Hizbollah with its enhanced missile capability, Iran naturally counted on Hizbollah to rush to assist it in the event of a US-Iran war, primarily by hitting Israeli targets as part of Iran's "extended deterrence strategy."[30] It was therefore highly unlikely that Iran would ever consent to compromise its valued ties with its powerful protege force irrespective of US pressure and or any future US offer of incentives. Still, this did not mean that a US-Iran dialogue involving Hizbollah was necessarily futile, for example, it could yield results in terms of Iran's willingness to influence Hizbollah to moderate its position on Israel and, for example, agree to refrain from provocative actions against Israel (so long as Israel

retreated from any unilateral offensive against Hizbollah). Similarly, Iran could also have a moderating influence on Palestinian groups such as Hamas and Islamic Jihad, although far less than Hizbollah because of the limited nature of Iran's connections to these groups. After all, Iran's main worries centered on its national security interests in vicinity of its own borders, primarily in Persian Gulf and Caspian Sea regions, and there were associated costs with an "overstretched" Iranian power involving the "out of area" Israel that, in the sanctions-hit Iran, potentially made it less likely that Tehran was seeking (in) direct conflict with Israel. In a sense, it was Israel's own litany of anti-Iran actions, such as pressuring Washington to discard the nuclear agreement and to re-impose sanctions on Iran, which invited a more bellicose Iranian approach toward Israel, that is, a case of Israeli "self-fulfilling prophecy." More than Israel, Iran was concerned about Saudi Arabia's march toward a Pax Saudica with much help from the Trump administration as well as the Israeli enablers, potentially instigating a fresh Iranian approach to regional issues, with its eyes set on finding "circuit breakers" for the emerging Saudi-US-Israeli axis against it. An Iranian re-entrenchment within its own borders was, within certain limits, a feasible scenario, so long as Iran was assured of its own national security and the absence of potential harm to its "proxy assets" that, on the whole, reflected Iran's "sphere of influence" politics stemming from parallel such efforts on the part of Iran's regional rivals. The problem with Israel, however, was that it enjoyed the benefits of a nuclear weapons monopoly in the Middle East and was opposed to the JCPOA partly as a result of the JCPOA-induced momentum for a regional disarmament engulfing Israel, reflected in Zarif's statement that Iran had met its disarmament obligations and "it is now Israel's turn."[31] The demise of JCPOA let Israel off the hook and, at the same time, raised the question of if Israel would ever consent to new US-Iran nuclear negotiations that, both deliberately and inadvertently, re-raise the unwanted specter of Israeli disarmament down the road? Indeed, this formed a nub of American dilemma, that is, how to proceed with Iran and enter a new agreement with Iran, which could have the unintended consequence of introducing new pressures on Israel with respect to its clandestine nuclear program? Another related issue was about Saudi Arabia's nascent nuclear program, which raised new concerns in Iran and the region, warranting further US guarantees that its nuclear assistance to Riyadh would not discriminate against Iran by helping the Saudis in a nuclear weapons program. All in all, Trump administration's stated desire for an all-inclusive "global" negotiation with Iran meant that such a negotiation had to address the behavior and programs of other nations in the region and provide certain guarantees to Iran, instead of seeking unilateral Iranian concessions in a vacuum of understanding of Iran's national security concerns. A Saudi race toward nuclear bombs had become an issue of concern on Iran's part, invoking memories of Iran's past concerns about the Baathist Iraqi regime's quest for nuclear weapons, which were a principal cause of post-revolutionary Iran's fateful decision to resurrect its nuclear program after ditching it following the downfall of the ancien regime. A nuclear-armed Saudi Arabia, dominated by its anti-Shiite Wahhabist Sunni leadership, was a supreme nightmare for Iran (as well as Shiite-dominated Iraq), particularly since the Trump administration did not seem to be willing to exert any meaningful pressure on Saudi Arabia. In theory, Israel shared some of Iran's concerns about a nuclearizing Saudi Arabia, which could be the basis for a new look at their policies toward each other, as two of the three non-Arab nations of the region (the other being Turkey). From the prism of Iran's national security, there were certain "structural limits" on the scope of Saudi-Israeli alliance against Iran, as it was unclear if the Saudi quest for hegemony in the Persian Gulf necessarily corresponded with Israel's national security. Recalling the past episode of Iran-Contra affair, spurred in part by Israel to enter into a tactical support for Iran against its arch Arab enemy Iraq as part of Israel's "balance of power approach," the new regional milieu drifting in the direction of a new Saudi hegemony raised the prospect of an alternative Israeli look at the regional picture at variance with the Saudi objectives aforementioned; the latter is much assisted by Trump, who has given a carte blanche to the Saudi rulers in the region while beefing them up militarily, turning a blind eye to their repressive mischiefs, and applying "maximum pressure" on Iran, the other regional pillar. Trump's confrontational Iran was likely calculated as a "war of attrition" to weaken Iran economically and (geo) strategically while simultaneously assisting the Saudis to improve their economy and military and security prowess to the point that a precious few years from now an economically-squeezed Iran would be "shrunk to size" and ultimately submit to the Saudi hegemony. However, the problem with this narrative was that it stemmed from an unrealistic assessment of the "realities on the ground," that is, the mere fact that Iran would never submit to Saudi hegemony and forfeit its historical role as a pivotal Persian Gulf power, no matter what the US pressure.

In conclusion, in our assessment, the confrontational US strategy on Iran scripted by the Trump administration was deeply flawed and fraught with major risks that were justifiable only from the perspective of an Iranophobic "threat inflation," one that deliberately ignored the important constraints on Iranian power in a fractious, and Arab-dominated, Persian Gulf. To bring this narrative to a close, in our view, the US foreign policy in the Middle East is much better served by pursuing a "post-interventionist" logic of action, whereby "offshore balancing" and inclusionary security policies went hand in hand, aimed at de-escalation of tensions and the pursuit of a peaceful and tranquil regional environment. This lofty objective was introduced in an embryonic fashion through the Iran nuclear deal, which held the promise for broader peaceful resolution of Middle East conflicts utilizing the unique resources of multilateral diplomacy. The Trump administration would need to engineer a diplomatic U-turn away from the compellence strategy and toward the traditional containment strategy, while exploring the possibilities for achieving a sustainable détente with Iran. To this effect, both countries need to approach each other with candid consideration of their points of agreement and disagreement, stemming from their national (security) interests. Only then, the present spiral toward a US-Iran conflict would be arrested and reversed in the direction of peaceful coexistence.

NOTES

1. "How Will Trump's Oil Gamble Affect the Global Economy?" *Al-Jazeera*, May 5, 2019, https://www.aljazeera.com/programmes/countingthecost/2019/05/trump-iran-oil-gamble-affect-global-economy-190504073832283.html.

2. "US Can't Be the World's Policeman, Trump to US Troop in Iraq," *Times of India*, December 27, 2018, https://timesofindia.indiatimes.com/world/us/us-cant-be-worlds-policeman-trump-to-us-troops-in-iraq/articleshow/67268197.cms.

3. Tim O' Connor, "Iran Defends Venezuela as U.S. Warns of 'All Options' against Two More Oil-Rich Nations," *Newsweek*, May 3, 2019, https://www.newsweek.com/iran-defends-venezuela-all-options-oil-1414237.

4. "North Korea 'Test Fires' Short-Range Missiles," *BBC*, May 3, 2019, https://www.bbc.com/news/world-asia-48158880.

5. "Iran's Mahan Air Launches Direct Flight to Venezuela," *Reuters*, April 7, 2019, https://www.reuters.com/article/iran-venezuela-airlines/irans-mahan-air-launches-direct-flights-to-venezuela-idUSL8N21Q11T.

6. For more on this see, Kaveh Afrasiabi and Seyedrasoul Mousavi, "A Power Shift to the East: Iran and the SCO," *Lobelog*, June 7, 2018, https://lobelog.com/a-power-shift-to-the-east-iran-and-the-sco/comment-page-2/. Until 2015, when the Iran nuclear deal was reached, the SCO's objection to Iran's membership was that, per its internal rules, countries under international (UN) sanctions could not be admitted. With the Iran nuclear deal (the Joint Comprehensive Plan of Action or JCPOA) effectively removing the UN sanctions, that legal hurdle has been lifted. There is now no important obstacle blocking Iran's bid to join the SCO.

7. Despite the new US sanctions on Iran, Moscow had vowed to increase its cooperation with Iran. See, "Russia Vows to Continue Relations with Iran despite US' Sanctions," *Business Standards*, May 5, 2019, https://www.business-standard.

com/article/news-ani/russia-vows-to-continue-relations-with-iran-despite-us-sanc
tions-119050500352_1.html.

8. Paul Pillar, "The MEK and the Bankrupt U.S. Policy on Iran," *National Interest*, November 13, 2018, https://nationalinterest.org/blog/paul-pillar/mek-and-bankru
pt-us-policy-iran-35982.

9. "Iran Welcomes Egypt's Reported Withdrawal from 'Arab NATO' Plan," *Al-Jazeera*, April 11, 2019, https://www.aljazeera.com/news/2019/04/iran-welcomes-eg
ypt-reported-withdrawal-arab-nato-plan-190411181116040.html.

10. Bill Chappell, "In Cairo, Pompeo Slams Obama's Mideast Policies, Says Era of 'American Shame' Is Over," *NPR*, January 10, 2019, https://lobelog.com/pompe
o-iran-threat-inflation-eludes-search-for-allies/comment-page-2/.

11. "Kuwait Emir Welcomes Close Ties to Iran," *Tehran Times*, December 18, 2018, https://www.tehrantimes.com/news/430839/Kuwait-Emir-welcomes-close-tie
s-with-Iran.

12. David M. Herszenhorn, "Europe Vows to Uphold Iran Nuclear Deal as Trump Raises Pressure," *Politico*, May 4, 2019, https://www.politico.eu/article/europe-v
ows-to-uphold-iran-nuclear-deal-as-trump-raises-pressure/.

13. Daniel Greenfield, "Max Boot: Israel and Foreign Leaders Control Trump," *Frontpage*, May 2, 2019, https://www.frontpagemag.com/point/273642/max-boot
-israel-and-foreign-leaders-control-trump-daniel-greenfield.

14. Nader Entessar and Kaveh Afrasiabi, "The Pitfalls of Trump's New Iran Strategy," *Belfer Center*, October 31, 2017, https://www.belfercenter.org/publication/pitf
alls-trumps-new-iran-strategy.

15. According to the British columnist Simon Tisdall, "Pompeo Belongs to a cold war generation that, despite mounting evidence of relative US decline, clings to delusional myths of American exceptionalism and US hegemony." See Simon Tisdall, "Pompeo, Bully Boy Calls at No. 10," *Guardian*, May 4, 2019, https://www.theguard
ian.com/us-news/2019/may/04/mike-pompeo-bully-boy-calls-at-no-10.

16. Kaveh Afrasiabi, "A Conversation with Iran's Foreign Minister Javad Zarif," *Lobelog*, April 30, 2019, https://lobelog.com/a-conversation-with-irans-foreign-m
inister-javad-zarif/

17. Edith M. Lederer, "Iran Minister: Trump Wants to Talk, Bolton Wants War," *Time*, April 24, 2019, http://time.com/5577723/iran-minister-trump-bolton-conflict/.

18. Afrasiabi, "A Conversation with Iran's Foreign Minister Javad Zarif.".

19. Suzanne DiMaggio, "Track II Diplomacy," *United States Institute of Peace*, 2010, https://iranprimer.usip.org/resource/track-ii-diplomacy.

20. Laura Rozen, "Iraq Offers to Mediate between Trump, Iran," *Al-Monitor*, October 3, 2018, https://www.al-monitor.com/pulse/originals/2018/10/iraq-new-
government-mediate-us-iran-tensions.html.

21. Phil Stewart, "With an Eye on Iran, U.S. Clinches Strategic Port Deal with Oman," *Reuters*, March 24, 2019, https://www.reuters.com/article/us-usa-oman-m
ilitary/with-an-eye-on-iran-u-s-clinches-strategic-port-deal-with-oman-idUSKCN1R
50JD.

22. For more on this subject see Robin Wright, "Trump's Strange, Tense Campaign against Iran," *New Yorker*, April 25, 2019, https://www.newyorker.com/news

/our-columnists/trumps-strange-tense-campaign-against-iran. Also, Kaveh Afrasiabi and Nader Entessar, "Trump and Rouhani Need to Talk," *New York Times*, September 5, 2018, https://www.nytimes.com/2018/09/05/opinion/trump-rouhani-summit-meeting.html.

23. Kaveh Afrasiabi, "Turmoil in Europe Is Poison for JCPOA," *Iran Diplomacy*, December 12, 2018, http://www.irdiplomacy.ir/en/news/1980591/turmoil-in-europe-is-poison-for-jcpoa.

24. Alaa Shahine, "As Bad as War? Trump's Steps Seen Deepening Iran's Economic Pain," *Bloomberg*, April 29, 2019, https://www.business-standard.com/article/news-ani/russia-vows-to-continue-relations-with-iran-despite-us-sanctions-119050500352_1.html.

25. John R. Bolton, "How to Get Out of the Iran Nuclear Deal," *National Review*, August 28, 2017, https://www.nationalreview.com/2017/08/iran-nuclear-deal-exit-strategy-john-bolton-memo-trump/.

26. Zachary Cohen, "Iran's President Says He'll Talk to Trump Right Now," *CNN*, August 7, 2018, https://www.cnn.com/2018/08/06/politics/rouhani-trump-us-iran-talks/index.html.

27. Wright, "Trump's Strange, Tense Campaign against Iran."

28. Kaveh Afrasiabi, "Yemen: Gateway to U.S.-Iran Dialogue?" *Lobelog*, November 21, 2018, https://lobelog.com/yemen-gateway-to-iran-u-s-dialogue/.

29. For more on this see, Kaveh Afrasiabi, "Trump's Syria Decision and Its Implications for Iran," *Lobelog*, December 31, 2018, https://lobelog.com/trumps-syria-decision-and-its-implications-for-iran/. Former US ambassador to NATO Robert Hunter has raised the question as to whether this decision is indicative of a larger transformation in the edifice of US foreign policy. This question owes itself partially to the reports that Trump is also considering pulling troops out of Afghanistan—although Trump had apparently issued no orders to that effect—while simultaneously pursuing a dialogue with Taliban and a cease-fire in Yemen. See Robert E. Hunter, "Will the United States Ever Think Seriously about the Middle East?" *Lobelog*, December 24, 2018, https://lobelog.com/will-the-united-states-ever-think-seriously-about-the-middle-east/.

30. Meysam Behravesh, "IRGC Change of Command Signals Tehran's New Offensive Approach," *Atlantic Council*, May 2, 2019, https://www.atlanticcouncil.org/blogs/iransource/irgc-change-of-command-signals-tehran-s-new-offensive-approach.

31. Javad Zarif, "Iran Has Signed the Nuclear Deal. It Is Now Israel's Turn," *Guardian*, July 31, 2015, https://www.theguardian.com/profile/javad-zarif. Iran was not the only Persian Gulf state calling for a nuclear weapons-free zone in the Middle East and Qatar echoed a similar sentiment. See, "Qatar Calls for Nuclear Weapons-Free Zone," *Gulf Times*, May 5, 2019, https://www.gulf-times.com/story/630659/Qatar-calls-for-nuclear-weapons-free-zone.

Postscript

There have been several significant developments signifying a substantial escalation of tensions between the United States and Iran since we completed the manuscript for this book in early 2019.[1] On the whole, these developments, ranging from a new "tanker warfare" in the Persian Gulf and its vicinity waters, to US deployment of a great deal of military assets in the region while citing "credible threats" from Iran, to Iran's downing a US spy plane followed by a US retaliatory strike that was called off at the last minute by President Trump citing humanitarian concerns, and to Iran's signaling the end of its "strategic patience" with US sanctions and European inaction by reducing its cooperation with the nuclear accord, and so forth, confirm the preceding chapters' analysis, particularly our prognostication of the various drivers for war as well as war-prevention and diplomacy. While edging closer to war, both the United States and Iran have simultaneously been pulled in the opposite direction of war-avoidance, their future relations caught at the crosswinds of war and peace. Tantamount to a fragile "neither peace, nor war" imbroglio, the geopolitical and geostrategic ramifications of the tense standoff between the two countries cast a dark pall on the stability of Persian Gulf, riven by opposing power blocs. As a result, divergent possibilities, such as a military confrontation potentially culminating in a regional conflagration or, conversely, a major de-escalation of tensions stemming from a conscious pursuit of an "off-ramp" solution with the help of both regional and extra-regional actors, loomed on the horizon. With a great deal of uncertainty surrounding the net outcome of the "maximum pressure" strategy of the United States on Iran, which refused to capitulate to Trump administration's demands, it was difficult to see how a peaceful exit from the growing crisis between the two countries could emerge, notwithstanding Trump's admission that he did not do an "exit strategy."[2] With far-reaching (secondary)

195

sanctions in place, including new sanctions on Iran's spiritual leader, which, in turn, diminished the already scant likelihood of bilateral negotiation, the Trump administration was saddled with its mission to cripple Iran's economy and weaken Iran's regional portfolio.[3] Iran, on the other hand, intent on neutralizing the American-led pressures, which it denounced as "economic terrorism," devised its own evolving "pushback" tactics and strategies that had both nuclear and non-nuclear components and included brinksmanship in the strategically important Strait of Hormuz, this while still vesting hope that the nuclear deal could be preserved and, perhaps, Trump could be persuaded by other JCPOA signatories and others both in the United States and in the region to reconsider his antagonistic approach and re-embrace the nuclear deal and its "bargaining table." Meanwhile, the European powers had intensified their efforts to preserve the JCPOA, in part through diplomacy with both Tehran and Washington and also in part by operationalizing the Iran-trade financial mechanism (i.e., INSTEX) after a six month delay and openly mulling the idea of using it not just for "humanitarian goods" but also oil trade with Iran. The EU's foreign policy chief Federica Mogherini played down Tehran's breaches of the Iran nuclear as not "significant enough" to trigger "snapback" UN sanctions.[4] Russia and China, the other two parties to the JCPOA, openly backed Iran in its on-going dispute with the United States, which they commonly blamed for the unilateral exit from the JCPOA, with Russian officials going so far as referring to Iran as an "ally" that would receive Russian assistance in the event of a US war on Iran.[5] Concerned about a radical re-mapping, the Middle East geopolitics detrimental to their interests nested by Trump's confrontational Iran policy, Beijing and Moscow represented two important pillars of support for Iran at the international level that, in turn, reduced Washington's chances for achieving its stated objectives on Iran. Irrespective, the Trump administration stubbornly clung to its compellence strategy and, in the aftermath of suspicious attacks on oil tankers in May and June 2019, added new feathers to this strategy by contemplating an international maritime force to escort oil tankers in the Persian Gulf. Such a move, reminiscent of the prior experience in 1987–1988, which culminated in the accidental US shooting down an Iranian passenger airplane and engaging in naval warfare with Iran, was a risky as well as a costly undertaking that could have the unintended consequence of piling tensions in the oil hub instead of defusing those tensions.

Henceforth, only a paradigmatic shift away from the compellence strategy and toward a more nuanced, and certainly less confrontational US strategy, could bring about a major de-escalation of tensions with Iran. Certainly, Iran needed to do its part, by taking proactive steps aimed at conflict-reduction in the region, to convince its adversaries in the region and beyond that, the Iran "threat" had been exaggerated and was a tissue of misperception, rather than a correct assessment of the country's external behavior. Tehran could, for instance, provide further assurance to the international community that it was not seeking to develop nuclear weapons and or to subvert its Arab neighbors, for example, by implementing a new "non-aggression pact" with those neighbors.[6] The latter included the UAE, which had wisely opted to pull its forces out of Yemen theater of conflict, much to the chagrin of their Saudi allies, in part as a friendly gesture toward Iran.[7] But, ironically, just as the mounting threat of war was dictating a fresh reconsideration of their anti-Iran positions on the part of some GCC states such as UAE, United Kingdom was threading the opposite path, for example, by openly contemplating joining the United States in a war with Iran and also lending a helping hand to US oil embargo by seizing an Iranian tanker off the coast of Gibraltar.[8] UK's hostile behavior toward Iran inevitably rekindled the memory of the Iraq war, leading some commentators to conclude that we were on the cusp of a historical deja vu. In turn, this represented a major foreign policy dilemma for President Trump, whose self-restraint in June 2019 aforementioned was in sharp contrast to the war drive of his key advisers and, in the words of a Gary Sick, a former US official, reflected an administration that was at "war with itself."[9] Also, the threat of war with Iran had resulted in a vote in the House of Representatives in favor of the war authorization act, mandating a prior congressional approval of any military campaign against Iran.[10] Thus, constrained both at home and abroad, Trump's Iran policy faced major challenges that were quite possibly capable of directing the administration toward contemplating a genuine diplomatic path toward Iran, instead of the initial pseudo-diplomatic gestures, which were intended as mere window dressing for the compellence strategy. But, what that strategy failing to yield any perceptible results in terms of weakening Iran's will to resist the American pressure, and the re-election imperatives of Trump dictating a more careful approach that would not backfire against his bid to win the presidency for a second term, the pressures on the administration to find a suitable adjustment of its Iran policy grew. In fact, the mere fact that United States and Iran almost went to war, which was avoided at the last minute by both sides showing self-restraint, was a turning point that, on Trump's part, reflected an evolution as Trump invoked the standard of proportionality to defend his decision against launching a retaliatory strike on Iran. Theoretically, this could be extended to the "maximum pressure" strategy that, as pointed out by several US experts such as Jeffrey Sachs, drew blood on Iran by victimizing many millions of Iranians, targeted for economic and medicinal deprivations by US sanctions deemed unjust.[11] That strategy was, in other words, questionable from the prism of "just war," which centers on the notion of proportionate response. Hypothetically speaking, then, Trump was apt to reconsider, and at least partially step back from, the maximalist compellence strategy, for example, by re-issuing oil waivers, in line with his newly invoked standard of proportionality.[12] Unfortunately, consistency and coherence was not a hallmark of Trump's presidency, notwithstanding Trump's vastly more threatening language of "obliterating" Iran in the event of war, which followed his restraint in June 2019; the latter as a matter of fact invoked the image of a "total war" that could conceivably involve the use of tactical nuclear weapons against Iran. Although a remote possibility at the time of this writing, the threat of a nuclear war in the Persian Gulf was real and was in line with the nuclear weapons posture of the United States, which openly contemplated the use of "smart" tactical nukes in conventional theaters.[13] Needless to say, this was a nightmare scenario with huge long-term implications for the future of non-proliferation, incubated by the sum of tensions that were building up between Iran and the United States. To ratchet down those tensions, a great deal of preliminary confidence-building steps between the two countries were necessary, such as a consistent messaging from the White House that its end-game on Iran was not regime change and that it was open to the possibility of a *modus vivendi* with the Islamic Republic of Iran. In that case, the regional allies of the United States, above all Israel and Saudi Arabia,[14] were guaranteed to redouble their efforts to steer the Trump administration toward confrontation rather than reconciliation with Iran, thus underscoring the need for the administration to insulate its Iran policy from third-party influences and make the necessary adjustments in that policy based on the national interests of the United States. After all, the United States and Iran shared parallel interests, for example, with respect to the stability of Iraq, Afghanistan, that, in turn, conveyed the sense of a non-zero-sum game between the two countries, inferred from the US waivers on Iran-Iraq trade and India's investments in Chah Bahar discussed in this book. These areas of mutual interests were in the danger of being eclipsed by the one-way imperatives of the compellence strategy, which net outcome could turn out to be a lose-lose conflict between the United States and Iran draining the resources of both countries.[15] With the help of peacemaking interlocutors as well as timely "back channel" diplomacy, Tehran and Washington could avert such an unwanted war that did not serve the interest of either nation and, then again, to a large extent this depended on the latter's recognition of the simple yet profound fact that its unilateral waging an economic warfare against Iran was indeed tantamount to paving the way to an open military warfare and not an alternative to it.

NOTES

1. For a brief chronology of developments in May through July 2019, see John Haltiwanger, "Timeline of How the Trump Administration Got into a Showdown

with Iran That Could Lead to War," *Business Insider*, July 1, 2019, https://www.bus inessinsider.com/timeline-of-how-trump-administration-got-into-a-showdown-with-i ran-2019-5.

2. Jessica Campisi, "Trump on Possible War with Iran: 'I Don't Need Exit Strategies'," *The Hill*, June 25, 2019, https://thehill.com/homenews/administration/450280 -trump-on-possible-war-with-iran-i-dont-need-exit-strategies.

3. Edward Wong, "Trump Imposes New Sanctions on Iran, Adding to Tensions," *New York Times*, June 24, 2019, https://www.nytimes.com/2019/06/24/us/politics/ira n-sanctions.html.

4. Rym Momtaz, "EU's Mogherini: Iran Breaches not 'Significant' to Escalate," *Politico*, July 15, 2019, https://www.politico.eu/article/iran-deal-not-dead-but-time-running-out-jeremy-hunt-says/.

5. Tom O'Connor, "Russia Warns U.S. and Israel That Iran Was Its 'Ally' and Was Right about the Drone Shoot Down," *Newsweek*, June 25, 2019, https://www.newsweek .com/russia-iran-us-israel-drone-ally-1445802. Similarly, Chinese President Xi Jinping told Iran's President Rouhani on the sideline of Shanghai Cooperation Organization summit in June 2019 that China sought the steady development of ties with Iran no matter how the international situation changed. See, "Xi Says China Will Promote Steady Ties with Iran," *Reuters*, June 14, 2019, https://www.reuters.com/article/us-mideast-at tacks/xi-says-china-will-promote-steady-ties-with-iran-idUSKCN1TF0IH.

6. "Russia Supports Iran's Proposal of a Non-Aggression Pact with Gulf Arab States," *Radio Farda*, May 27, 2019, https://en.radiofarda.com/a/russia-supports-i ran-s-proposal-of-a-non-aggression-pact-with-gulf-arab-states/29965818.html.

7. "UAE Pulls Most Forces from Yemen in Blow to Saudi War Efforts," *New York Times*, July 11, 2019, https://www.nytimes.com/2019/07/11/world/middleeas t/yemen-emirates-saudi-war.html. UAE officials also distanced themselves from the Trump administration's claim that Iran was responsible for the attacks on oil tankers off its coast in May 2019. Tom O'Connor, "U.S. and Saudi Ally UAE Says It Can't Blame Iran for Attacking Tankers: 'We Don't Have Evidence,'" *Newsweek*, June 26, 2019, https://www.newsweek.com/uae-us-russia-iran-tankers-blame-1446096.

8. For more on this issue, see Kaveh Afrasiabi, "UK's Misguided Bandwagoning with U.S. on Iran," *Lobelog*, July 9, 2019, https://lobelog.com/uks-misguided-b andwagoning-with-u-s-on-iran/.

9. Gary Sick, "U.S. Iran Policy Gives Me Vertigo," *Lobelog*, July 10, 2019, https ://lobelog.com/u-s-iran-policy-gives-me-vertigo/.

10. Connor O'Brien, "House Votes to Limit Trump's Iran War Powers," *Politico*, July 12, 2019, https://www.politico.com/story/2019/07/12/house-vote-limit-trump-iran-war-powers-1414943.

11. According to economist Jeffrey Sachs, US sanctions on Iran were causing a humanitarian crisis as they were sure to "cause a significant rise in mortality." Quoted in Farid Zakaria, "Trump Is Strangling Iran. It's Raising Tensions Across the Middle East," *Washington Post*, July 11, 2019, https://www.washingtonpost.com/opinions/ trump-is-strangling-iran-its-sowing-resentment-across-the-middle-east/2019/07/11 /511b13c4-a413-11e9-b732-41a79c2551bf_story.html?noredirect=on&utm_term=.ff 558683f34e.

12. A relevant article is by Ed Condon, "Drone Strikes and Proportionality: What is 'Just War'," *Catholic News Agency*, June 21, 2019, https://www.catholicnewsagency.com/news/drone-strikes-and-proportionality-what-is-just-war-30384.

13. Kaveh L. Afrasiabi and Nader Entessar, "A Nuclear War in the Persian Gulf?" *Bulletin of the Atomic Scientists*, July 2, 2019, https://thebulletin.org/2019/07/a-nuclear-war-in-the-persian-gulf/

14. Dario Leone, "Sabre-Rattling: Israel Warns Its Stealthy F-351 Can Reach Iran and Syria," *National Interest*, July 17, 2019, https://nationalinterest.org/blog/buzz/sabre-rattling-israel-warns-its-stealthy-f-35i-can-reach-iran-and-syria-67487.

15. Grace Shao, "US-Iran Conflict Will Be a 'Lose-Lose' Situation, Analysts Say," *CNBC*, June 21, 2019, https://www.cnbc.com/2019/06/21/us-iran-military-conflict-will-be-a-lose-lose-situation-analysts.html.

Selected Bibliography

Abbaspoor Baghabari, Abbas and Khajouei Ravari, Mohammad Hassan. "Barressi-e Emkan Sanjai-e Ijad-e Hamgarai-e Amniyati dar Hoozeh-e Jeopolitik-e Khaleej-e Fars az Manzar-e Realism-e Sarkhtari" (A Study of the Feasibility of Creating a Security Convergence in the Persian Gulf Geopolitical Area from the Perspective of Structural Realism). *Journal of Defense Policy*, vol. 23, no. 91, Summer 2015, pp. 131–163.

Abdul-Shafi, Wael, Hassan, Kawa, and Tabatabai, Adnan. "Victimized by Geopolitics: Iranian and Saudi Perspectives on the Refugee Crisis." Center for Applied Research and Partnership with the Orient (CARPO), *Brief*, no. 5, October 24, 2016, pp. 1–9.

Abedin, Mahan. "Why Oman's Embrace of Israel Is Bad News." *Middle East Monitor*, October 29, 2018. Available at: https://www.middleeastmonitor.com/201810 29-why-omans-embrace-of-israel-is-bad-news/

Abrahamian, Ervand. *The Coup: 1953, the CIA, and the Roots of Modern U.S.-Iranian Relations*. New York: New Press, 2013.

Abrar Cultural and Research Institute. *Parvandeh Hastei Iran: Ravandha va Nazarha* (Iran's Nuclear Project: Trends and Views). Tehran: Abrar Cultural and Research Institute, 2004.

Adebahr, Cornelius. *Europe and Iran: The Nuclear Deal and Beyond*. London and New York: Routledge, 2017.

———. *Inside Iran: Alte Nation, neue Macht?* (Inside: Iran: Old Nation, New Power?). Bonn, Germany: J.H.W. Dietz Nachf. GmbH, 2018.

Adib-Moghaddam, Arshin. *Iran in World Politics: The Question of the Islamic Republic*. New York: Columbia University Press, 2008.

———. *The International Politics of the Persian Gulf: A Cultural Genealogy*. New York and London: Routledge, 2006.

Afkhami, Gholamreza, ed. *Barnamehe Enrji-e Atomi-e Iran: Talashha va Taneshha, Interview with Akbar Etemad, Nokhosteen Raiis-e Sazeman-e Atomi-e Iran* (Iran's Atomic Energy Program: Mission, Structure, Politics: An Interview with Akbar

Etemad, The First Director of the Atomic Energy Organization of Iran). Washington, DC: Foundation for Iranian Studies, 1997.

Afrasiabi, Kaveh L. "A Conversation with Iran's Foreign Minister Javad Zarif." *LobeLog*, April 29, 2019. Available at: https://lobelog.com/a-conversation-with-irans-foreign-minister-javad-zarif/

———. "A Proposed Endgame for the Iranian Nuclear Crisis." *Bulletin of the Atomic Scientists*, February 25, 2013. Available at: http://thebulletin.org/proposed-end game-iranian-nuclear-crisis-0.

———. *After Khomeini: New Directions in Iran's Foreign Policy*. Boulder, CO: Westview Press, 1994.

———. "Debunking the Harvard Report on Iran Nuclear Past." *Eurasia Review*, May 2, 2019. Available at: https://www.eurasiareview.com/02052019-debunking-t he-harvard-report-on-iran-nuclear-past-oped/

———. "Europe's Unequal Exchange with Iran: The Missing Links." *Iranian Diplomacy*, October 5, 2018. Available at: http://irdiplomacy.ir/en/news/1979350/eu rope-s-unequal-exchange-with-iran-the-missing-links.

———. "Iran and the Khashoggi Crisis." *LobeLog*, October 22, 2018. Available at: https://lobelog.com/iran-and-the-khashoggi-crisis/

———. "Iran Debates Ties with Russia." *LobeLog*, July 19, 2018. Available at: https ://lobelog.com/iran-debates-ties-with-russia/

———. "Iran Nuclear Crisis II." *Bulletin of the Atomic Scientists*, September 26, 2018. Available at: https://thebulletin.org/2018/09/iran-nuclear-crisis-ii/

———. "Iran's Economic Populism: Antidote to U.S. Pressure." *LobeLog*, November 15, 2018. Available at: https://lobelog.com/irans-economic-populism-antido te-to-u-s-pressure/

———. "Letter to the American Experts." *Iranian Diplomacy*, April 5, 2019. Available at: http://www.irdiplomacy.ir/en/news/1982589/letter-to-the-american-experts.

———. "Realism, Not Idealism: Iran's Latent Nuclear Potential." *Harvard International Review*, May 2, 2005. Available at: http://hir.harvard.edu/archives/1403.

———. "Sanctions: Tools of American Hegemony." *Iranian Diplomacy*, August 18, 2018. Available at: http://www.irdiplomacy.ir/en/news/1978484/sanctions-tools-of -american-hegemony.

———. "The ICJ Ruling: An Interim Ruling for Iran and the World." *LobeLog*, October 5, 2018. Available at: https://lobelog.com/the-icj-ruling-an-interim-vict ory-for-iran-and-the-world/

———. "Trump's Iran Offensive: Regime Change by Other Names." *Islamic Republic News Agency (IRNA)*, August 18, 2018. Available at: http://www.irna.ir/en/ News/83004577.

———. "Trump's Iran Policy: Rollback or Containment?" *Iranian Diplomacy*, October 30, 2018. Available at: http://www.irdiplomacy.ir/en/news/1979828/tru mp-s-iran-policy-rollback-or-containment-

———. "Trump's Syria Decisions and Its Implications for Iran." *LobeLog*, December 31, 2018. Available at: https://lobelog.com/trumps-syria-decision-and-its-impli cations-for-iran/

———. "Understanding Trump's 'Game of Thrones' with Iran." *Iranian Diplomacy*, January 8, 2019. Available at: http://www.irdiplomacy.ir/en/news/1981014/und erstanding-trump-s-game-of-thrones-with-iran.

——— and Entessar, Nader. "A Nuclear War in the Persian Gulf?" *Bulletin of the Atomic Scientists*, July 2, 2019. Available at: https://thebulletin.org/2019/07/a-n uclear-war-in-the-persian-gulf/

———. "Iran Uses Hamas for Leverage in Nuclear Negotiations." *Aljazeera America*, August 13, 2014. Available at: http://america.aljazeera.com/opinions/2014/8/ iran-hamas-palestinenuclearnegotiations.html.

———. "Paradoxical Implications of the Ukraine Crisis for Iran Nuclear Talks." *Iran Matters*, Belfer Center for Science and International Affairs, Harvard University, March 13, 2014. Available at: http://iranmatters.belfercenter.org/blog/paradoxic al-implications-ukraine-crisis-iran-nuclear-talks.

———. "The Coming U.S.-Iran Showdown at UN." *LobeLog*, September 11, 2018. Available at: https://lobelog.com/the-coming-u-s-iran-showdown-at-un/

———. "The Trump Administration's Compellence Strategy and Iran's 'Melian' Dilemma." *Brown Journal of World Affairs*, vol. 25, no. 1, Fall/Winter 2018, pp. 70–77.

———. "Trump and Rouhani Need to Talk." *New York Times*, September 5, 2018. Available at: https://www.nytimes.com/2018/09/05/opinion/trump-rouhani-sum mit-meeting.html.

———. "United States and Iran: Confrontation or Dialogue?" Columbia University, *Journal of International Affairs*, August 8, 2018. Available at: https://jia.sipa.col umbia.edu/online-articles/united-states-and-iran-confrontation-or-dialogue.

——— and Kibaroglu, Mustafa. "Negotiating Iran's Nuclear Populism." *Brown Journal of World Affairs*, vol. 12, no. 1, Summer/Fall 2005, pp. 255–268.

——— and Maleki, Abbas. "Iran's Foreign Policy After 11 September." *Brown Journal of World Affairs*, vol. 9, no. 2, Winter/Spring 2003, pp. 255–265.

Agha, Hussein and Malley, Robert. "The Middle East's Great Divide Is Not Sectarianism." *The New Yorker*, March 11, 2019. Available at: https://www.newyorke r.com/news/news-desk/the-middle-easts-great-divide-is-not-sectarianism.

Ahmadian, Ali Akbar. "Tahdid Shenasi az Manzar-e Rahbaran-e Enghelab-e Eslami-e Iran" (Understanding Threats as Viewed by the Leaders of the Islamic Revolution of Iran). *Journal of Defense Policy*, vol. 23, no. 91, Summer 2015, pp. 9–39.

Ahmadian, Hassan and Mohseni, Payam. "Iran's Syria Strategy: The Evolution of Deterrence." *International Affairs*, vol. 95, no. 2, March 2019, pp. 341–364.

Ahmed, Salman and Bick, Alexander. "Trump's National Security Strategy: A New Brand of Mercantilism?" Carnegie Endowment for International Peace, *Paper*, August 17, 2017. Available at: https://carnegieendowment.org/2017/08/17/trum p-s-national-security-strategy-new-brand-of-mercantilism-pub-72816.

Ajorloo, Saeid. "Internal Discourses in Iran's Nuclear Diplomacy." *Discourse: An Iranian Quarterly*, vol. 11, no. 3, Winter 2017, pp. 97–112.

Akbarzadeh, Shahram and Baxter, Kylie. *Middle East Politics and International Relations: Crisis Zone*. London and New York: Routledge, 2018.

Akbarzadeh, Shahram and Conduit, Dara, eds. *Iran in the World: President Rouhani's Foreign Policy*. New York: Palgrave Macmillan, 2016.

Alaedini, Pooya and Razavi, Mohamad R., eds. *Industrial, Trade, and Employment Policies in Iran: Towards a New Agenda*. New York: Springer, 2018.

Alcaro, Riccardo. "All Is Not Quiet on the Western Front: Trump's Iran Policy and Europe's Choice on the Nuclear Deal." Instituto Affari Internazionali (IAI), *IAI Papers*, no. 18 | 07, April 2018, pp. 1–26.

———. *Europe and Iran's Nuclear Crisis: Lead Groups and EU Foreign Policy-Making*. New York: Palgrave Macmillan, 2018.

——— and Dessi, Andrea. "A Last Line of Defence: A Strategy for Europe to Preserve the Iran Nuclear Deal." Instituto Affari Internazionali (IAI), *IAI Papers*, no. 19, June 14, 2019, pp. 1–24.

Alimagham, Pouya. "America's Standard of 'Normal Nation' in the Middle East." *LobeLog*, May 5, 2019. Available at: https://lobelog.com/americas-standard-of -normal-nation-in-the-middle-east/

Alimardani, Mahsa and Pakzad, Roya. "Silicon Valley Preaches Diversity and Inclusion While Excluding Iranians." Atlantic Council, *IranSource*, April 8, 2019. Available at: https://www.atlanticcouncil.org/blogs/iransource/silicon-valley-p reaches-diversity-and-inclusion-while-excluding-iranians.

Alizadeh, Parvin and Hakimian, Hassan, eds. *Iran and the Global Economy: Petro Populism, Islam and Economic Sanctions*. London and New York: Routledge, 2013.

Allin, Dana H. and Simon, Steven. *The Sixth Crisis: Iran, Israel, America, and the Rumors of War*. New York: Oxford University Press, 2010.

Al-Monitor Staff. "Iranian Photographer Reclaims Iconic Image Used in Controversial Trump Tweet." *Al-Monitor*, February 12, 2019. Available at: https:// www.al-monitor.com/pulse/originals/2019/02/iran-yalda-moayyeri-trump-tweet-ic onic-image-photo-reclaimed.html.

Al-Rantawi, Oraib. "Oman's Mediation and Iran's Return to the Diplomatic Path." *Middle East Monitor*, August 1, 2018. Available at: https://www.middleeastmon itor.com/20180801-oman-mediation-and-irans-return-to-the-diplomatic-path/

Altaqi, Samir and Aziz, Esam. "Is Saudi-Iranian De-escalation Possible?" *Middle East Briefing*, vol. 3, no. 130, June 9, 2016. Available at: http://mebriefing. com/?p=2363.

Aman, Fatemeh. "Iran's Environment: The Grass Beneath Two Fighting Elephants." *LobeLog*, July 18, 2018. Available at: https://lobelog.com/irans-environment-th e-grass-beneath-two-fighting-elephants/

———. "Water Dispute Escalating Between Iran and Afghanistan." Atlantic Council, South Asia Center, *Issue Brief*, August 2016, pp. 1–10.

Amanat, Abbas. *Iran: A Modern History*. New Haven, CT: Yale University Press, 2017.

American College of National Security Leaders. "50+ Retired Generals and Diplomats Urge the United States to Reenter Iran Deal." *The National Interest*, March 11, 2019. Available at: https://nationalinterest.org/feature/50-retired-generals-and -diplomats-urge-united-states-reenter-iran-deal-46747.

Amirahmadi, Hooshang and ShahidSaless, Shahir. "Avoid Repeating Mistakes Toward Iran." *The Washington Quarterly*, vol. 36, no. 1, Winter 2013, pp. 145–162.

Anderson, Perry. *American Foreign Policy and Its Thinkers*. New York: Verso Books, 2017.

Applebaum, Anne. "Iran's Regime Could Fall Apart. What Happens Then?" *Washington Post*, November 23, 2018. Available at: https://www.washingtonpost.com/opinions/global-opinions/irans-regime-could-fall-apart-what-happens-then/2018/11/23/3b476d12-edc6-11e8-8679-934a2b33be52_story.html?utm_term=.f1b124954545.

Arabshahi, Mohammad. "Iran's Foreign Policy in Middle East's New Order." *Iranian Diplomacy*, February 11, 2017. Available at: http://www.irdiplomacy.ir/en/page/1966978/Iran%E2%80%99s+Foreign+Policy+in+Middle+East%E2%80%99s+New+Order.html.

Araud, Gérard and Vaez, Ali. "Iran Isn't Trying to Build a Bomb Tomorrow. It Wants Sanctions Relief." *Foreign Policy*, July 2, 2019. Available at: https://foreignpolicy.com/2019/07/02/iran-isnt-trying-to-build-a-bomb-tomorrow-it-wants-sanctions-relief-uranium-jcpoa-trump-enrichment/

Armbruster, Ben. "Team Trump's Iran War Rationales Are Nonsense." *LobeLog*, April 11, 2019. Available at: https://lobelog.com/team-trumps-iran-war-rationales-are-nonsense/

Arms Control Association. "Dismantling the Iran Deal Would Be Dangerous and Unwise." *Issue Brief*, vol. 8, no. 7, December 13, 2016. Available at: https://www.armscontrol.org/Issue-Briefs/2016-12-13/Dismantling-the-Iran-Deal-Would-Be-Dangerous-and-Unwise.

———. *Solving the Iranian Nuclear Puzzle: Toward a Realistic and Effective Comprehensive Nuclear Agreement*, 3rd edition. Washington, DC: Arms Control Association Briefing Book, June 2014.

———. "Understanding the Extension of the Iran Nuclear Talks and the Joint Plan of Action." *Issue Brief*, vol. 6, no. 12, December 23, 2014, pp. 1–4.

———. "Voting Up-or-Down on an Iran Nuclear Deal: Not as Easy as 123." *Issue Brief*, vol. 7, no. 4, February 11, 2015. Available at: http://www.armscontrol.org/issue-briefs/2015/02-11/Voting-up-or-Down-on-an-Iran-Nuclear-Deal-Not-as-Easy-as-123.

Arnold, Aaron. "Where Does Trump Get the Power to Reimpose Sanctions?" *Bulletin of the Atomic Scientists*, August 15, 2018. Available at: https://thebulletin.org/2018/08/where-does-trump-get-the-power-to-reimpose-sanctions/

———, Bunn, Matthew, Chase, Caitlin, Miller, Steven E., Mowatt-Larssen, Rolf, and Tobey, William H. "The Iran Nuclear Archive: Impressions and Implications." Belfer Center for Science and International Affairs, Harvard Kennedy School, *Belfer Center Report*, April 2019. Available at: https://www.belfercenter.org/sites/default/files/files/publication/The%20Iran%20Nuclear%20Archive.pdf.

Asgari, Mahmoud. "Iran's Defense Diplomacy." *Discourse: An Iranian Quarterly*, vol. 10, nos. 1–2, Winter-Spring 2012, pp. 167–191.

Asgharirad, Javad. "U.S. Public Diplomacy Towards Iran During the George W. Bush Era." Ph.D. dissertation submitted to the Department of History and Cultural Studies, the Freie Universität Berlin, 2012.

Astore, William. "The American Cult of Bombing and Endless War: The Tenets of Air Power That I Didn't Learn in the Air Force." *TomDispatch*, June 4, 2019. Available at: http://www.tomdispatch.com/blog/176571/

Avey, Paul C., Markowitz, Jonathan N., and Reardon, Robert J. "Disentangling Grand Strategy: International Relations Theory and U.S. Grand Strategy." *Texas National Security Review*, vol. 2, no. 1, November 2018. Available at: https://tnsr.org/2018/11/disentangling-grand-strategy-international-relations-theory-and-u-s-grand-strategy/

Axworthy, Michael and Milton, Patrick. "A Westphalian Peace for the Middle East: Why an Old Framework Could Work." *Foreign Affairs*, October 10, 2016. Available at: https://www.foreignaffairs.com/articles/europe/2016-10-10/westphalian-peace-middle-east.

Ayatollahi Tabaar, Mohammad. "As Islamism Fades, Iran Goes Nationalist." *New York Times*, April 3, 2019. Available at: https://www.nytimes.com/2019/04/03/opinion/iran-trump-sanctions.html.

———. *Religious Statecraft: The Politics of Islam in Iran*. New York: Columbia University Press, 2018.

Ayoob, Mohammed. "The Trump Administration's Foolish Endeavors in Iran." *The National Interest*, April 30, 2019. Available at: https://nationalinterest.org/blog/middle-east-watch/trump-administrations-foolish-endeavors-iran-55102.

Ayson, Robeert. "Adjusting to the Trump Presidency." *New Zealand International Review*, vol. 42, no. 3, May-June 2017, pp. 10–13.

Bacevich, Andrew J. *America's War for the Greater Middle East: A Military History*. New York: Random House, 2016.

———. "Less Than Grand Strategy: Zbigniew Brzezinski's Cold War." *The Nation*, December 17/24, 2018, pp. 33–36.

———. *Twilight of the American Century*. Notre Dame, IN: University of Notre Dame Press, 2018.

Bahgat, Gawdat. "Iran-Asia Energy Partnership: Economic and Strategic Implications." *Journal of South Asian and Middle Eastern Studies*, vol. 39, no. 4, Summer 2016, pp. 47–62.

———. "Iran's Ballistic-Missile and Space Program: As Assessment." *Middle East Policy*, vol. 26, no. 1, Spring 2019, pp. 31–48.

———. "Iran's Relations with Persian Gulf Arab States—Implications for the United States." *Journal of South Asian and Middle Eastern Studies*, vol. 38, no. 2, Winter 2015, pp. 12–26.

———. "Nuclear Proliferation: The Islamic Republic of Iran." *Iranian Studies*, vol. 39, no. 3, September 2006, pp. 307–327.

Bajoghli, Narges. "The Hidden Sources of Iranian Strength." *Foreign Policy*, May 15, 2019. Available at: https://foreignpolicy.com/2019/05/15/the-hidden-sources-of-iranian-strength/

———. "Why Trump's Iran Strategy Will Fail." *New York Times*, July 1, 2019, p. A23.

——— and Moosavi, Amir, eds. *Debating the Iran-Iraq War in Contemporary Iran*. London and New York: Routledge, 2018.

Bali, Asli U. "Negotiating Nonproliferation: International Law and Delegation in the Iranian Nuclear Crisis." *UCLA Law Review*, vol. 61, no. 2, January 2014, pp. 232–324.

———. "The US and the Iranian Nuclear Impasse." *Middle East Report*, vol. 36, no. 4, Winter 2006, pp. 12–21.

Banco, Erin and Ackerman, Spencer. "He's Trump's Point Man on Iran—and Under Investigation." *Daily Beast*, March 26, 2019. Available at: https://www.thedaily beast.com/brian-hook-is-trumps-point-man-on-iran-and-under-investigation.

Bandow, Doug. "The Saudi-UAW Alliance Is the Most Dangerous Force in the Middle East Today." *The American Conservative*, June 13, 2018. Available at: http://www.theamericanconservative.com/articles/the-saudi-uae-alliance-is-the-most-dangerous-force-in-the-middle-east-today/

Barnes-Darcey, Julien, Geranmayeh, Ellie, and Lovatt, Hugh. "The Middle East's New Battle Lines." European Council on Foreign Relations, *Policy Brief*, no. 259, May 2018, pp. 1–11.

Barzashka, Ivanka. "Using Enrichment Capacity to Estimate Iran's Breakout Potential." *Federation of the American Scientists Issue Brief*, January 21, 2011, pp. 1–16.

——— and Oelrich, Ivan. "Iran and Nuclear Ambiguity." *Cambridge Review of International Affairs*, vol. 25, no. 1, March 2012, pp. 1–26.

Barzegar, Kayhan. "Balance of Power in the Persian Gulf: An Iranian View." *Middle East Policy*, vol. 17, no. 3, Fall 2010, pp. 74–87.

———. "How Multilateral Diplomacy Can Defeat ISIS." *Discourse: An Iranian Quarterly*, vol. 11, no. 3, Winter 2017, pp. i–vi.

———. "Iran and the Shiite Crescent: Myths and Realities." *Brown Journal of World Affairs*, vol. 15, no. 1, Fall/Winter 2008, pp. 87–99.

———. "Iran's Foreign Policy Strategy After Saddam." *The Washington Quarterly*, vol. 33, no. 1, January 2010, pp. 173–189.

———. "Iran-US Relations in the Light of the Nuclear Negotiations." *The International Spectator*, vol. 49, no. 3, September 2014, pp. 1–7.

———. "Kontrol-e Hesab Shodeh-e Tangehe Hormouz?" (Managed Control of the Strait of Hormuz?) *Shargh*, July 23, 2018. Available at: http://sharghdaily.ir/fa/main/print/191986.

———. "Persia Is Back, But in a Different Form." Atlantic Council, *IranSource*, January 28, 2019. Available at: https://www.atlanticcouncil.org/blogs/iransource/persia-is-back-but-in-a-different-form.

———. "Rahbord-e Siyast-e Kharejiye Iran dar Tavozon-e Ghovaye Manteghei" (Iran's Foreign Policy Strategy for Regional Balance of Power), *Strategic Studies Quarterly* (Tehran), vol. 21, no. 4, Winter 2019, pp. 183–206.

———. "The Iranian Factor in the Emerging Balance of Power in the Middle East." Al Jazeera Centre for Studies, *Reports*, September 9, 2018, pp. 1–14.

———. "The Iranian Quagmire: How to Move Forward." *Bulletin of the Atomic Scientists*, vol. 66, no. 6, November 2010, pp. 109–114.

———. "The Paradox of Iran's Nuclear Consensus." *World Policy Journal*, vol. 26, no. 3, Fall 2009, pp. 21–30.

———. "The Trump Administration's Terrorist Label Is Strengthening the IRGC." Atlantic Council, *IranSource*, April 15, 2019. Available at: https://www.atlantic

council.org/blogs/iransource/the-trump-administration-s-terrorist-label-is-stren
gthening-the-irgc.

——— and Divsallar, Abdolrasool. "Political Rationality in Iranian Foreign Policy."
The Washington Quarterly, vol. 40, no. 1, Spring 2017, pp. 39–53.

——— and Rezaei, Masoud. "Ayatollah Khamenei's Strategic Thinking." *Discourse: An Iranian Quarterly*, vol. 11, no. 3, Winter 2017, pp. 27–54.

Basrur, Rajesh. "Nuclear Deterrence: The Wohlstetter-Blackett Debate Re-visited."
S. Rajaratnam School of International Studies, *RSIS Working Paper*, no. 271, April
15, 2014, pp. 1–15.

Bassiri Tabrizi, Aniseh. "Iran Still Doesn't Want an Escalation." *Foreign Policy*,
May 13, 2019. Available at: https://foreignpolicy.com/2019/05/13/iran-may-be-b
luffing/

——— and Bronk, Justin. "Armed Drones in the Middle East: Proliferation and
Norms." Royal United Services Institute (RUSI), *Occasional Paper*, December
2018, pp. 1–41.

Bassiri Tabrizi, Aniseh and Pantucci, Raffaello, eds. "Understanding Iran's Role in
the Syrian Conflict." Royal United Services Institute (RUSI), *Occasional Paper*,
August 2016, pp. 1–53.

Batmanghelidj, Esfandyar. "Pompeo, Religion, and Regime Change in Iran."
LobeLog, July 20, 2018. Available at: https://lobelog.com/pompeo-religion-and-
regime-change-in-iran/

——— and Hellman, Axel. "Europe, Iran and Economic Sovereignty: A New Banking Architecture in Response to US Sanctions." European Leadership Network and
Bourse & Bazaar, *Global Security Report*, June 2018, pp. 1–22. Available at: https
://www.europeanleadershipnetwork.org/wp-content/uploads/2018/06/Europe-Iran
-and-Economic-Sovereignty-07062018.pdf.

———. "How Europe Could Blunt U.S. Iran Sanctions without Washington Lifting
a Finger." *Foreign Policy*, December 3, 2018. Available at: https://foreignpolic
y.com/2018/12/03/how-europe-can-blunt-u-s-iran-sanctions-without-washington
-raising-a-finger-humanitarian-spv/

———. "Mitigating US Sanctions on Iran: The Case for a Humanitarian Special
Purpose Vehicle." European Leadership Network and Bourse & Bazaar, *Global
Security Policy Brief*, November 2018. Available at: https://www.europeanleade
rshipnetwork.org/wp-content/uploads/2018/11/FINAL-ELN-BB-HSPV-Policy-B
rief-271118-for-ONLINE.pdf.

———. "OFAC Off." *Foreign Policy*, June 15, 2018. Available at: http://foreignp
olicy.com/2018/06/15/ofac-off/

Batmanghelidj, Esfandyar and Mulder, Nicholas. "Lifting Sanctions Isn't as Simple
as It Sounds." *Foreign Policy*, April 15, 2019. Available at: hrrps://foreignpolic
y.com/2019/04/15/lifting-sanctions-isnt-as-simple-as-it-sounds-soudan-iran-bashi
r-rouhani-obama-trump-jcpoa-reconstruction/

Batmanghelidj, Esfandyar and Shah, Sahil. "Protecting Europe-Iran Trade to Prevent
War: A Provisional Assessment of INSTEX." European Leadership Network and
Bourse & Bazaar, *Global Security Policy Brief*, June 28, 2019. Available at: https

://www.europeanleadershipnetwork.org/policy-brief/protecting-europe-iran-trade-t
o-prevent-war-a-provisional-assessment-of-instex/

Beeman, William O. *The "Great Satan vs. the "Mad Mullahs": How the United
States and Iran Demonize Each Other*. Chicago: University of Chicago Press,
2008.

Behravesh, Maysam. "A Crisis of Confidence Revisited: Iran-West Tensions and
Mutual Demonization." *Asian Politics & Policy*, vol. 3, no. 3, July 2011, pp.
327–347.

Benjamin, Medea. "Israel and Saudi Arabia: Strange Bedfellows in the New Middle
East." *Foreign Policy in Focus*, May 18, 2016. Available at: http://fpif.org/israel-sa
udi-arabia-strange-bedfellows-new-middle-east/

———. *Kingdom of the Unjust: Behind the US-Saudi Connection*. New York: O/R
Books, 2016.

Bergman, Ronen. "When Israel Hatched a Secret Plan to Assassinate Iranian Scientists." *Politico Magazine*, March 5, 2018. Available at: https://www.politico.com/
magazine/story/2018/03/05/israel-assassination-iranian-scientists-217223.

Bew, John and Jones, David Martin. "A Trump Doctrine?" *The National Interest*, no.
153, January/February 2018, pp. 43–52.

Beydoun, Khaled A. and Zahawi, Hamada D. "Divesting From Sectarianism: Reimagining Relations Between Iran and the Arab Gulf States." *Journal of International Affairs*, vol. 69, no. 2, Spring/Summer 2016, pp. 47–63.

Bhadrakumar, M.K. "Trump Scores an Own-Goal in the Game Against Iran." *Asia
Times*, August 13, 2018. Available at: http://www.atimes.com/article/trump-scor
es-an-own-goal-in-the-game-against-iran/

Biswas, Shampa. *Nuclear Desire: Power and the Postcolonial Nuclear Order*. Minneapolis: University of Minnesota Press, 2014.

Blackwill, Robert D., ed. *Iran: The Nuclear Challenge*. New York: Council on Foreign Relations Press, 2012.

———. "Trump's Foreign Policies Are Better Than They Seem." Council on Foreign
Relations, *Council Special Report*, no. 84, April 2019, pp. 1–104.

Blanc, Jarrett. "Memo to Trump: Iran Is Not North Korea." *Politico Magazine*, July
24, 2018. Available at: https://www.politico.com/magazine/story/2018/07/24/
memo-to-trump-iran-isnt-north-korea-219032#

Blechman, Barry and Moore, R. Taj. *Iran in Perspective: Holding Iran to Peaceful
Uses of Nuclear Technology*, Washington, DC: Stimson Center, March 2012.

Bochkarev, Danila and Hanrath, Jan. "Envisioning the Future: Iranian and Saudi Perspectives on the Post-Oil Economy." Center for Applied Research in Partnership
with the Orient (CARPO), *Brief*, no. 7, April 18, 2017, pp. 1–9.

Boggs, Carl. *Fascism Old and New: American Politics at the Crossroads*. London
and New York: Routledge, 2018.

Boksa, Michal and Hendricks-Costello, Caitlyn. "U.S. Foreign Policy: From the
Force of Politics to the Politics of Force." Columbia University, *Journal of International Affairs*, October 11, 2018. Available at: https://jia.sipa.columbia.edu/onlin
e-articles/us-politics-of-force.

Bolourchi, Neda. "Lessons from the Iran-Iraq War: Iranian Minorities Won't Lead the Transformative Change." Atlantic Council, *IranSource*, August 17, 2018. Available at: http://www.atlanticcouncil.org/blogs/iransource/lessons-from-the-iran-iraq-war-iranian-minorities-won-t-lead-transformative-change.

———. "The Sacred Defense: Sacrifice and Nationalism Across Minority Communities in Post-Revolutionary Iran." *Journal of the American Academy of Religion*, April 18, 2018. Available at: https://doi.org/10.1093/jaarel/lfx089.

Bolton, John R. "How to Get Out of the Iran Nuclear Deal." *National Review*, August 28, 2017. Available at: https://www.nationalreview.com/2017/08/iran-nuclear-deal-exit-strategy-john-bolton-memo-trump/

———. "To Stop Iran's Bomb, Bomb Iran." *New York Times*, March 26, 2015, p. A23.

Borger, Julian. "Iran Makes 'Substantial' Nuclear Offer in Return for US Lifting Sanctions." *The Guardian*, July 18, 2019. Available at: https://www.theguardian.com/world/2019/jul/18/iran-nuclear-deal-trump-mohammad-javad-zarif-sanctions.

Bott, Uwe. "The Need for a U.S. Policy Pivot Towards Ira." *The Globalist*, October 24, 2018. Available at: https://www.theglobalist.com/united-states-middle-east-iran-saudi-arabia-oil/

Bourse & Bazaar. "When the Sun Sets in the East: New Dynamics in China-Iran Trade Under Sanctions." *Special Report*, January 2019, pp. 1–10.

Bowen, Wyn Q. and Brewer, Jonathan. "Iran's Nuclear Challenge: Nine Years and Counting." *International Affairs*, vol. 87, no. 4, July 2011, pp. 923–943.

Bowen, Wyn Q., Moran, Matthew and Esfandiary, Dina. *Living on the Edge: Iran and the Practice of Nuclear Hedging.* New York: Palgrave Macmillan, 2016.

Brands, Hal. *American Grand Strategy in the Age of Trump.* Washington, DC: Brookings Institution Press, 2018.

Brew, Gregory. "Misreading the 1953 Coup." *LobeLog*, May 20, 2019. Available at: https://lobelog.com/misreading-the-1953-coup/

Brody, David. "Exclusive—Secretary of State Pompeo to CBN News: God May Have Raised Up Trump Like He Raised Up Queen Esther." Christian Broadcasting Network, *CBN News*, March 21, 2019. Available at: https://www1.cbn.com/cbnnews/israel/2019/march/exclusive-secretary-of-state-pompeo-to-news-god-raised-up-trump-like-he-raised-up-queen-esther.

Bromwich, David. *American Breakdown: The Trump Years and How They Befell Us.* New York: Verso 2019.

Brumberg, Daniel. "Trump's Unprincipled 'Principled Realism' Benefits Trump, Not the World." *Arab Center*, Washington, DC, October 5, 2018. Available at: http://arabcenterdc.org/policy_analyses/trumps-unprincipled-principled-realism-benefits-trump-not-the-world/

Burns, William J. *The Back Channel: A Memoir of American Diplomacy and the Case for Its Renewal.* New York: Random House, 2019.

Burr, William. "A Brief History of U.S.-Iranian Nuclear Negotiations." *Bulletin of the Atomic Scientists*, vol. 65, no. 1, January/February 2009, pp. 21–34.

Busch, Nathan E. and Pilat, Joseph, H. *The Politics of Weapons Inspections: Assessing WMD Monitoring and Verification Regimes.* Stanford, CA: Stanford University Press, 2017.

Butt, Ahsan I. "Why did the United States Invade Iraq in 2003?" *Security Studies.* Published online on January 4, 2019. Available at: https://doi.org/10.1080/096364 12.2019.1551567.

Canadian Security Intelligence Service. *Between Hope and Fear: A New Iran?* Ottawa: Canadian Security Intelligence Service, 2016.

Carapico, Sheila, ed. *Arabia Incognita: Dispatches from Yemen and the Gulf.* Charlottesville, VA: Just World Books, 2016.

Carden, James. "This Think Tank Is Pushing Regime Change in Iran—and the White House Is Listening." *The Nation*, July 12, 2018. Available at: https://www.thenatio n.com/article/think-tank-pushing-regime-change-iran-white-house-listening/

Carlson, John. "Iran and a New International Framework for Nuclear Energy." *Discussion* Paper, Project on Managing the Atom, Belfer Center for Science and International Affairs, Harvard Kennedy School, November 2016, pp. 1–21.

Carnelos, Marco. "Pompeo's Falsified History of US-Iran Provocations." *Middle East Eye*, June 21, 2019. Available at: https://www.middleeasteye.net/opinion/us-iran -history-unprovoked-provocations.

———. "Qassem Soleimani Is a Master Strategist, Not a Cartoon Villain." *Middle East Eye*, March 15, 2019. Available at: https://www.middleeasteye.net/opinion/qa ssem-soleimani-master-strategist-not-cartoon-villain.

Carpenter, Ted Galen. "Ally Angst: Why America's Iran Policy Doesn't Have International Support." *The National Interest*, May 24, 2019. Available at: https://na tionalinterest.org/feature/ally-angst-why-americas-iran-policy-doesnt-have-inter national-support-59142.

———. *Gullible Superpower: U.S. Support for Bogus Foreign Democratic Movements.* Washington, DC: Cato Institute, 2019.

———. "How Iran Would Battle the U.S. in a War (It Would Be Bloody)." *The National Interest*, June 20, 2019. Available at: https://nationalinterest.org/blog/s keptics/how-iran-would-battle-us-war-it-would-be-bloody-64681.

———. "Wrong: Trump Is Not an Isolationist." *The National Interest*, June 23, 2019. Available at: https://nationalinterest.org/feature/wrong-trump-not-isolati onist-63552.

——— and Innocent, Malou. *The Ties That Bind: How the U.S.-Saudi Alliance Damages Liberty and Security.* Washington, DC: Cato Institute, 2018.

Carter, Ash. "The Logic of American Strategy in the Middle East." *Survival*, vol. 59, no. 2, April 2017, pp. 13–24.

CBS News, "Full Interview: Javad Zarif on 'Face the Nation'." April 28, 2019. Available at: https://www.cbsnews.com/news/full-interview-javad-zarif-on-face-t he-nation/

Center for Strategic Studies. *Diplomasiye Hastei: 678 Rooz Modiriyat-e Bohran* (Nuclear Diplomacy: 678 Days of Crisis Management). Tehran: Center for Strategic Studies, 2006.

Cho, Il Hyun. *Global Rogues and Regional Orders: The Multidimensional Challenge of North Korea and Iran.* New York: Oxford University Press, 2015.

Chubin, Shahram. *Iran's Nuclear Ambitions.* Washington, DC: Carnegie Endowment for International Peace, 2006.

———. "Iran's Power in Context." *Survival*, vol. 51, no. 1, February–March 2009, pp. 165–190.

———. *Iran's Security Policy: Intentions, Capabilities and Impact.* Washington, DC: Carnegie Endowment for International Peace, 1993.

———. "Is Iran a Military Threat?" *Survival*, vol. 56, no. 2, April–May 2014, pp. 65–88.

———. *Whither Iran? Reform, Domestic Politics and National Security.* Adelphi Paper 342. London: Routledge, 2002.

Cimino-Isaacs, Kathleen, Katzman, Kenneth, and Mix, Derek E. "Efforts to Preserve Economic Benefits of the Iran Nuclear Deal." Congressional Research Service, *In Focus*, June 27, 2018. Available at: https://fas.org/sgp/crs/nuke/IF10916.pdf.

Ciot, Melania-Gabriela. "Idiosyncrasies in Trump's Foreign Policy Decision Making." *Analele Universităţii din Oradea*, no. 8, 2016, pp. 43–60.

Cirincione, Joe. "Bolton's Big Iran Con." *Defense One*, January 12, 2019. Available at: https://www.defenseone.com/ideas/2019/01/boltons-big-iran-con/154109/?oref=d-river.

——— . "Trump's March to War with Iran." *LobeLog*, October 4, 2018. Available at: https://lobelog.com/trumps-march-to-war-with-iran/

——— and Kaszynski, Mary. "The Path to War with Iran Is Paved with Sanctions." *LobeLog*, April 23, 2019. Available at: https://lobelog.com/the-path-to-war-with-iran-is-paved-with-sanctions/

"Civilians Caught in Sanctions Crossfire Need Geneva Convention Protection, Says UN Expert." United Nations Human Rights, Office of the High Commissioner, November 8, 2018. Available at: https://www.ohchr.org/EN/NewsEvents/Pages/DisplayNews.aspx?NewsID=23847&LangID=E.

Clapper, James and Pickering, Thomas. "Trump's Iran Policy Cannot Succeed Without Allies." *The National Interest*, November 9, 2018. Available at: https://nationalinterest.org/blog/middle-east-watch/trumps-iran-policy-cannot-succeed-without-allies-35632.

Clarke, Colin P. and Tabatabai, Ariane M. "Is Major Realignment Taking Place in the Middle East? Why Turkey Is Pivoting Toward Iran and Russia?" *Foreign Affairs*, October 31, 2018. Available at: https://www.foreignaffairs.com/articles/turkey/2018-10-31/major-realignment-taking-place-middle-east.

———. "The Revolutionary Guards Are Ready to Strike Back." *Foreign Policy*, April 11, 2019. Available at: https://foreignpolicy.com/2019/04/11/the-revolutionary-guards-are-ready-to-strike-back/

Clawson, Patrick. "Iran's Vulnerabilities to U.S. Sanctions (Part 1): Finding the Weak Spots." The Washington Institute for Near East Policy, *Policy Watch 2983*, June 14, 2018. Available at: http://www.washingtoninstitute.org/policy-analysis/view/irans-vulnerabilities-to-u.s.-sanctions-part-1-finding-the-weak-spots.

Clifton, Eli. "FDD Aligned with State Department to Attack Supporters of Iran Diplomacy." *LobeLog*, June 1, 2019. Available at: https://lobelog.com/fdd-aligned-with-state-department-to-attack-supporters-of-iran-diplomacy/

———. "Large Payments to Bolton Might Explain His UANI Tweet." *LobLog*, February 26, 2019. Available at: https://lobelog.com/large-payments-to-bolton-might-explain-his-uani-tweet/

———. "Trump Has a $259 Million Reason to Bomb Iran." *LobeLog*, June 22, 2019. Available at: https://lobelog.com/trump-has-a-259-million-reason-to-bomb-iran/

Cockburn, Andrew. "Acceptable Losses: Aiding and Abetting the Saudi Slaughter in Yemen." *Harper's Magazine*, September 2016, pp. 61–68.

Cockburn, Patrick. *The Age of Jihad: Islamic State and the Great War for the Middle East*. New York: Verso Books, 2016.

Cohen, Avner. "Israel's Nuclear Future: Iran, Opacity and the Vision of Global Zero." *Palestine-Israel Journal*, vol. 16, no. 3 & 4, March 2010, pp. 6–19.

———. *The Worst-Kept Secret: Israel's Bargain with the Bomb*. New York: Columbia University Press, 2010.

Cohen, David S. and Weinberg, Zoe. "Sanctions Can't Spark Regime Change: The Trouble with Trump's Approach to Venezuela and Iran." *Foreign Affairs*, April 29, 2019. Available at: https://www.foreignaffairs.com/articles/united-states/2019-04-29/sanctions-cant-spark-regime-change.

Cohen, Eliot A. "Trump's Lucky Year: Why the Chaos Can't Last." *Foreign Affairs*, vol. 97, no. 2, March/April 2018, pp. 2–9.

———, Edelman, Eric, and Takeyh, Ray. "Time to Get Tough on Iran: Iran Policy After the Deal." *Foreign Affairs*, vol, 95, no. 1, January/February 2016, pp. 64–75.

Cole, Brendan. "Mike Pompeo Says Iran Must Listen to the U.S. 'If They Want Their People to Eat'." *Newsweek*, November 9, 2018. Available at: https://www.newsweek.com/mike-pompeo-says-iran-must-listen-us-if-they-want-their-people-eat-1208465.

Cole, Juan. "Pompeo's US Jingoism and Anti-Iran Warmongering Rejected by Mideast Public." *Informed Comment*, January 11, 2019. Available at: https://www.juancole.com/2019/01/jingoism-warmongering-rejected.html.

———. "The Cost of Trumpism in U.S. Policy toward the Middle East." Al Jazeera Centre for Studies, *Reports*, April 15, 2018, pp. 1–12.

———. "Top Ten Differences Between the Iraq War and Trump's Proposed Iran War." *Informed Comment*, May 15, 2015. Available at: https://www.juancole.com/2019/05/differences-between-proposed.html.

Connable, Ben, Campbell, Jason H., and Madden, Dan. *Stretching and Exploiting Thresholds for High-Order War: How Russia, China, and Iran Are Eroding American Influence Using Time-Tested Measures Short of War*. Santa Monica, CA: RAND Corporation, 2016.

Corbett, Jessica. "'A Reckless Advocate of Military Force': Demands for John Bolton's Dismissal After Reports He Asked Pentagon for Options to Strike Iran." *Common Dreams*, January 13, 2019. Available at: https://www.commondreams.org/news/2019/01/13/reckless-advocate-military-force-demands-john-boltons-dismissal-after-reports-he.

Cordesman, Anthony H. and Al-Rodhan, Khalid R. *Iran's Weapons of Mass Destruction: The Real and Potential Threat*. Washington, DC: Center for Strategic and International Studies, 2006.

Cordesman, Anthony and Harrington, Nicholas. *The Arab Gulf States and Iran: Military Spending, Modernization, and the Shifting Military Balance in the Gulf*. Washington, DC: Center for Strategic and International Studies, 2018.

Cordesman, Anthony and Toukan, Abdullah. *Iran and the Gulf Military Balance.* Washington, DC: Center for Strategic and International Studies, 2016.

———. *The National Security Economics of the Middle East: Comparative Spending, Burden Sharing, and Modernization.* Washington, DC: Center for Strategic and International Studies, 2017.

Costello, Ryan and Cullis, Tyler. "Restoring U.S. Credibility: Returning to the Iran Nuclear Agreement." National Iranian American Council (NIAC), *Report*, November 19, 2018. Available at: https://www.niacouncil.org/restoring-u-s-credibility-re turning-to-the-iran-nuclear-agreement/

Costello, Ryan and Toossi, Sina. "Mohammad bin Salman Is the Next Salman Hussein." *Foreign Policy*, October 29, 2018. https://foreignpolicy.com/2018/10/2 9/mohammed-bin-salman-is-the-next-saddam-hussein-mbs-iraq-iran-rumsfeld-rea gan-gulf-war/

Cotton, Shea and Varnum, Jessica C. "No, Iran Is Not Pursuing an ICBM (Yet)." Nuclear Threat Initiative (NTI), *Analysis-Articles*, August 2, 2017. Available at: https://www.nti.org/analysis/articles/no-iran-is-no-pursuing-an-icbm/

Council of the European Union. "Iran: Council Adopts Conclusions." *Press Release 65/19*, February 4, 2019. Available at: https://www.consilium.europa.eu/en/press/ press-releases/2019/02/04/iran-council-adopts-conclusions/pdf.

Crist, David. *The Twilight War: The Secret History of America's Thirty-Year Conflict with Iran.* New York: Penguin Press, 2012.

Cronberg, Tarja. *Nuclear Multilateralism and Iran: Inside EU Negotiations.* London and New York: Routledge, 2017.

Cullis, Tyler. "Does ISA Extension Violate the JCPOA?" *Sanction Law*, December 19, 2016. Available at: http://sanctionlaw.com/does-isa-extension-violate-the-j cpoa/

Czulda, Robert. "Russia Is a Clear Winner in US-Iran Tensions." Atlantic Council, *IranSource*, May 28, 2019. Available at: https://www.atlanticcouncil.org/blogs/ir ansource/russia-is-a-clear-winner-in-us-iran-tensions.

———. "The Defensive Dimension of Iran's Military Doctrine: How Would They Fight?" *Middle East Policy*, vol. 23, no. 1, Spring 2016, pp. 92–109.

Daalder, Ivo H. and Lindsay, James H. "The Committee to Save the World: America's Allies Must Step Up as America Steps Down." *Foreign Affairs*, vol. 97, no. 6, November/December 2018, pp. 72–83.

———. *The Empty Throne: America's Abdication of Global Leadership.* New York: PublicAffairs, 2018.

Dabashi, Hamid. "Is Trump a King Cyrus or a Queen Esther?" *Al Jazeera*, April 11, 2019. Available at: https://www.aljazeera.com/indepth/opinion/trump-king-cy rus-queen-esther-190411105108358.html.

———. "The Idea of Regime Change in Iran Is Delusional." *Al Jazeera*, June 6, 2018. Available at: https://www.aljazeera.com/indepth/opinion/idea-regime-c hange-iran-delusional-180604165615762.html.

———. "'The Ugly Americans': From Kermit Roosevelt to John Bolton." *Al Jazeera*, June 1, 2019. Available at: https://www.aljazeera.com/indepth/opinion/ ugly-americans-kermit-roosevelt-john-bolton-190531154843191.html.

Dalton, Melissa D. "How Iran's Hybrid-War Tactics Help and Hurt It." *Bulletin of the Atomic Scientists*, vol. 73, no. 5, 2017, pp. 312–315.

Danish Institute for International Studies (DIIS). *China and the Challenges in Greater Middle East: Conference Report.* Copenhagen: DIIS, 2016.

Darvish, Rezadad. "Tahavolat-e Baynolmelali va Chaharchoob-e Siyasat-e Khareji-e Trump" (International Development and a Framework for Understanding Trump's Foreign Policy). *Tehran Foreign Policy Studies Quarterly*, vol. 3, no. 10, Autumn 2018. Available at: http://tfpsq.net/fa/post.php?id=82.

Dassa Kaye, Dalia. "Israel's Iran Policies After the Nuclear Deal." *Perspective*, RAND Center for Middle East Public Policy, document number PE-207-CMEPP, 2016, pp. 1–24.

Davidson, Christopher. *Shadow Wars: The Secret Struggle for the Middle East.* London: Oneworld Publications, 2016.

Davis, Jacquelyn K. and Pfaltzgraff, Robert L., Jr. *Anticipating a Nuclear Iran: Challenges for U.S. Security.* New York: Columbia University Press, 2013.

Davis, Lynn E., Martini, Jeffrey, Nader, Alireza, Dassa Kaye, Dalia, Quinlivan, James T., and Steinberg, Paul. *Iran's Nuclear Future: Critical U.S. Policy Choices.* Santa Monica, CA: RAND Corporation, 2011.

Delpech, Therese. *Iran and the Bob.* London: Hurst & Co., 2006.

Del Sarto, Raffaella A., Malmvig, Helle, and Soler i Lecha, Eduard. "Interregnum: The Regional Order in the Middle East and North Africa After 2011." Middle East and North Africa Regional Architecture (MENARA), *Final Reports*, no. 1, February 2019, pp. 1–57.

Demir, Imran. "Domestic Determinants of the U.S.-Iran Rivalry." *Insight Turkey*, vol. 20, no. 2, Spring 2018, pp. 201–221.

DePetris, Daniel. "Trump's Geopolitical Mistake." *Washington Examiner*, August 12, 2018. Available at: https://www.washingtonexaminer.com/opinion/trumps-geopolitical-mistake.

Des Roches, David and Thafer, Dania, eds. *The Arms Trade, Military Services and the Security Market in the Gulf States: Trends and Implications.* Berlin: Gerlach Press, 2016.

DiMaggio, Anthony R. *Selling War, Selling Hope: Presidential Rhetoric, the News Media, and U.S. Foreign Policy since 9/11.* Albany, NY: State University of New York Press, 2016.

Divsallar, Abdolrasool. "Will Iran Adopt a 'Massive Retaliation' Doctrine?" *LobeLog*, May 28, 2019. Available at: https://lobelog.com/will-iran-adopt-a-massive-retaliation-doctrine/

Dizaji, Sajjad F. and Farzanegan, Mohammad R. "Do Sanctions Reduce the Military Spending in Iran?" University of Marburg, *Joint Discussion Paper Series in Economics*, no. 31, 2018. Available at: https://www.uni-marburg.de/fb02/makro/forschung/magkspapers/paper_2018/31-2018_dizaji.pdf.

Djalili, Mohammad-Reza and Kellner, Thierry. "Turkey and Iran, Allies or Rivals? Two Great Empires." *Le Monde diplomatique*, January 2017. Available at: http://mondediplo.com/2017/01/06empires.

Doost va Doshman-e Khod Ra Beshnaseem: Che Keshvarhai dar Jalaseh-e Shoraye Amniyat dar Moghabel-e Ziyadehkhahiy-e Amrika Alayhe Iran Eestadegi Kardand?" (Know Our Friends and Enemies: Which Countries Stood Up to America's Excessive Anti-Iran Demands at the UN Security Council?) *Raja News*, September 27, 2018. Available at: http://www.rajanews.com/node/293089?format=print.

Dorf, Michael C. "The Senators' Letter to Iran and Domestic Incorporation of International Law." *Political Science Quarterly*, vol. 131, no. 1, Spring 2016, pp. 45–68.

Dorfman, Zach and McLaughlin, Jenna. "The CIA's Communications Suffered a Catastrophic Compromise. It Started with Iran." *Yahoo News*, November 2, 2018. Available at: https://finance.yahoo.com/news/cias-communications-suffered-catas trophic-compromise-started-iran-090018710.html.

Dorraj, Manochehr and Entessar, Nader. *Iran's Northern Exposure: Foreign Policy Challenges in Eurasia*. Occasional Paper No. 13. Doha, Qatar: Center for International and Regional Studies, Georgetown University School of Foreign Service in Qatar, 2013.

Dorraj, Manochehr and Monshipouri, Mahmood. "Trump's Iran Policy: From Art of the Deal to the Mirage of Regime Change." *IranSource*, Atlantic Council, June 14, 2018. Available at: http://www.atlanticcouncil.org/blogs/iransource/trump-s-iran -policy-from-the-art-of-the-deal-to-the-mirage-of-regime-change.

Dorsey, James M. "Destabilisig Iran." *Countercurrents*, April 23, 2019. Available at: https://countercurrents.org/2019/04/destabilising-iran.

———. "Inside the Beltway: Iran Hardliners vs. Iran Hardliners." *International Policy Digest*, January 16, 2019. Available at: https://intpolicydigest.org/2019/01 /16/inside-the-beltway-iran-hardliners-vs-iran-hardliners/

———. "Talking to Rouhani: Trump Shooting from the Hip? Or Following a Script?" *The Globalist*, August 1, 2018. Available at: https://www.theglobalist. com/trum-rouhani-united-states-iran-jcpoa/

———. "Transition in the Middle East: Transition to What?" *National Security*, vol. 1, no. 1, August 2018, pp. 84–108.

———. "US's Iran Sanctions: Mixed Prospects and a Beyond-SWIFT Question." Al Jazeera Centre for Studies, *Reports*, December 27, 2018, pp. 1–13.

Drezner, Daniel W. "This Time Is Different: Why U.S. Foreign Policy Will Never Recover." *Foreign Affairs*, vol. 98, no. 3, May/June 2019, pp. 10–17.

Dugan, Andrew. "After Nuclear Deal, U.S. Views of Iran Remain Dismal." *Gallup*, February 17, 2016. Available at: http://www.gallup.com/poll/189272/after-nucle ar-deal-views-iran-remain-dismal.aspx.

Early, Bryan R. *Busted Sanctions: Explaining Why Economic Sanctions Fail*. Stanford, CA: Stanford University Press, 2015.

——— and Asal, Victor. "Nuclear Weapons and Existential Threats: Insights from a Comparative Analysis of Nuclear-Armed States." *Comparative Strategy*, vol. 33, no. 4, September–October 2014, pp. 303–320.

Ebadi, Shirin and Williams, Jody. "Maximum Diplomacy Can Prevent War with Iran." *New York Times*, July 8, 2019. Available at: https://www.nytimes.com/2 019/07/08/opinion/iran-trump.html.

Edelman, Eric and Takeyh, Ray. *Revolution and Aftermath: Forging a New Strategy toward Iran.* Stanford, CA: Hoover Institution Press, 2018.

Ehteshami, Anoushiravan and Molavi, Reza, eds. *Iran and the International System.* London and New York: Routledge, 2012.

Ehteshami, Anoushiravan, Quilliam, Neil, and Bahgat, Gawdat, eds. *Security and Bilateral Issues Between Iran and its Arab Neighbours.* London and New York: Palgrave Macmillan, 2017.

Ehteshami, Anoushiravan and Zweiri, Mahjoob, eds. *Iran's Foreign Policy: From Khatami to Ahmadinejad.* Reading, UK: Ithaca Press, 2011.

Einhorn, Robert. "Let's Get Realistic on North Korea and Iran." Brookings Institution, *Order from Chaos*, October 5, 2018. Available at: https://www.brookings.edu/blog/order-from-chaos/2018/10/05/lets-get-realistic-on-north-korea-and-iran/

———. "The JCPOA Should Be Maintained and Reinforced with a Broad Regional Strategy." Election 2016 and America's Future Series, Brookings Institution, September 29, 2016. Available at: https://www.brookings.edu/research/the-jcpoa-should-be-maintained-and-reinforced-with-a-broad-regional-strategy/

——— and Nephew, Richard. "The Iran Nuclear Deal: Prelude to Proliferation in the Middle East?" Brookings Institution, *Arms Control and Non-Proliferation Series Paper 11*, May 2016, pp. 1–61.

Eiran, Ehud and Malin, Martin B. "The Sum of All Fears: Israel's Perception of a Nuclear-Armed Iran." *The Washington Quarterly*, vol. 36, no. 3, Summer 2013, pp. 77–89.

Eisenstadt, Michael. "The Strategic Culture of the Islamic Republic of Iran: Operational and Policy Implications." Middle East Studies (MES), Marine Corps University, *MES Monographs*, no. 1, August 2011, pp. 1–19.

"Elaam-e Shoroot-e Jomhouri-e Eslami Iran Baraye Edame-e Barjam ba Oroopa" (Announcement of Iran's Conditions for the Continuation of the JCPOA with Europe). Aytollah Ali Khamenei's Specific Conditions that Europe Has to Meet for the JCPOA to Survive, May 23, 2018. Available at: http://farsi.khamenei.ir/news.content?id=39650.

Eland, Ivan. *War and the Rogue Presidency: Restoring the Republic After Congressional Failure.* Oakland, CA: Independent Institute, 2019.

ElBaradei, Mohamed. *The Age of Deception: Nuclear Diplomacy in Treacherous Times.* New York: Metropolitan Books, 2011.

Elleman, Michael. "Why Iran's Satellite Launch Does Not Amount to an ICBM Test." International Institute for Strategic Studies (IISS), *Analysis*, January 17, 2019. Available at: https://www.iiss.org/blogs/analysis/2019/01/iran-satellite-launch.

——— and Firzpatrick, Mark. "How to Strike a Missile Deal with Iran." *Foreign Policy*, August 6, 2018. Available at: https://foreignpolicy.com/2018/08/06/how-to-strike-a-missile-deal-with-iran-trump-ballistic-nuclear-warheads/

———. "No, Iran Does Not Have an ICBM Program." *War on the Rocks*, March 5, 2018. Available at: https://warontherocks.com/2018/03/no-iran-not-icbm-program/

Engelhardt, Tom. *A Nation Unmade by War.* Chicago: Haymarket Books, 2018.

———. "What Will Donald Trump Be Remembered for? The World According to The Don(ald)." *TomDispatch*, September 6, 2018. Available at: http://www.tomd ispatch.com/post/176464/tomgram%3A_engelhardt%2C_history%2C_memor y%2C_and_donald_trump/#more.

England, Andrew. "The Complex Brinkmanship Behind Iran's Nuclear Response." *Financial Times*, July 3, 2019. Available at: https://www.ft.com/content/75fd3f62 -9cd1-11e9-9c06-a4640c9feebb.

Entessar, Nader. "Iran's Nuclear Decision-Making Calculus." *Middle East Policy*, vol. 16, no. 2, Summer 2009, pp. 26–38.

———. "Iran's Nuclear Program and Foreign Policy." In Thomas Juneau and Sam Razavi, eds., *Iranian Foreign Policy Since 2001: Alone in the World*. London and New York: Routledge, 2013, pp. 70–86.

———. "Iran's Security Challenges." *The Muslim World*, vol. 94, no. 4, October 2004, pp. 537–554.

———. "Irańsko-saudyjska łamigłówka" (The Iran-Saudi Conundrum). In Robert Czulda, ed., *Islamska Republika Iranu na arenie międzynarodowej: Motywacje i kierunki polityki* (The Islamic Republic of Iran in the International Arena: Motivations and Policy Directions). Łódź, Poland: University of Łódź Press, 2019, pp. 285–309.

———. "Israel and Iran's National Security." *Journal of South Asian and Middle Eastern Studies*, vol. 27, no. 4, Summer 2004, pp. 1–19.

———. "Superpowers and Persian Gulf Security." *Third World Quarterly*, vol. 10, no. 4, October 1988, pp. 1427–1451.

———. "The Limits of Sports Diplomacy in US-Iran Relations." *LobeLog Foreign Policy*, February 9, 2017. Available at: http://lobelog.com/the-limits-of-sports-diplomacy-in-us-iran-relations/

———. "Uneasy Neighbors: Iran and the Kurdish Regional Government." *Journal of South Asian and Middle Eastern Studies*, vol. 41, no. 2, Winter 2018, pp. 73–84.

———. "Whither Iran's Nuclear Program?" *Bustan: The Middle East Book Review*, vol. 4, no. 1, 2013, pp. 33–41.

——— and Afrasiabi, Kaveh. *Iran Nuclear Accord and the Remaking of the Middle East*. Lanham, MD: Rowman & Littlefield, 2018.

——— and Afrasiabi, Kaveh. *Iran Nuclear Negotiations: Accord and Détente Since the Geneva Agreement of 2013*. Lanham, MD: Rowman & Littlefield, 2015.

——— and Afrasiabi, Kaveh. "Iran's Range of Options." *LobeLog*, April 6, 2018. Available at: https://lobelog.com/irans-range-of-options/

———. *Maraton-e Mozakerat-e Hasteii: Az Sa'ad Abad ta Koborg* (The Marathon of Iran Nuclear Negotiations: From Sa'ad Abad to Coburg). Translated by Saeid Jafari and Rouhollah Faghihi. Tehran: Ghoomes Publishing, 2016.

———. "Nuclear Deal Could Reset US-Iran Relations." *Boston Globe*. November 19, 2014. Available at: http://www.bostonglobe.com/opinion/2014/11/19/nucl ear-deal-could-reset-iran-relations/eovhBLrPdNOCG1Zn7eNDXN/story.html.

———. "Rebooting US-Iran Relations." *Boston Globe*, September 24, 2013, p. A13.

———. "The Iran Nuclear Accord and the Future of Nonproliferation: A Constructivist-Critical Approach." *Brown Journal of World Affairs*, vol. 22, no. 2, Spring/Summer 2016, pp. 177–195.

———. "The Strait of Hormuz: Iran's Potential Measures to US Hostility." *LobeLog*, August 14, 2018. Available at: https://lobelog.com/the-strait-of-hormuz-irans-pot ential-countermeasure-to-us-hostility/

Entous, Adam. "The Enemy of My Enemy: How Donald Trump, Israel, and the Gulf States Plan to Fight Iran—and Leave the Palestinians and the Obama Years Behind." *The New Yorker*, June 18, 2018, pp. 30–45.

Episkopos, Mark. "Behold: Iran's Mini-Submarine Force Is Dangerous (Partly Thanks to North Korea)." *The National Interest*, May 26, 2019. Available at: https ://nationalinterest.org/blog/buzz/behold-irans-mini-submarine-force-dangerous-pa rtly-thanks-north-korea-59562.

Erästö, Tytti. "Dissecting International Concerns About Iran's Missiles." Stockholm International Peace Research Institute (SIPRI), *Commentary/Backgrounders*, November 15, 2018. Available at: https://www.sipri.org/commentary/topical-back grounder/2018/dissecting-international-concerns-about-irans-missiles.

———. "The Lack of Disarmament in the Middle East: A Thorne in the Side of the NPT." Stockholm International Peace Research Institute (SIPRI), *SIPRI Insights on Peace and Security*, no. 2019/1, January 2019, pp. 1–23. Available at: https:// www.sipri.org/sites/default/files/2019-01/sipriinsight1901.pdf.

———. "Time for Europe to Put Iran's Missile Programme in Context." Stockholm International Peace Research Institute (SIPRI), *Commentary/Backgrounders*, October 30, 2017. Available at: https://www.sipri.org/commentary/topical-backgroun der/2017/time-europe-put-irans-missile-programme-context.

Erlich, Reese. *The Iran Agenda Today: The Real Story Inside Iran and What's Wrong with U.S. Policy*. London and New York: Routledge, 2018.

———. "The 'Trump Doctrine' Is Sinking Fast." *48 Hills*, June 28, 2019. Available at: https://48hills.org/2019/06/trump-doctrine-sinking/

———. "Trump Is Driving Iran into Russia's Arms." *Foreign Policy*, May 29, 2019. Available at: https://foreignpolicy.com/2019/05/29/trump-is-driving-iran-into-r ussias-arms-nuclear-deal-putin-rouhani-sanctions/

———. "What the Khashoggi Case Tells Us About Terrorism." *48 Hills*, October 19, 2018. Available at: https://48hills.org/2018/10/what-the-khashoggi-case-tel ls-us-about-terrorism/

Escobar, Pepe. "Economic War on Iran Is War on Eurasia Integration." *Asia Times*, August 14, 2018. Available at: http://www.atimes.com/article/economic-war-on -iran-is-war-on-eurasia-integration/

———. "EU Finally Stands Up to US 'Bullying' Over Iran Sanctions." *Asia Times*, September 30, 2018. Available at: http://www.atimes.com/article/eu-finally-stan ds-up-to-us-bullying-over-iran-sanctions/

Esfandiary, Dina, "No Country for Oversimplifications: Understanding Iran's Views on the Future of Regional Security Dialogue and Architecture." *Report, Arab Regional Security*, the Century Foundation, January 24, 2018. Available at: https:// tcf.org/content/report/no-country-oversimplifications/

——— and Fitzpatrick, Mark. "Sanctions on Iran: Defining and Enabling 'Success'." *Survival*, vol. 53, no. 5, October–November 2011, pp. 143–156.

——— and Tabatabai, Ariane M. "A Comparative Study of U.S. and Iranian Counter-ISIS Strategies." *Studies in Conflict & Terrorism*, vol. 40, no. 6, 2017, pp. 455–469.

———. "Moscow and Beijing Have Tehran's Back." *Foreign Policy*, July 25, 2018. Available at: https://foreignpolicy.com/2018/07/25/moscow-and-beijing-have-tehrans-back/

———. "Saudi Arabia Cares More About Iran Than Iran Does About Saudi Arabia." *The National Interest*, October 18, 2016. Available at: http://nationalinterest.org/feature/saudi-arabia-cares-more-about-iran-iran-does-about-saudi-18091.

———. "Will China Undermine Trump's Iran Strategy?" *Foreign Affairs*, July 20, 2018. Available at: https://www.foreignaffairs.com/articles/china/2018-07-20/will-china-undermine-trumps-iran-strategy.

Fabius, Laurent. "Inside the Iran Deal: A French Perspective." *The Washington Quarterly*, vol. 39, no. 3, Fall 2016, pp. 7–38.

Faghihi, Rohollah. "The App Destroying Iran's Currency." *Foreign Policy*, November 22, 2018. Available at: https://foreignpolicy.com/2018/11/22/the-app-destroying-irans-currency/

Farmanfarmaian, Roxane. "Can Iran's Shrewd Diplomacy Avert War with Washington?" *The Nation*, July 11, 2019. Available at: https://www.thenation.com/article/can-irans-shrewd-diplomacy-avert-war-with-washington/

Farrell, Henry and Newman, Abraham. "America's Misuse of Its Financial Infrastructure." *The National Interest*, April 15, 2019. Available at: https://nationalinterest.org/feature/america's-misuse-its-financial-infrastructure-52707.

Fathollah-Nejad, Ali. "German-Iranian Relations After the Nuclear Deal: Geopolitical and Economic Dimensions." *Insight Turkey*, vol, 18, no. 1, Winter 2016, pp. 59–77.

Faux, Jeff. "Why Is Iran Our Enemy?" *The Nation*, June 13, 2016. Available at: http://www.thenation.com/article/why-is-iran-our-enemy/

Fayazmanesh, Sasan. *Containing Iran: Obama's Policy of Tough Diplomacy.* Newcastle upon Tyne: Cambridge Scholars Publishing, 2013.

———. *The United States and Iran: Sanctions, Wars and the Policy of Dual Containment.* London and New York: Routledge, 2008.

Feffer, John. "The War Before the Iran War." *Foreign Policy In Focus*, August 1, 2018. Available at: https://fpif.org/the-war-before-the-iran-war/

Fehrs, Matthew. "Letting Bygones Be Bygones: Rapprochement in US Foreign Policy." *Foreign Policy Analysis*, vol. 12, no. 2, April 2016, pp. 128–148.

Fernandez, Belen. "Meet Amir Fakhravar, the 'Snake Oil Salesman' Pushing Regime Change in Iran." *Middle East Eye*, July 20, 2018. Available at: http://www.middleeasteye.net/columns/meet-amir-fakhravar-snake-oil-salesman-pushing-regime-change-iran-1990398486.

Fikenscher, Sven-Eric and Reardon, Robert J. "The Fool's Errand for a Perfect Deal with Iran." *The Washington Quarterly*, vol. 37, no. 3, Fall 2014, pp. 61–75.

Filkins, Dexter. "On the Warpath: Can John Bolton Sell an Isolationist President on Military Force?" *The New Yorker*, May 6, 2019, pp. 32–45.

Finer, Jon. "The Last War—and the Next? Learning the Wrong Lessons from Iraq." *Foreign Affairs*, May 28, 2019. Available at: https://www.foreignaffairs.com/reviews/review-essay/2019-05-28/last-war-and-next.

Fisher, Max and Taub, Amanda. "Sending Signals, and Lots of Noise, to Ira." *The Interpreter—New York Times*, May 16, 2019. Available at: https://static.nytimes.co m/email-content/INT_13285.html.

Fisk, Robert. "Rouhani's Victory Is Good News for Iran, But Bad News for Trump and His Sunni Allies." *Independent*, May 20, 2017. Available at: http://www.inde pendent.co.uk/voices/iran-election-rouhani-saudi-arabia-trump-bad-news-a774 6146.html.

———. "This Is the Aim of Donald Trump's Visit to Saudi Arabia—and It Isn't Good for Shia Communities." *Independent*, May 18, 2017. Available at: http://www.inde pendent.co.uk/voices/donald-trump-saudi-arabia-iran-iraq-kurdish-population-shia -muslims-a7742276.html.

Fischer, Joschka. "Trump's Lose-Lose Iran Strategy." *Project Syndicate*, June 28, 2019. Available at: https://www.project-syndicate.org/commentary/trump-losi ng-iran-strategy-by-joschka-fischer-2019-06.

Fitzpatrick, Mark. "An Order of Priorities in Confronting Iran." *Survival*, vol. 59, no. 2, April 2017, pp. 25–29.

———. "Assessing Iran's Nuclear Programme." *Survival*, vol. 48, no. 3, Autumn 2006, pp. 5–26.

———. "Can Iran's Nuclear Capability Be Kept Latent?" *Survival*, vol. 49, no. 1, Spring 2007, pp. 33–58.

———. "Iran and North Korea: The Proliferation Nexus." *Survival*, vol. 48, no. 1, Spring 2006, pp. 61–80.

———. "Iran: The Fragile Promise of the Fuel-Swap Plan." *Survival*, vol. 52, no. 3, June–July 2010, pp. 67–94.

———. "Iran Will Determine Obama's Legacy." *Survival*, vol. 54, no. 6, December 2012–January 2013, pp. 41–48.

———. "Khashoggi Case Exposes US Contradictions on Iran." International Institute for Strategic Studies (IISS), *Analysis*, October 23, 2018. Available at: https://ww w.iiss.org/blogs/analysis/2018/10/khashoggi-us-contradictions-iran.

———. "The IAEA's Diligent Investigation of Iran's 'Atomic Archive'." International Institute for Strategic Studies (IISS), *Analysis*, March 20, 2019. Available at: https://www.iiss.org/blogs/analysis/2019/03/the-iaeas-diligent-investigation-of-irans-atomic-archive.

———. *The Iranian Nuclear Crisis: Avoiding Worst-Case Outcomes*. Adelphi Paper 398. London: Routledge, 2008.

———, Elleman, Michael, and Izewicz, Paulina. *Uncertain Future: The JCPOA and Iran's Nuclear and Missile Programmes*. Adelphi Series 466–467. London: Routledge/IISS, 2019.

Flannery, Francis, Deaton, Michael L., and Walton, Timothy R. "Radical Apocalyp-ticism and Iranian Nuclear Proliferation: A Systems Oriented Analysis." *International Journal of Intelligence and Counterintelligence*, vol. 26, no. 4, 2013, pp. 693–729.

Flynn, Michael T. Lt. General (Ret.) and Ledeen, Michael. *The Field of Fight: How We Can Win the Global War Against Radical Islam and Its Allies*. New York: St. Martin's Press, 2016.

Forden, Geoffrey and Thomson, John. "Iran as a Pioneer Case for Multilateral Nuclear Arrangements." *Science, Technology and Global Security Working Group*, Massachusetts Institute of Technology, May 24, 2007, pp. 1–39.

Forozan, Hesam. *The Military in Post-Revolutionary Iran: The Evolution and Role of the Revolutionary Guards*. London and New York: Routledge, 2018.

FOX New Sunday, "Iran Foreign Minister Accuses US and Mideast Officials of Trying to Provoke a Conflict with Iran." April 28, 2019. Available at: https://video.f oxnews.com/v/6030800403001/#sp=show-clips.

Freedman, Guy. "Iranian Approach to Deterrence: Theory and Practice." *Comparative Strategy*, vol. 36, no. 5, 2017, pp. 400–412.

Friedman, Uri. "Trump, Iran, and the Dangers of Presidential Bluffing." *The Atlantic*, July 23, 2018. Available at: https://www.theatlantic.com/international/archive/ 2018/07/donald-trump-iran-bluff/565844/

Frum, David. "Take It From an Iraq War Supporter—War with Iran Would Be a Disaster." *The Atlantic*, May 15, 2019. Available at: https://www.theatlantic.com/ ideas/archive/2019/05/the-iraq-war-was-a-failurewar-with-iran-would-be-worse/ 589534/

Gaddis, John Lewis. *On Grand Strategy*. New York: Penguin Press, 2018.

Gaffar, Md. Abdul. "Regional Supremacy in West Asia: A Case Study of Iran and Saudi Arabia." *Journal of South Asian and Middle Eastern Studies*, vol. 39, no. 4, Summer 2016, pp. 63–83.

Ganji, Babak. *Main Currents in Iranian Strategy Since 9/11.* London: Conflict Studies Centre, 2005.

———. *Politics of Confrontation: The Foreign Policy of the USA and Revolutionary Iran*. London: I.B. Tauris/Tauris, 2006.

Gardner, Hall. *World War Trump: The Risks of America's New Nationalism*. Amherst, NY: Prometheus Books, 2018.

Gartner, John and Buser, Steven, ed. *Rocket Man: Nuclear Madness and the Mind of Donald Trump*. Asheville, NC: Chiron Publications, 2018.

Garver, John W. "China and Iran: An Emerging Partnership Post-Sanctions." Middle East Institute, *MEI Policy Focus 2016-3*, February 2016, pp. 1–8.

Gause III, F. Gregory. "'Hegemony' Compared: Great Britain and the United States in the Middle East." *Security Studies*, published online on June 3, 2019. Available at: https://www.tandfonline.com/doi/full/10.1080/09636412.2019.1604987.

———. *The International Relations of the Persian Gulf*. New York: Cambridge University Press, 2009.

Gearan, Anne, DeYoung, Karen, and Sonmez, Felicia, "Trump Says He's Willing to Meet Iranian President Rouhani 'Anytime' and Without Preconditions." *Washington Post*, July 30, 2018. Available at: https://www.washingtonpost.com/poli tics/trump-says-hes-willing-to-meet-iranian-president-rouhani-without-preconditi ons/2018/07/30/89bb6b66-93e3-11e8-80e1-00e80e1fdf43_story.html?utm_ter m=.50a7e58a45ab.

Geranmayeh, Ellie. "Extending the Iran Nuclear Talks: Not Ideal, but Not Defeat." *Arms Control Today*, vol. 45, no. 1, January/February 2015, pp. 8–10.

———. "How Europe Can Save What's Left of the Iran Nuclear Deal." *Foreign Policy*, July 12, 2019. Available at: https://foreignpolicy.com/2019/07/12/how-europe-can-save-whats-left-of-the-iran-nuclear-deal/

———. "The Case for Caution with Iran: Why Trump Should Tread Carefully." *Foreign Affairs*, April 20, 2017. Available at: https://www.foreignaffairs.com/articles/middle-east/2017-04-20/case-caution-iran.

———. "Three Years Later: Europe's Last Push on the Iran Nuclear Deal." *European Council on Foreign Relations*, July 16, 2018. Available at: https://www.ecfr.eu/article/commentary_three_years_later_europes_last_push_on_iran_nuclear_deal.

——— and Batmanghelidj, Esfandyar. "Bankless Task: Can Europe Stay Connected to Iran?" *European Council of Foreign Relations*, October 10, 2018. Available at: https://www.ecfr.eu/article/commentary_bankless_task_can_europe_stay_connected_to_iran.

Geranmayeh, Ellie and Liik, Kadri. "The New Power Couple: Russia and Iran in the Middle East." European Council on Foreign Relations, *Policy Brief*, no. 186, September 2016, pp. 1–15.

Gerecht, Reuel Marc and Takeyh, Ray. "Don't Fear Regime Change in Iran." *Wall Street Journal*, June 11, 2018. Available at: https://www.wsj.com/articles/dont-fear-regime-change-in-iran-1528756928.

Ghalehdar, Payam. "This Is Not the Regime Change Strategy You're Looking for." *The National Interest*, June 20, 2018. Available at: http://nationalinterest.org/feature/not-the-iran-regime-strategy-youre-looking-26351.

Ghassemi, Farhad and Poorjam, Bahareh. "Mosabegh-e Taslihati, Sobat-e Rahbordi va Nazm-e Mantaghe-e Khavar-e Miyaneh" (The Arms Race, Strategic Stability, and the Regional Order of the Middle East). *Journal of Defense Policy*, vol. 23, no. 90, Spring 2015, pp. 79–107.

Ghazanfari, Kamran. *Hassan Rouhani dar Yek Negah: Barressiye Savabegh, Amal-kardha va Mavaze* (A Look at Hassan Rouhani: Analysis of His Background, Performance and Stance). Tehran, 2018. Available at: http://razeghatname.ir/media/2018/04/%D8%B1%D9%88%D8%AD%D8%A7%D9%86%DB%8C-3.pdf.

Gilsinan, Kathy. "Trying to Kill the Iran Deal Could End Up Saving It." *The Atlantic*, March 17, 2019. Available at: https://www.theatlantic.com/politics/archive/2019/03/us-attempts-kill-iran-nuclear-deal-could-save-it/585109/

Giraldi, Philip. "Attacking Iran: Fake News About a Terrorist Connection Could Serve as a Pretext for War." *The Unz Review*, February 26, 2019. Available at: http://www.unz.com/pgiraldi/attacking-iran/

Giroux, Henry A. *American Nightmare: Facing the Challenge of Fascism*. San Francisco: City Lights Publishers, 2018.

———. *The Public in Peril: Trump and the Menace of American Authoritarianism*. London and New York: Routledge, 2017.

Glaser, Charles L. and Kelanic, Rosemary A., eds. *Crude Strategy: Rethinking the US Military Commitment to Defend Persian Gulf Oil*. Washington, DC: Georgetown University Press, 2016.

Glass, Charles. "From the Somme to the Persian Gulf, Lessons on Shows of Force." *Stratfor Worldview*, May 22, 2019. Available at: https://worldview.stratfor.com/article/somme-persian-gulf-lessons-shows-force.

Glazebrook, Dan. "Trump's Grand Strategy and the Coming War on Iran." *Counter-Punch*, vol. 24, no. 2, March 2017, pp. 14–17.

Goldberg, Jeffrey. "A Senior White House Official Defines the Trump Doctrine: 'We're America, Bitch'." *The Atlantic*, June 11, 2018. Available at: https://www.theatlantic.com/politics/archive/2018/06/a-senior-white-house-official-defines-the-trump-doctrine-were-america-bitch/562511/

———. "The Obama Doctrine." *The Atlantic*, vol. 317, no. 3, April 2016, pp. 70–90.

Goldenberg, Ilan. "What a War with Iran Would Look Like." *Foreign Affairs*, June 4, 2019. Available at: https://www.foreignaffairs.com/articles/iran/2019-06-04/what-war-iran-would-look.

Goodman, Melvin. "Donald the Destroyer." *CounterPunch*, July 25, 2018. Available at: https://www.counterpunch.org/2018/07/25/donald-the-destroyer/

Gordon, Philip H. "A Path to War with Iran: How Washington's Escalation Could Lead to Unintended Catastrophe." *Foreign Affairs*, May 20, 2019. Available at: https://www.foreignaffairs.com/articles/iran/2019-05-20/path-war-iran.

———. "A Vision of Trump at War: How the President Could Stumble Into Conflict." *Foreign Affairs*, vol. 96, no. 3, May/June 2017, pp. 10–19.

——— and Malley, Robert. "Trump's Magical Thinking on Iran Sanctions Won't Advance U.S. Interests." *Foreign Policy*, November 14, 2018. Available at: https://foreignpolicy.com/2018/11/14/trumps-iran-sanctions-are-built-on-magical-thinking-yemen-saudi-arabia-nuclear-foreign-policy/

Gresh, Alain. "Donald Trump, l'assassinat de Jamal Khashoggi et… l'Iran." *Orient XXI*, November 21, 2018. Available at: https://orientxxi.info/magazine/donald-trump-l-assassinat-de-jamal-khashoggi-et-l-iran,2777.

Gresh, Geoffrey. *Gulf Security and the U.S. Military: Regime Survival and the Politics of Basing*. Stanford, CA: Stanford University Press, 2015.

Gurol, Julia and Shahmohammadi, Parisa. "Turning Interdependence into Complimentary Action: EU-China Relations and the Quest to Save the Nuclear Agreement." Center for Applied Research in Partnership with the Orient (CARPO), *CARPO Report*, no. 7, May 15, 2019, pp. 1–28.

Gutfeld, Arnon. "Israel Approaches the Nuclear Threshold: The Controversies in the American Administration Surrounding the Israeli Nuclear Bomb 1968–1969." *Middle Eastern Studies*, vol. 52, no. 5, 2016, pp. 715–736.

Guzinger, Mark, with Dougherty, Chris. *Outside-In: Operating from Range to Defeat Iran's Anti-Access and Area-Denial Threats*. Washington, DC: Center for Strategic and Budgetary Assessments, 2011.

Gvosdev, Nikolas K. "How U.S. National Security Decisions Are Made." *Orbis*, vol. 61, no. 1, Winter 2017, pp. 27–33.

Haass, Richard. *A World in Disarray: American Foreign Policy and the Crisis of the Old Order*. New York: Penguin Books, 2018.

Hadian, Naser and Hormozi, Shani. "Iran's New Security Environment Imperatives: Counter Containment or Engagement with the US." *Iranian Review of Foreign Affairs*, vol. 1, no. 4, Winter 2011, pp. 13–55.

Haji-Yousefi, Amir M. "Iran's Foreign Policy during Ahmadinejad: From Confrontation to Accommodation." *Alternatives: Turkish Journal of International Relations*, vol. 9, no. 2, Summer 2010, pp. 1–23.

Haines, John R. "Divining a 'Trump Doctrine'." *Orbis*, vol. 61, no. 1, Winter 2017, pp. 125–136.

Hakimian, Hassan. "Can Trump's Sanctions Break Iran?" *Project Syndicate*, September 3, 2018. Available at: https://www.project-syndicate.org/commentary/will-trump-sanctions-break-iran-by-hassan-hakimian-2018-09.

Halff, Antoine. "The Art of the Opec Deal." *Report Published by the Center on Global Policy*, School of International and Public Affairs (SIPA), Columbia University, June 2018. Available at: http://energypolicy.columbia.edu/sites/default/files/pictures/The%20Art%20of%20the%20OPEC%20Deal_Halff_June%202018.pdf.

Hamblin, Jacob Darwin. "The Nuclearization of Iran in the Seventies." *Diplomatic History*, vol. 38, no. 5, November 2014, pp. 1114–1135.

Hanna, Michael Wahid and Dassa Kaye, Dalia. "The Limits of Iranian Power." *Survival*, vol. 57, no. 5, October–November 2015, pp. 173–198.

Hannay, David and Pickering, Thomas R. "Building on the Iran Nuclear Agreement." *Survival*, vol. 59, no. 2, April 2017, pp. 153–166.

Hanrath, Jan. "The EU's Balancing Act in the Middle East: How to Engage Iran Without Alienating GCC States." Center for Applied Research in Partnership with the Orient (CARPO), *Brief*, no. 4, July 8, 2016, pp. 1–10.

Harp, Seth. "Is the Trump Administration Pivoting the Fight in Syria Toward a War with Iran?" *The New Yorker*, November 26, 2018. Available at: https://www.newyorker.com/news/dispatch/is-the-trump-administration-pivoting-the-fight-in-syria-toward-a-war-with-iran#

Harrison, Ross. "Shifts in the Middle East Balance of Power: An Historical Perspective." Al Jazeera Centre for Studies, *Reports*, September 2, 2018. Available at: http://studies.aljazeera.net/en/reports/2018/09/shifts-middle-east-balance-power-historical-perspective-180902084750811.html.

———. "The Global and Regional Geopolitics of Civil War in the Middle East." Middle East Institute, *Policy Paper 2019-1*, January 2019, pp. 1–27.

———. "Toward a Regional Framework for the Middle East: Takeaways from Other Regions." Middle East Institute, *Policy Paper 2016-10*, December 2016, pp. 1–37.

———. "U.S. Policy Toward the Middle East: Pumping Air into a Punctured Tire." Arab Center for Research & Policy Studies (Doha), *Research Paper*, March 7, 2019, pp. 1–13.

——— and Salem, Paul, eds. *From Chaos to Cooperation: Toward Regional Order in the Middle East*. Washington, DC: Middle East Institute, 2017.

Harrop, William Scott. "Obama's Iran Policy: Mutual Respect Matters." *Iranian Review of Foreign Affairs*, vol. 1, no. 3, Fall 2010, pp. 63–84.

Hasan, Mehdi. "John Bolton Wants to Bomb Iran—and He May Get What He Wants." *The Intercept*, January 16, 2019. Available at: https://theintercept.com/ 2019/01/15/john-bolton-wants-to-bomb-iran-and-he-may-get-what-he-wants/

———. "Trump's 'Moderate' Defense Secretary Has Already Brought Us to the Brink of War." *The Intercept*, March 1, 2017. Available at: https://theintercept .com/2017/03/01/trumps-moderate-defense-secretary-has-already-brought-us-to -the-brink-of-war/

——— and Grim, Ryan. "Leaked State Department Memo Advised Trump Administration to Push for 'Islamic Reformation'." *The Intercept*, June 18, 2018. Available at: https://theintercept.com/2018/06/18/islamic-reformation-trump-administration/

Hashemi, Nader. "Donald Trump and the Strangling of Persia." *Al Jazeera*, July 11, 2019. Available at: https://www.aljazeera.com/indepth/opinion/donald-trump-strangling-persia-190710142907968.html.

——— and Postel, Danny, eds. *Sectarianization: Mapping the New Politics of the Middle East*. New York: Oxford University Press, 2017.

Hashim, Ahmed Salah. "Military Orientalism: Middle East Ways of War." *Middle East Policy*, vol. 26, no. 2, Summer 2019, pp. 31–47.

Hassan, Oz. "Trump, Islamophobia and US-Middle East Relations." *Critical Studies on Security*, vol. 5, no. 2, 2017, pp. 187–191.

Hatamzadeh, Azizollah and Mennati, Ayyoub. "Realism-e Enteghasdi va Siyast-e Khareji-e Jomhouri-e Eslami-e Iran" (Critical Realism and Foreign Policy of the Islamic Republic of Iran). *Journal of Foreign Policy*, vol. 31, no. 4, Winter 2018, pp. 5–40.

Haun, Phil. *Coercion, Survival, and War: Why Weak States Resist the United States*. Stanford, CA: Stanford University Press, 2015.

Hayden, Michael V. *The Assault on Intelligence: American National Security in an Age of Lies*. New York: Penguin Press, 2018.

Heer, Jeet. "Trump Administration Incoherence Could Lead to War." *The Nation*, June 20, 2019. Available at: https://www.thenation.com/article/trump-iran-forei gn-policy/

Heilbrunn, Jacob. "Iran's Foreign Minister Zarif: We Can't 'Discount' Possibility of War." *The National Interest*, July 18, 2019. Available at: https://nationalinterest. org/feature/irans-foreign-minister-zarif-we-cant-discount-possibility-war-67742.

———. "Trump Transformed." *The National Interest*, no. 160, March/April 2019, pp. 5–9.

Hersh, Seymour M. *The Killing of Osama Bin Laden*. New York: Verso Books, 2016.

Hicks, Kathleen H. and Dalton, Melissa, eds. *Deterring Iran After the Nuclear Deal*. Washington, DC: Center for Strategic and International Studies/Lanham, MD: Rowman & Littlefield, 2017.

Hildreth, Steven A. and Jabbari, Cyrus A. "Iran's Ballistic Missile and Space Launch Programs." Congressional Research Service, *In Focus*, August 1, 2018. Available at: https://fas.org/sgp/crs/nuke/IF10938.pdf.

Hiltermann, Joost, Vaez, Ali, Dickinson, Elizabeth, and Schneiderman, Daniel. "Iran's Ahvaz Attack Worsens Gulf Tensions." International Crisis Group, *Commentary*, September 24, 2018. Available at: https://www.crisisgroup.org/mi

ddle-east-north-africa/gulf-and-arabian-peninsula/iran/irans-ahvaz-attack-worsen s-gulf-tensions.

Himes, Joshua. *Iran's Two Navies: A Maturing Maritime Strategy*. Middle East Security Report I. Washington, DC: Institute for the Study of War, 2011.

Hinz, Fabian. "A Roadmap to Pragmatic Dialogue on the Iranian Missile Program." European Leadership Network, *Global Security Policy Brief*, March 2019, pp. 1–19.

Hirsh, Michael. "Is the Iran Deal Finally Dead?" *Foreign Policy*, September 25, 2018. Available at: https://foreignpolicy.com/2018/09/25/iran-nuclear-deal-last-stand/

Hiro, Dilip. "Can Donald Trump United the World (Against Himself)? The Rise of An Anti-Trump Movement Globally—and on His Home Turf." *TomDispatch*, August 23, 2018. Available at: http://www.tomdispatch.com/post/176461/tomgra m%3A_dilip_hiro%2C_trumping_trump/#more.

———. *Cold War in the Islamic World: Saudi Arabia, Iran, and the Struggle for Supremacy*. New York: Oxford University Press, 2019.

Hjelmgaard, Kim. "Exclusive: Iran Open to Talks with US if Trump Changes 'Approach' to Nuclear Deal, Top Diplomat Says." *USA Today*, November 5, 2018. Available at: https://www.usatoday.com/story/news/world/2018/11/05/iran-united-states-president-donald-trump-nuclear-deal-foreign-minister-mohammad-javad-zarif/1859375002/

Hobsbawm, Eric. *On Empire: America, War, and Global Supremacy*. New York: The New Press, 2008.

Homayounvash, Mohammad. *Iran and the Nuclear Question: History and Evolutionary Trajectory*. New York: Routledge, 2016.

Hong, Brendon. "China: Iran's Lifeline to Overcome Oil Sanctions." Atlantic Council, *IranSource*, October 3, 2018. Available at: http://www.atlanticcouncil.org/blog s/iransource/china-iran-s-lifeline-to-overcome-oil-sanctions.

Hook, Brian H. "Iran Should Reconcile with America." *New York Times*, April 8, 2019. Available at: https://www.nytimes.com/2019/04/08/opinion/iran-united-states.html.

Hooker, R.D., Jr., ed. *Charting a Course: Strategic Choices for a New Administration*. Washington, DC: National Defense University Press, 2016.

Howard, Brad. "Iran's New Fighter Is an Omen of Things to Come." *Task & Purpose*, August 24, 2018. Available at: https://taskandpurpose.com/iran-new-fighter-analysis.

Hulsman, John C. and Mitchell, A. Wess. *The Godfather Doctrine: A Foreign Policy Parable*. Princeton, NJ: Princeton University Press, 2009.

Hunter, Robert E. *Building Security in the Persian Gulf*. Santa Monica, CA: RAND Corporation, 2010.

———. "Dealing with Iran: Today's Yellow Journalism?" *LobeLog*, May 20, 2019. Available at: https://lobelog.com/dealing-with-iran-todays-yellow-journalism/

Hunter, Shireen T. *Arab-Iranian Relations: Dynamics of Conflict and Accommodation*. London: Rowman & Littlefield International, 2019.

———. "Can Hassan Rouhani Succeed where Muhammad Khatami Failed? Internal and International Politics of Reform in Iran." *Contemporary Review of the Middle East*, vol. 1, no. 3, September 2014, pp. 253–268.

———. *Iran's Foreign Policy in the Post-Soviet Era: Resisting the New International Order.* Santa Barbara, CA: ABC-CLIO/Praeger, 2010.

———. Iran's Geopolitical Predicament and Its Consequences. *LobeLog Foreign Policy*, March 7, 2017. Available at: http://lobelog.com/irans-geopolitical-predicament-and-its-consequences/

———. "Iran's Problems with America Won't End with Trump's Departure." *LobeLog*, September 17, 2018. Available at: https://lobelog.com/irans-problems-with-america-wont-end-with-trumps-departure/

Hussain, Agha. "Iran and Syria Signal 'Resistance' with Latakia Port Move." *The Iranian*, April 15, 2019. Available at: https://iranian.com/2019/04/15/iran-and-syria-signal-resistance-with-latakia-port-move/

Hutchins, Robert and Suri, Jeremi, eds. *Foreign Policy Breakthroughs: Cases in Successful Diplomacy.* New York: Oxford University Press, 2015.

"I am Part of the Resistance Inside the Trump Administration." An anonymous op-ed written by a senior official in the Trump administration, *New York Times*, September 5, 2018. Available at: https://www.nytimes.com/2018/09/05/opinion/trump-white-house-anonymous-resistance.html.

Ibish, Hussein. "A Sequential Framework for Iran-GCC Détente." *The Arab Gulf States Institute in Washington*, April 11, 2017. Available at: http://www.agsiw.org/sequential-framework-iran-gcc-detente/

Ilishev, Ildus G. "The Iran-Saudi Arabia Conflict and Its Impact on the Organization of Islamic Cooperation." Wilson Center, *Viewpoints*, no. 104, June 2016, pp. 1–5.

Imbert, Louis. "Ghassem Soleimani, le 'Che Guevara' iranien." *Le Monde*, May 12, 2017. Available at: http://www.lemonde.fr/proche-orient/article/2017/05/12/ghassem-soleimani-le-gardien-de-l-iran_5126707_3218.html#meter_toaster.

International Court of Justice. "Alleged Violation of the 1955 Treaty of Amity, Economic Relations, and Consular Rights (Islamic Republic of Iran v. United States of America), Request for the Indication of Provisional Measures—Order." *ICJ*, October 3, 2018. Available at: https://www.icj-cij.org/files/case-related/175/175-20181003-ORD-01-00-EN.pdf.

International Crisis Group. *How Europe Can Save the Iran Nuclear Deal.* Middle East Report No. 185, May 2, 2018, pp. 1–24.

———. *Implementing the Iran Nuclear Deal: A Status Report.* Middle East Report No. 173, January 16, 2017, pp. 1–27.

———. *Iran After the Nuclear Deal.* Middle East Report No. 166, December 15, 2015, pp. 1–29.

———. *Iran and the P5+1: Solving the Nuclear Rubik's Cube.* Middle East Report No. 152, May 9, 2014, pp. 1–56.

———. "Iran Nuclear Talks: The Fog Recedes." *Policy Briefing*, no. 43, December 10, 2014, pp. 1–15.

———. *Iran's Priorities in a Turbulent Middle East.* Middle East Report No. 184, April 13, 2018, pp. 1–39.

———. *On Thin Ice: The Iran Nuclear Deal at Three.* Middle East Report No. 195, January 16, 2019, pp. 1–37.

————. "The Illogic of the U.S. Sanctions Snapback on Iran." *Briefing*, no. 64, November 2, 2018. Available at: https://www.crisisgroup.org/middle-east-north -africa/gulf-and-arabian-peninsula/iran/b64-illogic-us-sanctions-snapback-iran.

————. "Turkey and Iran: Bitter Friends, Bosom Rivals." *Briefing*, no. 51, December 13, 2016. Available at: https://www.crisisgroup.org/middle-east-north-africa/ gulf-and-arabian-peninsula/iran/b051-turkey-and-iran-bitter-friends-bosom-rivals.

International Institute for Strategic Studies (IISS). *Iran's Ballistic Missile Capabilities: A Net Assessment.* An IISS Strategic Dossier. London: International Institute for Strategic Studies, 2010.

————. *Iran's Nuclear, Chemical and Biological Capabilities: A Net Assessment.* An IISS Strategic Dossier. London: International Institute for Strategic Studies, 2011.

————. *Missile-Defence Cooperation in the Gulf.* London: International Institute for Strategic Studies, 2016.

————. *Nuclear Programmes in the Middle East: In the Shadow of Iran.* An IISS Strategic Dossier. London: International Institute for Strategic Studies, 2008.

International Middle East Peace Research Center (IMPR). "Domestic Determinants of the US-Iran Rivalry." *IMPR Report*, April 2013, pp. 1–34.

International Monetary Fund. "Islamic Republic of Iran." *Staff Report for the 2016 Article IV Consultation*, February 9, 2017, pp. 1–50.

Iran Action Group, U.S. Department of State. "Outlaw Regime: A Chronicle of Iran's Destructive Activities." September 28, 2018. Available at: https://www.state.gov/ documents/organization/286410.pdf

"Iran Embraces ICJ's Ruling Against US." Official Statement of the Ministry of Foreign Affairs, Islamic Republic of Iran, on the Provisional Decision of the International Court of Justice Against the United States on Iran Sanctions, October 3, 2018. Available at: http://en.mfa.ir/index.aspx?siteid=3&fkeyid=&siteid=3&p ageid=36409&newsview=538292.

"Iran Sanctions Are Unjust and Harmful, Says UN Expert Warning Against Generalised Economic Warfare." United Nations Human Rights, Office of the High Commissioner, August 22, 2018. Available at: https://www.ohchr.org/EN/NewsE vents/Pages/DisplayNews.aspx?NewsID=23469&LangID=E.

Irwin, Douglas A. "The False Promise of Protectionism: Why Trump's Trade Policy Could Backfire." *Foreign Affairs*, vol. 96, no. 3, May/June 2017, pp. 45–56.

Islamic Revolutionary Guard Corps (IRGC). "Nesbat-e Khoroj-e Amrika az Barjam; az Elal va cheraii ta Payamadha; Senariyoha va Rahbordihaye Peeshro" (America's Exit from the JCPOA; From Causes to Messages; Scenarios and Forward-Looking Strategies). *Hadian Occasional Analysis*, May 2018, pp. 1–12.

Ismail, Raihan. *Saudi Clerics and Shi'a Islam.* New York: Oxford University Press, 2016.

Jaeger, Mark Daniel. *Coercive Sanctions and International Conflicts: A Sociological Theory.* London and New York: Routledge, 2018.

Jafari Movahhedi, Hossein. "Rabete-e Iran ba eyalat-e Mottahede-e Amrika: Emkan ya Emtenaa?" (Iran-United States Relations: Possible or Impossible?) *Journal of Foreign Policy*, vol. 29, no. 3, Autumn 2015, pp. 105–131.

Jahan News Managing Editor, "Negahi be Pasokh-e Mooshaki-e Sepah be Jenayat-e Ahvaz: Chand Payam-e Ekhtesasi ke Faqat Amrikaiha Dark Meekonand/Majeraye Estefadeh az Pahbadi Shabihe RQ-170 Amrikai" (A Look at the Islamic Revolutionary Guard Corps' Missile Response to the Ahvaz Crime: Special Messages that Are Understood Only by the Americans/What Was the Story of Using a Drone Similar to the American RQ-170?) *Jahan News*, October 2, 2018. Available at: http://www.jahannews.com/news/643904/

Jalilvand, David Ramin. "Between Dependence and Diversification: Making Sense of Iran's Energy." Center for Applied Research in Partnership with the Orient (CARPO), *Briefing*, no. 6, February 2, 2017, pp. 1–8.

Jarzabeck, Jaroslaw. "G.C.C. Military Spending in Era of Low Oil Prices." Middle East Institute, *MEI Policy Focus 2016–19*, August 2016, pp. 1–7.

Jebraily, Seyed Yasser. "How will the US Nuclear Deal Pullout Affect Iran's Economy?" *Al Jazeera*, May 29, 2018. Available at: https://www.aljazeera.com/inde pth/opinion/nuclear-deal-pullout-affect-iran-economy-180528104638815.html.

Jenkins, Peter. "Iranian Missiles: Hypocrisy and Paradox." *LobeLog*, December 17, 2018. Available at: https://lobelog.com/iranian-missiles-hypocrisy-and-paradox/

―――― and Dalton, Richard. "Iran's Nuclear Future." Chatham House, The Royal Institute of International Affairs, *Research Paper*, September 2014, pp. 1–18.

Jervis, Robert. "Getting to Yes with Iran: The Challenges of Coercive Diplomacy." *Foreign Affairs*, vol. 92, no. 1, January/February 2013, pp. 105–115.

――――. *Perception and Misperception in International Politics*, new edition. Princeton, NJ: Princeton University Press, 2017.

――――. "Understanding the Bush Doctrine: Preventive Wars and Regime Change." *Political Science Quarterly*, vol. 131, no. 2, Summer 2016, pp. 285–311.

――――, Gavin, Francis, Rover, Joshua, and Labrosse, Diane, eds., *Chaos in the Liberal Order: The Trump Presidency and International Politics in the Twenty-First Century*. New York: Columbia University Press, 2018.

Jett, Dennis C. *The Iran Nuclear Deal: Bombs, Bureaucrats, and Billionaires*. New York: Palgrave Macmillan, 2018.

Joint Comprehensive Plan of Action (JCPOA). July 14, 2015. Available at: https://s3.amazonaws.com/s3.documentcloud.org/documents/2165388/iran-deal-text.pdf.

Jones, Peter. *Track Two Diplomacy in Theory and Practice*. Stanford, CA: Stanford University Press, 2015.

Journal of International Affairs, "Iranian-American Negotiations: An Interview with Ambassador William J. Burns." *Journal of International Affairs*, vol. 69, no. 2, Spring/Summer 2016, pp. 177–183.

Joyner, Daniel H. *Interpreting the Nuclear Non-Proliferation Treaty*. New York: Oxford University Press, 2011.

――――. "Iran's Nuclear Program and International Law." *Penn State Journal of Law & International Affairs*, vol. 2, no. 2, 2013, pp. 282–292.

――――. *Iran's Nuclear Program and International Law: From Confrontation to Accord*. New York: Oxford University Press, 2016.

――――. "Is the U.S. Complying with the JCPOA?" *Arms Control Law*, July 6, 2016. Available at: https://armscontrollaw.com/2016/07/06/is-the-u-s-complying-with-t he-jcpoa/

————. "The Security Council as a Legal Hegemon." *Georgetown Journal of International Law*, vol. 43, no. 2, 2012, pp. 225–257.

————. "The United States' 'Withdrawal' from the Iran Nuclear Deal." *E-International Relations*, August 21, 2018. Available at: https://www.e-ir.info/2018/08/21/the-united-states-withdrawal-from-the-iran-nuclear-deal/

Juneau, Thomas. "If the U.S. Rejoins the JCPOA, Iran's Power Will Not Be Unshackled." *Lawfare*, May 5, 2019. Available at: https://www.lawfareblog.com/if-us-r ejoins-jcpoa-irans-power-will-not-be-unshackled#

————. "Iran Under Rouhani: Still Alone in the World." *Middle East Policy*, vol. 21, no. 4, Winter 2014, pp. 92–104.

————. "Iran's Costly Intervention in Syria: A Pyrrhic Victory." *Mediterranean Politics*, published online on May 30, 2018. Available at: https://doi.org/10.1080/1 3629395.2018.1479362.

————. "Iran's Policy Towards the Houthis in Yemen: A Limited Return on a Modest Investment." *International Affairs*, vol. 92, no. 3, May 2016, pp. 647–663.

————. *Squandered Opportunity: Neoclassical Realism and Iranian Foreign Policy.* Stanford, CA: Stanford University Press, 2015.

————. "The Enduring Constraints on Iran's Power After the Nuclear Deal." *Political Science Quarterly*, vol. 134, no. 1, Spring 2019, pp. 39–61.

———— and Razavi, Sam. "Costly Gains: A Cost-Benefit Assessment of Iran's Nuclear Program." *Nonproliferation Review*, vol. 25, nos. 1–2, 2018, pp. 69–86.

————, eds. *Iranian Foreign Policy since 2001: Alone in the World.* London and New York: Routledge, 2013.

Kahl, Colin H. "Pompeo's Dangerous Delusions: What the Trump Administration's Iran Policy Gets Wrong." *Foreign Affairs*, October 24, 2018. Available at: https://www.foreignaffairs.com/articles/iran/2018-10-24/pompeos-dangerous-delusions.

————, Dalton, Melissa G., and Irvine, Matthew. *Risk and Rivalry: Iran, Israel and the Bomb.* Washington, DC: Center for a New American, June 2012.

Kahl, Colin H. and Narang, Vipin. "Trump Thinks His North Korea Strategy Will Work on Iran. He's Wrong on Both." *Washington Post*, May 4, 2018. Available at: https://www.washingtonpost.com/outlook/trump-thinks-his-north-korea-st rategy-will-work-on-iran-hes-wrong-on-both/2018/05/04/9a430328-4e28-11e8-84 a0-458a1aa9ac0a_story.html?noredirect=on&utm_term=.cb35c7c85ce3.

Kahl, Colin H. and Wolfsthal, Jon. B. "It's John Bolton's World. Trump Is Just Living in It." *Los Angeles Times*, May 14, 2019. Available at: https://www.latimes.com/opinion/op-ed/la-oe-kahl-wolfsthal-john-bolton-trump-north-korea-iran-v enezuela-20190514-story.html.

Kaleji, Vali Kouzegar. *Siyast-e Khareji-e Amrika dar Asiaye Markazi: Ravandha va Cheshm Andazha* (U.S. Foreign Policy in Central Asia: Processes and Perspectives). Tehran: Center for International Research and Education, Foreign Ministry Publications, 2016.

Kamrava, Mehran. "Hierarchy and Instability in the Middle East Regional Order." *International Studies Journal (ISJ)*, vol. 14, no. 4, Spring 2018, pp. 1–35.

————, ed. *International Politics of the Persian Gulf.* Syracuse, NY: Syracuse University Press, 2011.

———. *Nuclear Question in the Middle East*. New York: Oxford University Press, 2012.

———. *Troubled Waters: Insecurity in the Persian Gulf*. Ithaca, NY: Cornell University Press, 2018.

Kaplan, Fred. "Iran Is Right." *Slate*, July 8, 2019. Available at: https://slate.com/ne ws-and-politics/2019/07/trump-iran-jcpoa-enrichment-uranium-deal.html.

Kaplan, Robert D. "Warning to Iran." *The Atlantic*, vol. 315, no. 1, January/February 2015, pp. 17–19.

Katz, Yaakov and Hendel, Yoaz. *Israel vs. Iran: The Shadow War*. Washington, DC: Potomac Books, 2012.

Katzman, Kenneth. *Iran: Politics, Gulf Security, and U.S. Policy*. Washington, DC: Congressional Research Service, March 30, 2016, pp. 1–53.

———. *Iran Sanctions*. Washington, DC: Congressional Research Service, January 4, 2019.

———. *Iran's Foreign and Defense Policies*. Washington, DC: Congressional Research Service, Updated January 16, 2019.

———. *Iran's Foreign Policy*. Washington, DC: Congressional Research Service, June 27, 2016.

Kaye, Dalia Dassa. "Bringing Back Sanctions Will Hurt U.S. Allies and Iran, But Will It Help the U.S.?" *The RAND Blog*, August 7, 2018. Available at: https://www.ran d.org/blog/2018/08/bringing-back-sanctions-will-hurt-us-allies-and-iran.html.

Kazianis, Harry J. "How Iran Could Use a Chinese Military Strategy to Wage War Against America." *The National Interest*, July 23, 2018. Available at: https://na tionalinterest.org/blog/buzz/how-iran-could-use-chinese-military-strategy-wage-w ar-against-america-26531.

———. "What a War Between Iran and America Would Look Like." *The National Interest*, July 21, 2017. Available at: https://nationalinterest.org/print/blog/the-b uzz/what-war-between-iran-america-would-look-21615.

Keck, Zachary. "5 Iranian Weapons of War America Should Fear." *The National Interest*, January 23, 2015. Available at: https://nationalinterest.org/feature/5-irania n-weapons-war-america-should-fear-12092.

———. "No Easy War Here: Why America Isn't Invading Iran Anytime Soon." *The National Interest*, July 23, 2018. Available at: https://nationalinterest.org/blog/b uzz/no-easy-war-here-why-america-isnt-invading-iran-anytime-soon-26586.

Kellner, Douglas. *American Nightmare: Donald Trump, Media Spectacle, and Authoritarian Populism*. Rotterdam: Sense Publishers, 2016.

Kemp, Geoffrey and Gay, John Allen. *War with Iran: Political, Military, and Economic Consequences*. Lanham, MD: Rowman & Littlefield, 2013.

Kemp, R. Scott. "The Nonproliferation Emperor Has No Clothes: The Gas Centrifuge, Supply-Side Controls, and the Future of Nuclear Proliferation." *International Security*, vol. 38, no. 4, Spring 2014, pp. 39–78.

Kenner, David. "Why Israel Fears Iran's Presence in Syria." *The Atlantic*, July 22, 2018. Available at: https://www.theatlantic.com/international/archive/2018/07/he zbollah-iran-new-weapons-israel/565796/

Kerr, Paul K. *Iran's Nuclear Program: Status.* Washington, DC: Congressional Research Service, April 27, 2017, pp. 1–63.

———. *Iran's Nuclear Program: Tehran's Compliance with International Obligations.* Washington, DC, Congressional Research Service, February 7, 2019, pp. 1–19.

Kerry, John. *Every Day Is Extra.* New York: Simon & Schuster, 2018.

Kershner, Isabel. "Israeli Leader Visits Oman, a Potential Back Channel to Iran." *New York Times*, October 26, 2018, p. A8.

Kesić, Ivan. "Along with Economic and Humanitarian Wars, the US Wages a Scientific War Against Iran." *Antiwar*, June 5, 2019. Available at: https://original.ant iwar.com/Ivan_Kesi/2019/06/04/along-with-economic-and-humanitarian-wars-the -us-wages-a-scientific-war-against-iran/

———. "A Reuters Report on Iran That Spurred US Diatribes." *Consortium News*, December 27, 2018. Available at: https://consortiumnews.com/2018/12/27/a-reute rs-report-on-iran-that-fueled-us-diatribes/

Keynoush, Banafsheh. *Saudi Arabia and Iran: Friends or Foes?* New York: Palgrave Macmillan, 2016.

Khailzad, Zalmay. *The Envoy: From Kabul to the White House, My Journey Through a Turbulent World.* New York: St. Martin's Press, 2016.

———. "Why America Needs Iran in Iraq." *Politico Magazine*, May 2, 2016. Available at: http://www.politico.com/magazine/story/2016/05/why-america-needs-iran-in-iraq-213865.

———. "Why Iran Will Choose to Negotiate with Trump." *Washington Post*, June 13, 2018. Available at: https://www.washingtonpost.com/news/global-opinions/wp/2018/06/13/heres-what-trump-should-do-next-on-iran/?utm_term=.2f984ca786f0.

Khalaf, Sawsan. "Gulf States' Jubilation After U.S. Violation of Iran Deal Is Myopic & Hypocritical." *Muftah*, May 11, 2018. Available at: https://muftah.org/gulf-s tates-celebration-of-us-violation-iran-deal-is-hypocritical-and-myopic/#.WyOrTfZ FyUl.

Khamenei, Ayatollah Ali. "Why Is the U.S. Frightened of Iran's Missile Capabilities?" January 27, 2018. Available at: http://english.khamenei.ir/news/5421/Why -is-the-U-S-frightened-of-Iran-s-missile-capabilities.

Khan, Mehreen. "Brussels Barters with Iran." *Financial Times*, September 26, 2018. Available at: https://www.ft.com/content/f6956310-c140-11e8-8d55-5419 7280d3f7.

Khan, Saira. *Iran and Nuclear Weapons: Protracted Conflict and Proliferation.* London and New York: Routledge, 2010.

Khani, Mohammad Hassan and Mohammadisirat, Hossein. "Ta'sir-e Ideoloji bar Manafe'-e Melli va Amniyat-e Melli dar Siyasat-e Khareji-e Jomhouri-e Eslami-e Iran; ba Ta'keed bar Andishe-e Imam Khomeini" (The Impact of Ideology on the National Interests and National Security [Discourse] in the Foreign Policy of the Islamic Republic of Iran; with an Emphasis on Imam Khomeini's Thought). *Quarterly Journal of Political Research in the Islamic World* (Tehran), vol. 6, no. 4, Winter 2017, pp. 91–117.

Kheel, Rebecca. "US Terminates 1950s Treaty with Iran After Court Orders Ease in Sanctions." *The Hill*, October 3, 2018. Available at: https://thehill.com/policy/def ense/409657-us-ending-treaty-with-iran-after-international-court-ruling.

Khodabandeh, Massoud. "Bolton vs. Zarif on MEK." *LobeLog,* May 2, 2019. Available at: https://lobelog.com/bolton-vs-zarif-on-mek/

———. "Bolton's Plans for a False Flag Op Involving MEK Are Already Underway." *The Iranian*, May 13, 2019. Available at: https://iranian.com/2019/05/13/boltons-plans-for-a-false-flag-op-involving-mek-are-already-underway/

Khoshroo, Gholamali. "Trump's Sanctions Against Iran Are a Clear Breach of International Law." *The Guardian*, August 8, 2018. Available at: https://www.the guardian.com/commentisfree/2018/aug/08/donald-trump-sanctions-iran-internat ional-law.

Kinch, Penelope. *The US-Iran Relationship: The Impact of Political Identity on Foreign Policy*. London and New York: I.B. Tauris, 2016.

Kinzer, Stephen. "Iran's Best Diplomat Takes on US Power." *Boston Globe*, September 28, 2018. Available at: https://www.bostonglobe.com/opinion/2018/09/28/ira n-best-diplomat-takes-power/nnrnpnTucFWpWylBCkeUnM/story.html.

Kissinger, Henry. *World Order*. New York: Penguin Press, 2014.

Klare, Michael T. "Entering a 1984 World, Trump-Style—Or Implementing the Sino-Russian Blueprint for a Triple World Order." *TomDispatch*, July 24, 2018. Available at: http://www.tomdispatch.com/dialogs/print/?id=176451.

———. "The Missing Three-Letter Word in the Iran Crisis: Oil's Enduring Sway in U.S. Policy in the Middle East." *TomDispatch*, July 11, 2019. Available at: http://www.tomdispatch.com/blog/176584/

———. "The Navy's War vs. Bolton's War: The Pentagon's Spoiling for a Fight—But with China, Not Iran." *Tom Dispatch*, June 2, 2019. Available at: http://www.tomdispatch.com/blog/176570/

Klion, David. "The Blob: Ben Rhodes and the Crisis of Liberal Foreign Policy." *The Nation*, November 12, 2018, pp. 27–31.

Klippenstein, Ken. "It's Not Just Bolton and Giuliani: Trump Team's Links to Iran 'Cult' Run Deep." *The Young Turks (TYT) Network*, August 8, 2018. Available at: https://tytnetwork.com/2018/08/08/its-not-just-bolton-and-giuliani-trump-teams-l inks-to-iran-cult-run-deep/

Knutsen, Torbjorn. *A History of International Relations Theory*, 3rd edition. Manchester, UK: Manchester University Press, 2016.

Kokabisaghi, Fatemeh. "Assessment of the Effects of Economic Sanction on Iranians' Right to Health by Using Human Rights Impact Assessment Tool: A Systematic Review." *International Journal of Health Policy and Management*, vol. 7, no. 5, May 2018, pp. 374–393.

Kondapalli, Srikanth. "China and the Iranian Nuclear Issue—Converting Challenges into Opportunities." *Contemporary Review of the Middle East*, vol. 3, no. 1, March 2016, pp. 63–76.

Koozegar-Kalej, Valiollah. "Bohran-e Gharebagh va Manafe'a Melli Iran: Tarseem Senariohayi Baraye Siyasat-e Kharejiye Iran" (The Karabakh Crisis and Iran's

National Interests: Alternative Scenarios for Iran's Foreign Policy). Institute for Iran-Eurasia Studies, *Occasional Paper*, no. 44, December 2016, pp. 9–17.

Korb, Lawrence J. "The Iran War Crisis: Are We Headed Towards a Gulf of Tonkin Incident?" *The National Interest*, May 25, 2019. Available at: https://nationa linterest.org/feature/iran-war-crisis-are-we-headed-towards-gulf-tonkin-incident -59167.

Kordzadeh Kermani, Mohammad. "Immorality and Illegality of Sanctions and Iranian Response." *Iranian Review of Foreign Affairs*, vol. 5, no. 1, Spring 2014, pp. 89–120.

Kovalik, Dan. *The Plot to Attack Iran: How the CIA and the Deep State Have Conspired to Vilify Iran*. New York: Skyhorse Publishing, 2018.

Kozhanov, Nikolay. *Iran's Strategic Thinking: The Evolution of Iran's Foreign Policy 1979–2017*. Berlin: Gerlach Press, 2018.

Kristian, Bonnie. "Sanctioning Iran Is Risky for America." *The National Interest*, November 15, 2018. Available at: https://nationalinterest.org/feature/sanctioning-i ran-risky-america-36162.

Kristiansen, Lars J. and Kaussler, Bernd. "The Bullshit Doctrine: Fabrication, Lies, and Nonsense in the Age of Trump." *Informal Logic*, vol. 38, no. 1, 2018, pp. 13–52.

Kristof, Nicholas. "The Terrorists the Saudis Cultivate in Peaceful Countries." *New York Times*, July 2, 2016. Available at: http://www.nytimes.com/2016/07/03/o pinion/sunday/the-terrorists-the-saudis-cultivate-in-peaceful-countries.html?_r=0.

Kroenig, Matthew. *A Time to Attack: The Looming Iranian Nuclear Threat*: New York: Palgrave Macmillan, 2014.

———. "The Case for Trump's Foreign Policy: The Right People, the Right Positions." *Foreign Affairs*, vol. 96, no. 3, May/June 2017, pp. 30–34.

———. "Time to Attack Iran: Why a Strike Is the Least Bad Option." *Foreign Affairs*, vol. 91, no. 1, January/February 2012, pp. 76–86.

Lahoud, Nelly. "Al-Qa'ida's Contested Relationship with Iran: The View from Abbottabad." New America, *International Security Report*, September 2018. Available at: https://s3.amazonaws.com/newamericadotorg/documents/Al-Qaida s_Contested_Relationship_with_Iran_2018-08-20_151707.pdf.

Laipson, Ellen. "A New Strategy for US-Iran Relations in Transition." Atlantic Council, *Strategy Paper No. 6*, October 2016, pp. 1–24.

———. "Does Trump Think U.S.-Iran Relations Have to Get Worse to Get Better?" *World Politics Review*, April 25, 2017, pp. 1–3.

———. "Is Iran Actually Losing Ground in the Shifting Geopolitics of the Middle East?" *World Politics Review*, March 21, 2017. Available at: http://www.worldpoli ticsreview.com/articles/21585/is-iran-actually-losing-ground-in-the-shifting-geo politics-of-the-middle-east.

Lakshmanan, Indira A.R. "Inside the Plan to Undo the Iran Nuclear Deal." *Politico Magazine*, July 15, 2016. Available at: http://www.politico.com/magazine/story/2 016/07/iran-nuclear-deal-foreign-policy-barack-obama-hassan-rouhani-javad-z arif-israel-john-kerry-214052#ixzz4ETLpq3ni.

Larison, Daniel. "How 'President Bolton' Gets His Way." *The American Conservative*, January 21, 2019. Available at: https://www.theamericanconservative.com/larison/how-president-bolton-gets-his-way/

———. "Iraqis Want No Part of Trump's Iran Obsession." *The American Conservative*, February 4, 2019. Available at: https://www.theamericanconservative.com/larison/iraqis-want-no-part-of-trumps-iran-obsession/

Lawson, Fred H. *Implications of the 2011–13 Syrian Uprising for the Middle Eastern Regional Security Complex.* Occasional Paper No. 14. Doha, Qatar: Center for International and Regional Studies, Georgetown University School of Foreign Service in Qatar, 2014.

Layne, Christopher. "The Big Forces of History: Can the Era of America's Global Dominance Be Sustained?" *The American Conservative*, vol. 16, no. 1, January/February 2017, pp. 10–14.

Lebovic, James H. "Red Lines and Green Lights: Iran, Nuclear Arms Control, and Nonproliferation." *Strategic Studies Quarterly*, vol. 10, no. 1, Spring 2016, pp. 10–42.

Lee, Bandy X. *The Dangerous Case of Donald Trump: 27 Psychiatrists and Mental Health Experts Assess a President.* New York: Thomas Dunne Books, 2017.

Leslie, Jonathan, Marashi, Reza, and Parsi, Trita. "Losing MORE Billions: The Cost of Iran Sanctions to the U.S. Economy." A report published by the National Iranian American Council, December 2016, pp. 1–26.

Leupp, Gary. "Bolton, MERK and Trump Iran Strategy." *Counterpunch*, July 11, 2018. Available at: https://www.counterpunch.org/2018/07/11/bolton-mek-and-trump-iran-strategy/

———. "What Right Has Britain to Seize an Iranian Tanker Off Spain?" *Counterpunch*, July 16, 2019. Available at: https://www.counterpunch.org/2019/07/16/what-right-has-britain-to-seize-an-iranian-tanker-off-spain/

Leverett, Flynt and Mann Leverette, Hillary. "American Hegemony (and Hubris), the Iranian Nuclear Issue, and the Future of Sino-Iranian Relations." The Dickinson School of Law, Pennsylvania State University, *Legal Research Paper No. 39-2014*, September 25, 2014, pp. 1–26.

———. *Going to Tehran: Why the United States Must Come to Terms with the Islamic Republic of Iran.* New York: Metropolitan Books, 2013.

Levine, Nathan. "China Will Be the True Winner of a U.S.-Iran War." *The National Interest*, May 29, 2019. Available at: https://nationalinterest.org/feature/china-will-be-true-winner-us-iran-war-60052.

Levinson, Chaim and Shezaf, Hagar. "$6 Billion of Iranian Money: Why Israeli Firm Black Cube Really Went After Obama's Team." *Haaretz*, October 26, 2018. Available at: https://www.haaretz.com/israel-news/.premium-6-billion-of-iranian-money-why-israeli-firm-black-cube-went-after-obama-s-team-1.6593965.

Levite, Ariel E. "Looking Beyond the Interim Deal." *Arms Control Today*, vol. 45, no. 1, January/February 2015, pp. 11–13.

Lew Jacob J. and Nephew, Richard. "The Use and Misuse of Economic Statecraft: How Washington Is Abusing Its Financial Might." *Foreign Affairs*, vol. 97, no. 6, November/December 2018, pp. 139–149.

Lewis, Jeffrey. "Nuclear Deals and Double Standards: American Hypocrisy Is Harming Nonproliferation Efforts." *Foreign Affairs*, October 2, 2018. Available at: https://www.foreignaffairs.com/articles/2018-10-02/nuclear-deals-and-double-stan dards.

Lim, Kevjn and Baram, Gil. "Iran Is Mastering the Final Frontier." *Foreign Policy*, March 14, 2019. Available at: https://foreignpolicy.com/2019/03/14/iran-is-maste ring-the-final-frontier/

Limber, John. "Iran Nuclear Deal: One-time Event or Breakthrough?" *LobeLog Foreign Policy*, May 2, 2016. Available at: http://lobelog.com/iran-nuclear-deal-one -time-event-or-breakthrough/

———. *Negotiating with Iran: Wrestling the Ghosts of History*. Washington, DC: United States Institute of Peace, 2009.

———. "Pompeo and Iran: A Bizarre Mentality." *LobeLog*, July 24, 2018. Available at: https://lobelog.com/pompeo-and-iran-a-bizarre-mentality/

———. "The Trump Administration's Iran Fiasco." *The American Prospect*, June 5, 2019. Available at: https://prospect.org/article/trump-administrations-iran-fiasco.

Litwak, Robert. *Iran's Nuclear Chess: After the Deal*, updated edition. Washington, DC: Wilson Center, 2015.

———. "Living with Ambiguity: Nuclear Deals with Iran and North Korea." *Survival*, vol. 50, no. 1, February–March 2008, pp. 91–118.

———. *Outlier States: American Strategies to Change, Contain, or Engage Regimes*. Baltimore: Johns Hopkins University Press, 2012.

Lob, Eric. "The Islamic Republic of Iran's Foreign Policy and Construction Jihad's Developmental Activities in Sub-Saharan Africa." *International Journal of Middle East Studies*, vol. 48, no. 2, May 2016, pp. 313–338.

Lovell, Joseph. "Americans Can't Give Up the Cult of War." *Foreign Policy*, April 9, 2019. Available at: https://foreignpolicy.com/2019/04/09/americans-cant-giv e-up-the-cult-of-war/#

Luers, William, Pickering, Thomas, and Walsh, Jim. "Congress and the Future of Iran Talks." *Arms Control Today*, vol. 45, no. 1, January/February 2015, pp. 14–15.

Lukyanov, Fyodor, ed. *Russia and the Middle East: Viewpoints, Policies, Strategies*. Minneapolis, MN: East View Press, 2019.

Lupovici, Amir. "Securitization Climax: Putting the Iranian Nuclear Project at the Top of the Israeli Public Agenda (2009–2012)." *Foreign Policy Analysis*, article first published online October 17, 2014, DOI: 10.1111/fpa.12081.

Lynch, Marc. "The New Arab Order: Power and Violence in Today's Middle East." *Foreign Affairs*, vol. 97, no. 5, September/October 2018, pp. 116–126.

———. *The New Arab Wars: Uprisings and Anarchy in the Middle East*. New York: PublicAffairs, 2016.

Mabon, Simon. *Saudi Arabia and Iran: Power and Rivalry in the Middle East*, new edition. London: I.B. Tauris, 2015.

Machlis, Elisheva. "Al-Wefaq and the February 14 Uprising: Islam, Nationalism and Democracy—The Shi'i-Bahraini Discourse." *Middle Eastern Studies*, vol. 52, no. 6, 2016, pp. 978–995.

————. "The Islamic Republic: A Bastion of Stability in the Region?" *Middle East Critique*, published online on August 11, 2016, pp. 1–23. Available at: http://dx. doi.org/10.1080/19436149.2016.1213946.

Mackey, Robert. "Here's John Bolton Promising Regime Change in Iran by the End of 2018." *The Intercept*, March 23, 2018. Available at: https://theintercept.com/ 2018/03/23/heres-john-bolton-promising-regime-change-iran-end-2018/

Mahapatra, Chintamani. "US-Iran Nuclear Deal: Cohorts and Challenger." *Contemporary Review of the Middle East*, vol. 3, no. 1, March 2016, pp. 36–46.

Mahboubian, Cyrus. "Washington's Sunni Myth and the Civil Wars in Syria and Iraq." *War on the Rocks*, August 16, 2016. Available at: http://warontherocks.com/ 2016/08/washingtons-sunni-myth-and-the-civil-wars-in-syria-and-iraq/

Majd, Hooman. "Pride and Prejudice in Tehran: To Understand Iran's Foreign Policy, You Need to Learn a Little Farsi." *Foreign Policy*, no. 229, July 2018, pp. 8–9.

Makinsky, Michel. "Iran: Trump, Bolton, Pompeo et la justice a l'ouest de l'Hudson." *Les cles du Moyen-Orient*, October 10, 2018. Available at: https://www.lesclesd umoyenorient.com/Iran-Trump-Bolton-Pompeo-et-la-justice-a-l-ouest-de-l-Huds on.html.

Maleki, Abbas. "Iran's Nuclear File: Recommendations for the Future." *Daedalus*, vol. 139, no. 1, Winter 2010, pp. 105–116.

———— and Tirman, John, eds. *U.S.-Iran Misperceptions: A Dialogue*. New York: Bloomsbury, 2014.

Malekzadeh, Shervin. "Boys Go to Baghdad, Real Men Go to Tehran." *LobeLog*, June 15, 2018. Available at: https://lobelog.com/boys-go-to-baghdad-real-men-go -to-tehran/

————. "What Trump Doesn't Get About Ideology in Iran. It's About Nationalism, Not Theocracy." *Washington Post*, June 25, 2018. Available at: https://www.was hingtonpost.com/news/monkey-cage/wp/2018/06/25/what-trump-doesnt-get-a bout-ideology-in-iran-its-about-nationalism-not-theocracy/?utm_term=.c2b31e 466776.

————. "What It Means to Be Iranian in America: Forgetting the Revolution." *Foreign Affairs*, May 3, 2019. Available at: https://www.foreignaffairs.com/articles/ iran/2019-05-03/what-it-means-be-iranian-america.

Malici, Akan and Walker, Stephen G. *Role Theory and Role Conflict in U.S.-Iran Relations: Enemies of Our Own Making*. London and New York: Routledge, 2016.

Maloney, Suzanne. "Iran Isn't Taking Trump's Twitter Bait—for Now." *The Atlantic*, July 25, 2018. Available at: https://www.theatlantic.com/international/archive/ 2018/07/trump-pressure-iran-rouhani/566000/

————. "Trump Wants a Bigger, Better Deal with Iran. What Does Tehran Want?" Brookings Institution, *Order from Chaos*, August 8, 2018. Available at: https://ww w.brookings.edu/blog/order-from-chaos/2018/08/08/trump-wants-a-bigger-bette r-deal-with-iran-what-does-tehran-want/

Mamedov, Eldar. "Iran's Own Never Forget, Never Again Mantra." *Muftah*, July 31, 2018. Available at: https://muftah.org/iran-never-forget-never-again-mantra/#.W2 cGn_ZFyUl.

———. "Pompeo Gets Cold-Shouldered on Iran in Brussels." *LobeLog*, May 14, 2019. Available at: https://lobelog.com/pompeo-gets-cold-shouldered-on-iran-in-b russels/

Mandelbaum, Michael. "How to Prevent an Iranian Bomb: The Case for Deterrence." *Foreign Affairs*, vol. 94, no. 6, November/December 2015, pp. 19–24.

———. "The New Containment: Handling Russia, China, and Iran." *Foreign Affairs*, vol. 98, no. 2, March/April 2019, pp. 123–131.

Marandi, Seyed Mohammad. "Iran Faces US Aggression and European Hypocrisy, But This Time It's Ready." *Middle East Eye*, July 12, 2019. Available at: https://www.middleeasteye.net/opinion/iran-faces-us-aggression-and-european-hypocrisy-time-its-ready.

———. "Regime Chang? This Isn't 1953 and Khamenei Isn't Mosaddegh." *Middle East Eye*, July 27, 2018. Available at: http://www.middleeasteye.net/columns/reg ime-change-beware-isn-t-1953-and-khamenei-isn-t-mosaddegh-1182820278.

Marschall, Christin. *Iran's Persian Gulf Policy: From Khomeini to Khatami*. London and New York: Routledge, 2003.

Martini, Jeffrey, Wasser, Becca, Dassa Kaye, Dalia, Egel, Daniel, and Ogletree, Cordaye. *The Outlook for Arab Gulf Cooperation*. Santa Monica, CA: RAND Corporations, 2016.

Mason, Robert. *Foreign Policy in Iran and Saudi Arabia: Economics and Diplomacy in the Middle East*. London: I.B. Tauris, 2015.

———, ed. *Egypt and the Gulf: A Renewed Policy Alliance*. Berlin: Gerlach Press, 2017.

———, ed. *Reassessing Order and Disorder in the Middle East: Regional Imbalance or Disintegration?* Lanham, MD: Rowman & Littlefield, 2017.

Mazzetti, Mark, Bergman, Ronen, and Kirkpatrick, David D. "Saudis Close to Crown Prince Discussed Assassinating Enemies a Year Before Khashoggi Killing." *New York Times*, November 11, 2018. Available at: https://www.nytimes.com/2018/1 1/11/world/middleeast/saudi-iran-assassinations-mohammed-bin-salman.html.

McChrystal, Stanley. "Iran's Deadly Puppet Master." *Foreign Policy*, no. 231, Winter 2019, pp. 36–38.

McGurk, Brett. "American Foreign Policy Adrift." *Foreign Affairs*, June 5, 2019. Available at: https://www.foreignaffairs.com/articles/united-states/2019-06-05/american-foreign-policy-adrift.

McKenzie, Kenneth F., Jr. "Rising to the Threat: Revitalizing America's Military and Political Power." Remarks by General Kenneth F. McKenzie, Commander, U.S. Central Command, Presented at the Foundation for Defense of Democracies, May 8, 2019. Available at: https://www.fdd.org/wp-content/uploads/2019/05/Transcri pt-CMPP-McKenzie.pdf.

McNerney, Michael J., et al. *National Will to Fight: Why Some States Keep Fighting and Others Don't*. Santa Monica: CA: RAND Corporation, 2018.

McInnis, J. Matthew. *The Future of Iran's Security Policy: Inside Tehran's Strategic Thinking*. Washington, DC. American Enterprise Institute, May 2017.

Mearsheimer, John J. *The Great Delusion: Liberal Dreams and International Realities*. New Haven, CT: Yale University Press, 2018.

Mennell, Stephen. "Trump's America: International Relations and the Construction of They-Images." *International Relations and Diplomacy*, vol. 6, no. 10, October 2018, pp. 527–536.

Menon, Rajan. "Will Trump Shred the Iran Nuclear Deal? Or Is That the Least of Our Problems When It Comes to U.S.-Iranian Relations?" *TomDispatch*, January 12, 2017. Available at: http://www.tomdispatch.com/blog/176230.

Merat, Arron. "Terrorists, Cultists—or Champions of Iranian Democracy? The Wild Wild Story of the MEK." *The Guardian*, November 9, 2018. Available at: https ://www.theguardian.com/news/2018/nov/09/mek-iran-revolution-regime-trump-ra javi.

Merom, Gil. "The Logic and Illogic of and Israeli Unilateral Preventive Strike on Iran." *Middle East Journal*, vol. 71, no. 1, Winter 2017, pp. 87–110.

Mesbahi, Mohiaddin. "Free and Confined: Iran and the International System." *Iranian Review of Foreign Affairs*, vol. 2, no. 5, Spring 2011, pp. 9–34.

Miller, Aaron David and Sokolsky, Richard. "Trump Isn't Just Reversing Obama's Foreign Policies. He's Making it Impossible for His Successor to Go Back to Them." *Politico Magazine*, April 23, 2019. Available at: https://www.politico.com/magazine/story/2019/04/23/trump-obama-foreign-policy-226708.

———. "What Is Trump Getting for Sucking up to Saudi Arabia?" *Politico Magazine*, August 29, 2018. Available at: https://www.politico.com/magazine/story/2018/08/29/trump-mbs-saudi-arabia-yemen-middle-east-foreign-policy-219617.

Miller, John W. "Defusing Tensions at Sea: U.S.-Iran Maritime Relations in the Persian Gulf." Middle East Institute, *MEI Policy Focus 2016-16*, July 2016, pp. 1–11.

Miller, Nicholas. "The Trump Administration's New 'Iran Action Group' Won't Work—For These 3 Reasons." *Washington Post*, August 29, 2018. Available at: https://www.washingtonpost.com/news/monkey-cage/wp/2018/08/29/the-trum p-administrations-new-iran-action-group-wont-work-for-these-3-reasons/?utm_ term=.b613e515c17d.

Mills, Curt. "Ex-Military Brass Line Up Against War in Iran." *The National Interest*, May 30, 2019. Available at: https://nationalinterest.org/feature/ex-military-brass-line-against-war-iran-60207.

Mills, Robin. "Iran and Oil Sanctions." Report published by the Center on Global Energy Policy, School of International and Public Affairs, Columbia University, May 2018. Available at: http://energypolicy.columbia.edu/sites/default/files/pi ctures/Iran%20Oil%20and%20Sanctions_CGEP_Mills.pdf.

Ministry of Foreign Affairs, Islamic Republic of Iran. "Foreign Ministry's Statement on Re-imposition of US Sanctions." November 3, 2018. Available at: http://en.mfa. ir/index.aspx?siteid=3&fkeyid=&siteid=3&pageid=36409&newsview=543101.

Mintz, Alex and Wayne, Carly. *The Polythink Syndrome: U.S. Foreign Policy Decisions on 9/11, Afghanistan, Iraq, Iran, Syria, and ISIS*. Stanford, CA: Stanford University Press, 2016.

Miremadi, Tahereh. "Learning Process in Public Diplomacy: The Case of Iranian Nuclear Diplomacy." *Iranian Review of Foreign Affairs*, vol. 5, no. 1, Spring 2014, pp. 29–55.

————. "The Role of Domestic Factors in Science and Technology Diplomacy: The Case of Iran's Nuclear Program." *Iranian Review of Foreign Affairs*, vol. 6, no. 2, Summer-Fall 2015, pp. 93–122.

Mizokami, Kyle. "How Iran Could Sink a Navy Aircraft Carrier in Battle." *The National Interest*, April 18, 2013. Available at: https://nationalinterest.org/blog/t he-buzz/how-iran-could-sink-navy-aircraft-carrier-battle-25435.

Moaveni, Azadeh. "How the Trump Administration Is Exploiting Iran's Burgeoning Feminist Movement." *New Yorker*, July 9, 2018. Available at: https://www.new yorker.com/news/news-desk/how-the-trump-administration-is-exploiting-irans-burgeoning-feminist-movement.

Modaress, Susan. "Did Trump's Double-Speak 'Blow' Chances of Rouhani Meeting?" *Al-Monitor*, August 14, 2018. Available at: https://www.al-monitor.com/pulse/or iginals/2018/08/iran-us-direct-talks-trump-rouhani-new-york-unga-jcpoa.html.

Monshipouri, Mahmood, ed. *Inside the Islamic Republic: Social Change in Post-Khomeini Iran*. London: Hurst & Company, 2016.

Monteireo, Nuno P. *Theory of Unipolar Politics*. New York: Cambridge University Press, 2014.

Morello, Carol. "Iran to Avoid Sanctions by Dodging U.S. Dollar." *Washington Post*, September 30, 2018, p. A12.

Morley, Jefferson. "The Growing Obsession with Linking Iran to Terrorism." *The New Republic*, April 10, 2019. Available at: https://newrepublic.com/article/153 537/growing-obsession-linking-iran-terrorism.

Morris, Edwin Kent. "Inversion, Paradox, and Liberal Disintegration: Towards a Conceptual Framework of Trumpism." *New Political Science*, vol. 41, no. 1, March 2019, pp. 17–35.

Moshirzadeh, Homeira. "Discursive Foundations of Iran's Nuclear Policy." *Security Dialogue*, vol. 38, no. 4, December 2007, pp. 521–543.

Mostofifar, Farzaneh and Erzi, Maryam. "Humanitarian Consequences of Sanctions: Medical Equipment, Medicine, Trade, and Transportation Sectors." Organization for Defending Victims of Violence, *Report No. 4*, March 2019, pp. 1–20.

Mousavi, Mohammad Ali and Norouzi, Yasser. "Iran-US Nuclear Standoff: A Game Theory Approach." *Iranian Review of Foreign Affairs*, vol. 1, no. 1, Spring 2010, pp. 121–152.

Mousavian, Seyed Hossein. "A Win-Win for Iran and the Region." *The Cairo Review of Global Affairs*, no. 33, Spring 2019, pp. 107–118.

————. "Can We Stop the Slow Slide to a U.S.-Iran War?" *The National Interest*, May 5, 2019. Available at: https://nationalinterest.org/feature/can-we-stop-slow-s lide-us-iran-war-55727.

————. "EU-Iran Relations After Brexit." *Survival*, vol. 58, no. 5, 2016, pp. 83–94.

————. "How Iran Sees Its Standoff with the United States." *Foreign Affairs*, July 12, 2019. Available at: https://www.foreignaffairs.com/articles/iran/2019-07-12/ how-iran-sees-its-standoff-united-states.

————. "How US, Iranian Regional Security Strategies Diverge." *Al-Monitor*, March 22, 2019. Available at: https://www.al-monitor.com/pulse/originals/2019/03/iran -us-regional-security-strategies-pmud-basij-syria-iraq.html.

———. "Iran, Saudi Arabia and a History of American Aggression." *Middle East Eye*, November 22, 2018. Available at: https://www.middleeasteye.net/columns/ir an-saudi-arabia-and-history-us-aggression-1345006352.

———. "Saudi Arabia Is Iran's New National Security Threat." *Huffington Post*, June 3, 2016. Available at: http://www.huffingtonpost.com/seyed-hossein-mousav ian/saudi-arabia-iran-threat_b_10282296.html.

———. "The Iran-Saudi/Arab Conflict and the Path to Peace." *Islamic Republic News Agency (IRNA)*, September 15, 2018. Available at: http://www.irna.ir/en/ News/83033599.

———. *The Iranian Nuclear Crisis: A Memoir*. Washington, DC: Carnegie Endowment for International Peace, 2012.

———. "Trump's 'Arab NATO' Project Is Doomed." *Newsweek*, October 16, 2018. Available at: https://www.newsweek.com/trumps-arab-nato-project-doomed-opi nion-1170368.

———, with Shahidsaless, Shahir. *Iran and the United States: An Insider's View on the Failed Past and the Road to Peace*. New York: Bloomsbury, 2014.

——— and Afrasiabi, Kaveh. "Eight Reasons Why Waltz Theory on Nuclear Iran Is Wrong." *Al-Monitor*, July 16, 2012. Available at: http://www.al-monitor.com/puls e/originals/2012/al-monitor/eight-reasons-why-the-waltz-theo.html.

——— and Toossi, Sina. "Assessing U.S.-Iran Nuclear Engagement." *The Washington Quarterly*, vol. 40, no. 3, Fall 2017, pp. 65–95.

Mowlana, S. Hamid and Mohammadi, Manouchehr. *Siyast-e Khareji-e Jomhouri-e Eslami-e Iran dar Dolat-e Ahmadinejad* (Foreign Policy of the Islamic Republic of Iran in Ahmadinejad's Government). Tehran: Dadgostar, 2008.

"Mozakereh ba Amrika: Tajrobeh-e Namovafagh Koreh-e Shomali" (Negotiating with the United States: The Failed Lesson of North Korea). Tehran, Majlis Research Center, October 21, 2018, pp. 1–18.

Mueller, Benjamin. "British Leaks Describe Trump's 'Act of Diplomatic Vandalism' on Iran Deal." *New York Times*, July 13, 2019. Available at: https://www.nytimes. com/2019/07/13/world/europe/britain-leaks-press-freedom.html.

Mulder, Nicholas. "Correlation Does Not Equal Compellence: The Weak Evidence for Sanctions." *Fellow Travelers*, February 25, 2019. Available at: https://fellowt ravelersblog.com/2019/02/25/correlation-does-not-equal-compellence-the-weak -evidence-for-sanctions/

Mulligan, Stephen P. *Withdrawing from International Agreements: Legal Framework, the Paris Agreement, and the Iran Nuclear Agreement*. Washington, DC: Congressional Research Service, May 4, 2018, pp. 1–28.

———. "Withdrawal from the Iran Nuclear Deal: Legal Authorities and Implications." *Legal Sidebar*, Congressional Research Service, May 17, 2018. Available at: https://fas.org/sgp/crs/nuke/LSB10134.pdf.

Murray, Donette. *US Foreign Policy and Iran: American-Iranian Relations since the Islamic Revolution*. London and New York: Routledge, 2010.

Nabavian, Seyyed Mahmood. *Chalesh-e Hastei* (The Nuclear Challenge). Vol. 1. Tehran: Islamic Revolution Documentation Center, 2018.

"Nagofteha-i az Mozakerat-e Iran va Amrika dar Doreh-e Ahmadinejad/Vasete-e Omani-e Mozakerat ke Bood? (The Untold Story of the Iran-U.S. Negotiations

During the Ahmadinejad Era/Who Was the Omani Intermediary?) *Tasnim News Agency*, September 16, 2018. Available at: https://www.tasnimnews.com/fa/news/1397/06/25/1828116/

Nakhleh, Emile. "How the Saudis with U.S. Help Made the Middle East 'A Very Dangerous'." *LobeLog*, November 26, 2018. Available at: https://lobelog.com/how-the-saudis-with-u-s-help-made-the-middle-east-a-very-dangerous-place/

———. "MbS: The New Saddam of Arabia?" *LobeLog*, October 30, 2018. Available at: https://lobelog.com/mbs-the-new-saddam-of-arabia/

———. "The Islamic Revolution's Impact on Political Islam and the Middle East." *LobeLog*, February 6, 2019. Available at: https://lobelog.com/the-islamic-revolutions-impact-on-political-islam-and-the-middle-east/

———. "The Middle East in Trump's Wake." *LobeLog*, June 14, 2018. Available at: https://lobelog.com/the-middle-east-in-trumps-wake/

———. "Trump's War Hysteria Against Iran Ignores Middle East Realities." *LobeLog*, August 1, 2018. Available at: https://lobelog.com/trumps-war-hysteria-against-iran-ignores-middle-east-realities/

Narwani, Sharmine. "US Officials Offered My Friend Cash to Take to Take Down Tehran's Power Grid." *Medium*, March 14, 2019. Available at: https://medium.com/@sharminen/us-officials-offered-my-friend-cash-to-take-down-tehrans-power-grid-628435bc61f8.

Nasr, Vali R. "A Saudi Murder Becomes a Gift to Iran." *New York Times*, November 12, 2018. Available at: https://www.nytimes.com/2018/11/12/opinion/saudi-murder-jamal-khashoggi-iran.html.

———. "Trump Is About to Make the Defining Mistake of His Foreign Policy." *Washington Post*, October 12, 2017. Available at: https://www.washingtonpost.com/opinions/trump-is-about-to-make-the-defining-mistake-of-his-foreign-policy/2017/10/12/17c87b96-af6b-11e7-be94-fabb0f1e9ffb_story.html?utm_term=.f599f54e7910.

National Security Archive, "Excessive U.S. Sanctions Could Push Iran 'Over the Brink': UAE Official to U.S. in 1995." *Briefing Book*, August 8, 2018. Available at: https://nsarchive.gwu.edu/briefing-book/iran/2018-08-08/excessive-us-sanctions-could-push-iran-over-brink-uae-official-us-1995.

"National Security Strategy of the United States." *The White House*, December 2017. Available at: https://www.whitehouse.gov/wp-content/uploads/2017/12/NSS-Final-12-18-2017-0905.pdf.

"National Strategy for Counterterrorism of the United States of America." *The White House*, October 2018. Available at: https://www.whitehouse.gov/wp-content/uploads/2018/10/NSCT.pdf.

Navazeni, Bahram, Ghasemi, Hakem, and Farsaei, Shahram. "Arzyabi-e Mahafel-e Gharbi az Payamadhaye Khavarmiyanei Barjam Baraye Siyasat-e Kharaji-e Iran" (The Western Circles' Evaluation of the Middle East Consequences of the JCPOA's for Iran's Foreign Policy). *Journal of Foreign Policy*, vol. 29, no. 4, Winter 2016, pp. 7–26.

Nedal, Dani and Nexon, Daniel. "Trump's 'Madman Theory' Isn't Strategic Unpredictability. It's Just Crazy." *Foreign Policy*, April 18, 2017. Available at: https://

foreignpolicy.com/2017/04/18/trumps-madman-theory-isnt-strategic-unpredictabi
lity-its-just-crazy/

Nephew, Richard. "Six Month Later: Assessing the Implementation of the Iran Nuclear Deal." Center on Global Energy Policy, Columbia University, July 2016, pp. 1–22.

———. *The Art of Sanctions: A View from the Field.* New York: Columbia University Press, 2017.

———. "The U.S. Drive to End Iranian Oil Exports: Expectations, Risks and Outcomes." Center on Global Energy Policy, Columbia University, April 23, 2019. Available at: https://energypolicy.columbia.edu/research/commentary/us-drive-en d-iranian-oil-exports-expectations-risks-and-outcomes.

———. "The US Withdrawal from the JCPOA: What to Look Out for Over the Next Year." Center on Global Energy Policy, Columbia University, November 2018, pp. 1–6.

Neubauer, Sigurd. "Is Oman Helping Netanyahu Make Peace with Saudi Arabia and Iran?" *LobeLog*, October 30, 2018. Available at: https://lobelog.com/is-oman-he lping-netanyahu-make-peace-with-saudi-arabia-and-iran/

Nili, Mas'ud. *Eqtesad-e Iran be Kodam Su Miravad?* (Which Direction Is the Iranian Economy Headed To?). Tehran: Donya-ye Eqtesad, 2017.

Ningthoujam, Alvite Singh. "Iranian Nuclear Program: A Chronology." *Contemporary Review of the Middle East*, vol. 3, no. 1, March 2016, pp. 111–122.

Nissenbaum, Dion. "John Bolton Energizes Trump's Agenda—and His Own." *Wall Street Journal*, November 18, 2018. Available at: https://www.wsj.com/articles/j ohn-bolton-energizes-trumps-agendaand-his-own-1542546003.

———. "White House Sought Options to Strike Iran." *Wall Street Journal*, January 13, 2019. Available at: https://www.wsj.com/articles/white-house-sought-options -to-strike-iran-11547375404.

Nixon, John. *Debriefing the President: The Interrogation of Saddam Hussein.* New York: Blue Rider Press/Penguin Random House, 2016.

Noori, Alireza. "Russia and Iran's Nuclear Program." *Discourse: An Iranian Quarterly*, vol. 11, nos. 1–2, Fall 2013–Winter 2014, pp. 155–178.

Nuclear Energy Iran. *What Are Iran's "Practical Needs" and Why Does Iran Want to Fuel Reactors on Its Own?* Tehran: Nuclearenergy.ir, July 2014, pp. 1–12.

Nye, Joseph. S., Jr. "Limits of American Power." *Political Science Quarterly*, vol. 131, no. 2, Summer 2016, pp. 267–283.

Oakeshott, Isabel. "Trump Axed Iran Deal to Spite Obama: How the British Ambassador Called the President's Actions 'Diplomatic Vandalism' Fueled by 'Personality Reasons'—as Revealed in More Explosive Cables That Have Sparked a Free Speech Row While Iran Tensions Mount." *Daily Mail*, July 13, 2019. Available at: https://www.dailymail.co.uk/news/article-7244539/Trump-axed-Iran-deal-spite-Obama-British-ambassador-says-Trumps-actions-diplomati c-vandalism.html.

Oborne, Peter and Morrison, David. *A Dangerous Delusion: Why the West Is Wrong About Nuclear Iran.* London: Elliott & Thompson, 2013.

Ochmanek, David, Wilson, Peter, A., Allen, Brenna, Meyers, John Speed, and Price, Carter C. *U.S. Military Capabilities and Forces for a Dangerous World:*

Rethinking the U.S. Approach to Force Planning. Santa Monica, CA: RAND Corporation, 2017.

O'Connor, Tom. "U.S. vs. Iran: Military Action 'On the Table,' Trump Administration Says After Senate Vote Threatens Saudi Arabia Support." *Newsweek*, November 29, 2018. Available at: https://www.newsweek.com/us-military-action-iran-t able-saudi-support-1237100.

Ollivant, Douglas A. and Gaston, Erica. "The Problem with the Narrative of 'Proxy War' in Iraq." *War on the Rocks*, May 31, 2019. Available at: https://warontherock s.com/2019/05/the-problem-with-the-narrative-of-proxy-war-in-iraq/

Omidi, Ali. "Is the Complaint Field with UN against Iran by Kuwait and Saudi Arabia Valid?" *Iran Review*, August 1, 2016. Available at: http://www.iranreview.org /content/Documents/Is-the-Complaint-Filed-with-the-UN-against-Iran-by-Kuwai t-and-Saudi-Arabia-over-Iran-s-Alleged-Marine-Transgressions-Valid-.htm.

Osman, Tarek. "Iran's Play for Middle Eastern Leadership: Where It Comes from and Why It Can't Last." *Foreign Affairs*, January 20, 2017. Available at: https ://www.foreignaffairs.com/articles/middle-east/2017-01-20/iran-s-play-middle-eas tern-leadership.

Ostovar, Afshon. "From Tehran to Mosul: Iran and the Middle East's Great Game." *Foreign Affairs*, November 4, 2016. Available at: https://www.foreignaffairs.com/ articles/iran/2016-11-04/tehran-mosul.

———. "Sectarian Dilemmas in Iranian Foreign Policy: When Strategy and Identity Politics Collide." Carnegie Endowment for International Peace, November 2016, pp. 1–32.

———. *Vanguard of the Imam: Religion, Politics, and Iran's Revolutionary Guards*. New York: Oxford University Press, 2016.

O'Toole, Brian. "Trump Policy, Not Sanctions, to Blame for Poor US Response to Iran Floods." Atlantic Council, *IranSource*, April 11, 2019. Available at: https ://www.atlanticcouncil.org/blogs/iransource/trump-policy-not-sanctions-to-blame- for-poor-us-response-to-iran-floods.

Padeanu, Iulia E. "Is the Trump Administration Bound by the Iran Deal?" *Yale Journal of International Law*, December 1, 2016. Available at: http://campuspress.yale. edu/yjil/is-the-trump-administration-bound-by-the-iran-deal/

Pande, Savita. "The Joint Comprehensive Plan of Action: Impacts on Pakistan-Iran Relations." *Contemporary Review of the Middle East*, vol. 3, no. 1, March 2016, pp. 77–94.

Pandey, Sanjay Kumar and Behboodinejad, Ghodratollah. "Payamadhaye Tavafogh-e Hastei bar Siyasathaye Mantaghei-e Iran" (The Consequences of the Nuclear Deal for Iran's Regional Foreign Policy). *Journal of Foreign Policy*, vol. 29, no. 3, Autumn 2015, pp. 57–78.

Pant, Girijesh. "Iran Returns to Global Energy Market: Issues and Prospects." *Contemporary Review of the Middle East*, vol. 3, no. 1, March 2016, pp. 23–35.

Pape, Robert A. "Why Economic Sanctions Do Not Work." *International Security*, vol. 22, no. 2, Fall 1997, pp. 90–136.

Parsi, Rouzbeh and Esfandiary, Dina. "An EU Strategy for Relations with Iran After the Nuclear Deal." Directorate-General for External Policies, Policy Department, European Parliament, June 2016, pp. 1–24.

Parsi, Trita. "America's Confrontation with Iran Goes Deeper Than Trump." *The Nation*, June 20, 2019. Available at: https://www.thenation.com/article/iran-war-tr ump/

———. "America's Effort to Isolate Iran Will Backfire: John Bolton and Mike Pompeo Are Pushing Trump Down a Proven Path of Failure." *The National Interest*, February 12, 2019. Available at: https://nationalinterest.org/feature/americas-effo rt-isolate-iran-will-backfire-44342.

———. *A Single Role of the Dice: Obama's Diplomacy with Iran*. New Haven, CT: Yale University Press, 2013.

———. "Iran Is Not North Korea: Trump's Regional Allies Prefer Civil War to Peace." *Middle East Eye*, January 13, 2018. Available at: http://www.middleeas teye.net/columns/iran-not-north-korea-why-trumps-goal-iran-may-go-well-beyo nd-regime-change-604890459.

———. *Losing an Enemy: Obama, Iran, and the Triumph of Diplomacy*. New Haven, CT: Yale University Press, 2017.

———. *Treacherous Alliance: The Secret Dealings of Israel, Iran, and the United States*. New Haven, CT: Yale University Press, 2007.

———. "Trump's 'Genocidal' Tweets Against Iran Come with a Price." *Truthout*, May 21, 2019. Available at: https://truthout.org/articles/trumps-genocidal-tweets-a gainst-iran-come-with-a-price/

———. "Trump's Iran Terrorist Designation Is Designed to Lock in Endless Enmity." *The Guardian*, April 12, 2019. Available at: https://www.theguardian. com/commentisfree/2019/apr/12/trump-iran-us-terror-designation-revolutionary -guards-latest.

———. "War with Iran Won't Be Iraq All Over Again. It'll Be Much Worse." *Huffington Post*, March 30, 2018. Available at: https://www.huffingtonpost.com/entry/ opinion-parsi-war-with-iran_us_5abd46fde4b055e50acc2e82.

———. "Warsaw Summit was a Failure for Trump—But a Win for Netanyahu." *Middle East Eye*, February 15, 2019. Available at: https://www.middleeasteye.net/ opinion/warsaw-summit-was-failure-trump-win-netanyahu.

———. "Why Trump's Hawks Back the MEK Terrorist Cult." *New York Review of Books*, July 20, 2018. Available at: https://www.nybooks.com/daily/2018/07/20/ why-trumps-hawks-back-the-mek-terrorist-cult/

——— and Azodi, Sina. "Is Trump's Iran Policy Meant to Start a War?" *The National Interest*, October 15, 2018. Available at: https://nationalinterest.org/print/ blog/skeptics/trump%E2%80%99s-iran-policy-meant-start-war-33541.

Parsi, Trita and Toossi, Sina. "Beware the Foreign Regime Change Charlatans." *The American Conservative*, January 24, 2019. Available at: https://www.theameri canconservative.com/articles/beware-the-regime-change-cottage-industry/

Parsi, Trita and Weinstein, Adam. "Iranian Hegemony Is a Figment of America's Imagination." *Foreign Policy*, January 25, 2017. Available at: http://foreignpolicy .com/2017/01/25/irans-proxy-wars-are-a-figment-of-americas-imagination/

Patrikarakos, David. *Nuclear Iran: The Birth of an Atomic State*. London: I.B. Tauris, 2013.

Paulraj, Nansi. "The JCPOA and Changing Dimensions of the Russia-Iran Relations." *Contemporary Review of the Middle East*, vol. 3, no. 1, March 2016, pp. 95–110.

Peled, Miko. "For the US and Israel, Iran Works Best as a Perpetual Threat." *Mint Press News*, June 3, 2019. Available at: https://www.mintpressnews.com/for-t he-us-and-israel-iran-works-best-as-a-perpetual-threat/258942/

Perkovich, George. "Compliance Versus Bargaining: An Implication of the Iran Nuclear Deal." *Arms Control Today*, vol. 46, no. 8, October 2016, pp. 32–35.

Perry, Mark. "Mattis's Last Stand Is Iran." *Foreign Policy*, June 28, 2018. Available at: https://foreignpolicy.com/2018/06/28/mattiss-last-stand-is-iran/

Phillips, Christopher. *The Battle for Syria: International Rivalry in the New Middle East*. New Haven, CT: Yale University Press, 2018.

Pieper, Moritz. "From Zero Problems with Neighbors to Zero Neighbors without Problems: Turkish-Iranian Relations Before and After the Syrian Crisis." In Amour, Philipp O., ed. *The Middle East Reloaded: Revolutionary Changes, Power Dynamics and Regional Rivalries Since the Arab Spring*. London and Washington, DC: Academic Press, 2018, pp. 171–198.

———. *Hegemony and Resistance Around the Iranian Nuclear Programme: Analysing Chinese, Russian and Turkish Foreign Policies*. London and New York: Routledge, 2017.

Pillar, Paul R. "Bolton's War." *LobeLog*, May 6, 2019. Available at: https://lobelog.com/boltons-war/

———. "Iran Policy and Misusing the Fear of Terrorism." *LobeLog*, September 25, 2018. Available at: https://lobelog.com/iran-policy-and-misusing-the-fear-of-ter rorism/

———. "Lessons from the Gulf of Tonkin Incident." *LobeLog*, May 21, 2019. Available at: https://lobelog.com/lessons-from-the-gulf-of-tonkin-incident/

———. "Maximum Pressure on Iran Still Isn't Working." *LobeLog*, April 2, 2019. Available at: https://www.lobelog.com/maximum-pressure-on-iran-still-isnt-worki ng/

———. "Sixty-Five Years On: Iran Regime Change Advocates Haven't Learned from Coup." The Atlantic Council, *IranSource*, August 15, 2018. Available at: http://www.atlanticcouncil.org/blogs/iransource/sixty-five-years-on-iran-regime-change-advocates-haven-t-learned-from-coup.

———. "Straining to be Anti-Iran." *The National Interest*, April 22, 2015. Available at: http://nationalinterest.org/blog/paul-pillar/straining-be-anti-iran-20318?page=s how.

———. "The Corruption of the Terrorist Group List." *LobeLog*, April 15, 2019. Available at: https://lobelog.com/the-corruption-of-the-terrorist-group-list/

———. "The MEK and the Bankrupt U.S. Policy on Iran." *LobeLog*, November 13, 2018. Available at: https://lobelog.com/the-mek-and-the-bankrupt-u-s-policy-on-i ran/

———. "The Paradox of Persian Power." *The National Interest*, no. 155, May/June 2018, pp. 29–39.

———. "The Role of Villain: Iran and U.S. Foreign Policy." *Political Science Quarterly*, vol. 131, no. 2, Summer 2016, pp. 365–385.

———. "The Sources of Iranian Conduct." *The National Interest*, December 12, 2018. Available at: https://nationalinterest.org/print/blog/paul-pillar/sources-irani an-conduct-38527.

———. "The Ugly Destination of Trump's Iran Policy." *LobeLog*, July 23, 2018. Available at: https://lobelog.com/the-ugly-destination-of-trumps-iran-policy/

———. "Washington Has Become a Warmonger's Paradise." *The National Interest*, May 21, 2019. Available at: https://nationalinterest.org/blog/paul-pillar/washingto n-has-become-warmongers-paradise-58832.

———. "What Makes Iran Look Like an Immediate Threat." *LobeLog*, May 16, 2019. Available at: https://lobelog.com/what-makes-iran-look-like-an-immediate-threat/

———. *Why America Misunderstands the World: National Experience and Roots of Misperception.* New York: Columbia University Press, 2016.

———. "Why Saudi Arabia Will Acquire Nuclear Weapons." *The National Interest*. November 26, 2018. Available at: https://nationalinterest.org/print/blog/paul-pilla r/why-saudi-arabia-will-acquire-nuclear-weapons-37197.

———. "Will the Trump Administration Start a War with Iran?" *The National Interest*, December 7, 2016. Available at: http://nationalinterest.org/blog/paul-pillar/ will-the-trump-administration-start-war-iran-18652.

Pintak, Lawrence. *America & Islam: Soundbites, Suicide Bombs and the Road to Donald Trump.* London: I.B. Tauris, 2019.

Plumer, Andrew G. "Iranian Sanctions: An Actor-Centric Analysis." M.A. Thesis, Naval Posdtgraduate School, Monterey, CA, March 2012.

Polk, William R. "A Trump War on Iran Would Destroy That Country, But Would It Brig Down the US as Well?" *Informed Comment*, September 10, 2018. Available at: https://www.juancole.com/2018/09/destroy-country-bring.html.

Pollack, Kenneth M. *The Persian Puzzle: The Conflict Between Iran and America.* New York: Random House, 2005.

———. *Unthinkable: Iran, the Bomb, and American Strategy.* New York: Simon & Schuster, 2013.

Pompeo, Michael R. "A Force for Good: America Reinvigorated in the Middle East." Full Text of the US Secretary of State Mike Pompeo's Speech at the American University in Cairo, January 10, 2019. Available at: https://www.state.gov/secretar y/remarks/2019/01/288410.htm.

———. "After the Deal: A New Iran Strategy." Full Text of the US Secretary of State Mike Pompeo's Speech at the Heritage Foundation, May 21, 2018. Available at: https://www.heritage.org/defense/event/after-the-deal-new-iran-strategy.

———. "Confronting Iran: The Trump Administration's Strategy." *Foreign Affairs*, vol. 97, no. 6, November/December 2018, pp. 60–70.

———. "Remarks to the Media." Full Text of the US Secretary of State Mike Pompeo's Remarks About the Termination of the 1955 Treaty of Amity with Iran, October 3, 2018. Available at: https://www.state.gov/secretary/remarks/2018/ 10/286417.htm.

———. "Supporting Iranian Voices." Full Text of the US Secretary of State Mike Pompeo's Speech at the Ronald Reagan Presidential Foundation and Library, July 22, 2018. Available at: https://www.state.gov/secretary/remarks/2018/07/284292. htm#.W1WWM57F-jw.mailto.

———. "The U.S.-Saudi Partnership Is Vital." *Wall Street Journal*, November 27, 2018. Available at: https://www.wsj.com/articles/the-u-s-saudi-partnership-is-vi tal-1543362363.

Porter, Gareth. "Do Iranian 'Threats' Signal Organized U.S.-Israel Subterfuge?" *The American Conservative*, May 21, 2019. Available at: https://www.theamericanconservative.com/articles/do-iranian-threats-signal-organized-u-s-israel-subterfuge/

———. "How Corporate Media Are Fueling a New Iran Nuclear Crisis." *Truthdig*, July 17, 2019. Available at: https://www.truthdig.com/articles/how-corporate-media-are-fueling-a-new-iran-nuclear-crisis/

———. "How 'Operation Merlin' Poisoned U.S. Intelligence on Iran." *Consortium News*, March 3, 2018. Available at: https://consortiumnews.com/2018/03/03/how-operation-merlin-has-poisoned-u-s-intelligence-on-iran/

———. "Israel's Construction of Iran as an Existential Threat." *Journal of Palestine Studies*, vol. 43, no. 1, Autumn 2015, pp. 43–62.

———. "Lies About Iran Killing US Troops in Iraq Are a Ploy to Justify War." *Truthout*, July 9, 2019. Available at: https://truthout.org/articles/lies-about-iran-killing-us-troops-in-iraq-are-a-ploy-to-justify-war/

———. *Manufactured Crisis: The Untold Story of the Iran Nuclear Scare*. Charlottesville, VA: Just World Books, 2014.

———. "Pentagon's Phony Iran 'Evidence': New Rationale for U.S. Intervention?" *Salon*, June 3, 2019. Available at: https://www.salon.com/2019/06/03/pentagons-phony-iran-evidence-new-rationale-for-u-s-intervention/

———. "Rouhani's Dual Message and Iran's Security Strategy." *Middle East Eye*, September 30, 2015. Available at: http://www.middleeasteye.net/columns/rouhanis-dual-messages-and-iran-s-security-strategy-1712351174.

———. "The Latest Act in Israel's Iran Nuclear Disinformation Campaign." *Consortium News*, May 3, 2018. Available at: https://consortiumnews.com/2018/05/03/the-latest-act-in-the-israels-iran-nuclear-disinformation-campaign/

———. "The Permanent-War Complex." *The American Conservative*, vol. 17, no. 6, November/December 2018, pp. 28–32.

———. "The Right May Finally Get Its War on Iran." *Truthdig*, February 27, 2019. Available at: https://www.truthdig.com/articles/the-right-may-finally-get-its-war-on-iran/

Porter, Patrick. "A World Imagined: Nostalgia and Liberal Order." Cato Institute, *Policy Analysis*, no. 843, June 5, 2018, pp. 1–24.

Posch, Walter. "Ideology and Strategy in the Middle East: The Case of Iran." *Survival*, vol. 59, no. 5, October–November 2017, pp. 69–98.

———. "Iranian Regional Security Policies: The Case of Iraq and Syria." *Al Sharq Forum*, May 21, 2018. Available at: http://www.sharqforum.org/2018/05/21/iranian-regional-security-policies-the-cases-of-iraq-and-syria/

Posen, Barry R. "The Rise of Illiberal Hegemony: Trump's Surprising Grand Strategy." *Foreign Affairs*, vol. 97, no. 2, March/April 2018, pp. 20–27.

Postel, Danny and Hashemi, Nader. "Playing with Fire: Trump, the Saudi-Iranian Rivalry, and the Geopolitics of Sectarianization in the Middle East." European Institute of the Mediterranean (IEMed), *IEMed Mediterranean Yearbook 2018*. Barcelona: IEMed, 2018, pp. 58–63.

Potter, William and Mukhatzhanova, Gaukhar. *Nuclear Politics and the Non-Aligned Movement*. Adelphi Paper 427. London: Routledge, 2012.

Potts, Daniel Thomas. "Iran and America: A Forgotten Friendship." *The Conversation*, July 31, 2018. Available at: https://theconversation.com/iran-and-america-a-forgotten-friendship-99350.

Pourebrahim, Nasser. "Turkish-Saudi Relations: A Regional Perspective (2003–2015). *Iranian Review of Foreign Affairs*, vol. 6, no. 2, Summer–Fall 2015, pp. 69–92.

Pourtaher, Elham. "For Iranians, the War Has Already Begun." *LobeLog*, May 13, 2019. Available at: https://lobelog.com/for-iranians-the-war-has-already-begun/

Prashad, Vijay. *The Death of the Nation and the Future of the Arab Revolution.* Berkeley, CA: University of California Press, 2016.

Preble, Christopher A. "Here's How the Road to Iraq Is Repeating Itself with Iran." *The National Interest*, July 5, 2018. Available at: http://nationalinterest.org/blog/skeptics/heres-how-road-iraq-repeating-itself-iran-25097.

Pugwash Conference on Science at World Affairs. Tehran Meeting on JCPOA. "Pugwash-IPIS Roundtable Report." July 10, 2019. Available at: https://pugwashconferences.files.wordpress.com/2019/07/20190624_tehran_jcpoa-report-1.pdf.

Qaidaari, Abbas. "President Hassan Rouhani's Defense Policy." *Atlantic Council*, February 11, 2016. Available at: http://www.atlanticcouncil.org/blogs/new-atlanticist/president-hassan-rouhani-s-defense-policy.

Raas, Whitney and Long, Austin. "Osirak Redux? Assessing Israeli Capabilities to Destroy Iranian Nuclear Facilities." *International Security*, vol. 31, no. 4, Spring 2007, pp. 7–33.

Rafati, Nysan. "Regional Risks of U.S.-Iran Rivalry." International Crisis Group, *Commentary*, November 1, 2018. Available at: https://www.crisisgroup.org/middle-east-north-africa/gulf-and-arabian-peninsula/iran/regional-risks-rising-us-iran-rivalry.

——— and Vaez, Ali. "Europe Tests the Boundaries on Iran: A New Trade Vehicle Could Preserve the Nuclear Deal's Core Bargain." *Foreign Affairs*, February 4, 2019. Available at: https://www.foreignaffairs.com/articles/iran/2019-02-04/europe-tests-boundaries-iran.

Rafi, Mohammad. "When It Comes to War with Iran: Less Is Not More." *TelosScope*, May 27, 2019. Available at: http://www.telospress.com/when-it-comes-to-war-with-iran-less-is-not-more/

Rahigh-Aghsan, Ali and Jakobsen, Peter Viggo. "The Rise of Iran: How Durable, How Dangerous?" *Middle East Journal*, vol. 64, no. 4, Autumn 2010, pp. 559–573.

Rajendram Lee, Lavina. *US Hegemony and International Legitimacy: Norms, Power and Fellowship in the Wars on Iraq.* London and New York: Routledge, 2010.

Raji, Mehdi, ed. *Aghay-e Safir: Goftogo ba Mohammad Javad Zarif, Safir-e Pishin-e Iran dar Sazman-e Mellal-e Mottahed* (Mr. Ambassador: A Dialogue with Mohhamad Javad Zarif, the Former Ambassador of Iran to the United Nations). Tehran: Nashr-e Ney, 2013.

Rajiv, S. Samuel C. "Deep Disquiet: Israel and the Iran Nuclear Deal." *Contemporary Review of the Middle East*, vol. 3, no. 1, March 2016, pp. 47–62.

Ram, Haggai. *Iranophobia: The Logic of an Israeli Obsession.* Stanford, CA: Stanford University Press, 2009.

Ramazani, R.K. *Independence Without Freedom: Iran's Foreign Policy.* Charlottesville, VA: University of Virginia Press, 2013.

Randjbar-Daemi, Siavush. *Quest for Authority in Iran: A History of Presidency from Revolution to Rouhani.* London: I.B. Tauris, 2017.

Rashid, Ahmed. "Iran's Game in Aleppo." *New York Review of Books*, December 1, 2016. Available at: http://www.nybooks.com/daily/2016//12/01/iran-game-in-a leppo-syria/

Ratner, Michael. "Iran's Threats, the Strait of Hormuz, and Oil Markets: In Brief." Congressional Research Service, *CRS Report*, August 6, 2018, pp. 1–8.

Rauf, Tariq and Kelley, Robert. "Assessing the IAEA 'Assessment' of 'Possible Military Dimensions' of Iran's Nuclear Program'." Stockholm International Peace Research Institute (SIPRI), December 15, 2015. Available at: http://www.sipri.org /pdfs/final-assessment-iaea-december-2015.

Razoux, Pierre. *The Iran-Iraq War.* Translated by Nicholas Elliott. Cambridge, MA: Harvard University Press, 2015.

Reda, Latife. "Origins of the Islamic Republic's Strategic Approaches to Power and Regional Politics: The Palestinian-Israeli Conflict in Khomeini's Discourse." *Middle East Critique*, vol. 25, no. 2, June 2016, pp. 181–203.

Reisinezahd, Arash. "Why Iran Needs to Dominate the Middle East." *The National Interest*, April 10, 2015. Available at: https://nationalinterest.org/print/feature/wh y-iran-needs-dominate-the-middle-east-12595.

Rezaei, Farhad. *Iran's Foreign Policy After the Nuclear Agreement: Politics of Normalizers and Traditionalists.* New York: Palgrave Macmillan, 2018.

Rezaian, Jason. "The State Department Has Been Funding Trolls. I'm One of Their Targets." *Washington Post*, June 4, 2019. Available at: https://www.washingt onpost.com/opinions/2019/06/04/state-department-has-been-funding-trolls-im-one-their-targets/

———. "Why Does the U.S. Need Trolls to Make Its Iran Case?" *Washington Post*, June 11, 2019. Available at: https://www.washingtonpost.com/opinions/2019/ 06/11/why-does-us-need-trolls-make-its-iran-case/

Rhodes, Ben. *The World as It Is: A Memoir of the Obama White House.* New York: Random House, 2018.

Riedel, Bruce. "Lessons from America's First War with Iran." *The Fletcher Forum of World Affairs*, vol. 37, no. 2, Summer 2013, pp. 101–106.

Risen, James. *State of War: The Secret History of the CIA and the Bush Administration.* New York: Free Press, 2006.

Ritter, Scott. "America Just Declared War on Iran and Nobody Blinked." *The American Conservative*, April 11, 2019. Available at: https://www.theamericanconserv ative.com/articles/america-just-declared-war-on-iran-and-nobody-blinked-irgc-ter rorists/

———. *Deal Breaker: Donald Trump and the Unmaking of the Iran Nuclear Agreement.* Atlanta: Clarity Press, 2018.

———. *Deal of the Century: How Iran Blocked the West's Road to War.* Atlanta: Clarity Press, 2017.

————. "Iran Deserves Credit for the Ruin of ISIS." *The American Conservative*, October 17, 2018. Available at: https://www.theamericanconservative.com/artic les/iran-deserves-credit-for-the-ruin-of-isis/

————. "Propaganda Aiming to Prove Iran Supplied Missiles Backfires." *The American Conservative*, December 26, 2017. Available at: https://www.theamericanco nservative.com/articles/propaganda-exercise-aiming-to-prove-iran-supplied-missil es-backfires/

————. *Target Iran: The Truth About the White House's Plans for Regime Change.* New York: Nations Books, 2006.

————. "The Trouble with Defectors: What Informants Taught an Intelligence Officer." *Harper's Magazine*, January 2017, pp. 31–35.

Robinson, Heather M., Connable, Ben, Thaler, David E., and Scotten, Ali G. *Sectarianism in the Middle East: Implications for the United States*, Santa Monica, CA: RAND Corporation, 2018.

Rodríguez Toribio, Isabel and González Aldea, Patricia. "U.S. Foreign Policy in Clinton and Trump's Presidential Campaign. Discourses on ISIS in the Media." *Doxa Comunicación*, vol. 25, 2017, pp. 13–42.

Rogers, Paul F. "Military Action Against Iran: Impact and Effects." Oxford Research Group, *Briefing Paper*, July 2010, pp. 1–14.

Rome, Henry. "Why Iranian Waits: Staying in the Nuclear Deal Is Its Worst Option, Except for All the Others." *Foreign Affairs*, January 10, 2019. Available at: https ://www.foreignaffairs.com/articles/iran/2019-01-10/why-iran-waits.

Rose, Gideon and Tepperman, Jonathan, eds. *Iran and the Bomb: Solving the Persian Puzzle.* New York: Council on Foreign Relations Press, 2012.

Rosenberg, Elizabeth. "The EU Can't Avoid U.S. Sanctions on Iran." *Foreign Affairs*, October 10, 2018. Available at: https://www.foreignaffairs.com/articles/ europe/2018-10-10/eu-cant-avoid-us-sanctions-iran.

Ross, Dennis. "Iran Is Throwing a Tantrum but Wants a Deal." *Foreign Policy*, August 15, 2018. Available at: https://foreignpolicy.com/2018/08/15/iran-is-throw ing-a-tantrum-but-wants-a-deal/

Rouhani, Hassan. *Amniyat-e Melli va Diplomasiye Hastei* (National Security and Nuclear Diplomacy). Tehran: Center for Strategic Studies, 2012.

————. "Europe Should Work with Iran to Counter US Unilateralism." *Financial Times*, November 1, 2018. Available at: https://www.ft.com/content/3ecaed5e-dcfc -11e8-b173-ebef6ab1374a.

————. "Iran Is Committed to Honest Dialogue. Is Trump?" *Washington Post*, September 21, 2018. Available at: https://www.washingtonpost.com/opinions/iran-is-committed-to-honest-dialogue-is-trump/2018/09/21/7c1a2754-bdb4-11e8-be70 -52bd11fe18af_story.html?utm_term=.811fa253b39b.

————. "JCPOA Lost 1 Out of 5+1." President Rouhani's televised address to the Iranian people after President Trump's withdrawal from the Iran nuclear deal, May 9, 2018. Available at: http://president.ir/en/104282.

Rouhi, Mahsa. "Iranians Will Tolerate Hardship But Not Capitulation." *Foreign Policy*, May 13, 2019. Available at: https://foreignpolicy.com/2019/05/13/iranians-will-tole rate-hardship-but-not-capitulation-rouhani-trump-bolton-sanctions-eu-instex/

Rubin, Michael. "The Mojahedin e-Khalq Aren't America's Friends." *The National Interest*, March 28, 2019. Available at: https://nationalinterest.org/print/blog/middl e-east-watch/mojahedin-e-khalq-arent-americas-friends-49547.

Russell, James A. "A Tipping Point Realized? Nuclear Proliferation in the Persian Gulf and Middle East." *Contemporary Security Policy*, vol. 29, no. 3, December 2008, pp. 521–537.

Saab, Bilal Y. "Can Mohamed bin Salman Reshape Saudi Arabia? The Treacherous Path to Reform." *Foreign Affairs*, January 5, 2015. Available at: https://www.for eignaffairs.com/articles/saudi-arabia/2017-01-05/can-mohamed-bin-salman-res hape-saudi-arabia.

——— and Elleman, Michael. "Precision Fire: A Strategic Assessment of Iran's Conventional Missile Program." Atlantic Council, *Issue Brief*, September 2016, pp. 1–10.

Sachs, Jeffrey D. *A New Foreign Policy: Beyond American Exceptionalism*. New York: Columbia University Press, 2018.

———. "America's Economic Blockades and International Law." *Project Syndicate*, June 28, 2019. Available at: https://www.project-syndicate.org/commentary/trump -reliance-on-economic-sanctions-by-jeffrey-d-sachs-2019-06.

Sadeghi-Boroujerdi, Eskandar. "The Iran Nuclear Deal, Regime Change, and the Perils of the 'Third Way'." *Jadaliyya*, June 12, 2018. Available at: http://www .jadaliyya.com/Details/37649/The-Iran-Nuclear-Deal,-Regime-Change,-and-the-Perils-of-the-%E2%80%9CThird-Way%E2%80%9D.

Sadeghinia, Mahboubeh. *Security Arrangements in the Persian Gulf, with Special Reference to Iran's Foreign Policy*. Reading, UK: Ithaca Press, 2011.

Sadjadpour, Karim. "The High-Stakes Confrontation Between Trump and Khamenei." *The Atlantic*, April 29, 2019. Available at: https://www.theatlantic.com/ideas/ archive/2019/04/trump-and-khamenei/588250/

Saeedi, Rouholamin. "Rahkar-e Ideolojik baraye Gozar az Ideoloji dar Siyasat-e Khareji: Naqdi bar Yaddasht-e Mohammad-e Quochani" (An Ideological Solution to the Transition from Ideology in Foreign Policy: A Critique of Mohammad Quochani's Memo). *Asr-e Andisheh*, April 21, 2018. Available at: http://www.asre andisheh.ir/Home/Content/444.

Safdari, Hossein. "Ahamiyat-e Rahbordiye Piroozihaye Artesh-e Sooriye dar Sharghe Halab dar Negah-e Dabir-e Shorarye Aliye Amniyat-e Iran" (The Strategic Importance of the Syrian Army's Victory in Eastern Aleppo from the Perspectives of the Secretary of Iran's Supreme National Security Council). *Tehran Foreign Policy Studies Quarterly*, vol. 1, no. 2, Winter 2017. Available at: http://tfpsq.ne t/?page=article&language=persian&id=14.

Sagan, Scott D. and Valentino, Benjamin A. "Revisiting Hiroshima in Iran: What Americans Really Think About Using Nuclear Weapons and Killing Noncombatants." *International Security*, vol. 42, no. 1, Summer 2017, pp. 41–79.

Sahimi, Muhammad. "Pompeo, Bolton, and Iran's 'Fake Opposition'." *LobeLog*, February 6, 2019. Available at: https://lobelog.com/pompeo-bolton-and-irans-f ake-opposition/

Saikal, Amin, ed. *The Arab World and Iran: A Turbulent Region in Transition*. New York: Palgrave Macmillan, 2016.

Sajjadpour, Seyed Kazem. "Chahar Chobi Mafhoomi va Farageer baray-e Dark va Tahlil-e Siyasat-e Khareji-e Iran" (An Inclusive Conceptual Framework for Understanding and Analyzing Iranian Foreign Policy), *Foreign Policy* (Tehran), vol. 32, no. 4, Spring 2019, pp. 27–42.

Salama, Sammy and Weber, Heidi. "Arab Nuclear Envy." *Bulletin of the Nuclear Scientists*, vol. 63, no. 5, September/October 2007, pp. 44–63.

Salehi, Ali Akbar. *Gozari dar Tarikh: Khaterat-e Doktor Ali Akbar Salehi* (Passage in History: Memoirs of Dr. Ali Akbar Salehi). Tehran: Ministry of Foreign Affairs of the Islamic Republic of Iran Publications, 2018).

Salehi, Seyyed Javad and Farahbakhsh, Abbas. "Paygah Sazi-e Nezami dar Gharb-e Asia (Khavar-e Miyaneh) va Baz Darandigiy-e Jomhoori-e Eslami-e Iran" (Military Basing in West Asia (Middle East) and the Islamic Republic of Iran's Deterrence Policy). *Journal of Defense Policy*, vol. 24, no. 96, Fall 2016, pp. 33–65.

Salehi-Isfahani, Djavad. "The Cost of Sanctions for Iran's Economy." *Tyranny of Numbers*, July 23, 2018. Available at: https://djavadsalehi.com/2018/07/23/the-cost-of-sanctions-for-irans-economy/

———. "Yes, Iran's Economy Is Suffering—But It's Not All About the U.S." *Foreign Affairs*, September 25, 2018. Available at: https://www.foreignaffairs.com/arti cles/iran/2018-09-25/yes-irans-economy-suffering-its-not-all-about-us.

Salehiyan, Tajeddin and Simbar, Reza. "Manabe'e Ejtemaiye Siyast-e Kharejiye Jomhoriye Eslamiye Iran" (Social Sources of the Islamic Republic of Iran's Foreign Policy). *Public Policy Strategic Studies Quarterly* (Tehran), vol. 8, no. 26, Spring 2018, pp. 165–186.

Sanati, Reza. "Beyond the Domestic Picture: The Geopolitical Factors That Have Formed Contemporary Iran-US Relations." *Global Change, Peace & Security*, vol. 26, no. 2, 2014, pp. 125–140.

Sankaran, Jaganath and Fetter, Steve. "A Path to Reducing Iran's Missile Threat and Reconfiguring U.S. Missile Defenses." *Arms Control Today*, vol. 48, no. 6, July/August 2018, pp. 12–17.

Sardarnia, Khalil and Chitsazian, Mohammad Reza. "The Future of Iran-Iraq Relations: Possible Scenarios." *Iranian Political Studies*, vol. 1, no. 1, May 2019, pp. 43–59.

Sariolghalam, Mahmood. "Prospects for Change in Iranian Foreign Policy." Carnegie Endowment for International Peace, February 20, 2018. Available at: https://carnegieendowment.org/2018/02/20/prospects-for-change-in-iranian-foreign-poli cy-pub-75569.

Sauer, Tom. "Coercive Diplomacy by the EU: The Iranian Nuclear Weapons Crisis." *Third World Quarterly*, vol. 28, no. 3, April 2007, pp. 613–633.

Saunders, Elizabeth N. "Is Trump a Normal Foreign-Policy President? What We Know After One Year." *Foreign Affairs*, January 18, 2018. Available at: https://www.foreignaffairs.com/articles/united-states/2018-01-18/trump-normal-foreign -policy-president.

Scahill, Jeremy. "More Than Russia—There's a Strong Case for the Trump Team Colluding with Saudi Arabia, Israel, and the UAE." *The Intercept*, June 10, 2018. Available at: https://theintercept.com/2018/06/10/more-than-just-russia-theres-a-strong-case-for-the-trump-team-colluding-with-saudi-arabia-israel-and-the-uae/

Schake, Kori. "Republican Foreign Policy After Trump." *Survival*, vol. 58, no. 5, October-November 2016, pp. 33–52.

Schmerler, David. "Iran's Space Launch: ICBM or Space Program Development?" Foreign Policy Research Institute, Middle East Program, *E-Notes*, January 22, 2019. Available at: https://www.fpri.org/article/2019/01/irans-space-launch-icbm -or-space-program-development/

Schmid, Dorothée and Brillat, Adrian Giorgio. "Beyond the JCPOA: The Renewal of Iranian Diplomacy." In Italian Institute for International Political Studies (ISPI), ed. *Building Trust: The Challenge of Peace and Stability in the Mediterranean*. Mediterranean Dialogues 2018. Rome: ISPI, 2018, pp. 44–47.

Schmitt, Eric and Barnes, Julian E. "White House Reviews Military Plans Against Iran, in Echoes of Iraq War." *New York Times*, May 13, 2019. Available at: https:// www.nytimes.com/2019/05/13/wold/middleeast/us-military-plans-iran.html.

Schneider, Mark B. "Has Iran Covertly Acquired Nuclear Weapons?" *Comparative Strategy*, vol. 32, no. 4, September 2013, pp. 308–312.

Schweller, Randall. "Three Cheers for Trump's Foreign Policy: What the Establishment Misses." *Foreign Affairs*, vol. 97, no. 5, September/October 2018, pp. 133–143.

Scobell, Andrew and Nader, Alireza. *China in the Middle East: The Wary Dragon*. Santa Monica, CA: RAND Corporation, 2016.

Scott, Catherine V. *Neoliberalism and U.S. Foreign Policy: From Carter to Trump*. New York: Palgrave Macmillan, 2018.

Scott-Clark, Cathy and Levy, Adrian. *The Exile: The Stunning Inside Story of Osama bin Laden and Al Qaeda in Flight*. New York: Bloomsbury Publishing, 2017.

Sebenius, James K. and Singh, Michael K. "Is a Nuclear Deal with Iran Possible? An Analytical Framework for the Iran Nuclear Negotiations." *International Security*, vol. 37, no. 3, Winter 2012/13, pp. 52–91.

Serfaty, Simon. "Trump's Moment in History." *The National Interest*, no. 152, November/December 2017, pp. 32–38.

Sestanovich, Stephen. "The Brilliant Incoherence of Trump's Foreign Policy." *The Atlantic*, May 2017, pp. 92–102.

Shabani, Mohammad Ali. "Why US Sanctions Won't 'Starve' Iran of Means to Pursue Its Regional Policy." *Al-Monitor*, November 30, 2018. Available at: https:// www.al-monitor.com/pulse/originals/2018/11/iran-regional-policy-sanctions-imp act-pompeo-starve-syria.html.

Shaddel, Mehdy. "Donald Trump Thinks It's His Fault that Iran's Currency Is in Meltdown. He Shouldn't Be So Arrogant." *Independent*, September 18, 2018. Available at: https://www.independent.co.uk/voices/iran-us-rial-currency-crisis -explained-a8543086.html.

Shahabi Sirjani, Farhad. "Iran's Nuclear Fatwa." *Iranian Review of Foreign Affairs*, vol. 4, no. 2, Summer 2013, pp. 57–80.

Shahidsaless, Shahir. "Signs of a Spectacular Policy Shift in Iran." Atlantic Council, *IranSource*, October 19, 2018. Available at: http://www.atlanticcouncil.org/blogs/ iransource/signs-of-a-spectacular-policy-shift-in-iran.

———. "Trump versus Iran: Three Flashpoints that Could Spark War." *Middle East Eye*, February 3, 2017. Available at: http://www.middleeasteye.net/columns/iso lationist-trump-could-be-dragged-one-america-s-worst-wars-256134427.

Shameer, Modongal and Mousavian, Seyed Hossein. "Why Iran Has Not Developed the Nuclear Weapons: Understanding the Role of Religion in Nuclear Policies of Iran." *Bandung: Journal of the Global South*, vol. 6, no. 1, June 2019, pp. 132–152.

Shams, Shamil. "Pakistan on Collision Course with Iran?" *Deutsche Welle*, April 25, 2017. Available at: https://amp-dw-com.cdn.ampproject.org/c/amp.dw.com/en/pakistan-on-collision-course-with-iran/a-38578700.

Sharifi, Farzad Cyrus. *Arab-Iranian Rivalry in the Persian Gulf: Territorial Disputes and the Balance of Power in the Middle East*. London and New York: I.B. Tauris, 2015.

Shehadeh, Raja and Johnson, Penny, eds. *Shifting Sands: The Unraveling of the Old Order in the Middle East*. Northampton, MA: Olive Branch Press, 2016.

Sherman, Wendy R. "How We Got the Iran Deal: And Why We'll Miss It." *Foreign Affairs*, vol. 97, no. 5, September/October 2018, pp. 186–197.

———. *Not for the Faint of Heart: Lessons in Courage, Power, and Persistence*. New York: PublicAffairs, 2018.

Sherwood, Harriet. "The Chosen One? The New Film That Claims Trump's Election Was an Act of God." *The Guardian*, October 3, 2018. Available at: https://www.theguardian.com/us-news/2018/oct/03/the-trump-prophecy-film-god-election-mark-taylor.

Shinkman, Paul D. "Trump Pick for Saudi Ambassador: Iran Threat Outweighs Other Concerns." *US News & World Report*, March 6, 2019. Available at: https://www.usnews.com/news/politics/articles/2019-03-06/trumps-saudi-ambassador-nominee-argues-iran-threat-outweighs-human-rights-concerns.

Shokri Kalehsar, Omid. "Iran-Azerbaijan Energy Relations in the Post-Sanctions Era." *Middle East Policy*, vol. 23, no. 1, Spring 2016, pp. 136–143.

Shoup, Laurence H. *Wall Street's Think Tank: The Council on Foreign Relations and the Empire of Neoliberal Geopolitics, 1976–2019*, new edition. New York: Monthly Review Press, 2019.

Simes, Dimitri K. "Poised for Success?" *The National Interest*, no. 156, July/August 2018, pp. 5–12.

Simon, Steven. "Iran and President Trump: What Is the Endgame?" *Survival*, vol. 60, no. 4, August-September 2018, pp. 7–20.

——— and Stevenson, Jonathan. "Iran: The Case Against War." *New York Review of Books*, July 17, 2019. Available at: https://www.nybooks.com/articles/2019/08/15/iran-case-against-war/

———. "Trump's Dangerous Obsession with Iran: Why Hostility Is Counterproductive." *Foreign Affairs*, August 13, 2018. Available at: https://www.foreignaffairs.com/articles/iran/2018-08-13/trumps-dangerous-obsession-iran.

Simpson, Emile. *War from the Ground Up: Twenty-First Century Combat as Politics*. Revised updated edition. New York: Oxford University Press, 2018.

Singh, Michael. "The Case for Zero Enrichment in Iran." *Arms Control Today*, vol. 44, no. 2, March 2014, pp. 12–14.

Slavin, Barbara. *Bitter Friends, Bosom Enemies: Iran, the U.S., and the Twisted Path to Confrontation*. New York: St. Martin's Press, 2007.

Smith, Keith. "Realist Foreign Policy Analysis with a Twist: The Persian Gulf Security Complex and the Rise and Fall of Dual Containment." *Foreign Policy Analysis*, vol. 12, no. 3, July 2016, pp. 315–333.

Sobelman, Daniel. "Restraining an Ally: Israel, the United States, and Iran's Nuclear Program, 2011–2012." *Texas National Security Review*, vol. 1, no. 4, August 14, 2018. Available at: https://tnsr.org/2018/08/restraining-an-ally-israel-the-united-st ates-and-irans-nuclear-program-2011-2012/

Solomon, Jay. *The Iran Wars: Spy Games, Bank Battles, and the Secret Deals that Reshaped the Middle East.* New York: Random House, 2016.

Soltanifar, Ehsan, Aghazadeh, Hashem, and Ansari, Manochehr. "Tahlili Siyasati bar Mohit-e Tose'e Hamkariye Tejari-Eqtesadi Miyan-e Iran va Faranse" (A Policy Analysis of the Environment for the Expansion of Trade-Economic Cooperation Between Iran and France). *Public Policy Strategic Studies Quarterly* (Tehran), vol. 8, no. 26, Spring 2018, pp. 207–237.

Sonne, Paul. "Can Saudi Arabia Produce Ballistic Missiles? Satellite Imagery Raises Suspicions." *Washington Post*, January 23, 2019. Available at: https://www.was hingtonpost.com/world/national-security/can-saudi-arabia-produce-ballistic-missi les-satellite-imagery-raises-suspicions/2019/01/23/49e46d8c-1852-11e9-a804-c35766b9f234_story.html?utm_term=.f34a94f4a727.

Soufan, Ali. "Qassem Soleimani and Iran's Unique Regional Strategy." Combating Terrorism Center at West Point, *CTC Sentinel*, vol. 11, no. 10, November 2018, pp. 1–12.

Sperandei, Maria. "Bridging Deterrence and Compellence: An Alternative Approach to the Study of Coercive Diplomacy." *International Studies Review*, vol. 8, no. 2, June 2006, pp. 253–280.

Srđa, Trifković. "Trump's Foreign Policy: A Victory for the Deep State." *Politeia*, vol. 7, no. 13, 2017, pp. 28–52.

Stacey, Jeffrey, A. "Strengthen Iran's Moderates Before It's Too Late: Running Out of Time in Iran." *Foreign Affairs*, March 2, 2017. Available at: https://www.for eignaffairs.com/articles/iran/2017-03-02/strengthen-irans-moderates-its-too-late.

Starr-Deelen, Donna. *Counter-Terrorism from the Obama Administration to President Trump: Caught in the Fait Accompli War.* New York: Palgrave Macmillan, 2018.

"Statement by the High Representative of the European Union and the Foreign Ministers of France, Germany and the United Kingdom." Foreign & Commonwealth Office, the United Kingdom, May 4, 2019. Available at: https://www.gov.uk/ government/news/statement-by-the-high-representative-of-the-european-union-a nd-the-foreign-ministers-of-france-germany-and-the-united-kingdom.

Stephens, Bret. "The Foreign Policy Fiasco That Wasn't." *New York Times*, March 30, 2019, p. A27.

Stiglitz, Joseph E. *Globalization and Its Discontents Revisited: Anti-Globalization in the Era of Trump.* New York: W.W. Norton & Company, 2017.

Stimpson, Cassandra and Harris, Nia. "The Lobby for War with Iran." *Inkstick*, June 26, 2019. Available at: https://inkstickmedia.com/the-lobby-for-war-with-iran/

Stone, Richard. "Science in Iran Languishes After Trump Re-Imposes Sanctions." *Science*, August 31, 2018. Available at: http://www.sciencemag.org/news/2018/08/ science-iran-languishes-after-trump-re-imposes-sanctions.

Straw, Jack. *The English Job: Understand Iran and Why It Distrusts Britain.* London: Biteback Publishing, 2019.

Sullivan, Eileen. "Trump Calls His Intelligence People 'Naïve'." *New York Times*, January 30, 2019. Available at: https://www.nytimes.com/2019/01/30/us/politics/trump-isis-north-korea.html.

Sullivan, Jake. "The World After Trump: How the System Can Endure." *Foreign Affairs*, vol. 97, no. 2, March/April 2018, pp. 10–19.

Sun, Degang with Zhang, Dandan. *Diplomacy of Quasi-Alliances in the Middle East*. Translated from the Chinese by Jinan Wang. Berlin: Gerlach Press, 2019.

Tabatabai, Adnan. "The Logic Behind Iran's Regional Posture." *LobeLog*, December 11, 2017. Available at: http://lobelog.com/the-logic-behind-irans-regional-posture/

Tabatabai, Ariane M. "How Iran Will Determine the Nuclear Deal's Fate." *Foreign Affairs*, May 16, 2018. Available at: https://www.foreignaffairs.com/articles/iran/2018-05-16/how-iran-will-determine-nuclear-deals-fate.

———. "Maximum Pressure Yields Minimum Results." *Foreign Policy*, March 6, 2019. Available at: https://foreignpolicy.com/2019/03/06/maximum-pressure-yields-minimum-results/

———. "Negotiating the 'Iran Talks' in Tehran: The Iranian Drivers that Shaped the Joint Comprehensive Plan of Action." *Nonproliferation Review*, vol. 24, nos. 3–4, 2017, pp. 225–242.

———. *No Conquest, No Defeat: Iran's National Security Strategy*. London: Hurst Publishers, 2019.

———. "Other Side of the Iranian Coin: Iran's Counterterrorism Apparatus." *Journal of Strategic Studies*, vol. 41, nos. 1–2, 2018, pp. 181–207.

——— and Esfandiary, Dina. "Cooperating with Iran to Combat ISIS in Iraq." *The Washington Quarterly*, vol. 40, no. 3, Fall 2017, pp. 129–146.

———. *Triple Axis: China, Russia, Iran and Power Politics*. London: I.B. Tauris, 2018.

Tabatabai, Ariane M. and Hassan, Kawa. "KNOW Your Enemy—Iranian and Saudi Perspectives on ISIL." Center for Applied Research and Partnership with the Orient, *Brief*, no. 3, April 22, 2016, pp. 1–9.

——— and Samuel, Annie Tracy. "What the Iran-Iraq War Tells Us About the Future of the Iran Nuclear Deal." *International Security*, vol. 42, no. 1, Summer 2017, pp. 152–185.

Tabrizi, Jafar Sadegh, Pourasghar, Faramarz, and Gholamzadeh Nikjoo, Raana, "Status of Iran's Primary Health Care System in Terms of Health Systems Control Knobs." *Iranian Journal of Public Health*, vol. 46, no. 9, September 2017. Available at: https://www.ncbi.nlm.nih.gov/pmc/articles/PMC5632316/pdf/IJPH-46-1156.pdf.

Tajbakhsh, Kian. "Getting Real About Iran." *Foreign Affairs*, March 19, 2019. Available at: https://www.foreignaffairs.com/articles/iran/2019-03-19/getting-real-about-iran.

———. "Who Wants What from Iran? The Post-Nuclear Deal U.S. Policy Debate." *The Washington Quarterly*, vol. 41, no. 3, Fall 2018, pp. 41–61.

Tajvidi, Alireza. "US Policy Toward Iran: An Interview with Richard Cottam." *Critique: Critical Middle Eastern Studies*, vol. 6, no. 11, Fall 1997, pp. 5–19.

Takeyh, Ray. *Guardians of the Revolution: Iran and the World in the Age of the Ayatollahs*. New York: Oxford University Press, 2009.

————. *Hidden Iran: Paradox and Power in the Islamic Republic.* New York: Times Books, 2006.

Takht Ravanchi, Majid. "The U.S. Policy of Maximum Pressure Against Iran Has Failed." *Washington Post*, May 24, 2019. Available at: https://www.washingt onpost.com/opinions/global-opinions/the-us-policy-of-maximum-pressure-again st-iran-has-failed/2019/05/24/1db2f7b8-7e61-11e9-8ede-f4abf521ef17_story.html.

Tankel, Stephen. *With US and Against Us: How America's Partners Help and Hinder the War on Terror.* New York: Columbia University Press, 2018.

Taremi, Kamran. "Iranian Perspectives on Security in the Persian Gulf." *Iranian Studies*, vol. 36, no. 3, September 2003, pp. 381–391.

Teisseire, Pierre-Jacques. "Les contre-performances des armees du Golfe auYemen: Analyse militaire d'un fiasco." *OrientXXI*, May 26, 2016. Available at: http://ori entxxi.info/magazine/les-contre-performances-des-armees-du-golfe-au-yemen,1 341,1341.

Terhalle, Maximilian. "Revolutionary Power and Socialization: Explaining the Persistence of Revolutionary Zeal in Iran's Foreign Policy." *Security Studies*, vol. 18, no. 3, July–September 2009, pp. 557–586.

Tertrais, Bruno. "A Nuclear Iran and NATO." *Survival*, vol. 52, no. 6, December 2010–January 2011, pp. 45–61.

The Iran Project. *Iran and Its Neighbors: Regional Implications for U.S. Policy of a Nuclear Agreement.* New York: The Iran Project, 2014.

————. *Looking to a Comprehensive Nuclear Agreement with Iran: Assessing Claims and Counter Claims Over New Sanctions.* New York: The Iran Project, 2013.

————. *Strategic Options for Iran: Balancing Pressure with Diplomacy.* New York: The Iran Project, 2013.

————. *Weighing Benefits and Costs of International Sanctions Against Iran.* New York: The Iran Project, 2012.

Therme, Clément. "How Will Iran Rise to the Challenge of America's Escalation?" *Orient XXI*, August 7, 2018. Available at: https://orientxxi.info/magazine/how-will -iran-rise-to-the-challenge-of-america-s-escalation,2575.

————. "Les relations Iran-Europe au défi de l'administration Trump." *Telos*, December 17, 2018. Available at: https://www.telos-eu.com/fr/politique-francai se-et-internationale/les-relations-iran-europe-au-defi-de-ladministrati.html.

Thielmann, Greg. "Try Taming Rather Than Laming Iran's Missile Program." Atlantic Council, *Iran Source*, February 25, 2019. Available at: https://www.atlanticcounc il.org/blogs/iransource/try-taming-rather-than-laming-iran-s-missile-program.

Thompson, Jack. "Trump and the Future of US Grand Strategy." Center for Security Studies (CSS), ETH Zurich, *CSS Analyses in Security Policy*, no. 212, September 2017, pp. 1–4.

————. "Trump's Middle East Policy." Center for Security Studies (CSS), ETH Zurich, *CSS Analyses in Security Policy*, no. 233, October 2018, pp. 1–4.

Thomson, John. "The Iranian Nuclear Crisis: A Risk Assessment." British American Security Information Council, *Discussion Paper Series*, no. 2, March 2007, pp. 1–9.

"Time for Iran-US Talks, Former Deputy FM Argues." *Iran Front Page*, January 18, 2019. Available at: https://ifpnews.com/exclusive/time-for-iran-us-talks-former-deputy-fm-argues/

Tisdall, Simon. "Mike Pompeo" A Bully Boy Calls at No 10." *The Guardian*, May 4, 2019. Available at: https://www.theguardian.com/us-news/2019/may/04/mike-po mpeo-bully-boy-calls-at-no-10.

Toosi, Nahal. "Trump Has Tough Sell Recruiting Iranian-Americans in Campaign Against Tehran." *Politico*, July 18, 2018. Available at: https://www.politico.com/ story/2018/07/18/trump-iran-iranian-americans-pompeo-731736.

Torabi, Ghasem. "Arab Revolutions and Iran's Security." *Discourse: An Iranian Quarterly*, vol. 10, nos. 1–2, Winter–Spring 2012, pp. 97–117.

Toukan, Abdullah and Cordesman, Anthony. *Iran, Israel and the Effects of a Nuclear Conflict in the Middle East*. Washington, DC: Center for Strategic and International Studies, June 1, 2019.

Townsend, Mark and Borger, Julian. "Revealed: Trump Team Hired Spy Firm for 'Dirty Ops' on Iran Arms Deal." *The Guardian*, May 5, 2018. Available at: https ://www.theguardian.com/uk-news/2018/may/05/trump-team-hired-spy-firm-dirty-ops-iran-nuclear-deal.

Transfeld, Mareike. "Iran's Small Hand in Yemen." *Sada*, Carnegie Endowment for International Peace, February 14, 2017. Available at: http://carnegieendowment. org/sada/67988.

Traub, James. "Trump's Ego Is Officially a Foreign Policy Crisis." *Foreign Policy*, June 30, 2019. Available at: https://foreignpolicy.com/2019/06/30/trumps-ego-is-officially-a-foreign-policy-crisis-iran/

Trenin, Dmitri. *What Is Russia up to in the Middle East?* Cambridge, UK: Polity Press, 2017.

Trickett, Nicholas. "US Policy on Russia Aims for Iran." *YaleGlobal Online*, September 13, 2018. Available at: https://yaleglobal.yale.edu/content/us-policy-russ ia-aims-iran.

Trump, Donald J. "My Number-One Priority: Dismantle the Disastrous Deal with Iran." Address delivered at the American Israel Public Affairs Committee, 2016 Policy Conference, Washington, DC, March 21, 2016. *Vital Speeches of the Day*, vol. 82, no. 5, May 2016, pp. 136–139.

———. "Remarks on United States Strategy Towards Iran." *Daily Compilation of Presidential Documents*, October 13, 2017, pp. 1–4.

Udall, Tom and Durbin, Richard J. "Trump Is Barreling Toward War with Iran. Congress Must Act to Stop Him." *Washington Post*, March 5, 2019. Available at: https ://www.washingtonpost.com/opinions/2019/03/05/trump-is-barreling-toward-war -with-iran-congress-must-act-stop-him/?utm_term=.5c3e325d7828.

Ulrichsen, Kristian Coates. "Israel and the Arab Gulf States: Drivers and Directions of Change." Center for the Middle East, Rice University's Baker Institute for Public Policy, September 2016, pp. 1–14.

———, ed. *The Changing Security Dynamics of the Persian Gulf*. New York: Oxford University Press, 2017.

Unger, Craig. *House of Trump, House of Putin: The Untold Story of Donald Trump and the Russian Mafia*. New York: Dutton, 2018.

United States Government Accountability Office (GAO). *Iran Nuclear Agreement: The International Atomic Agency's Authorities, Resources, and Challenges.*

Washington, DC: GAO-16-565, June 2016. Available at: http://www.gao.gov/a ssets/680/677783.pdf.

U.S. Department of State. "Maximum Pressure Campaign on the Regime in Iran." *Fact Sheet*, April 2, 2019. Available at: https://content.govdelivery.com/attachments/U SSTATEBPA/2019/04/02/file_attachments/1185553/Iran%20Fact%20Sheet.pdf.

———. "The Iranian Regime's Transfer of Arms to Proxy Groups and Ongoing Missile Development." Special Briefing by Brian Hook, Senior Policy Advisor to the Secretary of State and Special Representative for Iran. Joint Base Anacosita—Bolling, Washington, DC, November 29, 2018. Available at: https://www.state.gov/r/ pa/prs/ps/2018/11/287661.htm.

Vaez, Ali. "The Risks of Maximising Pressure on Iran." International Crisis Group, *Commentary*, April 24, 2019. Available at: https://www.crisisgroup.org/middle-east-north-africa/gulf-and-arabian-peninsula/iran/risks-maximising-pressure-iran.

———. "Trump's 'Maximum Pressure' Won't Make Iran Yield." *The Atlantic*, May 12, 2019. Available at: https://www.theatlantic.com/ideas/archive/2019/05/why-t rumps-sanctions-iran-arent-working/589288/

———. "Why Would Iran Want to Talk to Trump Anyway?" *The Atlantic*, July 31, 2018. Available at: https://www.theatlantic.com/international/archive/2018/07/ir an-trump-precondition-meeting-nuclear-deal/566426/

Vaïsse, Justin. *Zbigniew Brzezinski: America's Grand Strategist*. Translated by Catherine Porter. Cambridge, MA: Harvard University Press, 2018.

Vakhshouri, Sara. "Iran's Strategy to Tackle Sanctions: Pre-selling Oil." Atlantic Council, *Iran Source*, July 11, 2019. Available at: https://www.atlanticcouncil.org/ blogs/iransource/iran-s-strategy-to-tackle-sanctions-pre-selling-oil.

Vakil, Sanam. "Iran and the GCC: Hedging, Pragmatism and Opportunism." Chatham House, Middle East and North Africa Programme, *Research Paper*, September 2018. Available at: https://www.chathamhouse.org/sites/default/files/public ations/research/2018-09-13-iran-gcc-vakil.pdf.

———. "The Art of a New Iran Deal: What the World's Diplomats Really Think of Trump's Endgame in Iran." *Foreign Affairs*, May 9, 2019. Available at: https://ww w.foreignaffairs.com/articles/iran/2019-05-09/art-new-iran-deal.

Valipour Zeroomi, Seyyed Hossein. *Goftemanhay-e Amniyat-e Melli dar Jomhouri-e Eslami-e Iran* (Discourse on National Security in the Islamic Republic of Iran). Tehran: Strategic Research Institute, 2005.

Vatanka, Alex. "Iran and the United States Can Be Friends." *Foreign Policy*, November 28, 2018. Available at: https://foreignpolicy.com/2018/11/28/iran-and-the-united-states-can-be-friends/

———. "Iran's Use of Shi'i Militant Proxies: Ideological and Practical Expediency versus Uncertain Sustainability." Middle East Institute, *Policy Paper 2018-5*, June 2018, pp. 1–24.

———. "U.S.-Iran Relations: Recommendations for the Next President." Middle East Institute, *MEI Policy Focus 2016–17*, July 2016, pp. 1–9.

Vishwanathan, Arun. "Iranian Nuclear Agreement: Understanding the Nonproliferation Paradigm." *Contemporary Review of the Middle East*, vol. 3, no. 1, March 2016, pp. 3–22.

Vivaldelli, Roberto." Interview with Mearsheimer." *LobeLog*, March 22, 2019. Available at: https://lobelog.com/interview-with-mearsheimer/

Von Daniels, Laura. "German 'Iran Ban' to Save Nuclear Agreement." German Institute for International and Security Affairs (SWP). *Point of View*, June 13, 2018. Available at: https://www.swp-berlin.org/en/point-of-view/2018/german-iran-bank -to-save-nuclear-agreement/

Von Rennenkampff, Marik. "The Reaganesque Approach to Iran? Embrace the Moderates." *War on the Rocks*, June 6, 2019. Available at: https://warontherocks.com /2019/06/the-reaganesque-approach-to-iran-embrace-the-moderates/

Voskopolos, George. "Transatlantic Relations, Alliance Theory and the Limits of Soft Power: A Realist Perspective." *IUP Journal of International Relations*, vol. 5, no. 2, July 2011, pp. 1–18.

Wagner, Wolfgang and Onderco, Michal, "Accommodation or Confrontation? Explaining Differences in Policies Toward Iran." *International Studies Quarterly*, vol. 58, no. 4, December 2014, pp. 717–728.

Walt, Stephen M. "America's Polarization Is a Foreign Policy Problem, Too." *Foreign Policy*, March 11, 2019. Available at: https://foreignpolicy.com/2019/03/11/ americas-polarization-is-a-foreign-policy-problem-too/

———. "Dear President Trump, Let's Talk About Iran." *Foreign Policy*, June 24, 2019. Available at: https://foreignpolicy.com/2019/06/24/dear-president-trump-le ts-talk-about-iran/

———. "Great Powers Are Defined by Their Great Wars." *Foreign Policy*, September 21, 2017. Available at: https://foreignpolicy.com/2017/09/21/great-powers -are-defined-by-their-great-wars/

———. "If Nobody Knows Your Iran Policy, Does It Even Exist?" *Foreign Policy*, May 6, 2019. Available at: https://foreignpolicy.com/2019/05/06/if-nobody-kno ws-your-iran-policy-does-it-even-exist-bolton-trump/#

———. "The End of Hubris: And the New Age of American Restraint." *Foreign Affairs*, vol. 98, no. 3, May/June 2019, pp. 26–35.

———. *The Hell of Good Intentions: America's Foreign Policy Elite and the Decline of U.S. Primacy*. New York: Farrar, Straus and Giroux, 2018.

———. "The Islamic Republic of Hysteria: The Trump Administration's Middle East Strategy Revolves Around a Threat that Doesn't Exist." *Foreign Policy*, no. 227, January 2018, pp. 3–5.

Waltz, Kenneth N. "Why Iran Should Get the Bomb: Nuclear Balancing Would Mean Stability." *Foreign Affairs*, vol. 91, no. 4, July/August 2012, pp. 2–5.

Warnaar, Maaike, Zaccara, Luciano, and Aarts, Paul, eds. *Iran's Relations with the Arab States of the Gulf: Common Interests Over Historic Rivalry*. Berlin: Gerlach Press, 2016.

Ward, Alex. "How the Trump Administration Is Using 9/11 to Build a Case for War with Iran." *Vox*, June 14, 2019. Available at: https://www.vox.com/platform/a mp/2019/6/14/18678809/usa-iran-war-aumf-911-trump-pompeo.

Warde, Ibrahim. "Trump's Iranian Diktat." *Le Monde diplomatique*, June 2016. Available at: https://mondediplo.com/2018/06/03iranwarde.

Wastnidge, Edward. *Diplomacy and Reform in Iran: Foreign Policy under Khatami.* London and New York: I.B. Tauris, 2016.

Watling, Jack. "Iran's Objectives and Capabilities: Deterrence and Subversion." Royal United Services Institute (RUSI), *Occasional Paper*, February 2019, pp. 1–38. Available at: https://rusi.org/sites/default/files/20190219_op_irans_objectives_and_capabilities_web.pdf.

Webb, Whitney. "Neocons Concoct Threat of 'Iranian Hackers' to Justify Preemptive 'Counterattack' Against Iran." *Mint Press News*, August 9, 2018. Available at: https://www.mintpressnews.com/neocons-hype-threat-of-iranian-hackers-to-justify-preemptive-counterattack/247369/

White House. "Statement from President Donald J. Trump on Standing with Saudi Arabia." November 20, 2018. Available at: https://www.whitehouse.gov/briefings-statements/statement-president-donald-j-trump-standing-saudi-arabia/

WikiLeaks. *The WikiLeaks Files: The World According to US Empire.* New York: Verso Books, 2016.

Wilkerson, Lawrence. "I Helped Sell the False Choice of War Once. It's Happening Again." *New York Times*, February 5, 2018. Available at: https://www.nytimes.com/2018/02/05/opinion/trump-iran-war.html.

———. "Pompeo: The Real Threat to U.S. National Security." *LobeLog*, February 19, 2019. Available at: https://lobelog.com/pompeo-the-real-threat-to-u-s-national-security/

Williams, Katie Bo. "'It's Complete Folly': Hagel Says Trump Administration Can't Threaten Iran Out of Syria." *Defense One*, October 4, 2018. Available at: https://www.defenseone.com/politics/2018/10/its-complete-folly-hagel-says-trump-administration-cant-threaten-iran-out-syria/151808/

Wilson, Geoff and Cirincione, Joe. "The Cavalier Crusade for a War with Iran." *War Is Boring,* May 17, 2018. Available at: https://warisboring.com/the-cavalier-crusade-for-a-war-with-iran/

Wiseman, Geoffrey. *Isolate or Engage: Adversarial States, US Foreign Policy, and Public Diplomacy.* Stanford, CA: Stanford University Press, 2015.

Wolf, Albert B. "After the Iran Deal: Competing Visions for Israel's Nuclear Posture." *Comparative Strategy*, vol. 35, no. 2, 2016, pp. 124–130.

Wolff, Michael. *Fire and Fury: Inside the Trump White House.* New York: Henry Holt and Company, 2018.

———. *Siege: Trump Under Fire.* New York: Henry Holt and Company, 2019.

Woodruff, Betsy and Banco, Erin. "Saudi Spy Met with Team Trump About Taking Down Iran." *Daily Beast*, October 25, 2018. Available at: https://www.thedailybeast.com/saudi-spy-met-with-team-trump-about-taking-down-iran.

Woodward, Bob. *Fear: Trump in the White House.* New York: Simon & Schuster, 2018.

"Worldwide Threat Assessment of the US Intelligence Community." Statement for the Record, Daniel R. Coats, Director of National Intelligence, Senate Select Committee on Intelligence, January 29, 2019. Available at: https://www.dni.gov/files/ODNI/documents/2019-ATA-SFR---SSCI.pdf.

Wright, Robin. "Is Trump Yet Another U.S. President Provoking a war?" *The New Yorker*, May 13, 2019. Available at: https://www.newyorker.com/news/our.colum nists/is-trump-yet-another-us-president-provoking-a-war.

———. "The Adversary: Is Iran's Nuclear Negotiator, Javad Zarif, for Real?" *The New Yorker*, May 26, 2014, pp. 40–49.

———. "The United States and Iran: It's Like '50 First dates'." *The New Yorker*, October 1, 2018. Available at: https://www.newyorker.com/news/news-desk/the-united-states-and-iran-its-like-50-first-dates.

———. "Trump's Strange, Tense Campaign Against Iran." *The New Yorker*, April 25, 2019. Available at: https://www.newyorker.com/news/our-columnists/trum ps-strange-tense-campaign-against-iran.

———. "Trump's Utter Denial About Saudi Arabia and Its Crown Prince." *The New Yorker*, November 20, 2018. Available at: https://www.newyorker.com/news/news -desk/trumps-utter-denial-about-saudi-arabia-and-its-crown-prince.

———. "Who Will Last Longer: Trump or Iran's Theocrats?" *The New Yorker*, August 6, 2018. Available at: https://www.newyorker.com/news/news-desk/who-will-last-longer-trump-or-irans-theocrats.

———, ed. *The Iran Primer: Power, Politics, and U.S. Policy.* Washington, DC: United States Institute of Peace, 2010.

Wright, Thomas. "Trump's Foreign Policy Is No Longer Unpredictable." *Foreign Affairs*, January 18, 2019. Available at: https://www.foreignaffairs.com/articles/ world/2019-01-18/trumps-foreign-policy-no-longer-unpredictable.

Yarhi-Milo, Keren. "After Credibility: American Foreign Policy in the Trump Era." *Foreign Affairs*, vol. 97, no. 1, January/February 2018, pp. 68–77.

Zaccara, Luciano. "Iran and the Intra-GCC Crisis: Risks and Opportunities." Instituto Affari Internazionali, *IAI Papers 19*, no. 11, May 2019, pp. 1–17.

Zahedi, Ardeshir and Vaez, Ali. "The U.S. Should Strive for a Stable Iran. Instead, It Is Suffocating It." *Washington Post*, June 20, 2019. Available at: https://www.was hingtonpost.com/opinions/global-opinions/the-us-should-strive-for-a-stable-iran-instead-it-is-suffocating-it/2019/06/20/1ac393ee-9380-11e9-aadb-74e6b2b46f6 a_story.html?utm_term=.e931290f1e1a.

Zakaria, Fareed. "Does a Trump Doctrine on Foreign Policy Exist? Ask John Bolton." *Washington Post*, May 2, 2019. Available at: https://www.washingtonpost.com/opin ions/does-a-trump-doctrine-on-foreign-policy-exist-ask-john-bolton/2019/05/02/6d 209220-6d1c-11e9-a66d-a82d3f3d96d5_story.html?utm_term=.56fbae754ae2.

———. "The Self-Destruction of American Power." *Foreign Affairs*, vol. 98, no. 4, July/August 2019, pp. 10–16.

Zakheim, Dov S. "Trump's Perilous Path." *The National Interest*, no. 156, July/ August 2018, pp. 13–21.

Zare', Mohammad. "Iran's Changing Approach to the Shanghai Cooperation Orga-nization." *Iran Review*, July 2, 2016. Available at: http://www.iranreview.org/ content/Documents/Iran-s-Changing-Approach-to-the-Shanghai-Cooperation-Org anization.htm.

Zarif, Mohammad Javad. "FM Zarif's Letter to the United Nations Secretary Gen-eral." Iranian government's official protest letter to the UN about the Trump administration's designation of the Islamic Revolutionary Guard Corps (IRGC), and official branch of Iran's armed forces, as a terrorist group. Ministry of Foreign Affairs, Islamic Republic of Iran, April 10, 2019. Available at: http://en.mfa.ir/upl oads/4_5874983243329045903_175386.pdf.

———. "Overcoming Regional Challenges in the Middle East: An Iranian Perspective." A talk delivered at Chatham House, the Royal Institute of International Affairs, London, United Kingdom, February 4, 2016. Available at: https://www.chathamh ouse.org/sites/files/chathamhouse/events/special/16%201Q%20Iran.pdf.

———. "Rid the World of Wahhabism." *New York Times*, September 14, 2016, p. A27.

———. "Siyasat-e Khareji-e Iran az Doroon-e Mozakereh-e Mobtani bar Ghodrat" (An Insider's View of Iranian Foreign Policy; Negotiating from Strength). *Foreign Policy* (Tehran), vol. 32, no. 4, Spring 2019, pp. 5–26.

———. "Speech by Iranian Foreign Minister Mohammad Javad Zarif at Munich Security Conference." Ministry of Foreign Affairs, Islamic Republic of Iran, February 17, 2019. Available at: http://en.mfa.ir/index.aspx?siteid=3&fkeyid=&sitei d=3&pageid=36409&newsview=558232.

———. "Statement by Minister of Foreign Affairs of the Islamic Republic of Iran at the High-Level Meeting of the General Assembly to Commemorate and Promote the International Day of Multilateralism and Diplomacy for Peace." Ministry of Foreign Affairs, Islamic Republic of Iran, April 24, 2019. Available at: http://en.mfa.ir/ind ex.aspx?siteid=3&fkeyid=&siteid=3&pageid=36409&newsview=567104.

———. "US Foreign Policy in Crisis." Article written by Iran's Foreign Minister Zarif in response to the US Secretary of State Pompeo's 12-point demand from Iran and posted on the website of the Ministry of the Foreign Affairs of the Islamic Republic of Iran, June 21, 2018. Available at: http://en.mfa.ir/index.aspx?siteid= 3&fkeyid=&siteid=3&pageid=36409&newsview=521164.

———. "Why Is Iran Building Up Its Defenses." *Washington Post*, April 20, 2016. Available at: https://www.washingtonpost.com/opinions/zarif-what-critics-get-wr ong-about-iran-and-the-nuclear-agreement/2016/04/20/7b542dee-0658-11e6-a12f -ea5aed7958dc_story.html.

———, Sajjadpour, S.M. Kazem, and Molaei, Ebadollah. *Doran Gozar-e Ravabet-e Baynolmelal dar Jahan-e Pasa Gharbi* (Transition in International Relations of the Post-Western World). Tehran: Center for International Research and Education, 2017.

Ziaee, Seyed Yaser. "Jurisdictional Countermeasures versus Extraterritoriality in International Law." *Russian Law Journal*, vol. 4, no. 4, 2016, pp. 27–45.

Index

al-Abadi, Haider, 92
Abdullah, King of Jordan, 25
Additional Protocol, 66
Additional Protocol plus, 67
Afghanistan, 20, 88, 89, 148, 183
Al-Ahmad, Sheikh Sabah, 145, 179
Ahmadinejad, Mahmoud, 119
Albright, Madeleine, 22, 65
Algiers Accord (1981), 16
Amano, Yukiya, 65
AML/CFT. *See* anti-money laundering,
  combating terrorism financing
  (AML/CFT)
Andrey, Yu, 98
anti-Americanism, 18, 99
anti-Iran alliance, 17, 145–46
anti-money laundering, combating
  terrorism financing (AML/CFT), 131
anti-Shiite sectarianism, 150
Arab League, 148, 151, 197
Arab NATO, 7, 141, 179
Arabs, 10, 129, 154; democratic
  movements, 50n99; misgiving
  about Faustian bargain, 26; missile
  systems, 169; nationalism, 146–47
Arab Spring, 23, 25, 50n99
Araghchi, Abbas, 67
Arank, 39
al-Assaf, Ibrahim, 152

asymmetrical warfare, 165, 167
aufhebung, 44n24
Austria, 125
Authorization for Use of Military Force
  Act (2001), 162

Baathist regime, 18–19, 147, 190
Baath Party, 149
backlash states, 19, 48n73
Bahrain, 16, 23, 25, 146, 147
Baker, James, 25
ballistic missile activities, 22, 25, 30,
  37, 56, 58, 117, 168, 169, 171, 184
Bank of Kunlun, 88
Bannon, Steve, 15
El-Baradei, Mohammad, 65
Barzegar, Kayhan, 51n109
Bazargan, Mehdi, 22
Bellinger, Jon, 32
Berger, Samuel, 65
Bill, James, 101
Blinken, Anthony, 10
blocking statute, 121–23
Bolton, John, 15–16, 72n33, 155, 164,
  179; complaints against Iran, 78–79;
  diplomacy, 182; on Europe, 119–20;
  opposition to Chabahar exemption,
  91; opposition to JCPOA, 61–62,
  185

Vehicle (SPV) and United States,
102–3
human rights: issues, 21; violation of,
16
Hunter, Robert, 193n29
Huntington, Samuel, 101
Hussain, Saddam, 17, 147, 149, 168,
179

IAEA. *See* International Atomic Energy
Agency (IAEA)
ICBM program, 169, 171
IMF. *See* International Monetary Fund
(IMF)
India, 87, 88, 89, 98; Chabahar project,
91
INSTEX. *See* Instrument for Supporting
Trade Exchanges (INSTEX)
Instrument for Supporting Trade
Exchanges (INSTEX), 131, 162, 183,
196
Intermediate-Range Nuclear Forces
Treaty, 12
International Atomic Energy Agency
(IAEA), 30, 56; agreement with Iran,
33, 66; defense of the JCPOA, 65;
"inspections anytime, anywhere"
provision, 57
International Crisis Group, 104n6
International Institute for Strategic
Studies, 166
International Monetary Fund (IMF),
105n14
Iran: ballistic missile program. *See*
ballistic missile activities Chabahar
project, 77, 88–91, 98; civilian
nuclear program, military dimensions
to, 33–34; compliance with the
terms of the JCPOA, 59, 64, 65–66,
116; compromise of NPT rights,
68; conflict-reduction in the region,
196–97; containment policy, 17, 24–
25; control of the shared waterway
with Iraq, 93; counter-compellence
strategy in the Persian Gulf, 154–55;

counter-terrorism strategy, 154;
currency depreciation, 82; defense
approach, 165–69; deterrence
strategy, 167–68; discounts on its
crude, 96; and Dubai, 146; economic
counter-strategy, 98–101; economic
policies, 7, 98; economic populism,
78, 99–101, 103; economy recession,
79–80; elections-based sources of
legitimacy in, 101; expansionism, 57,
139; extensive obligations under the
JCPOA, 34–35; financial support of
its regional proxies, 57; and foreign
banks, 80; foreign direct investment
in, 82–83; future generation fund,
97; future relations with the West,
10; and IAEA agreement(s), 33,
36, 66–67, 187; involvement in
Syrian conflict, 28–29, 141; and
Lebanon, 19; "Melian dilemma," 4;
military modernization and military
dominance, 147; missile categories,
170; missile threat, and US Navy,
165; navy, warning message to
the U.S., 164–65; nuclear-capable
missile tests, 57; as a nuclear
threat, 63; oil exports to Europe,
83; oil importers from, 97–98; oil
tankers, 85; Persian Gulf waters,
brinksmanship in, 164; presidential
elections 2009, 26; primacy thesis,
152–53; prohibited activities,
staying clear of, 36–37; proto-
nuclear weapons status, 181; ration
system, 99; regional portfolio, 196;
relations with its Arab neighbors,
10; resistance, 179; resorts to
International Court of Justice,
101–4; "rogue behavior" complain,
15, 21–22, 27–28, 48n73, 56–59,
63, 140; and Saudi Arabia, 146–55;
SCO's objection to membership,
191n6; social-welfare policies, 101;
space launch vehicle (SLV), 169; tax
extraction, 97; tourism, 92; unwanted

37; and UNSC Resolution 2231 (*see*
UNSC Resolution 2231) verification
cost provision, 74n54
al-Jubeir, Adel, 152
Juncker, Jean-Claude, 121, 125, 129,
138n71
Justice and Development Party, Turkey,
94
just war, 197

Kaeser, Joe, 83
Kamrava, Mehran, 19
Karzai, Hamid, 49n83
Kerry, John, 1, 40, 65, 66, 74n57, 80,
186
Khalidi, Rashid, 47–48n64
Khamenei, Ayatollah Seyed Ali, 10, 127
Khashoggi, Jamal, 143, 144
Khatami, Mohammad, 148
Khomeini, Ayatollah Ruhollah, 147
Kim, Jong-un, 11
Kinzer, Stephen, 18
Kissinger, Henry, 66
Kurdish separatism, 95
Kushner, Jarred, 12, 143
Kuwait, 145, 167, 179
Kuwait crisis, 20
Kuwait War, 144

Laderman, Charlie, 14
Lake, Anthony, 48n73
Lavrov, Sergei, 74n57
Lebanon, 140, 148–49
Le Maire, Bruno, 121
Leonard, Mark, 132n5
Libya, 23, 25
Luxembourg, 125
Lynch, Marc, 150

Macron, Emmanuel, 58, 117–18, 125,
133n19, 143, 183
Maduro, Nicolas, 178
Malley, Robert, 111n87
Martel, William C., 41n2
Mattis, James, 60, 172n7

maximalism, 69
maximalist (rollback) strategy. *See*
rollback strategy
"maximum pressure" compellence
strategy. *See* compellence strategy
May, Theresa, 118, 129
McMaster, H. R., 15, 60
Mearsheimer, John J., 17, 22
Mehdizadeh, Jaafar, 81
MEK (*Mojahedin-e Khalgh
Organization*), 16, 46n46, 179
Menezes, Mark, 86
Merkel, Angela, 116, 118, 129,
133n19
Middle East, 2–3, 7, 11, 20; broader
disarmament in, 10; defense
approach, 165–66; Obama's policy,
23; sectarian conflict in, 25; weapons
exports to, 142. *See also specific
countries*
military confrontation, 115, 195
minimalism, 10, 22
missiles, 25, 169–71; ballistic missile
activities, 22, 25, 30, 37, 56, 58, 117,
168, 184
Mogherini, Federica, 117, 122, 129,
196
Momtaz, Djamchid, 103
Moniz, Ernest, 65, 67, 74–75n61
Mossadegh, Mohammad, 18
Mousavian, Seyed Hossein, 168
Munich Security Conference (2019),
118
Murphy, Chris, 72n31
Murray, Donette, 17, 47n60
Muslim Brotherhood, in Egypt, 25

NAFTA. *See* North American Free
Trade Agreement (NAFTA)
Nasser, Gamal Abdul, 147
Natanz, 34
National Development Fund of Iran,
112–13n106
National Iranian Oil Company, 81
National Security Strategy, 56

About the Authors

Nader Entessar is a professor emeritus of political science at the University of South Alabama where he chaired the department of political science and criminal justice for several years before his retirement in 2017. A specialist in Iran's defense and foreign policy, and security issues in the Persian Gulf, he is the coauthor, most recently, of *Iran Nuclear Negotiations: Accord and Détente since the Geneva Agreement of 2013* (Rowman & Littlefield, 2015) and *Iran Nuclear Accord and the Remaking of the Middle East* (Rowman & Littlefield, 2018).

Kaveh L. Afrasiabi is an Iranian-American political scientist and author. He has taught political science at the University of Tehran, Boston University, and Bentley University, and was a visiting scholar at Harvard University, the University of California, Berkeley, Binghamton University, and the Center for Strategic Research, Tehran. He is the coauthor, most recently, of *Iran Nuclear Negotiations: Accord and Détente since the Geneva Agreement of 2013* (Rowman & Littlefield, 2015) and *Iran Nuclear Accord and the Remaking of the Middle East* (Rowman & Littlefield, 2018).